TURKEY: BRIGHT SUN, STRONG TEA

ON THE ROAD WITH A TRAVEL WRITER

BY

TOM BROSNAHAN

Tom Brosnahan

TRAVEL INFO EXCHANGE, INC.,
CONCORD, MA USA
WWW.BRIGHTSUNSTRONGTEA.COM

Library of Congress Cataloging-in-Publication Data

Brosnahan, Tom.
  Turkey--bright sun, strong tea : on the road with a travel writer / by Tom
Brosnahan.
    p. cm.
  Includes bibliographical references.
  ISBN 0-9767531-0-3 (alk. paper)
  1. Turkey--Description and travel. I. Title.
  DR429.4.B76 2005
  915.6104'3--dc22

                                                            2005008187

ଧଙ

ଧଙ

Cover photography and design: Tom Brosnahan
Design and Production: Digital Design Group, Newton, MA USA
    (www.ddgdesign.com)
Printer: Webcom Ltd., Toronto, Canada

Photographs and other information regarding this book are at
www.BrightSunStrongTea.com

TABLE OF CONTENTS

For Jane

(Heh)

FOREWORD

When I was young I did not know there were people who traveled all over the world and wrote about their adventures and got paid to do it. That's why, at the age of fifteen, I thought I was going to starve.

I wasn't actually hungry at the time. I lived in a small town just outside Bethlehem, Pennsylvania and got plenty to eat, but the outlook was bleak. I knew that soon I'd graduate from high school, then college, then look for a job.

That's when I'd starve, because I knew I couldn't go to work in an office every day the way my father did. I just couldn't.

I watched my father get up every morning, wash and shave, smoke a cigarette, have his cereal and coffee while listening to the radio, then drive off and work in an office at Bethlehem Steel Corporation. At five o'clock he'd drive home, sit in his easy chair, have a drink, relax and read the paper, and that was his day.

I just couldn't do it. I'd sit with Jane, my high school girlfriend, and fret over how I was going to earn a living.

So what *would* I do? Besides starve, that is.

I thought perhaps I'd be a diplomat because diplomats get to travel and live in exotic places and don't always work in offices. Some of them even write interesting books about their travels.

I thought I'd be the sort of diplomat who, in the evening, sat on the verandah of his tropical villa overlooking the emerald jungle and the broad, shining lake and wrote books on the manners and customs of the local tribes while a gin and tonic dripped condensation at his elbow. Or I'd be a consul in a timeless old city, sipping strong spiced coffee while renewing passports and keeping tabs on local export markets for a few hours each day. The rest of my time I'd spend researching the arcane inscriptions on ancient monumental arches and forgotten tombs. Or I'd hobnob with other diplomats in crumbling *Second Em-*

pire palaces built by French colonial governors, trade theories on what made the local dictator tick, and when the dictator was, inevitably, overthrown in a paroxysm of colorful violence, I'd write all about his wretched life, his cronies, his hundred mistresses, and his numbered Swiss bank accounts.

I should have been dreaming about being a travel writer, but I didn't know what travel writers were, or what they did, or how they did it, let alone whether or not it kept them from starving.

Now I do. I've written more than three dozen travel guidebooks to a dozen countries, and lots of articles for magazines, and made a decent living at it. I didn't have to be a diplomat after all. (Diplomats work for the *government*, for godsake.)

Best of all, I didn't starve.

I can scarcely credit how lucky I was to stumble into this career—and I do mean stumble. For several years after I became a bona fide travel writer I refused to believe I even was one. I went about engrossed in the fiction that I was on my way to becoming a history professor. (Yes, I know, professors spend time in offices and —worse—committee meetings. But they spend most of their time in classrooms, and they also get long sabbaticals when they can travel.) In any case, I came to my senses in time and realized I was a travel writer at heart and in fact.

I wanted to travel because I needed to figure out how the world worked and why I was here. Travel writing was perfect because it required me to learn about all sorts of things: architecture, art, botany, business, commerce, cuisine, culture, geography, government, history, languages, music, religion, society and even a bit of zoology.

It taught me a lot about people: who they are, what they think, and why they do what they do. It shouldn't have surprised me to discover that, when you finally make your way through all the cultural baloney, people are pretty much the same no matter where you go. To discover this, I had to live in a strange country and learn a strange language so I could talk to the people directly, but it was worth it.

The strange language was Turkish, by the way, and the country was Turkey. I could have lived in Austria or England or France—and in fact I did live in all those places at one time or another—but I wouldn't have learned all I learned by living in countries that are familiar, prosperous, western, European, and predominantly Christian. It had to be some place very different which, in the 1960s at least, Turkey certainly was.

"A cup of coffee gives memories for forty years," according to an old Turkish proverb. Of course it depends on where and with whom you slurp the coffee. Considering the amount of caffeine I've ingested in Turkey, I should be set with memories for the next millennium.

Some of my coffee (and tea) memories are in this book, the ones I thought might be amusing. To protect their privacy, I've changed the names of my friends and Peace Corps colleagues (except for Jane). You'll meet my favorite Turks, too. There are lots more where they came from and, because I've discovered how travel can open your eyes to the value of other people, I urge you to go meet your own.

Speaking of languages, there are some strange Turkish words in this book, along with a few in English, Farsi, French, German, Greek and Latin. They're all explained in the Glossary at the back, where you can also find a key to Turkish pronunciation.

This book is about other things besides Turkey: what it's like to be a travel writer, and a guidebook author in particular. About the bright side of Islam and its relationship to, of all things, champagne. About love sought and found, and lost, and found again, and so on—you know how that goes. About life's little jokes and absurdities, which seem far more abundant than is strictly necessary. About what we're all supposed to be doing on this planet...—but more of that later.

∞

1

Champagne in the Air

The champagne was at 31,000 feet and by happy circumstance so was I, cruising along at 500 miles per hour in a Boeing 707 chartered from Pan American World Airways by the United States Government. It was September, 1967, the end of the Summer of Love, and the plane was full of Peace Corps Volunteers who, having just completed an intensive three-month training program, were on their way overseas to fight communism by helping Third World countries with their economic development. The champagne was courtesy of Pan Am, which donated it in a gesture of thanks to the brave young people off to do good in the world.

We had our airline tray dinners in front of us, and we held up our wine glasses to be filled by the smiling stewardesses—which is what everybody called flight attendants back then. After our wine glasses were filled we held up our water glasses, and then our coffee cups. The stewardesses filled them all. Pan Am was being exceedingly generous with the bubbly.

This was too good! We had been chosen for Peace Corps service because of our resourcefulness, intrepidness and initiative, so no one was surprised when a few of us got up from our seats, cajoled the stewardesses out of their service aprons and took over pouring the champagne. We popped corks and formed a bottle brigade, passing bottles hand to hand from the stern galley to the forward bulkhead. Wine glasses, water glasses and coffee cups refilled, we sipped, joked, and toasted our future. If this was the Peace Corps, it was going to be a hoot.

We were a homogeneous bunch of upper middle-class twentysomething men and women, Christians, Jews and agnostics, the leading edge of the Baby Boom, most of us fresh out of college. We volunteered for the Peace Corps out of idealism, a taste for travel and adventure, and in the case of the men, an antipathy to having small pieces of swiftly-flying lead lodge painfully in our bodies. For most of us men of Selective Service (ie, military conscription) age, Peace Corps service was the only viable patriotic alternative to service on the front lines in Vietnam. For the women, it was a foreign adventure and philanthropic service before settling down to career and/or family.

Right now the Peace Corps was a college fraternity party high in the sky, and it went on until we were over Holland.

A story later circulated that not everyone who got on the plane as a virgin got off as one. The accomplishment of coital union in a Boeing 707 seat (or perhaps two), camouflaged only by a thin airline blanket, would have taxed the contortional powers of a Mongolian gymnast, but this was, after all, the Summer of Love, and far be it from me to cast doubt on the capabilities of my fellow PCVs (Peace Corps Volunteers). Pregnancy was strictly forbidden by Peace Corps regulations, by the way, which I'm sure was on everybody's mind as we knocked back the bubbly in the oxygen-poor air of the troposphere.

It was deathly quiet in the plane as we entered Dutch airspace and the full extent of our champagne hangover took hold. We returned the aprons to the flight attendants and allowed them to serve us espresso-strength coffee—quietly.

We stopped in Amsterdam for an hour to re-fuel, then took off again bound for Ankara, the Turkish capital. There was little sound in the 707's cabin except for the occasional low moan.

Until the moment when the Pan Am captain eased back on the throttle, lowered the plane's nose and dropped the wheels to land in Ankara, my future as a Peace Corps Volunteer teaching English in Turkey had been entirely theoretical. Now here it was right in front of me. I saw a brown, dusty landscape of low rolling steppe, treeless and barren. My mind conjured a vision of the lush forests of Pennsylvania where I had been raised. Oh God, was this ever gonna be different.

I disembarked into blast-furnace-style mid-September Middle Eastern heat which was even less bearable with a hangover. Where was I? What on earth had I done? It had all seemed so plausible, so worthy, so innocently good, a few weeks ago at Peace Corps training in Texas.

Turkey via Texas

Texas? Is that where you go to learn about Turkey? Apparently so, at least according to the jolly logic of government programs. I graduated from Tufts University near Boston then flew to Austin which at the time was a sleepy town of state government offices, the sprawling University of Texas, and little else. It would later develop rapidly as a high-tech development and manufacturing center, but in June of 1967 it was small and surrounded by open fields. Rich university students cruised its wide but short boulevards in convertibles sucking McDonald's milkshakes. In the summer, when the sun baked it at temperatures above 100°F, the university was nearly deserted. It had plenty of empty dormitory facilities to rent to the Peace Corps for its training programs. This was not the first year that PCVs had trained here. A group was training at the U of T the year before on August 1st when Charles Whitman, a Texas firearms enthusiast who was having a bad day, hauled a footlocker filled with legally-acquired guns, ammo and food to the top of the university tower, settled in, got comfy and took potshots at all and sundry for no apparent reason except that he was grossly unhappy. Other than that it was a nice clear day, good for practicing marksmanship (Charles had been a Marine), with lots of alluring moving targets strolling slowly across the plaza below. Charles murdered 16 people and wounded another 31 (none of them Peace Corps trainees) from his cozy nest before he himself was shot and killed by two fearless Austin police officers. A lot of Marines, present and former, were pretty upset with him for murdering innocent people and probably would have killed him had he not already been dead, but in any case his guns became highly-sought collectors' items among his fellow Texas firearms enthusiasts.

We thought about this when we arrived on the U of T campus for Peace Corps training. By the look of it, Peace Corps training in Texas might not be all that different from the front line in Vietnam, except that in Vietnam we would presumably have had our own weapons and would have been able, at least in principle, to shoot back.

Thereafter the university tower was closed to visitors, whether hauling cordite-filled trunks or not and, the shooting over, the Peace Corps signed a three-month summer lease on the Santa Rita Apartments, a modern private dormitory with several floors of rooms surrounding a central swimming pool. We moved in: 77 trainees, a number of American trainers and administrators, and a dozen or so Turkish teachers and language instructors. Groups of PCVs, two or three groups per year, had been going to Turkey since 1962. Our training group was designated "Turkey 15-Austin."

Right away we met our Turkish teachers. For most of us, they were the first and only Turks we had ever met. All spoke fluent English. Most lived in the USA now, either as university students, graduate students or professionals.

They were a diverse bunch. The director of the language training program was a short, dark, middle-aged, balding, sombre and serious man named Necdet whose sole goal in life seemed to be to drill a difficult language into us. Among the younger teachers was Halil, a tall, cheerful, athletic guy who spoke American English with such a perfect accent and played such good basketball that we called him "the kid from Cincinnati." René was just the opposite. He looked just like my stereotypical conception of a Turk: short, big head, dark mustache and goatee, his face with an eternally serious if-you-only-knew expression. I don't know where I acquired this stereotype. I knew virtually nothing about Turkey or Turks, but René fit the image, which shows you what stereotypes are worth because René was a Greek. An İstanbul Greek, to be sure, a Turkish citizen who spoke both Turkish and Greek as his mother tongues—*Grec-sujet turc* as 19th-century diplomats would have put it—but an orthodox-Christian-Greek nonetheless.

There were female teachers as well. Hülya was a slender, beautiful late-twentyish woman of medium height with long jet-black hair and exquisitely fine features. She was my initial definition of Turkish feminine beauty, and came close to being an ideal. Her beauty came with a ready smile, abundant energy and a no-nonsense American-style attitude toward getting the job done—in this case, teaching us Turkish.

Basic Training

The training program was intensive. We worked 14 hours a day, 6½ days a week. Every day started at 6 am with calisthenics and a one-kilometer run around the neighborhood before breakfast. The rest of the morning was spent studying the Turkish language. After lunch came more language training and classes in Turkish history, society and culture. After dinner we studied late into the night.

We learned that *Bey* meant Mr and *Hanım* meant Ms, and these titles were used with the given name, not the surname. (Yes! Turkey never did have titles such as Miss and Mrs to distinguish between married and unmarried women. They had Ms long before we did.) So *Mehmet Bey* was "Mr Mehmet" and *Ayşe Hanım* was "Ms Ayşe."

Turkish wasn't all that difficult to pronounce if you had studied French or German, which most of us had. The hard part was remembering its little weird-nesses, such as that 'c' in Turkish is pronounced like the 'j' in English, so *can*, the word for "soul," is pronounced "jahn." Turkish also has a weird "soft g" (ğ), that for some reason wasn't pronounced at all, but who are we English speakers to complain about other peoples' silent letters? Turkish has two 'i's, one with a dot (i) and one without (ı), which is perhaps the supreme weirdness. The one without a dot is pronounced "uh" as in "duh." We say that sound a lot in English (as in "love" and "hum"), but somehow it sounded weirder in Turkish.

We were taught Turkish by the aural-oral method: Hülya Hanım would say a simple sentence such as *Acaba buralarda bir postane var mı?* ("I wonder, is there a post office around here?") and we would repeat it aloud, again and again. We repeated it endlessly, mindlessly. She would then substitute one word for another in the sentence: *Acaba buralarda bir lokanta var mı?* ("I wonder, is there a restaurant around here?") We'd repeat that sentence over and over until we could say it in our sleep. Actually, according to reports by several insomniacs, most of us did say it in our sleep.

The aural-oral method was brain-numbing, but it worked. After a few weeks we could say simple phrases to one another in Turkish. We were tested on our progress every day. To remain in the program we had to pass the tests, so we studied hard.

Among our Turkish instructors was a family with a seven-year-old son. Though his parents were Turkish, little Murat had been born and raised in the USA. His parents spoke Turkish at home, but he spoke English with his friends and in school, so he was perfectly bilingual. At test time, Murat was the most popular boy in Texas. All of us university-educated young adults would gather around him and beseech:

"Murat! How do you say 'It's going to rain' in Turkish?

"Murat! What's the past tense of *gider* (to go)?

"Murat! I'll give you a piece of candy if you show me the mistakes in this piece of writing!"

Turkish history was more interesting to me than the language training, probably because I had majored in history at Tufts. The Turks rode westward from Asia a thousand years ago and took over what had been the later Roman, or Byzantine, empire—basically, all the land around the eastern Mediterranean. In 1453 the Turks breached the mighty walls of Constantinople itself, made it their capital and it became İstanbul.

By the mid-1500s the Ottoman Empire was Europe's greatest land and sea power, and its sultan, Süleyman the Magnificent (1520–1566), was the richest, most powerful and most resplendent of Renaissance monarchs, outshining his royal "brothers" François I of France, Henry VIII of England, and the Holy Roman Emperor Charles V. The sultan eventually ruled most of eastern Europe, the Middle East and North Africa, and western Europe shook in its boots fearing that the Turkish armies of Islam would soon overrun the continent completely. Twice the sultan's armies actually threatened the gates of Vienna, but could not break through.

By the 1700s the Reformation had largely freed Europe from the strictures of medieval religious law. The Inquisition was over, and Europe surged ahead in agriculture, science, commerce, education and exploration while Ottoman society remained stuck in the Middle Ages with Islamic Sharia the law of the land. "Nefarious innovation," as it was called, was not merely unwelcome but actively condemned within the sultan's domains. Soon Europe's modern, innovative armies and navies were breaching the sultan's far-flung borders, and the glorious reign of Süleyman the Magnificent was no more than a proud memory.

By the late 1800s the Turkish empire was on the point of collapse. The great powers of Europe could have toppled it at any time, but they refrained because they feared that once the empire collapsed there would be a frightful dogfight over the pieces. The tenuous balance of Great Power greed allowed the sultan to keep his throne until the early 20th century, but World War I blew the system apart, bringing down not only the Ottoman Empire but those of Austria-Hungary, Germany and Russia as well. In 1918 the victorious European powers, especially Great Britain, France and Italy, carved up the sultan's lands, taking what they wanted and leaving the Turks almost nothing.

Threatened with the disappearance of their country, in 1919 the Turks fought back. An Ottoman general and war hero named Mustafa Kemal organized armed resistance when Greece, supported by Great Britain, invaded the Turkish heartland bent on recreating the Byzantine Empire. In bitter fighting—including the longest pitched battle in history—Kemal's Turkish republican armies pushed the invaders out of Anatolia. Kemal went on to fashion a modern democratic nation-state, the Turkish Republic, and became known as *Atatürk* (Father of the Turks).

We learned this and a lot more, and even, occasionally, had a few moments to relax.

Home on the Range

Our only free time was Sunday afternoon. Actually, Sunday afternoon wasn't really free, it was for doing everything we had no time to do during the week: buy razor blades and stamps, write letters home, talk with other volunteers about things *not* Turkish, and fall in love.

Yes, fall in love.

On Sunday evenings we'd collapse in chairs and read, drink chilled Cold Duck (sparkling red wine) because it was cheap and insouciant and alcoholicly effective—and mostly because we didn't know any better and had terrible taste in drinks. We'd watch TV or go for walks, venturing out of the air-conditioned confines of the Santa Rita Apartments into the blazing air of a Texas summer, like walking into a pizza oven without the scorched cheese smell. We'd walk down to a nearby gully where there were trees and sit in the cool (or at least not so hot) shade and talk. My favorite companion on walks to the gully was Linda, a statuesque, forthrightly gorgeous West Coast girl who had a body that could raise men from the dead and that airy oh-wow California chick enthusiasm that mesmerized us stiff-shirt Easterners during the 1960s. Linda and I sat in the shade and talked and sighed and gazed meaningfully into one another's eyes, and then walked back to the Santa Rita through the Texas blast furnace and studied Turkish verb structures.

We were told at the beginning of training that most likely there would be at least one wedding among volunteers during our three-month training period. Linda and I never even got to first base, but sure enough, Turkey 15-Austin had one marriage during training, and more later in Turkey.

One weekend the Peace Corps administrators went wild and took us out on the range for a Texas barbecue. Turks and all, we emptied out of the Santa Rita, boarded a chartered bus and rode out to a Texas ranch complete with sagebrush, cacti, parched soil and rattlesnakes. The moment we reached the ranch our Turkish teachers, at least the male ones, stripped off their shirts and started a vigorous game of soccer. At that time soccer, called simply "football" in the rest of the civilized world, was not a familiar sport in the USA. To us, it was one of those weird and inferior things Europeans and Latin Americans did. The truly American games were baseball, basketball and American football, games for which there were real equipment markets.

Our male Turkish teachers were good soccer players. We were amazed, which shows you how ignorant we were and how much we had yet to learn about Turkey. We sat around a campfire and sang "Ay, ay, ay, ay," which in Turkish means "Moon, moon, moon, moon," and sure enough pretty soon we witnessed a spectacular moonrise. Ah, I can see it now....

Submitting to God's Will

Perhaps our greatest ignorance was about Islam, one of the most popular and populous religions in the world. We learned the basic tenets: *Islam* means "submission to God's will." A *muslim* is one who has submitted to God's will. There is only one god, and Muhammed is His Messenger, who miraculously brought the Holy Kur'an, God's word, to humankind. The Kur'an completes God's revelations which started with Judaism and the Torah, continued with Christianity and the Bible, and are completed and perfected by Islam and the Kur'an.

To become a Muslim, you need only say, understand and believe that "There is no god but God, and Muhammed is His Prophet." To be a good Muslim you must pray five times a day: at dawn, noon, mid-afternoon, dusk and after dark.

Pray five times a day? Holy Moses! Where we came from, God was lucky to get our attention once a week, if that. The very thought of praying five times a day wore us out.

The rest of Islam mostly looks easy compared to praying five times a day: give alms to the poor; fast during daylight hours in the holy month of Ramazan (but then you get to party all night); make the Haj, the pilgrimage to Mecca, at least once in your life if you can; beware the sins of fraud, usury, slander and gambling.

There is of course the shellfish-pork-and-booze thing, namely that you can't have any of them. We soon learned that many Turkish Muslims strictly observe the prohibition against pork and stiffen their resolve against the Evil Meat by imbibing numerous belts of rakı, the pungent, powerful anise-flavored grape brandy that is Turkey's national tipple. So pork is a no-no but booze is okay, at least for many Turks. Shellfish is a grey area.

It reminded me of the Pennsylvania Dutch region where I grew up. Some of the conservative religious people akin to the Amish didn't really go for driving a horse-and buggy. They decided it was okay to drive a car so long as the car wasn't "ostentatious," which meant that all the chrome had to be painted black.

Turkey's Islam was thus moderated by the demands and delights of the modern secular lifestyle even though Sharia, or Islamic religious law, had been the law of the land during the Ottoman Empire.

Luckily, Atatürk had removed religion from government just as the founders of the United States had done. It was a revolutionary act in both cases. Not long before, during the 1600s, both Europe and the Ottoman Empire were ruled by religious law, and it was pretty grim. In 1633 Galileo was tried and convicted by a court of the Inquisition for teaching the Copernican theory that the earth revolved around the sun and not vice-versa. It didn't matter that he was right, it mattered only that the church, comfortable in its dogma, didn't like what he was saying.

Ironically, it was Muslim astronomers, working from the 9th through 13th centuries, who had translated and expanded upon the great astronomical treatises of ancient Greece and India, making Galileo's work possible. But in the Ottoman Empire of the 17th century, as in the Europe of the Inquisition, you got into deep trouble if you spouted new science that ticked off the clerics.

Where'd You Learn to Say That?

Speaking of having a lot to learn, one afternoon we learned how to curse and swear in Turkish. Our Turkish teachers were called away to a trumped-up teachers' meeting and we were left with our American instructors, most of whom were former PCVs who had served in Turkey. We crowded into the Santa Rita's cafeteria.

"Close the doors," the senior instructor said. "Somebody stand guard. If a Turk comes, holler."

With security in place, he continued.

"Now you're going to learn all the words and phrases the Turks would rather die than teach you."

They taught us the words to watch out for: the words for sex and for bodily functions, the curses, obscenities and so's-your-mothers that could get you into a brawl. We learned all the obscene hand and facial gestures, and what to expect if we used them—probably a quick but exquisitely painful death.

These words and gestures meant nothing to us. It was funny, sitting there in a dormitory cafeteria in Texas, happily hurling Turkish obscenities at one another. We felt no emotions at all except an irresistible urge to guffaw. If a Turk had seen us he would have thought us certifiably insane.

We would never have been able to say the same words in the same way in our own language.

What's the difference?

We're all trained from an early age to load certain words and gestures with huge emotional charges. At first they're just meaningless sounds, innocent as milk bottles. But fill the milk bottle with gasoline, jam in a piece of cloth, light it and throw it, and you've got a Molotov cocktail that can cause real mayhem.

The room went quiet as we thought it over. We imagined a crowd of young Turks sitting in a cafeteria at İstanbul University cursing in English, happily hollering words we'd shrink from saying in public. The absurdity of taboo language was right in front of us. It was hilarious except that in Turkey—actually, in most places—it could lead to bodily perforation by heavy bits of metal if you weren't careful.

Yeah, but You'll Miss It When It's Over

Peace Corps training was one of those experiences in which a long, slow time passes in an instant: each 14-hour day was tedious and difficult, but the three summer months flew by in less time than it takes to hurl a Turkish insult (*Eşeği oğul eşek!* for example: "Ass and son of an ass").

August came to its blazing end and so did Peace Corps training. I flew to Pennsylvania for two weeks of home leave before flying off to live who-knows-where on the other side of the planet in a Muslim country without TV, refrigerators, working telephones or dental floss.

This seemed like a good time to visit my girlfriend.

Not that anytime at all wasn't a good time to visit your girlfriend. I had met mine at Tufts. Her name was Jane, which was something of a happy coincidence because my high school girlfriend's name was Jane, too. I didn't collect Janes on purpose despite the obvious and felicitous convenience factor. I simply fell in love with two Janes in a row.

College Jane was foreign and exotic. Well, sort of. She came from Canada originally, which is in fact a whole 'nother country despite what Americans think, and I didn't hold it against her exoticism that she was presently living in New Jersey and had in fact lived there for years. She had dark brown hair and a squinty-eyed 1000-watt smile, spoke French (from her earlier life in Montréal), was brilliantly smart, soft spoken, a feminist, a good singer, and eager to travel. Most amazing of all, perhaps, she laughed at my jokes.

We fled to my parents' cabin in the Pennsylvania mountains for forest walks, soulful talks, and certain other activities—all fairly innocent, I assure you. Or mostly innocent.

"Speak Turkish to me," she said one day. I parroted a few of the stock phrases I had learned, ending with "*Efendi.*"

"*Efendi,*" she repeated, caressing the exotic syllables and smiling. "*Efendi!* It sounds like something out of a historical romance." Romance, eh? I'll get plenty of history and plenty of Turkish where I'm going, but precious little romance.

Soon our time together was over. We both had to go, I to Turkey and she to Naples, where she would spend a post-graduate year. We said a tearful, sob-filled goodbye, not knowing when or even if we would ever see one another again. We promised to write.

My parents drove me the three hours to New York's Kennedy Airport, I boarded the chartered Boeing 707, floated across the Atlantic in a champagne haze, and arrived in blazing Ankara.

Not a Word? Not One?

The first thing I noticed about Ankara was that everybody was speaking Turkish except me. After three months of intensive instruction, the equivalent of a two-year university course, I opened my mouth to answer the questions of the customs and immigration officials at the airport and nothing came out. Dust and heat went in, but no Turkish words came out.

This was profoundly discouraging. The officials had probably been told, no doubt as a *jeu d'esprit* in bad taste, that all these young Americans spoke Turkish. The officials politely switched to English and stamped us in.

We were bussed to Middle East Technical University (METU), a bilingual (Turkish and English) institution substantially supported by US government largesse, where we were lodged in a dormitory. A few hours later, with jet-lag added to our hangover, we were in terrible shape, which is when the Peace Corps chose to issue our site assignments; that is, we were told where we'd be living and working for the next two years.

When we enlisted in the Peace Corps we had agreed to go wherever the Peace Corps posted us. The least desirable posts, almost always reserved for single men, were the small, remote villages in which the PCV would be the only teacher, the only foreigner, probably the only *gavur* (infidel) anyone in the village had ever laid eyes on. No modern apartment buildings, no hot water showers, no restaurants, no cinemas, no English-language newspapers, no English-speaking friends. Only the day's work and, in the evening, the village *çay evi* (tea house) with its talk of seeds, fertilizer, irrigation, crops and harvests, births, deaths and family feuds. Only these for months at a time.

The most desirable posts were the cities: Ankara, İstanbul, İzmir. Ankara was looked upon as the best because it was relatively modern (in a Third-World kind of way) and had the largest concentration of PCVs as well as many American diplomatic and military personnel. A PCV in Ankara always had friends nearby. For young, single unattached males and females, this was an important consideration.

Cosmopolitan İstanbul was many people's dream assignment—certainly it was mine—but it wasn't really a possibility because there were so few Peace

Corps-type jobs there. İstanbul already had plenty of English teachers both Turkish and foreign, so the Peace Corps wasn't needed. Having been the capital of the civilized world for at least a millennium, İstanbul could apparently take care of itself without the help of inexperienced young Americans.

İzmir was a close second to Ankara because it was a beautiful modern Aegean city with beaches nearby and a big Turkish-American military base just north of the city at Çiğli. With the base on the outskirts and NATO's Southeast European headquarters on the waterfront boulevard, İzmir had a significant American presence. Anyone with a radio could receive American news, music and sports programs on Armed Forces Radio. İzmir was beautiful and Turkish, but with lots of English speakers and hamburgers for moments of homesickness.

I got my assignment. It was to İzmir Koleji (İzmir College), an elite prep school with a beautiful pine-shaded campus amid the vineyards of the Aegean University in Bornova, a suburb of İzmir. My salary would be TL1070 ($118) per month.

I was delighted. Most of my PCV colleagues were envious.

After getting our assignments some of us took a bus from METU to Kızılay, Ankara's main square, to celebrate—or commiserate, as the case might be—and to see the Turkish capital. We spotted a new cafeteria several stories above street level on the open-air terrace of the GİMA department store. We sat outside under a full moon in the balmy late September evening air and dined on grilled fish, rice pilav, Turkish desserts and local beer. Music was provided by a British juke box which ran on sixpences. To play a song you bought a sixpence from a waiter, put it in the machine, and picked your tune.

Charming, but…

A few of the current PCV teachers at İzmir Koleji had traveled from Bornova to Ankara to escort us new teachers to İzmir and Bornova. At seven o'clock on the hot morning of September 23rd we gathered with them at the Ankara railway station and boarded our train for the 13-hour ride via Eskişehir, Kütahya, Balıkesir and Manisa to İzmir's Basmane Station. Our second-class tickets cost less than TL80 (US$9). We packed bread, cheese and pastries for lunch, figuring that we couldn't afford a meal in the dining car on a teacher's salary.

The train pulled out of the station right on time at 7:30 am and rumbled across the Anatolian plateau, treeless, dry, dusty and hot after four months without rain.

During the long journey we got to know our guides, the PCVs who had already spent a year teaching at "our" school. Foremost was Rob, a movie-star handsome guy with the easy, assured manner of those whose good looks generate smiles and open doors automatically. He was fairly tall, with swept-back blond hair, an easy, casual way of moving and walking, and a brilliant smile which was mostly real and turned on virtually all the time. Females, whether PCVs or Turks, immediately took an interest in Rob.

Rob had trained in Austin in 1966 and had been walking within sight of the university tower on the day Charles Whitman carried out his murderous target practice.

"Yeah, we heard this popping-and-whizzing sound around us," he said, recalling August 1st, "and somebody yelled 'Take cover!' We did."

Our other guide was named Dave. With a round head, dark hair cut short, round glasses with thick lenses and a wide range of emotional moods, he was the antithesis of Rob. They were different as day and night but they shared an apartment in Bornova, and got along fine.

Besides me, there were two new female teachers, Lily and Carol.

Lily was from Alaska, to which her parents had emigrated from Japan before she was born. Tall, easy-going, hip, intelligent and strikingly attractive, she was a Japanese traditional beauty turbocharged by an American high-protein diet. Lily had just graduated from a prestigious university in Boston and was out to see the world.

Carol was a short, compact blonde from farming country in the Midwest, friendly with a simple, homey appeal, a good heart and a ready smile. To the PCVs who had grown up on the more cosmopolitan Atlantic and Pacific coasts she seemed naïve, a bumpkin girl out of her depth.

We reached Eskişehir before noon. West of the city, the countryside became more fertile and lush with rows of tall, slender poplars rising from the stream banks in every village. As the day and the trip wore on, we allowed ourselves the extravagant purchase of pudding, ice cream and bottles of lukewarm *kola* (the local Coke knock-off) from station vendors.

We approached Karşıyaka, the suburb north of İzmir, at 8:30 pm as the last light of the day was fading and the lights of İzmir were twinkling on across the bay.

"See how the lights twinkle?" Rob asked, pouring on the charm for our benefit. "I've heard they only twinkle like that in İzmir."

It was the rankest claptrap but we lapped it up.

Just before 9 pm our train pulled into Basmane Station in the heart of İzmir, the big city with a small-town soul.

ເວເ

2
BORNOVA

Iron-rimmed horse cart wheels rattled noisily over granite paving stones on my first morning in Bornova, a town of 30,000 people (almost four times the size of my hometown in Pennsylvania). Roosters crowed, donkeys brayed, the late September sun came up bright and hot, hucksters wandered the streets calling out their wares, and I found myself dossed in the hallway of Rob and Dave's apartment wrapped in a blanket.

I got up and wondered out loud about coffee.

"No coffee," Rob said. "Too expensive. How 'bout some tea?"

He poured dark Turkish tea from a small pot into a little gold-rimmed tulip-shaped glass, added hot water from a big aluminum kettle, and handed it to me along with a spoon and a bowl of sugar. As I sipped the hot tea, Rob continued the lesson he had begun yesterday on the train from Ankara.

"Bornova's basically a farming town," Rob said, "even though the university and the *kolej* are here."

After breakfast I took a look around. Farmers drove horse carts through the streets on their way to and from the fields. Small shops along the main street sold groceries, clothing, stationery, yogurt. Old men sat at tea houses around the *meydan*, the town square, smoking *nargiles* (water pipes). Hidden here and there among its many low, old-fashioned red-tile-roofed Turkish houses and its few modern concrete apartment blocks were large classical-style Mediterranean villas with spacious gardens surrounded by high walls. The villas, Rob told me, were owned by "Levantines," mysterious people of European and American stock who had lived their entire lives in Turkey. So Bornova was a farming town with roosters and donkeys for alarm clocks, but with a university, and posh villas, and it was right next to Turkey's third largest city.

The Turkish standard of living was not bad, but many things were far less convenient than in the USA. The normal Turkish home in a town like Bornova had electricity and a radio but no hot water or television (which wouldn't arrive in Turkey until the 1980s). The waiting list for a telephone took about seven years to get to your name unless you paid a lot of money to buy someone else's place farther up the list. If like most people you didn't have a phone, you went to the PTT (*Posta Telefon Telgraf*, the postal, telephone and telegraph office), filled out a form for a long-distance call, got a place on the waiting list and sat there until your call went through, which might be hours. Most people sent telegrams instead because then you didn't have to wait around.

For washing dishes or clothes you heated water on the stove. For showers you went to the corner shop and bought a plastic bag of wood chips soaked in kerosene, put a pile of them in the bottom of a tall water heater, added sticks for fuel, lit the fire, and came back in an hour or two when the water was hot. For baths, you went to the *hamam*, or Turkish bath, of which there was always one in every neighborhood. It was usually right near the mosque because cleanliness is akin to godliness in Islam and most Muslims take a long steam bath at least once a week, preferably on Friday, the Muslim holy day.

What did people do for amusement without TV? The men sat around in tea houses, usually dingy places with tables inside and also on the sidewalk out front. They discussed politics, sports, crops, business, food. They played checkers and dominos, but most of all *tavla* (backgammon). They smoked cigarettes and water pipes, and drank gallons of strong, bracing Turkish tea grown on the humid mountain slopes of the eastern Black Sea coast, brewed fresh every hour or so, and heavily sugared in the glass. They drank Turkish coffee less frequently because it was more expensive.

The women worked, often harder than the men, in the house, in the fields and sometimes in the workshops and bazaars. They knitted, crocheted, made exquisite lace and wove gorgeous Turkish carpets and, when they had a few free minutes, drank tea at home with other women.

The kids mostly played soccer (football) because it was cheap and readily available. All you needed was an open space and a ball, and if you didn't have a ball you could use rags wrapped up in a ball. Few kids had bikes or other fancy toys, though they might find an old barrel hoop or bicycle tire, get a stick and play hoop-and-stick like kids in those old Victorian engravings. They might also play with the animals—goats, sheep, cats, chickens—because they were usually in charge of them.

"There's not much to do in Bornova," Rob said. "If you want something to do, you take a minibus into İzmir." So we did.

Despite having hosted foreign merchants and traders since 1535, İzmir in 1967 didn't feel particularly cosmopolitan. It was bigger and had more culture and commerce than a provincial town, but not much more sophistication. Its role as a major international commercial center had ended with the great fire during the War of Independence in 1923. Most İzmirlis (citizens of İzmir) looked upon it as home, but "the city" was İstanbul, the place you went to have fun and do business. Ankara, by contrast, was where you went to beseech petty bureaucrats to make incremental advances on matters important to you but trivial to them.

İzmir's market district bustled with crowds every day except Sunday, but otherwise the city had an agreeable, unhurried Mediterranean ambience. Every Sunday evening the waterfront boulevard called the Birinci Kordon (First Cordon) was closed to cars so that families could stroll in the balmy evening air and hormone-charged teens could assume looks of nonchalance while surreptitiously x-raying members of the alternate gender.

Along its waterfront from Republic Square to Konak, İzmir in 1967 was strongly reminiscent of 19th-century Smyrna, with its rough stone dockside warehouses, old-style five-story office buildings, and rows of kayıks, wooden coastal freight boats, tied up to the quay unloading bulk grain, sand, lumber, and coal. Walking through its streets the fragrant scent of tobacco came from the great warehouses and mixed with the salt air of the bay and the smell of manure dropped by cart and fayton (carriage) horses to create a complex, pleasant, earthy smell.

An Actual Job

On Monday, the second day after I arrived, we had a staff meeting at İzmir Koleji. For the first (and last) time in my life, I was on a staff and, like the other seven PCV teachers at the school, I had to get up and go to work.

İzmir Koleji was a preparatory middle and high school operated by the Ministry of Education. The students, who had to pass an examination to get in, entered at the age of 10 for a year of preparatory classes which included intensive training in English. Thereafter, some classes were taught in Turkish, others in English. The goal was to develop bilingual students who could participate internationally in science, engineering, government and commerce. The ministry's strategy was prescient and highly successful given the present-day dominance of English in all these fields.

The school had been founded in an old Levantine villa at the end of a kilometer-long private drive shaded by a double row of fragrant pines. The villa's spacious grounds had been developed into a school campus including modern classroom buildings, dormitories, a dining hall, a gymnasium and sports fields.

At the staff meeting we were introduced to Süleyman Bey, the headmaster, Necdet Bey the assistant headmaster, and our Turkish colleagues, male and female, on the teaching staff.

Süleyman Bey was a classic headmaster: grey-haired, soft-spoken, digni-fied, impeccably dressed, outwardly serene, occasionally imperious, and mostly remote. He was the monarch of the school, representing it at prestigious oc-casions but not involving himself in nitty-gritty daily operations. That was the preserve of Necdet Bey, who was short, muscular and blunt, a long-suffering, chain-smoking fireplug of a man with the eternally furrowed brow that is the occupational hazard of school administrators.

The Ministry of Education and its representatives Süleyman and Necdet seemed uncertain whether they really wanted PCVs in Turkey. Both of them were unfailingly polite and correct in their dealings with the PCV teachers, but they generally dealt with us warily, and with good reason. We were loose can-nons. The headmasters couldn't be sure exactly what we would do or say in our classes. They were happy to have the US government pay our wages, but would rather have had older, more experienced teachers who were completely under ministry control. They were almost certain we would cause them headaches, and they were right.

Our colleagues on the teaching staff were also courteous, polite and friendly to us, welcoming us among them and according us a professional respect which we did not merit, at least not this early in our teaching careers. Although we were idealistic and hard-working, we had nowhere near their depth of training or experience.

Teaching is a highly respected profession in Turkey and all teachers, present and former, are addressed as *hocam* (My Teacher). It's not just students or former students who call their teachers *hocam*. Everybody addresses every teacher as *hocam*, so that's how Turks addressed us. Here we were, inexperienced twenty-something foreigners who had taught for a few weeks at most being addressed as My Teacher by dignified older Turks, many the parents of our students, some of them prominent figures in the community, at least one of them an Oxford graduate! It was so undeserved an honor that it made us wince, though secretly we were deeply grateful for this splendid Turkish courtesy. Nobody had ever given us much in the way of respect up to this point, and even unearned respect was welcome.

The PCVs who had taught at İzmir Koleji during the previous school year had warned us to beware of only one teacher: Özcan Bey. He seemed to take pleasure in veiled denigration of our efforts, which was ironic because he was the only non-PCV teacher who had ever set foot in the USA. In fact, he had lived there for seven years. He dressed American-style, wore a fedora, drove an American station wagon, and had adopted many other middle-class American habits. He told us confidently that he "knew everything there was to know about America." Having grown up and lived our entire lives in America, we felt we had barely begun to learn about our own country, but Özcan Bey knew everything about us and our country after only seven years. This alone would qualify him for jerkdom. I suspect there was a heavy inferiority complex working its way through Özcan Bey. Unfortunately, he ended up projecting it on us when in fact there were far easier targets nearby, some of whom I would learn about the very next day.

This is the Peace Corps?

"I've got an invitation to the consul-general's house tonight. Wanna come?" Rob said on Tuesday, the third day after my arrival. "Lots of good food and free booze."

"Are you coming, Dave?" I asked.

"No, I don't really go for that stuff," he said.

Rob was the socialite. With his good looks and practiced manners he glided smoothly through any social situation, charming everyone. He was impossible to dislike. Even when he got angry, which was very, very seldom, it was alright. You were angry *with* him, even if you were the one he was angry at. He was just so *nice* about it. It seemed like stage anger and therefore didn't have as big an emotional charge. And yet he was completely sincere—a thoroughly likable guy, well balanced, conscious of his charm and willing to use it when he wanted something, but always honest and without guile.

Dave was endearing in his own way. Far more serious and less outgoing than Rob, he was still good company, intelligent and insightful, and helpful in explaining the situation at the school where we would all be teaching. In fact, he seemed absorbed in his work. He would add interesting insights to our conversations about Turkey and the Turks, but when the talk turned to the school, he came to life with impassioned opinions and observations. Clearly, cocktail parties were not his thing.

Rob and I went. The consul's villa was high on a ridge overlooking İzmir Bay, which was now filled with warships of the US Navy: the Sixth Fleet was in port for R & R. The consul's spacious living room was filled with Sixth Fleet naval officers paying their respects to the local dignitaries. The consul's reception was in their honor, and included diplomats from other countries and prominent local government, business and cultural leaders.

We chatted amiably, the naval officers poised, polite and formal, with interesting things to say. The Turkish guests were sophisticated, urbane, and spoke excellent English. We ate, we drank, we chatted, we laughed, we ate and drank some more. This was the Peace Corps?

Meanwhile, far beneath us on the waterfront Yankee sailors were storming ashore, their pockets full of dollars, their pants full of horn, their throats parched for booze. Many of them headed straight for the dicey *pavyons* (cheap nightclubs) that dotted the waterfront, followed at a safe distance by US military police. The next morning the local newspapers were filled with grainy photos of wasted American sailors black and blue from fights over girls. Many of the gobs had gotten so drunk they could nearly speak Turkish spontaneously. They wrecked *pavyons* for what must have seemed good and sufficient reasons at the time, though less so the next morning from the confines of the brig.

Tuesday and its aftermath demonstrated unmistakably to me that the citizens of İzmir had a love-hate relationship with America and Americans. Actually, it's wrong to call it a relationship. America blessed or inflicted, and the Turks enjoyed or suffered. They didn't have much of a choice. The major afflictions at the moment were the Cyprus crisis, the Vietnam war, the US Sixth Fleet, and the huge US Air Force base north of the city at Çiğli. That base and the Southeast European headquarters of NATO right in the center of İzmir brought significant wealth to the city in the form of big-spending foreign military personnel and well-paying jobs supplying their wants and needs, but it was also an unmistakable symbol of American political hegemony and monstrous military power. This power was ostensibly being exercised to protect American allies like Turkey from the steely grip of communist dictatorship, but the Turks feared they might end up being "protected" the way the Vietnamese were.

Between 1965 and 1969 US forces dropped or shot more than four million metric tons of bombs, ammunition and other explosives on the poor, backward country of Vietnam. The uneducated, ill-equipped, underfed but plucky Vietnamese kept fighting.

Many young American men in my situation shared a common view of this "anti-communist" war: communism was an idealistic but unworkable economic system that was used as a cover by political dictators and oligarchs. Yes, America needed to fight for democracy and free enterprise, but this was not our battle. The Vietnam War was a civil war between the northern and southern halves of a former French colony, both halves of which had more or less corrupt, dictatorial governments.

This poor little southeast Asian country couldn't possibly pose a threat to the United States of America. The United States had no real interest there, so what was to win? World War II had been a righteous war. The Korean War had a clear purpose. Vietnam was important to those who believed in the "domino effect" whereby countries falling to communism brought other countries down with them; but to those of us who didn't believe in that theory, Vietnam meant nothing. However, as we were discovering, the symbol of Vietnam meant a lot to people in other Third World countries, and it certainly colored their thinking about the Americans living among them, whether they were US soldiers, visiting US sailors, or Peace Corps teachers.

The US air base at Çiğli was a constant influence in İzmir. Many of its officers lived in plush apartments with west-facing (ie, sunset) sea views along the Birinci Kordon, the posh waterfront boulevard that was İzmir's prestige address, housing out of reach to all but the wealthiest locals. The US officers' club was in this posh waterfront space as well. The officers club and all the other American facilities—the combination supermarket/ department store known as the base exchange, the cinema, the medical clinic, the library, etc—were off limits to Turks. Actually, these military facilities were off limits to everyone without some role in the US military, government or NATO establishments, including civilian Americans (like me). Civilian Turks were equally excluded from Turkish military facilities such as officers' clubs and base exchanges. But to Turks it looked as though only they were being kept out of the US facilities so prominent in their midst.

The two most prominent symbols of this love-hate relationship were Coca Cola and Armed Forces Radio.

Coca Cola had penetrated markets and shops in Turkey just as it had in other countries, elbowing aside healthful traditional drinks such as fruit juice, *ayran* (a yogurt drink) and plain water with expensive caffeine-laced sugar syrup. Some Turks would express their independence, when within view of Americans, by ostentatiously ordering bottles of locally-made *gazoz* (lemon soda), *kola* or *Fruko* (orange soda) instead of Coke. When no Americans were around many of them would revert to Coke because they preferred the taste. Unbeknownst to most Turks, Fruko was manufactured by the Coca-Cola Company. Even so, I sort of admired the Turks' principled though doomed effort to escape the tentacles of Big Sweet Bubble Water.

The American Armed Forces Radio Network had a low-power AM broadcasting station on the Çiğli base. According to the joint military protocol signed by Turkey and the USA, low-power AM stations were allowed to transmit a signal only strong enough to reach to the limits of the military base, but in fact the signal reached all the way to, through and beyond İzmir to the satisfaction of all Americans and many Turks.

So the İzmir to which I came was essentially a pleasant, easygoing place, no longer a small town but not yet a big city; no longer a cosmopolitan Mediterranean port but not completely provincial; playing host to an intrusive foreign military presence that was both welcome and unwelcome at the same time.

İzmir's sensitivity may have been increased because of its role in the Turkish War of Independence. "Infidel Smyrna" had had a large non-Muslim population before the war. It was the final battleground in the war against foreign intervention in the Turkish homeland, and the battle had been commanded by none other than the Commander-in-chief, Mustafa Kemal (Atatürk).

Fred, or, the Importance of Atatürk

"Have you noticed Fred yet?" one of my PCV friends asked with a smirk soon after I arrived. "Fred. You must have noticed."

"Who's Fred?" I asked, ready to suffer the ignominy of ignorance.

He pointed at a plaster bust, painted gold, of Atatürk, Turkey's national hero.

"Meet Fred," he said.

Wha'?

In Turkey, images of Atatürk (1881-1938) are inescapable: on the money, on the walls, in the public squares, even on mountainsides, where white and black stones are arranged into giant rustic mosaic portraits. His words grace classroom walls, statue plinths, newspaper banners, anything and everything. Roll up the cults of Lenin, Stalin, Mao, JFK, Elvis and Britney into one and they still wouldn't get the audience penetration Atatürk gets in Turkey.

I thought of the books we had read in Austin, among them Lord Kinross's biography of Atatürk.

Mustafa Kemal (Atatürk) became famous during the Gallipoli campaign of 1915 which had been instigated by the 40-year-old British First Lord of the Admiralty, Winston Churchill. When the warships carrying the powerful British imperial and French expeditionary force appeared at Gallipoli, Lieutenant Colonel Mustafa Kemal alone predicted accurately where the enemy would come ashore. Acting to some extent without orders, and commanding right from the front line, he thrust his infantry regiment into a suicidal assault against the advancing ANZAC (Australian-New Zealand) troops. Kemal's regiment was wiped out in unspeakable hand-to-hand combat, and Kemal survived only by a miracle (the watch in his breast pocket stopped a piece of shrapnel that would otherwise have driven right through his heart), but the furious ANZAC advance was stopped. The invaders dug in and thereafter the two armies fell into a pattern of unwinnable trench warfare. Churchill's short, sharp battle for the heights of Gallipoli was lost.

Kemal won the battle but the Allies won the war, occupied İstanbul, and proceeded to carve up the country. Unable to bear the dismemberment of his homeland, Kemal escaped from occupied İstanbul into Anatolia where he organized the resistance and fought off the advancing armies of four countries under the most difficult conditions imaginable. When the smoke finally cleared and Turkey's borders were secure, he chucked out the sultan and established a republic.

Granted the honorific surname Atatürk—"Father of the Turks"—by a grateful parliament, Kemal went on to reform Turkish society utterly, making Turkey a secular state by instituting European-style civil law in place of religious law (Sharia) and encouraging the adoption of European customs. He saw to it that women became doctors, lawyers, university professors, administrators, pilots and members of parliament. The Turkish Constitutional Court had a woman justice decades before the US Supreme Court did. The personality cults of Atatürk's contemporaries, dictators like Stalin, Hitler, and Mao, were tools to strengthen these men's stranglehold on political power. Atatürk, on the contrary, used his substantial—sometimes dictatorial—power and influence for the establishment of democracy. He didn't take an independent parliament and turn it into a rubber stamp. He took a rubber stamp and made it independent. Just because such things seldom happen doesn't mean they never do.

Not everyone reveres Atatürk, of course. Minorities of Islamists and ultra-conservatives dream of undoing his work and of recreating a sprawling empire based on Turkish ethnicity or strict Islamic law. No wonder, then, that the country's democratic, secularist government defended Atatürk's vision. As in many countries, Turkey has lese-majesty laws against insulting or belittling the national symbols such as the flag and the Founder, which brings us back to Fred.

For us Peace Corps volunteers the lese-majesty laws posed a bit of a problem. We were intensely interested in Turkey, the Turks, Turkish history, society and culture, and we discussed these topics endlessly. We were also light-hearted twentysomething Americans who, being the very first Television Generation, saw life and the world as one big sitcom. Weak jokes, bad puns, mindless repartee and laugh-track put-downs were integral to our conversation.

If we talked about Atatürk, there was a good chance we might inadvertently mention him in a TV-like context. The snippet of conversation might be overheard and misinterpreted by a Turk, who might well take offense. This could be quite dangerous, the equivalent of joking in an airport about hijacking a plane. A few PCVs did in fact get into trouble when references to Turkish patriotic symbols were overheard and misunderstood.

Hence "Fred." He was Atatürk in class, and our friend Fred elsewhere. Call it bizarre, but it was convenient, and protected both Fred and us from nasty surprises.

Chicken Dreams

A week after my arrival in Bornova I found a place to live, a dark ground-floor apartment that had been rented by two PCVs the previous year. The Peace Corps paid the rent over the summer and used it to store furniture. The place was stuffed with stuff. My problem in furnishing the apartment was not finding furniture but getting rid of furniture. That and Rıza Bey's chickens.

Rıza Bey, my new landlord, was an eager, nervous man. The day after I moved in he came knocking at my door.

"Good morning, sir. How are you? Are you well?" he asked excitedly. He was eager to get to know his new foreign tenant and to provide whatever I needed. His agitation made me agitated, which scared my few words of Turkish back deep into my skull. They would not come out.

What I wanted from my brain was the words for "chicken," "noise," and "silence," or, better yet, "summary execution." Rıza Bey, I discovered to my dismay, was an enthusiastic chicken farmer. The hens occupied a sizable coop in his back garden right beneath my bedroom window. They set up an unbearable racket anytime there was daylight. And the rooster—the rooster! Every dream I had in that apartment was of throttling the rooster.

I wrote home about the apartment: "The best I can say is that it's not a suitcase."

The chickens were hard to bear, but I really had to leave because of the rent: TL325 a month, nearly a third of my salary. Rob and Dave paid TL188 each for their sunny, airy third-floor apartment with two bedrooms, three balconies, fine views of the town and the countryside beyond, a new bathroom, kitchen, salon, hallway (my former temporary home) and study. And no chickens. I wanted to pay less money for a place to sleep and have more money available for travel.

Lily and Carol found an apartment on an upper floor in a new building in the center of Bornova. Lily the bi-coastal sophisticate and Carol the Midwestern farm girl made a bizarre twosome, but as the only two new female PCV teachers they were pretty much destined to share an apartment, like it or not. They had a fine view, lots of sunlight, modern plumbing, and a landlady who looked upon them as a prime catch: two young foreign teachers who would pay their fairly high rent reliably. Landlords loved having young single women as tenants just as they feared having young single men.

Taking a hint from Rıza Bey's chickens, I spent a lot of my time trying to figure out how to fly the coop.

In It but Not of It

One day during the week when I was staying at Rob and Dave's, a young man named Franz appeared at the door. Franz was our age, of middle height, with brown hair, thick eyebrows and an engaging smile. He spoke fluent English, French and Turkish and carried a German passport. His Turkish was perfect and unaccented because he had been born and raised in Bornova and educated in Turkish schools.

Franz and his parents held both German and Turkish citizenship. They had been born in Turkey, as had parents and grandparents before them. Franz had never been to Germany and didn't speak German. As a Turkish citizen, he had already completed his service in the Turkish army, but Franz didn't think of himself as a Turk, and Turks didn't think of him as a Turk either. Franz was a "Levantine," the descendant of European traders who had moved to the Ottoman Empire and lived in Turkey ever since. In 1535 Sultan Süleyman the Magnificent and King François I of France made the first commercial treaty between a European country and the Ottoman Empire. The sultan allowed France, and later other European countries, to send traders to his dominions to foster commerce.

The traders had to live in a small fenced-in district on the İzmir waterfront that came to be called "Frankish Street" (Frenk Sokak). It was near where the Church of St. Polycarp (1630) still stands. The "Franks," as the French (and later all Europeans) were called, were soon joined by the English, then the Dutch and the Italians. They built their warehouses and offices along Frenk Sokak, with their living quarters above, and could not travel outside the restricted area without the sultan's permission.

Over the centuries living restrictions were eased. During the 1800s the prosperous Franks, now called Levantines (from "Levant," the eastern Mediterranean) built spacious villas inland where they could escape the city's summer heat and contagious diseases. Some of the families resident in İzmir and its garden suburbs such as Bornova in 1967 traced their ancestry to traders who had arrived more than a century before. They held British, French, German, Italian or American passports, but may never have set foot in those countries.

Franz lived with his parents in a big old villa in the center of Bornova. He took us to see it. The rambling one-story stuccoed stone house was a series of rooms surrounding a central courtyard, a logical layout for this relatively mild Mediterranean climate. It was furnished in 19th-century European Mediterranean style with some antique furniture and lots of fine Turkish carpets.

Franz spoke French because it had been Europe's lingua franca since the time of Napoleon, and also the language of international travel, trade and diplomacy. He had learned English because it was becoming the new international language of commerce, diplomacy, and learning. His accent in English sounded vaguely British, but I realized later that it was an accent unique to the Turkish Levantine community.

We had no telephone—most people in Turkey had no telephone in 1967—so Franz dropped by Rob and Dave's apartment in his old 1951 Chevrolet every now and then to invite them to take a drive. After I arrived, they included me. We'd go to the beach, or for walks in the hills.

One chilly evening Franz dropped by and invited me to a party at his grandfather's villa, which was not far from where we lived. The great house was a living museum of genteel 19th-century Ottoman social life. The lofty salons were decorated with dark oil paintings, and the floors, walls and sofas were covered in rich Turkish carpets which his grandfather and staff had gotten in the villages from which they bought their stocks of tobacco. Fist-sized lumps of coal, piled high in coal grates in the shallow fireplaces, glowed with warmth. I couldn't help thinking of Jane, and how she would have loved to see this grand old place. But she was in Naples, seeing grand old places of her own.

Franz's grandfather was tall, formal and austere, but he welcomed us young Americans with a smile and the appropriate Turkish greeting: *hoş geldiniz*. I tried to answer in Turkish but didn't get very far. I switched to French, which I spoke better, but not much better.

"My grandfather speaks English," Franz said, "and eleven other languages."

We chatted amiably about the house and its history. We nibbled stuffed vine leaves and flaky pastries, sipped Turkish wine and beer, and talked about Bornova and İzmir, the past and the future.

Sometime later I wanted to visit Franz's grandfather at his tobacco warehouse in İzmir. I telephoned for an appointment.

Buyrun ("Yes, please") said the voice at the other end of the line. I assumed it was a Turkish receptionist or clerk, so I tried to ask for an appointment in Turkish but didn't do too well. I switched to French, and so did the voice at the other end of the line, but that wasn't much better. It's difficult speaking a foreign language you don't know well and don't use much, but it's three times as difficult to do it over the phone. In exasperation I blurted something out in English.

"Turkish, French, English—make up your mind!" said the exasperated voice. We continued in English. It was no receptionist, but Franz's grandfather in person. He suggested 2 o'clock.

The huge barn-like warehouse was suffused with the rich, sweet aroma of drying tobacco. Its owner worked in a small, simple office amid the fragrant bales, commercial quarters that were the exact opposite of his grand villa. There were no forklifts or conveyor belts or hard hats or computers, just *hamals* (porters) carrying loads of tobacco here and there on their backs and an old man tallying figures in big ledger-books. Like the villa, it was a glimpse of the Ottoman past that was fast disappearing in the face of Turkey's rapid modernization.

I imagined the fragrant bales being loaded into ships and sent to America where the light, tasty Turkish leaf would be blended with heartier Virginia and dark Burley to make full-flavored pipe tobacco and the better-tasting stogies and fags.

"Turkish cigarettes don't cause cancer, only American ones do," my Turkish friends told me. I found this statement hilarious at the time, but later discovered that fragrant Turkish leaf does in fact have much less tar. Because of US tobacco companies' efforts to ruin the simple pleasure of an occasional smoke by goosing up their products' nicotine hit and addictive properties, it's much less hilarious now.

Soon after arriving in Turkey I took up smoking. Like it or not, tobacco is an aromatic herb. It tastes good. I didn't care about the nicotine hit. I guess I was lucky because I've never been addicted. I'd smoke two cigarettes a day, or ten, or one, or none.

Although I still enjoy the occasional cigar (about as frequently as the solstice), I haven't bought a pack of cigarettes in decades, but it's not because tobacco has been demonized. I don't think Turkish tobacco hurt me much. Maybe my Turkish friends were right. Maybe their tobacco really isn't so bad for you. These are the people who gave us Smyrna figs, dried apricots, fruit leather and yogurt, for godsake.

Besides, I never inhaled.

❧

3

WHO'S TEACHING WHOM?

All I did was open the door, step into the classroom and gently say "Good morning, class."

SOWL!

Thirty-three ten-year-olds leapt to their feet, stood rigid as boards and bellowed SOWL! at me. The force of it almost blew out the windows.

What was that all about? I struggled with my few Turkish words and asked them to sit.

SOWL, I soon learned, was actually *Sağ ol* ("Very good, sir"). It's what Turkish soldiers say early and often to their commanders, and it's how Turkish school children greet their teachers in the morning.

My first accomplishment that day was teaching them to stand at ease, smile and answer "Good morning, Mr. Brosnahan!" in a calm voice when I entered.

These 10-year-old *Hazırlık* (Preparatory) students, most of whom had not yet reached puberty, were the best students at İzmir Koleji. Not having the opposite gender on their minds all the time they were orderly, enthusiastic, friendly, serious and hard working. Nothing gave them more pleasure than to do well in school, if you can imagine. Turkey was—and still is—at that stage of development where an education is a precious gift, not a hassle.

Most of the students were Turkish Muslim boys, with a few Turkish girls, two Iranian girls, and three Turkish-Jewish students, two boys and a girl. All of them learned quickly and were a joy to teach.

One morning early in the year little Moşe raised his hand and said "Mr. Brosnahan, you didn't give us enough homework last night. We finished it and still had study time left over." The other students nodded in agreement. I was careful after that to suggest additional work that could be done in any "extra" time.

My young students were naturally curious about me. As a foreigner who spoke only a little Turkish I was exotic. They frequently asked questions about me, my family, my friends, and my country. I was happy for their curiosity. Teaching them about the world outside their own country was part of my job.

One morning Ahmet asked, "Mr. Brosnahan, I'm Turkish, what are you?" The rest of the class waited eagerly to hear what I'd say.

"I'm American" I answered.

That's not the answer they were looking for.

"Excuse me," he said, "but isn't everybody in America from somewhere else?"

"Except for the *Kızıldereliler* (Redskins)," little Ayse added.

"Yes, except for the *Kızıldereliler*," Ahmet confirmed.

"But I come from America," I said. "So I'm an American."

"No, no," he said, frustrated. "What are you *really*?"

"I'm *really* an American" I said, smiling.

Ahmet stood there vexed, his brain racing. Finally, he had an idea.

"What are your parents?"

"My parents are Americans, too."

"What are your grandparents?"

"They're Americans."

"What were their parents and grandparents?"

With the third and fourth generations he got his prize.

"My great-grandparents and great-great-grandparents were from England, Scotland, Ireland, Germany and France," I said. There was a huge sigh throughout the classroom. Victory! The students' faces lit up with smiles.

"So you're a mixture of bloods!" Ahmet said in triumph.

My secret was out.

Pounding his little chest he exclaimed "We, we're pure Turkish!"

I looked across the classroom at my beautiful students. Little Ahmet had the Asian eyes, dark complexion and black hair of a warrior in a Turkish miniature. Geylani had the blond hair and fair skin of a cherub in a Renaissance painting. The other students ran the gamut between.

"Americans are proud to be a mixture of bloods," I said, smiling. "We think it makes us strong."

"Yes, alright," Ahmet said finally. "But pure Turkish is good, too."

"Of course," I said, "of course."

Don't Smile Before Christmas
This was the fun part, but for all of us, teachers and students, most days were hard work. Peace Corps guidelines called for us to carry a course load (number

of classes) of 16 or 18 hours per week. Assuming the normal ratio of two hours' preparation for each hour of class, that meant we'd be working about 48 hours per week. In fact, with too few English teachers, we had at least 25 hours of classes. One day per week I taught every single hour—seven hours, from the first class of the day to the last. The other days I had fewer classes, but it still added up to at least a 70-hour week, and this was for huge classes of 40 to 45 students.

At first it didn't matter. We PCVs were young and unattached. The only people we knew in Turkey were our PCV colleagues and our Turkish colleagues. Our Turkish colleagues mostly had families and friends of their own. Because of this and the language barrier, we didn't socialize much outside of school time, which may be why we socialized with our students during school hours, which turned out to be a serious error.

Before the school year began Rob and Dave had warned us: "Don't smile before Christmas." It was important to establish a serious mood and to preserve discipline. If a teacher smiled, particularly a young foreign teacher unfamiliar with the customary formality and strict discipline of a Turkish classroom, the students would sense weakness and, like students anywhere, exploit it. Our Turkish colleagues never fraternized with students during the lunch hour or after classes. They were paternal and maternal authority figures, and expected the students to treat them as such, which they did.

Against the sage advice of our experienced colleagues, we insouciant PCVs from training group Turkey 15 fraternized with the students, enjoying their company and treating them as equals.

"You're not much older than we are," they'd point out.

I'd chat with them during recess, joke with them over lunch, and discuss weighty matters such as the Vietnam War as we walked along the lane back to Bornova after school.

This was one of the problems Süleyman Bey feared, with good reason. It made more work for us, and for him.

With hindsight, lack of discipline was not all bad. It allowed some unforgettable moments, like the day I entered a 10th grade classroom on the second floor. Across the room, five students were laughing and closing a big swinging window...right onto the hands of a student who was hanging outside clinging to the window frame! He was about to fall and break his neck!

"What are you doing? Stop!" I shouted, running to the window, pushing them aside, pulling back the window. They roared with laughter, including the student "hanging" outside, who was actually standing on a broad concrete ledge. He climbed back in. I did my best to calm them down and teach a class. After school I laughed all the way back to Bornova. They would never have pulled such antics in a classroom ruled by one of my Turkish colleagues.

Peace Corps Cuisine

We worked hard, and when we came home in the evening we wanted a good dinner. Unfortunately, what we got instead was Peace Corps cuisine.

With no clue how to cook and no inclination to learn, PCV men ate a lot of plain rice with margarine or innumerable bowls of noodles. A common dish for male Bornova PCVs was boiled semolina ("cream of wheat"). We'd cook too much, eat some with sugar and margarine for breakfast, and leave the rest in the pot to cool. When we came home from school it would have congealed into a rubber-like slab. We'd flop the slab into a pan and fry it in olive oil for dinner—this in the midst of a country with some of the cheapest, most delicious food in the world.

Luckily for our bodies, Turkish sourdough bread was delicious, healthful, cheap, and always fresh because it was baked twice a day, early morning and late afternoon. The fruit was cheap, abundant and excellent as well. Superb Black Sea butter was out of our price range, so we used Sana, a flavorful margarine better than any American margarine I had ever tasted.

Fresh yogurt was the other surprise. In 1967 you could find yogurt in New York and a few other big American cities with immigrant populations of Arabs, Armenians, Bulgarians, Greeks, Israelis, Turks or other yogurt-eaters, but most Americans had never heard of yogurt and when they did hear of it they reacted with fear and loathing.

At the American library in İzmir I picked up a copy of *Teen* magazine with a travel article about Turkey. The teenaged writer had toured Turkey and marveled at the Blue Mosque, Topkapı Palace, Ephesus and Pamukkale. She met a Turkish family who took her to dinner. The dinner included yogurt.

"What is it?" she asked.

"Soured milk," they answered.

"Ewwww! While my hosts weren't looking, I fed my soured milk to the cat," she reported.

Come to think of it, the great empires of the past have all been based on yogurt. David no doubt knocked back a goodly amount of *laban* and *eshel* before going out to topple Goliath. Genghis Khan spread yogurt culture (pun intended) across half the world. (Luckily, most of the world didn't take to that other Mongol practice: tenderizing beefsteaks by putting them under their saddles.) I'll bet the Romans had yogurt because they didn't have refrigerators to keep their milk cold. Of all the things Roman milk became when it was no longer fresh, yogurt must've been one of them.

The British didn't have yogurt, so they sent ships all over the world looking for it.

America without yogurt would be incomprehensible to any kid with a lunch box. How could America have achieved world-power status without yogurt? It doesn't seem possible.

In Bornova we had several shops that made and sold only yogurt. I went first thing in the morning to get it fresh. The *yoğurtçu* (yogurt-maker), armed with an oversized spoon, approached the large bowl that had clabbered overnight. Its mirror-like surface resembled a glacial milk pond, but we both knew its secret: the clever *Lactobacillus bulgaricus* had performed its magic. The milk now had substance, *gravitas*. With a gleam in his eye the master lowered the spoon, canted it slightly to one side, and eased it gently into the milky mass. Lubed by microscopic globules of partially digested milk-fat, the steel edge penetrated smoothly, slicing into the low-viscosity semi-liquid, the shallow bowl of the utensil quickly disappearing below the formerly pristine, virgin surface.

The yoğurtçu paused, pursed his lips, and slowly, majestically, raised the spoon straight upward and … SHHHHHHLLLLLLOOOOOOOOP!…carved out a pothole of yogurt and flopped it into a plastic tub. Breakfast!

Another lifesaver for undernourished PCVs were the little hand-grenade-shaped bottles of dark glass made by the Tamek company and filled with fruit nectar.

"You've got to try this. It's unbelievable," a friend said to me when first he tasted one. It was pure, thick fruit nectar. The smallest sip filled your mouth with an explosion of essential flavor. Peach, apricot, pear, Morello cherry…Turkish fruit was superb, and each little bottle held the quintessence, the very spirit of the fruit. The little bottles were expensive but worth it. In America there was nothing like it.

"It's too good," another friend said. "It can't last. Someone will come here and teach them to add water and sugar and stretch one of these little bottles into five and raise their profits fourfold."

A decade later food engineers arrived from Germany and did just that. Now Turkey has the same sort of thin, artificially sugared and flavored juice drinks as America. But for a few years, Turkey was a fruit nectar-lover's paradise.

We drank *Tekel Birası*, made by the government. Everyone drank government beer because there was no other beer sold in Turkey, if you discount the shiploads of Budweiser sold only to, and guzzled by, the 40,000 American troops. Tekel Birası was made by Tekel, the Turkish State Monopolies, a holdover from Ottoman times when the government added to its coffers by controlling a few essential products such as salt, matches, tobacco and certain alcoholic beverages. It was semi-flavorful, semi-flat and sometimes semi-sour, but it's what there was if you wanted beer.

President Gerald Ford famously said he was glad the US government didn't make beer because if it did they'd have to sell it for $50 a six-pack. Well, the

Turkish government made beer but would have sold none of it for $50, so it made and sold it cheap. Or, probably, made it expensively and sold it cheap in that irony of ironies, the government of a Muslim country subsidizing the production and sale of alcoholic beverages. In any case, a certain lighthearted attitude toward quality is what you'd expect of a monopoly, whether it be Tekel or Microsoft.

We drank sparkling mineral water (*maden sodası*), also a government monopoly, which was expensive and difficult to find in America back then but cheap and good in Turkey.

As for wine, we drank mostly Tekel's Güzel Marmara white. At 20¢ a bottle (plus 5¢ deposit) it was undeniably cheap but, like Tekel beer, one bottle would taste like Puligny-Montrachet, the next like pig whizz. Among the Tekel reds we drank mostly Buzbağ (pronounced BOOZ-bah, not buzz-bag). Buzbağ is full-flavored but usually contains so much tannin that after a few sips you have to sort out your puckered mouth with a screwdriver. Wines from the non-Tekel Kavaklıdere company were better, but they were substantially more expensive, and therefore only for special occasions.

On weekend evenings when we couldn't stand our own so-called cooking any longer we'd catch a minibus to İzmir and make a beeline for Nuri's.

Nuri's was a bare, simple cookshop on Anafartalar Caddesi near Basmane Station. It was patronized mostly by market merchants. We walked in as a group and Nuri rushed from his kitchen to greet us as though we were the mayor and city council. He fussed over us while we got seated and beamed with delight as we ordered his simple stews and pilavs. We ate our fill. The food was delicious. The bill was rarely even a dollar per person. We paid happily, and we still owe Nuri for keeping us alive and nutrified during the grossest of our bachelor years.

Once a month—usually just after we got paid—we'd go to a fish restaurant on the waterfront between the two main squares of Republic and Konak. The restaurant was pretty basic but fancier than Nuri's, and it served booze. We'd order a dozen plates of *meze* (Turkish hors d'oeuvres): sheep's-milk cheese, potato fritters, stuffed vine leaves, white beans vinaigrette, creamy eggplant purée, *sigara böreği* (pastry fritters stuffed with white cheese), tomato and cucumber salads, black olives, *taramasalata* (red caviar spread), whatever we liked. We talked and laughed and wondered aloud about our future. We drank, and when the bottle of cheap white wine was empty we ordered another.

Twilight turned to evening, then to night. The little bit of daytime traffic along this unfashionable part of the waterfront boulevard slowly disappeared, leaving the broad cobbled street empty and dark. The lights of Karşıyaka glowed and twinkled above the dark water on the far side of İzmir Bay. The brightly lit ferryboats glided swiftly and silently across the darkling horizon. The air was fragrant with the scent of tobacco, fish, figs, and the sea. Tomorrow again the work would crowd our brains, but tonight was perfect enjoyment, the richest of banquets. The bill never exceeded $3 per person.

The wine loosened our tongues, and the dinner table conversation would turn philosophical. Why did we have wars? Why couldn't people get along? Germany and Japan, the scourge of the world a few decades ago, were now among America's closest allies. After the terrible war in Vietnam, that country would no doubt return to the relative obscurity and neutrality it had enjoyed before the 1950s. It certainly seemed to us that the best way to eliminate ignorance and foster mutual understanding was to travel abroad, meet the people of other countries, hear what they had to say, and tell them about ourselves and our own country.

Our favorite waiter was a friendly guy who had worked for years on a ship, traveled the world and learned to speak surprisingly good colloquial English (with a bit of a Brooklyn accent). He was our uncle, he took care of us, he recommended the best—and cheapest—mezes and fish. He was intelligent, sensitive, and always half-drunk from rakı swigged straight from the bottle between courses.

"Ever try a *nargile*, a water pipe?" he asked one evening. None of us had.

"You gotta try it. Gives you a real nice buzz."

I tried a *nargile*. He was right. The powerful tobacco was nearly a narcotic. Mixed with generous doses of rakı, it was enough to make even the most bitter beached sailor happy he was ashore.

But we didn't need psychedelics. We were learning something new and priceless from Turkey and the Turks: the spirit of quiet contentment too often neglected by overworked Americans. We were discovering what the Turks call *keyf*.

Profesör Doktor Abdullah

"Mr. Brosnahan," the student messenger said, "Necdet Bey would like to speak with you in his office."

In the office Necdet Bey stood with another man of medium height, in late middle age. He was introduced as Professor Doctor Abdullah Kızılırmak, chairman of the astronomy department at Aegean University.

"Abdullah Bey has a proposal for you," Necdet Bey said.

Abdullah had lived and taught in the USA. Now that he was back in Turkey he was forgetting the English he had learned. He wanted some practice so he wouldn't forget. His spacious apartment in the faculty apartment block had a spare bedroom.

"You could stay there and give me English lessons," he said.

My Peace Corps apartment was lonely, too expensive for one person, had no central heat or hot water, and had Rıza Bey's chickens. The faculty apartment block in which Abdullah lived had central heating, hot water several days per week, and no chickens. The deal was that I'd give Abdullah one formal English lesson a week, and speak English with him whenever we were together. My head filled with visions of steamy showers every other morning.

Abdullah was friendly and knowledgeable. He had taught in South Carolina, married an American woman and had a son. They later separated and the professor returned to live in Turkey, making trips to America now and then to visit his son.

I pondered his offer, but the rush of events helped me to make my decision.

There were violent anti-American demonstrations in İzmir. They didn't affect us in Bornova, but they were frightening when we saw them in İzmir. Lily and I were strolling along Gaziosmanpaşa Bulvarı toward Republic Square on October 21st. Demonstrators gathered in the square, then began to run, flags and banners waving, up Gaziosmanpaşa Bulvarı right toward us. Mob mentality makes no fine distinctions, and my imagination raced to scenes of the mob surrounding us, challenging us, denouncing us,… trampling us? Who knows? Lily could pass for Japanese, but in a city with a large minority American population, I was obviously—far too obviously—a Yank. I really didn't want to find out what the mob would do with us.

I looked around for an escape route. There was none.

Just as the mob surged toward us, a small black Mercedes sedan raced up next to us and squealed to a stop. In the driver's seat was Abdullah.

"Get in!" he said, which is what we were doing as he said it. He floored it and tore down a side street to safety.

Not one to miss so obvious an omen, I packed up my things and hired a horse cart from the main square in Bornova to move them to the faculty apartment building. A junkman came to buy the cheap furniture in my old place in Rıza Bey's house.

"*Amerikan mı?*" he asked, pointing to objects of mysterious provenance. Is it American-made? He knew what the locally-made stuff was worth: not much. He was interested in the odd American-made items like a clothes iron or a radio that he could sell at a premium.

On my first morning on the third floor in the faculty apartment, I awoke to a strange loud puffing noise. I left my room and found Abdullah outside on a tiny balcony doing vigorous exercises in the misty morning air, huffing like a locomotive. We had breakfast together, in English.

"My students in America studied hard. Turkish students don't work hard," he said. "They don't want to study. For that matter, Turkish professors don't work hard."

Politely, I begged to differ, but he would have none of it.

"Look at me. I've published the books for my courses. My students are required to buy them. Everything is in the book. I lecture from the book. It's too easy."

Abdullah was ahead of me in seeing the differences between our two countries. He knew more about America than I knew about Turkey. Although I was supposed to be helping him with his English, in fact he ended up helping me just as much with my Turkish. He didn't mind, so long as we mostly communicated in English.

He was learning to play the *saz*, the long-necked traditional Turkish stringed instrument, taking lessons from a master who played at the local radio station. After Abdullah's lesson, given in the apartment, he, the saz teacher and I drank tea and chatted in Turkish, which was excellent practice for me. Saz music was "foreign" and exotic, with its system of *makams* (modes) and quarter-tones, but many of the centuries-old chords and tonalities sounded surprisingly modern.

Another morning I sat down at breakfast and found Abdullah in a bad mood. He had returned late the night before, driving home in his little old Mercedes through the rain and dark. During the day a road crew dug a deep ditch along one side of the road for a new sewer line. They had not put up any warning signs, markers or barriers. Visibility was bad in the rain, there were no street lights, and Abdullah had driven right into the ditch. His car had fallen in and was now stuck there, badly damaged.

"This is what I get for living in an undeveloped country!" Abdullah grumped. In America there would've been warning signs, barriers, flashing lights.

"...for living in a country under rapid development," I said. "No development, no new sewer lines, no ditches to fall into."

He smiled ruefully. The thought helped but only theoretically. His car was still dead and buried.

Tobacco Village

The door buzzer at Abdullah's apartment buzzed one morning, and I opened it to find Franz smiling at me.

"Would you like to visit a village?" Franz asked. "I'm going out to where we buy tobacco. You can come along if you like."

I liked. We went.

We spent most of our time in one village. Franz was received as a visiting dignitary, with formal greetings from the *muhtar* (headman), the *imam* (preacher), the teacher, the head of the tobacco cooperative, and virtually all of the kids. We were taken to the home of Mustafa, the head of the tobacco cooperative, led to the main salon and offered the seats of honor. The traditional pleasantries of formal greetings, tea, cigarettes and sweets were offered. After some talk about crops and tobacco market rates we adjourned to lunch in the adjoining room.

This was my introduction to Turkish village hospitality. The table was completely covered in food. There must have been 100 plates: olives, cheeses, breads, salads, purées, böreks, grills, stews and desserts. Had we been a significant detachment of the Turkish army we wouldn't have gone away hungry. As it was we barely made a dent in the bounty, though the food was so good we did our best to make the dent a big one.

After lunch came coffee, and after coffee, soccer. Franz stripped off his shirt, rolled up his trouser legs, and held up well against the local youths playing on a rocky, un-level field of packed earth. I begged off as a total klutz and watched in admiration. I can't remember who won the match, but of course it didn't matter. I returned to Bornova with a new appreciation for Franz's social, business and soccer skills, and for Turkish home cooking.

Sometime later Franz invited me to join him for an evening at the Levantines' club. We drove to a modest one-story building off by itself in a grove of trees. Simply but comfortably furnished, the club was busy with men and women of a half-dozen ethnic backgrounds, including Turks. Conversation was in a mixture of English, French, Italian, German and Turkish, with occasional lapses into other tongues. Most of the club members were, like Franz's grandfather, hugely polyglot, so it didn't matter which language they used. To me they spoke English; the few who didn't know English spoke to me in French because my Turkish was still weaker than my French.

We had a drink and chatted. I was struck by the number of older men who had young, beautiful women sitting next to them. The young women fawned on the old guys and looked as though they'd rather be sitting on them than next to them. I wonder how they managed that. It would be useful information for me to have. I got the impression that money—lots of it—had something to do with it. I also got the impression that my TL1070 a month wasn't going to turn these girls' heads.

Franz sat down to play a few hands of poker and cheerfully lost the equivalent of my monthly salary.

"Wanna play?" he asked.

"No thanks," I answered, stifling the desire to add "I'd rather eat and have a place to sleep."

"I won last time," he said, "so now I'm even."

"I can't take the chance," I admitted. "I have no money to lose."

"Lose money? At poker? That's nothing," he said. "Look here."

We went through a curtained doorway and into a back room where men were sitting around a circular table playing cards. On the green baize cloth was a card "shoe" which the dealer pushed around to the players as they asked for it. They were playing *chemin de fer*. In the pot were hundreds and hundreds of dollars, about a year's PCV salary. I figured—correctly, as it turned out—that high-stakes gambling was illegal in Turkey (as in the USA), and that's why they were in the back room behind a curtain.

The men played, asking for the shoe in French, mumbling curses in Turkish if the card wasn't what they wanted, bidding in English, joking with one another in German, Italian and Greek.

I couldn't even play in one language, though I was certain I could make more money disappear than the entire United Nations if given half a chance. We finished our drinks and left.

Action at Ephesus

I enjoyed a constant stream of visitors. Every PCV wanted to see İzmir because of an imagined resemblance to San Francisco. Turkey's "City on the Bay" took on a California sheen and eventually drew every young American with an un-scheduled weekend and sufficient bus fare.

When they came to İzmir they expected me to show them around. This was an early intimation of my later calling, but I didn't know it at the time and had I known it I probably would've hit them up for a tour-guide fee.

As part of their İzmir tour they wanted to see Ephesus, the capital of Asia Minor in Roman times which lay a mere two-hour bus ride to the south. Most of them had at least heard of St. Paul's Letter to the Ephesians, and they wanted to see where the Ephesians, the people of Ephesus, had lived.

School was out for Republic Day (October 29th), Turkey's national day, and I shepherded a pack of my colleagues onto a bus for the ride south to Ephesus. When we arrived, dark clouds were gathering over the Aegean to the west. We bought our admission tickets and were strolling down the Arcadian Way, the ancient city's main avenue, rich with colonnades and the remnants of fine buildings, when the clouds moved toward us. Ephesus was about to get drenched.

"If we run we can make it to the restaurant," one of them said. They took off.

I looked at the dark rumbling clouds speeding ominously towards me, heralded by chaotic gusts sweet with ozone. I turned and ran back up the Arcadian Way and into the 25,000-seat Great Theater. Vaulting up the ranks of seats two at a time I reached the top and tore through the scrub atop Mount Pagus to a 10-foot-high fragment of city wall that stood alone, a forlorn relic of the city's once-mighty defenses. Crouching beside the wall—which really only provided shelter in my imagination—I stared at the racing storm.

The rain followed the clouds in, teeming in sheets, now at St Paul's Prison on its hillock beyond the end of the Arcadian Way, now storming across the dark silted fields that had once been Ephesus's great harbor.

The wall of airborne water hit the western end of the Arcadian Way, slowed just a bit, then proceeded up the ancient street, drenching the white marble pavement and turning it to silver which shone in the dark, mysterious storm light. The silver sheen spread eastward, up from the pavement to the monumental fountains and the ranks of marble columns that bordered the avenue. Soon it had sped all the way along the Arcadian Way to the Marble Way which, because it was parallel to the storm front, was changed to silver in an instant by the elemental alchemy.

My eyes swept the scene: Ephesus as precious metal! Was God laughing at the silversmiths? It was their guild that had driven St Paul out of Ephesus because his Christian preaching was ruining their business making silver votive trinkets. Ancient pilgrims came to the great temple of Cybele-Artemis, Anatolia's traditional fertility goddess, to pay homage, and often bought votive trinkets to leave as tokens.

The Great Theater was next, the silver rain passing quickly across the marble stage and racing up the ranks of seats to the top. Soon the storm reached me and the furious wind whipped the scrub, raising dust, twigs, leaves and dead grass. A freshet of rain, only a handful by heaven's gauge, sprayed down on me, settling the dust and spotting my bit of rubble wall with dark circles but leaving me no worse than slightly damp.

That was it. The fury of the squall was a mile wide and a few hundred yards deep. I turned and watched it race inland, and when I looked westward again the sun was shining on the rain-slicked marble of the Arcadian Way. If it had been silver before, now it was gold.

I stood up, strolled down the hill through brush bejeweled by raindrops, descended into the *cavea* of the theater, over the wet stage, through the *scaena* and out the other side to where my friends were waiting. From down here, the Arcadian Way was merely wet marble. The vision was gone.

The unsettled weather at İzmir Koleji would not pass so quickly or agreeably, however. In fact, it was about to get much worse.

No matter. We climbed back on the bus and returned to İzmir, where we went out and had a good dinner. My friends treated me to lots of wine as a thank-you gesture for my service as their guide, and I forgot all about returning to school, a prospect about as attractive as brain surgery.

ဩ

4
Spy!

The young blond American gets out of the minibus at Basmane and enters the railway station. He looks around, scans the platforms and the waiting room, takes out a notebook and begins to write. He sits and orders tea. A train arrives. He searches the faces of the passengers, writes more notes, gets up and goes away.

It was I. Am I a spy?

Many Turks thought so. Why would young, prosperous Americans trained in Turkish history, culture and language come to Turkey, spread throughout the country and take low-paying jobs? There must be some hidden agenda.

Neither the staff, nor the faculty, nor the students at İzmir Koleji could truly understand why we PCVs were at the school at all. What would make us volunteer to learn a different language, travel halfway around the world, live in an unfamiliar culture, and teach in a school that paid us a fraction of what we could be earning in an American school?

It didn't make sense to them.

We explained that we volunteered to help Turkey to develop, and to resist communism. It was an accurate but incomplete explanation, so we added that we also wanted to "see the world," to live in another country, earn our living there, get to know it well. This was even less credible.

My Turkish colleagues and students all had the notion, widely held at the time, that the USA was highly developed, that Turkey was one of many "underdeveloped" countries, and that given the choice between the two any sane person would opt to live in the highly developed country. This was logical but only partly true. Economic development is not culture, and by several definitions Turkey had as much or more culture than the USA. Furthermore, people are people no matter what the level of development. They work and play, they laugh and cry, they find the beauties and joys of life. Those beauties and joys are often different in Turkey than at home, and we wanted to experience them. Besides, we PCVs expected to return to the USA after our term of service, so it was not as though we were leaving home forever (although some of us ultimately did).

This confusion of motives and explanations often produced the conviction that PCVs were in fact spies infiltrated into Turkey to gather intelligence on Turkish society. This intelligence could supposedly be used to control Turkey, an important US ally, and thus to rob it of its independent national will.

We laughed at this. PCVs, who enlisted for two-year terms, had few of the benefits of being US government employees—very few. Legally we were not really government employees at all. Our pay was very low by US standards, but was intended to be similar to what people were paid in the "host country." Because prices were lower in host countries, the pay was usually adequate, if only barely. A small amount of money (about $1500) was also deposited in an account for each PCV during the term of service, and the total amount paid to the PCV upon termination to help readjust to life in America and to find a job.

Although we were paid by the US government and had limited access to a few of its facilities and privileges abroad, we were theoretically employees of the Ministry of Education. The lowest soldier on a US base in Turkey had far more power and privilege within US officialdom than we had.

We should not have laughed at this suspicion of spying. It was logical and filled the void unsatisfied by the other explanations. Some of our students, particularly the more outspoken ones, would tell us to our faces that they believed PCVs were American spies. With traditional Turkish courtesy they would exclude us, saying "We don't think you're a spy, but all the other Peace Corps people are."

Our response was to ask what exactly we were supposedly spying on. We had no access to Turkish military or diplomatic installations. We had no special equipment or training, and very little money. We couldn't even travel as extensively (or as well) as the average tourist because we had full-time jobs. What would we spy on, and how?

This defense occasionally worked concerning those of us who were posted to cities, but what about my friend Dan?

Dinner With Dan

Dan was from a wealthy New York family. Of medium height with dark hair, strong Jewish features and a powerfully ironic, often hilarious sense of humor, he had been posted to Şirinova ("Pleasant Valley"), a tiny new village next to an agricultural station far from any big town or city. He was the only American in the village. It was simply incredible for Turks to believe he was living and working there by choice. They wouldn't do it themselves. Even the villagers wouldn't have stayed if they had had an alternative. Why would he?

Dan always had money to spend when he came to İzmir because there was nothing to spend it on in Şirinova. He received nearly the same pay as we did even though his rent, heat and food costs were very low. He worked, ate, slept, banked his money and came to İzmir to blow it.

"I hab a terrible code," he said on one occasion. "I cadt sbell a thig. What's the best place for didder?"

"The Bonjour Café in Alsancak," I answered. "But it's really pretty expensive. With your cold you won't be able to taste anything." In his condition even *vindaloo* wouldn't have been able to carve through the mucus.

"I dobt care. I wadt the Bodjour. How do we get there?"

The Bonjour was İzmir's only upscale European-style café-bistrot, a hangout for Levantine and Turkish gilded youth in the tony Alsancak district. It had a European gloss, with sidewalk tables in front, pretty good food, and European-style prices, which is to say that part of the reason you went to the Bonjour was to show that you could afford to go to the Bonjour. We went. Dan ate.

"How was it?"

"Goob. Wurf it. Nothig like it id Şiridoba."

How could we explain Dan and the other rural PCVs to our Turkish friends? Life in Turkey in 1967 was too close to the age-old edge of privation to allow for such gross altruism. Sure, you helped out your extended family and your friends, but travel to the other side of the world to help people who were not even your own, whom you had never even met before? It didn't compute.

There was no answer. A spy-hunt is a witch-hunt. If the "spy" is able to convince people that he is not a spy, it only proves how truly clever a spy he is.

Mostly, the charge of spying hurt our spirit. We respected Turkey and its people more than we did the foreign policy of the US government, which was sending American youth—not to mention Vietnamese youth—to death and destruction in a pointless war.

The charges of spying, which were even "proven" in a popular Turkish exposé book entitled *The Peace Corps Through Secret Documents* just discouraged us further. The book was a perfect example of a conspiracy alarmist at work: the author had gotten hold of innocuous documents from the Peace Corps office and read all sorts of sinister meanings into them. It called for "all [Turkish] thinkers, revolutionaries and patriots" to fight the Peace Corps by any and all means and to drive it "and its agents" out of Turkey as soon as possible.

See the World Without a Gun

The story of the Peace Corps was in fact even stranger than simple spying. Founded by President Kennedy in the early 1960s, the Peace Corps was an apparently idealistic government program which sent young American women and men to less economically developed countries throughout the world. Peace Corps Volunteers aided economic development by teaching English, training farmers in modern agricultural methods and health workers in the latest medical procedures, and helping villagers to build useful things like pipelines for drinking water.

A less overt purpose of the Peace Corps was to convince people in other countries that a free-enterprise economy was preferable to a command economy. In other words, that capitalism and democracy were better than communism and dictatorship. We were volunteers for capitalism.

The hidden purpose behind the Peace Corps, unmentioned even in America, was demographic. Imagine several million unwillingly-celibate soldiers coming home from the battlefields of World War II. Nine months later the Baby Boom began and the US birth rate surged. By 1960, when John F Kennedy was elected president, the baby boomers were becoming teenagers, and many of them would soon be going to college. The huge number of boomers meant there might not be enough jobs and university places for all of them.

Young people between 16 and 23 are idealistic and energetic. The government's plan was to channel their idealism away from politics, the crowded job market and universities, and put it to good use helping people abroad while spreading a positive image of the USA. The alternative was to let these energetic, idealistic young people fend for themselves, which almost certainly meant there would be riots in the streets.

In fact, the US got both.

Yet another goal of the Peace Corps was to educate a pool of young Americans about other peoples, their countries, cultures and languages because the US government had been embarrassed by a popular novel, *The Ugly American*, by William Burdick and William Lederer. In the novel, US government policy in Southeast Asia is inept and ill-informed, made and carried out by government bureaucrats who have little knowledge of the countries, peoples, languages or cultures in which they operate. However, an American engineer, an ugly-looking but kind-hearted man, works among the people of Southeast Asia, speaking their language and honoring their customs. Although he is ugly to look at, he is the most beloved American in the region because he understands the people, forms a true bond of friendship with them, and helps them to better their lives.

PCVs were supposed to be the "Handsome Americans," learning the local languages and customs, and later perhaps following careers in government service and helping to improve US government policy and programs.

Thoughts of Summer

Despite all of our problems, life had its moments, mostly in the form of simple daily pleasures.

If the weather was good I enjoyed walking to school. It was about a mile and a half and took less than thirty minutes. I'd walk from my apartment down the cobbled streets, across the railroad tracks and the Ankara highway, past the buildings of Aegean University, and down the long school lane beneath the dark, fragrant canopy of overarching pines. On both sides of the lane were the broad experimental vineyards of the university's Agricultural Faculty. On the summit of a mountain in the distance was its astronomical observatory where Abdullah conducted observations every Thursday evening.

The school car, a Land Rover, was available to drive faculty from Bornova's main square to the school each morning, but I rarely took it.

It was quiet walking down the lane, with only the cheerful chirp of birds and the soft sound of the wind in the pines to break the silence.

I had been on the job at İzmir Koleji barely two months when the Peace Corp's administrative schedule required that I make a big decision: what was I going to do next summer when the school was on vacation? I thought about it as I strolled beneath the canopy of pines toward another tough day at school.

The US government wasn't about to pay PCVs $118 a month to sit around. Each of us had to plan and carry out a summer project that would contribute to Turkey's development. Some teachers tutored their regular students who needed extra help, others went to villages and gave summer classes. I had no idea what to do. If I didn't submit a plan soon, the Peace Corps office would assign me to one. Who knows what or where?

I had not yet had a chance to travel much in Turkey, but from what I could see Turkey was perfect for tourism: beautiful, friendly and cheap, with lots of good beaches, important historical sites, great architecture and good food. Few people knew this.

What about a project that told the world's travelers about Turkey?

I knew of only two travel guidebooks to Turkey, the stuffy old Hachette *Blue Guide* and the more modern *Fodor's*, both used by people who stayed at the Hilton and saw the sights by chauffeured car. What Turkey needed was a book for the normal traveler who couldn't afford the Hilton and who traveled by bus.

I immediately thought of Arthur Frommer's *Europe on $5 a Day*. It had caused a revolution in guidebook publishing. Before Frommer, guidebooks had been written for rich people on the grand tour: they bought expensive airline tickets to Europe or they sailed there in comfort on ocean liners. They spent months and wads of money touring Europe. Frommer, on the other hand, had been a US soldier in Europe after World War II, and he toured Europe on a soldier's pay. He traveled by third-class train, stayed in family pensions, dined in market cookshops, and visited museums on discount day. He discovered that he could travel decently like a European for little more than $5 per day for a bed and three meals. His first travel guide was a small pamphlet written for his fellow soldiers. It was so popular that when he returned to the USA and civilian life he expanded it into a book.

The book was an instant, huge success. Instead of the stilted prose of the stuffy old academic guides, Frommer's friendly, conversational tone was like having an enthusiastic, travel-savvy friend along with you. It gave specific directions, exact prices in both dollars and the local currency, and showed you how to immerse yourself in another country and another culture. Frommer truly believed—and he still believes—that traveling cheap is better than traveling rich. By traveling budget class you experience more, learn more, enjoy more, and are enriched more than if you go first class.

Frommer's guidebook was one of four elements which converged to revolutionize tourism. The other three were the Baby Boom, the strong postwar dollar, and the Boeing 707, the first jet passenger aircraft. In the late 1960s, Baby Boomers were old enough that they wanted to see Europe, the land of their ancestors and a large part of their culture. Arthur Frommer told them how to do it on five strong dollars a day, and the 707 took them across the ocean swiftly and safely at a price they could afford.

I used *Europe on $5 a Day* on my first trip to Europe in 1966, as did all my friends and most of my PCV colleagues. The Frommer travel philosophy was perfect for a PCV living on $118 a month, and perfect for Turkey, where a few dollars easily bought a clean bed and three good meals.

Mr Frommer had covered the major cities of Europe, and even many of the smaller ones, in one guidebook. Athens was included. Why not İstanbul? I could write a chapter on İstanbul and Frommer could include it in his guide.

Here was the summer project for me! Not only would I get to travel, I'd base myself in historic İstanbul for the summer. It was perfect. Maybe I could even convince Jane to come to Turkey and travel around with me! By the time I reached the end of my walk, I had composed two letters in my head.

After school that day I wrote the first one and mailed it to the Peace Corps office in Ankara. I wrote the second one to Mr Frommer asking what he thought of the idea. Then I planned my lessons for the next few days, which were going to be harder than ever because of Cyprus.

Cyprus Splinters

On November 15th, 1967, Greek Cypriot soldiers attacked two Turkish Cypriot villages and massacred 23 Turkish Cypriots. The day following the outrage, Ankara and İstanbul exploded with anti-Greek demonstrations. By November 19th Turkish marines were waiting for the order to invade Cyprus.

A week after the crisis began, American diplomat Cyrus Vance arrived in Ankara to mediate. The 26th was widely seen as "D Day," the day on which war would break out between Turkey and Greece. In İzmir, auto owners painted their headlights dark blue so they could drive through air raids. War fever was on.

"Mr Brosnahan, you can celebrate Christmas in Athens. It will be Turkish by then," my older students told me.

Cyprus is one of those sticky Middle East-type ethnic problems that defy solution for generations. Today its people are mostly ethnic Greeks even though the island is hundreds of miles east of the Greek mainland, but only 40 miles south of the Turkish coast (and 60 miles west of Syria). Its strategic location on the main maritime routes in the eastern Mediterranean has always made it desirable for conquerors, especially those in ships. Through the centuries it was conquered by Alexander the Great, the Egyptians, the Romans, the Byzantines, and even England's Richard the Lionhearted.

The Ottomans conquered Cyprus from the Venetians in 1571 and held it for over three centuries before yielding it to Great Britain again after World War I. The British made it a crown colony in 1925 and used it as a military and naval base, which is why the Germans dropped clouds of paratroopers on it during World War II. After the war, George Grivas's EOKA guerillas started a terrorism campaign to drive out the Brits, "ethnically cleanse" the island of Turks, and unite it with mainland Greece, a goal known as *enosis*.

By 1960 the British had decided that Cyprus was nothing but a huge headache. To get out, they set up a complicated governance plan that shared power between the island's ethnically Greek majority (78%) and its Turkish minority (22%). Greece, Turkey and Britain signed a treaty to jointly guarantee Cyprus' independence and good behavior, but it didn't stick. EOKA kept the pot boiling and the bombs exploding. Massacres occurred regularly, keeping tension over Cyprus high right into the late 1960s when I arrived.

November 26th came and went and war didn't break out, however. By December 1st the crisis was winding down, and by the 8th, Greek soldiers exceeding the treaty quota were said to have been withdrawn from Cyprus, although they may just have doffed their uniforms, tied on aprons and opened restaurants, waiting for another opportunity to serve up enosis.

The crisis was over for the moment, but in my letters home I assured my parents that war would indeed break out in Cyprus. It was only a matter of time. Both Greece and Turkey were strong and important American allies, and Greece had a powerful lobby in Washington, which meant that a war between them could only harm Turkish-American relations, including our status as PCVs. But that wouldn't, and didn't, stop it from happening later.

The Yogurt Pot

Speaking of writing home, Jane and I were exchanging letters, but we seemed to be drifting apart. She was absorbed in her new life in Naples just as I was in mine in Bornova. Our letters became less frequent, not helped much by the slow mail service.

Her birthday was coming up, though. Here's a chance to strike a spark, I thought: I'll send her a present.

I went to the bazaar in İzmir and bought her a gift, a shiny little traditional brass yogurt pot. I collected packing materials and went to the post office in Bornova to send it off.

Shipping packages out of Turkey is a hassle because of the illegal trade in antiquities. In 1967 the contents of any package being mailed out of the country had to be inspected by a government official to make sure you weren't exporting Hittite figurines or Greek coins or Byzantine icons or Ottoman tiles. I showed Jane's yogurt pot to the post office clerk, a dignified grey-haired man in his sixties.

"Nice pot," he said. "What'd you pay for it?"

"Forty-five liras," I said. About five dollars.

"You got a good deal. Here, look, there's a date on it."

The date incised on the rim was Ottoman, meaning it was in the Arabic script and the Hijri (Islamic) lunar calendar which starts from the Hegira, Muhammed's escape from Mecca to Medina in 622 AD.

The clerk, who had learned the Ottoman calendar as a boy, mumbled to himself as he calculated.

"Eleven fifty-nine Hijri, let's see, that'd be, uh, that'd be about 1745 Milâdi [Gregorian]. So your little pot here is about two hundred, actually two hundred and twenty-three years old. Yeah, you got a good deal on it."

I was thunderstruck. My little five-dollar brass pot was older than the United States of America.

"Wrap it up," the clerk said. Apparently a two-century-old pot is not an antiquity in Turkey. I sent it off to Jane. It had the desired effect. In fact, she still has it, only it's even older now.

Slow to Fast

The thunder woke me before dawn on December 3rd, but when I was fully awake I realized the deep, low booming sound, vigorous, rhythmic, and very close, was not thunder. I leapt from my bed, rushed to the window, and in the faint pre-dawn light saw three men walking below beating huge drums.

"Ramazan," Abdullah explained as I slurped my morning tea. "The drummers wake people so they can eat before dawn. At dawn the fast begins." Abdullah wasn't fasting. He was slurping along with me.

Fasting. I had heard about it during training in Texas, but it was academic until the drums boomed me out of bed. Fasting! Not a bite of food, not a sip of water, not a chew of gum or a puff of smoke from dawn to dusk. Muslims were also supposed to refrain from sex during Ramazan.

Ramazan (Ramadan in other countries) is a month of the lunar Muslim calendar. Because the lunar year is about eleven days shorter than the solar year, the Muslim new year falls eleven days earlier each year, and so do its holidays.

I went to school. From what I could see at lunchtime, all of my students and teaching colleagues chowed down with a good appetite. Tea was served in the teachers' lounge as always, with no abstentions. From what I could see, Turkey was being secular about Ramazan, the way many people in Christian countries are about Lent. You keep it in mind, but it doesn't change your daily life much.

He Likes It, He Likes It Not

One of life's big, important questions for me during Ramazan in 1967 was this. would my summer travel-writing project be approved? When a letter finally arrived on Frommer's stationery, I was surprised, delighted, apprehensive. What if he didn't go for it?

I opened the letter. He didn't go for it.

"*Europe on $5 a Day* is my book," he wrote, "and it's good the way it is. I don't think it would work to add a chapter on Turkey."

"However," he went on, "Turkey is certainly a country worth knowing about. If you were to write your own guidebook, I can't promise that I would accept it for publication, but I assure you that I would give it a prompt and sympathetic reading."

So that was that. My summer project was off.

Or was it?

As I walked to work along the school lane the morning after reading Frommer's letter, my brain churned. Could I write a whole book on Turkey?

But a book was not a summer project. It would take at least a year, maybe more. Could I even finish it by the end of my Peace Corps service in 1969? Would the Ministry of Education and the Peace Corps allow me to give up teaching to write a whole guidebook? A travel guidebook as a Peace Corps project?

Why not? PCVs are supposed to think outside the box.

I wrote to the Peace Corps office in Ankara. They were intrigued. At the request of the Turkish government, the Peace Corps had recently begun a small tourism program. The first project was to establish ski patrols at Uludağ, the fledgling ski resort near Bursa. My guidebook plan might fit into the new little tourism program.

"We'll work on it," the Peace Corps office said. They contacted a Ministry of Tourism official named Edvin Ryzy, a Turkish citizen of Polish heritage. Mr Ryzy liked the idea and promoted it within the ministry.

That was enough for a rank optimist, so I got to work. Knowing a little bit about how governments worked, I realized it was entirely possible that approval for the project would come through when there was no longer enough time left in my Peace Corps service to get the job done. I'd better get started as soon as possible. One good reason was that I didn't have the foggiest idea how to write a travel guidebook. I had no experience. I'd better get some. Most of the restaurants in secular, liberal İzmir were open and serving even though it was Ramazan. I could check them out, write them up, and learn how to be a travel writer.

My work at school in December consisted of listening to my students' oral reports. I corrected the reports right in class, which meant I had little work outside of school hours. By December 17th an İzmir mini-guide, my first travel-writing project, was well under way.

Are You Really Gonna Drink That?

I saved my money for travel, dreams of which occupied the minds of PCVs just below sex, food and booze in the pleasure hierarchy. At vacation time everyone was planning trips to Beirut ("the Paris of the East"), Cairo (under Nasser) or Tehran (under the Shah). We weren't supposed to go to Europe, we were supposed to concern ourselves with the betterment of the Third World even when we were on vacation, so London and Paris—and Naples, where I could see Jane—were out. I decided to go to İstanbul and Athens.

Travel in Turkey was easy for us, but travel abroad brought us face to face with the moral dilemma of currency exchange. The liras with which we were paid were "blocked" funds: the US government had "loaned" the Turkish government millions of dollars in military and commercial support to help it resist Soviet communism. The sweet deal allowed Turkey to repay these loans in liras which, the US agreed, would not be taken out of the country or exchanged for hard currency. So the US embassy in Ankara was awash in unconvertible liras. It paid all its local bills with them, and paid us, too. The American embassy could have bought half the real estate in Ankara and it still would have had enough blocked liras to build a bridge across the Bosphorus.

At that time Turkish liras were a "soft" currency not readily convertible into "hard" currencies such as the US dollar and British pound. If we went into a Turkish bank to exchange liras for dollars, we would be allowed to convert only a small amount, and that at a very bad rate of exchange. It was technically illegal to take liras out of the country, but if we did, the exchange rate in a foreign bank would be even worse. To get full value, we had to convert our liras on the black market. Mostly we did what any Turk did who wanted hard currency: we'd hang around the tourist areas and offer to sell Turkish liras to tourists. They needed liras, we needed dollars. It would have been perfect if it hadn't been against the law.

At the end of December came our first real vacation. School went into recess for New Year's Day, and just after the New Year's recess came *Ramazan bayramı*, the three-day holiday which follows the end of Ramadan.

The Peace Corps had summoned us to Ankara for a conference during the New Year's holiday. I flew to Ankara on a Peace Corps-provided plane ticket on December 30th. The next day there was a New Year's party Peace Corps style, which means ultra cheap: it was held not in some nice restaurant but in the Peace Corps office. The celebratory punch was made of fruit juice spiked with *ispirto*, vivid blue Turkish duplicating-machine alcohol.

Two things made my heart rejoice that weekend: discovering that the Peace Corps liked my guidebook idea, and drinking Tekel beer instead of the punch.

My air ticket would get me back to İzmir, but that's not where I wanted to go. I wanted to go to İstanbul and Athens, and so I needed a source of cheap plane tickets. I asked some Ankara PCVs what to do.

"You want really cheap plane tickets, you go to Alp," one of them told me. Alp was a guy who worked in a downtown Ankara travel agency, for which the PCV gave me an address. "You'll need an official-looking letter saying you're a student," the PCV went on. "Get some college letterhead and write one. Fake the dean's signature, or the president's for all it matters. Take a quarter coin, ink it in a stamp pad and press it over the signature as a seal. If you can get a Kennedy half dollar or a silver dollar you can just roll the paper over it to 'emboss' it. Alp makes a photocopy of the letter, and you get your student discount."

Alp always came through, he said. The fare written on the ticket might be $100, but I'd pay $30 for it. I got some college stationery, a quarter and a stamp pad, and I was a student again, as I had been a few months before, and as I would be yet again a few years later.

The conference ended and, cheap ticket in hand, I flew to İstanbul with Lily, Dan, and a few other PCV friends.

A Glimpse of the Palace

City of history, intrigue, palaces, bazaars, romance,…. With my major love interest in Italy there was not much hope of romance for me, but at least I could see the sultan's palace, Hagia Sophia and the Blue Mosque.

Our plane touched down at Yeşilköy (later Atatürk) Airport on the dismal evening of January 3rd. The derelict airline bus trundled us along darkened streets slicked and glaring with rain. I wiped the funky haze from the cold, rain-smeared bus window, trying to see the glittering city. No glitter, just drab and dark.

The bus dropped us at Taksim Square and rumbled off into the murk. We asked a guy for directions to the Otel Santral, off Billurcu Sokak, one of a few hotels favored by PCVs because they were cheap and central. It turned out that the aptly-named Otel Santral ("Central Hotel") was only a few blocks away.

In its ornate little lobby a middle-aged black-haired woman welcomed us and checked us in for a three-day stay.

İstanbul! I was here! History was all around me. I was in the New Rome, the city of Constantine, of the crusaders, the sultans and their harems. Forget dinner, I wasn't hungry. I wanted a bite of big-city romance. I wanted to see Dolmabahçe Palace.

I picked up a simple map from the reception desk and walked back to Taksim Square, past the grand old villa of the chairman of the Ottoman Bank and down Gümüşsuyu Caddesi toward the Bosphorus. It was dark and damp and wet, with only the occasional car gliding by, its tires hissing on the wet macadam. The street lamps glared as I walked past the art deco Park Oteli and the palatial West German consulate. I passed İstanbul Technical University, looked over the edge of the hill toward the Bosphorus shore and there it was spread out along the shore for a quarter mile: Dolmabahçe Palace, its roofs black in the rain but its floodlit marble walls and ornate gates glimmering like silver. Beyond the palace the dark Bosphorus was busy with ships. Ferryboats whooped their sirens and swept the sea lanes with powerful searchlights as they steamed through the dark waters.

I walked downhill to the huge marble gates and peered through. The 285-room palace was silent and lifeless. I breathed in the foggy air, touched with the chill of winter and the sweet-acrid smell of burning coal, and dreamed of its past glories. One or two cars passed, but otherwise I was alone with my visions of the glittering evenings and luxurious days. The sultan, the harem, troops of liveried servants. Visiting emperors, kings, queens and princesses. Intrigue, treachery, sumptuous luxury, romance. This is where it had all happened.

Dolmabahçe embodied for me the splendor and tribulation of the 19th-century Ottoman Empire, of a country and people with a glorious history caught out of step with the times. In my dreams I saw the palace blazing with light and filled with elegantly dressed men and women. I remembered a fact from the history books: Sultan Abdülmecid, the builder of Dolmabahçe, spent more on furniture and dresses for the ladies of his harem than he spent on the entire Ottoman army in Thrace (European Turkey)—which is probably why the imperial Russian army found it so easy to breach the empire's borders and cut through Thrace like a hot knife through butter and come almost to the walls of İstanbul in 1877. Terrified of the Russian horde, the sultan's ladies shook in their bejeweled slippers.

I drank in the scene, felt the dank, chill night air and splashes of rain on my cheeks, then turned and walked slowly back uphill to Taksim Square and my small, plain, dark green room at the Otel Santral.

During the next three days we PCVs saw the big-city sights: Hagia Sophia, the Blue Mosque, Topkapı Palace, (but alas not Dolmabahçe Palace, which was open only at certain times, none of which fit our schedule). We ordered *Wienerschnitzel* and *palatschinken* at the restaurant run by Frau Fischer, a German émigrée. We splurged on chicken Kievsky and lemon vodka at the *Yeni Rejans* (New Regency), run by octogenarian White Russian refugees from the Bolshevik Revolution.

One evening we wandered into the Aya Triyada Greek Orthodox church just off Taksim Square. Something important was going on. The church was packed. We stood around in the crowd. All at once a path was cleared through the throng and His All-holiness Athenagoras, Ecumenical Patriarch of Constantinople, made his way slowly and solemnly into the church sprinkling holy water left and right. It was Orthodox Christmas eve! It seemed appropriate to be Greekly moistened because the next day we boarded a flight for Athens.

Beatles in Greece

We knew nothing about Greece but we thought we did. From an early age American children hear about "the greatness of ancient Greece and Rome" and equate ancient Rome with modern Italy, and ancient Greece with modern Greece. This is not completely accurate, but I didn't know it then.

In 1964, Nobel prize-winning author Nikos Kazantzakis's novel *Zorba the Greek* was made into a movie. With a tuneful musical score by Mikis Theodorakis and top actors like Anthony Quinn, Irene Pappas, Lila Kedrova and Alan Bates, it was a huge success. It won several Oscars. Its joyful bouzouki music echoed through university campuses across America, including Tufts. In Boston, which has a large Greek-American community, cars appeared with bumper stickers that read "*Yassou!*", "It's chic to be Greek!" and "This car powered by *ouzo*." It was a triumph of Greek popular culture and the Greek national image.

Besides Kazantzakis, many Baby Boomers had read the novels of Lawrence Durrell and Henry Miller, absorbing their praise of Athens, of the Greek islands, of the "Greek spirit." Yes, we thought we knew Greece. With the strong dollar and cheap airfares, young Americans flocked to the land of Zorba.

I flew to Athens on January 7th with my friends. We dropped our bags at Madame Cleo's pension, a rooming house near Syntagma Square recommended by other PCVs. Athens seemed more open, progressive, prosperous, modern and liberal than İstanbul. People were dressed more stylishly, and men and women held hands in public, something forbidden by law in Turkey, even between husband and wife (though not between friends of the same gender). In Greece we found no evidence of an inferiority complex such as dogged our relationship with Turks. If anything, Greeks had the opposite problem: because of 19th-century philhellenism and the 20th-century success of *Zorba the Greek*, they tended to be a bit cocky.

We hiked up to the Acropolis, went to the cinema, dined in a few restaurants. It was rainy, cold and dark most of the time—this was January, after all. We returned to Madame Cleo's late at night, borrowed a record player from her, gathered in my tiny room and listened to *Magical Mystery Tour*, the new Beatles album which Dan had just received from his parents and, in a moment of inspiration, shoved into his suitcase.

It was heartening, listening to the refreshing music. I made everyone laugh by reminding them that our students at İzmir Koleji knew all the Beatles songs and could sing every one in perfect Liverpudlian without a trace of a Turkish accent.

"Why can't you pronounce your class lessons that well?" we'd ask them.

"That's different," they'd say. "It's school."

We pondered this and life's other little absurdities. We pondered our fate and our future.

We lived in an exotic foreign country. We missed our friends and family, our girlfriends and boyfriends, especially on holidays. We loved our students and got along pretty well with our fellow teachers, but anti-Americanism engendered by the Vietnam war dogged us every day, affecting everything we did. Our work was hard and progress slow, if indeed there was any progress at all. A few PCVs were so dejected they were thinking of packing it in and going home to America.

We pondered the big questions, but Athens gave us no answers. On January 13th we flew back to İstanbul and İzmir, right into the teeth of a historic cold wave. The salt-water Gulf of Izmit, just east of İstanbul, froze over. In the eastern city of Ağrı, out by the Iranian border, the temperature dropped to −54°F. It was enough to give new meaning to the Iranian word for snow, which is *barf*.

ളൗ

5

BOOMERS GO BOOM!

1967 saw the Summer of Love. 1968 saw the Big Boom.

No American alive and politically conscious in 1968 is likely to forget it: the battles at the Democratic National Convention in Chicago, the violent protests and the equally violent police reaction. It was not just in America, but worldwide.

There seemed to be student protests everywhere. The post-World War II baby boom demographic surge affected lots of countries. In the USA the bumper crop of boomers, combined with the American government's schizophrenic foreign and military policies, resulted in just the sort of domestic turmoil which the Peace Corps, in shipping liberal young people overseas, had sought to avoid.

By putting us PCVs under suspicion, the Vietnam war made our work nearly impossible, as proven by what happened to Dave.

"Terrible beating incident at İzmir Koleji!" shouted the newspaper headline. "Sadism!" trumpeted the text of the article. A small İzmir newspaper reported that a Peace Corps Volunteer teacher at İzmir Koleji had beaten a student severely, torturing him by pulling hair right out of his head for some trivial offense.

Not all of the PCV teachers were soft on discipline. Dave had taught at our school for a year before I arrived and had established a reputation for strictness that equaled or exceeded that of any of our Turkish colleagues except perhaps the formidable Necdet Bey.

Unlike the rest of us, Dave was a born and dedicated teacher. The rest of us would go on to other careers after we left the Peace Corps, but teaching was Dave's life's work. He took a personal interest in each of his students. His goal was to teach them English so their adult lives would be better, and he was dedicated to the achievement of that goal.

To his students he was like an Old Testament God: feared, respected, loved. He paced the classroom propelled by nervous energy. Students who were not paying attention, or who hadn't done their homework, or who looked like they were cheating on a test, were subjected to his famous "Bak." *Bak* means "look" in Turkish. Dave would remove his glasses, open his eyes as wide as possible, stick his face right up to the student's and glare. He looked insane! The student would freeze in abject terror. The Bak was a harmless but surprisingly effective disciplinary tool.

As Richard Nixon was soon to teach us, allowing people to think you were unbalanced was not the worst thing in the world. It had its uses.

Under Dave's impassioned tutelage his students learned at an exhilarating pace. He would skewer a student with his gaze, ask a question, and if the answer was right he'd bark "Correct!" and the student would nearly explode with pride.

Hitting or slapping students was done in Turkish schools, just as it was done in American schools, British schools, and indeed in many schools around the world. I had been struck by teachers several times in high school in Pennsylvania when I was out of order. I deserved it and I hated it—which is what made it effective. The shame of having been struck was far worse than the minor physical pain. Today physical punishment is rightly prohibited, but in those days it wasn't uncommon.

As PCVs, we had to be careful. Turkish teachers might get away with traditional discipline but parents and the public would be particularly sensitive to foreigners striking Turkish students.

Dave thought he had found the perfect compromise, physical punishment that was stressful and therefore effective but never injurious: he'd grab a few strands of a student's hair close to the scalp and pull for a second or two.

Rooting for Dave

On the day of the incident a student was disrupting the class so Dave stormed back to his desk, grabbed a tuft of hair and pulled. The student didn't react because it didn't hurt. It didn't hurt because the hair came right out. The student was suffering from some illness that loosened hair.

Dave stared in shock at the tuft of hair between his fingers. All around him, eighty junior-high eyeballs froze on his fingers as though he had just plucked out the student's heart. The emotional level in Dave's classroom was always high, and now it exploded: students leapt from their chairs and ran to Necdet Bey's office.

Necdet Bey was now in the hot seat. He knew the incident was minor but he couldn't treat it that way because of the anti-American tension. When, the next day, it got into the newspapers, he had to do something. Dave was temporarily suspended from teaching.

The PCV teachers met on February 22nd and decided to support Dave. We would not return to our classes until he was absolved. We agreed to put this ultimatum to Süleyman Bey the next morning.

I went to bed late that night but couldn't get to sleep. I was still reading in bed at 12:40 am when someone began shaking my bed. Wait a minute... Something wrong here! I was alone in my room, and it wasn't just the bed that was shaking. Across the room on my dresser, the pages of an open book were bobbing up and down. The whole room was shaking, the whole building. The whole earth!

I leapt out of bed. What should I do? I put on my sneakers. By the time the laces were tied, the earthquake was over. Door frame! I was supposed to have run to a door frame and stood in it. Putting on my sneakers was a brilliant move that would have made the rescue workers who found my crushed body in the rubble wonder why I wore shoes to bed and why I hadn't used them—excellent traction in those rubber jobs!—to get to a door frame.

I took off my sneaks and got back in bed, wondering if I'd wake up in Bornova or in heaven, and, given the dismal situation at my school, which of those alternatives I might prefer.

Unfortunately the administrative earthquake at İzmir Koleji didn't stop so quickly or with so little damage. Süleyman Bey was predictably displeased and angered by our ultimatum. Our Turkish teaching colleagues didn't understand either.

"Why are you putting your jobs at risk? It's just him! He's the one who made the mistake, not you," they said. "Let him pay for it." Devil take the hindmost.

"He didn't do anything wrong," we replied. "Some teachers are much more severe. It's an arbitrary judgment. If he can be disciplined just for doing what lots of people do, there's no security for any of us."

E pluribus unum! Don't tread on me! We must all hang together or we shall surely all hang separately! We were being very American about it.

In early March Dave was suspended from teaching until a decision came down from the Ministry of Education. Ministry officials and Peace Corps officers worked out a compromise: Dave would leave İzmir Koleji, move to Ankara and finish his tour of duty at a teachers' institute, teaching older students.

With surpassing irony, Dave had been sacrificed just in time for Kurban Bayramı, the "Sacrifice Holiday." Called 'Eid el-Adha or 'Eid el-Kebir in many Muslim countries, it's the most important religious holiday of the Muslim year, commemorating Abraham's near-sacrifice of his son Isaac in obedience to God's command. It's described in the Book of Genesis, Chapter 22:

> *And [God] said, Take now thy son, thine only son Isaac, whom thou lovest, and get thee into the land of Moriah; and offer him there for a burnt offering upon one of the mountains which I will tell thee of....*

In the Kur'an, it's in Sura (Chapter) 37:

> *...he said, "My son, I see in a dream that I shall sacrifice thee; consider, what thinkest thou?"*
>
> *He said, "My father, do as thou art bidden; thou shalt find me, God willing, one of the steadfast."*

Seeing that Abraham is willing to do whatever God orders, even to sacrificing his own beloved son, God absolves Abraham of the obligation and orders him to sacrifice a ram instead.

By tradition in Turkey the head of the household procures a ram and sacrifices it on the first morning of the four-day holiday. The animal is then butchered and cooked, providing a feast for the household, a generous portion of it going to the poor, and the sheepskin to charity. Kurban Bayramı is a time for feasting and rejoicing, for visiting friends and family and exchanging greeting cards, gifts and treats—though there's little rejoicing for the sheep, two and a half million of which *baaa* their last on that day in Turkey alone.

This is a lot of dead sheep, but it pales in comparison to the 125 million turkeys who gobble their last at Thanksgiving in the USA.

Lily and Carol Pack It In

The brouhaha over Dave was the last straw for Lily and Carol, whose living situation had turned into a disaster due to culture clash. Their landlady had become their worst enemy.

With few other English-speaking friends in Bornova, we PCVs sought our own society, gathering at one another's apartments to share a meal, a glass of tea, or a beer and talk about students, classes and coming vacations. Lily and Carol had no romantic interest in any of the male PCV teachers, and we respected their feelings.

How did it look to the landlady? Many Friday and Saturday evenings, even some week nights, strange men climbed the stairs to the girls' apartment, stayed an hour or so, then tromped back downstairs. The girls had no chaperone, no family member or older person to protect their honor. And men were *men*!

The landlady decided she had made a terrible mistake. A respectable woman running a respectable apartment building, she wanted to get rid of these two foreign hookers. She gave them dirty looks. She turned off the water to their apartment during the daytime, turning it on again only in the middle of the night to fill up the toilet tanks.

The whole situation was too much for Carol. She had nothing in common with her roommate, or most of her other PCV colleagues for that matter. She was out of her element. Her parents, reading her anguished letters home, urged her to return. "Your own country needs you," they wrote. She packed her bags, headed out of Bornova and out of Turkey, and never looked back. Yankee go home! She got the message.

Lily, left without a place to live and not much reason to live there if she had one, left as well. We were down to four PCV teachers at İzmir Koleji—but the same number of classes, so our workload was even more crushing. The only good thing to come out of the mess was that I inherited Dave's class of 10-year old prep students, who were not only delightful kids but better at English than all the rest.

Rooming with Rob

The year dragged on and winter turned to spring. A letter arrived from the Peace Corps office on April 1st. My guidebook project had been approved, subject, as always in Turkey, to further approvals. I hoped this wasn't an April Fool's joke.

A few days later I decided to move out of Abdullah's and in with Rob. With Dave's departure for Ankara, Rob was left without a roommate and both halves of the rent to pay.

I was fairly happy at Abdullah's, but it was a bit lonely and a long walk from anywhere. I didn't feel comfortable inviting Peace Corps friends to visit me at Abdullah's because we might disturb him. Rob's apartment was bright, sunny, and closer to the school. I packed my trunk, my suitcase, my typewriter and my case of books, thanked Abdullah, and he wished me well.

I went to the main square in Bornova. Men with pickup trucks gathered there each morning, and people who needed their services hired them. I asked a group of drivers what it would cost to move my things. They gave me a price. It wasn't much, but I couldn't afford it. "Then you need a horse and wagon," they suggested. I found a man with a horse and wagon, and sure enough his price was lower. We piled my stuff into the wagon and trundled over to Rob's apartment on Çiftçi Caddesi.

Rob's apartment was on the second floor above a small stationery shop run by a kind old man named Neşe. He had been a printer at the university, and the shop was his way of adding a bit of money to his pension. He had an old-fashioned habit of licking the point of his pencil before writing with it. A wet pencil point writes darker than a dry point. Unfortunately, he held onto this habit when the pencil was replaced by the ballpoint pen as the writing implement of choice, so his tongue was always blue and you could see it when he licked a point.

Rob's landlady was a cheerful woman named Hatice. She enjoyed talking to Rob and having him as a tenant because of his movie-star looks, his good manners and unfailing charm.

Hatice's husband drove a minibus between Bornova and İzmir. We'd often ride with him when we went to the city. Coming back at night he followed the custom, common at the time, of turning off his headlamps when he stopped to drop off or pick up passengers. Thinking no doubt of candles and oil lamps, he believed this saved fuel and "wear" on the light bulbs. In fact it did neither, and eventually cost him big. One night another vehicle smashed into his unlit minibus as it waited at the side of the road, killing him and injuring several of his passengers, all victims of Turkey's rapid development from a land of candles and oil lamps to one of motors and electric light.

Spring in Bornova and İzmir was beautiful, the air filled with the scent of flowers. I set up my desk in Rob's apartment facing a window with a beautiful view of the city in the distance and Kadifekale (Mount Pagus), topped by Alexander the Great's fortress, rising behind it.

The Wolves of Ephesus

One fine spring Saturday morning I fled Bornova, climbed on a bus in İzmir and headed south to Selçuk. The bus dropped me in the town center and I walked the three kilometers to Ephesus along the old tree-lined road.

In the guard shack at the edge of the site sat a uniformed guard. He wore a gigantic revolver on his belt. Propped beside his chair was a long gun, a shotgun or a rifle, I can't remember which. It made a big impression, which probably means it was a shotgun. Maybe even a pump shotgun, which makes a really big impression, especially on its targets.

The guard was also the ticket-seller. I bought a ticket.

"Why the heavy artillery?" I asked. My Turkish had improved considerably over the winter.

"Wolves," he answered. A big smile lit his face with the unexpected pleasure of being asked a question in Turkish by a foreigner. "We've had a pretty bad winter this year, you know? They get hungry. When they get hungry enough, they come down out of the hills and into the ruins, especially in spring."

I toured the ruins on my own. Much of what you see today was still buried back then. There was much less to see, but also far fewer people out to see it. Actually, on this fine spring morning in April before Turkey became a popular tourist destination, I had the place to myself.

Having covered the main spots—the Great Theater, Arcadian Way, Marble Way, Library of Celsus (unrestored), and Curetes Way, I set out westward across the freshly-plowed fields for the little fort known as St Paul's Prison. Nightingale Mountain (Bülbül Dağı) loomed to the south, with fragments of Ephesus's ancient city walls running along its pine-clad crest from east to west.

I trudged through the farmer's furrows, the soft soil yielding easily as it sank beneath my boots. I looked down and noticed a piece of broken clay pot. A potsherd! I picked it up. It was dull red, a quarter-inch thick, and smaller than my palm. It felt damp and cool.

A potsherd! I was thrilled. Look at this! It could be ancient! Perhaps I should take it to the museum right away. They'd want to see this artifact. What luck!

I put it in my pocket and walked on. I noticed another potsherd, and another, and another. Dozens. Hundreds. Thousands of them. The ground was half earth and half potsherds. Dull red potsherds were—literally—as common as dirt.

I became more discriminating. I found thin potsherds of lighter clay with decorative painting on them. Surely these must be valuable! I emptied my pockets of the dull red rough clay ones and saved the thin painted ones.

It was no good. Millions of potsherds were scattered for miles in every direction. Well, what did I expect? Ephesus was a good 2000 years old, and this area had been settled for a few thousand years even before the city was founded.

I threw away the thin painted potsherds and walked on.

Set on a hillock above what was once the harbor, St Paul's Prison was a strong point in the walls. It is highly unlikely that St Paul ever spent any time here, or even set foot in it. It's another of those things that tourists, tourist guides, or locals get wrong, or make up for fun. The misinformation spreads and soon takes on a life of its own, an early example of the urban myth, like the alligators in the New York City sewers or the seeds from King Tut's tomb capable of germination.

St Paul was not in his cell when I came to call. Unfazed, I set out to follow the walls up and over Nightingale Mountain. The mountain wasn't high, the day was bright and clear, the walk a few miles at most.

Some places the wall was in good enough condition that I could walk on it. In others I had to push through the scrubby pines and gorse that surrounded it. The pushing got tougher as I climbed higher, but the view was magnificent and got progressively magnificenter.

I was less than a half hour from the summit when I saw the quick flick of a bushy grey tail in the scrub, and a flash of animal arse. A fox, I thought. But it was grey, not red. Foxes aren't grey, and they're not that big. It was bigger than a fox. What's grey and bigger than a fox?

One wolf? One wolf, and him a little guy. No problem. I kept walking.

One wolf.... Where does one find only one wolf? Wolves travel in packs, I thought. Wolves are not particularly communal, but they hunt in packs. This gives them the hunting ability of a far larger, more powerful beast like, say, a bear. But a pack of wolves is faster than a bear. In fact, a pack of wolves is a mortal threat and two wolves constitute a minimum pack. All I needed was one more wolf and I could serve them a nice fresh, hearty lunch of me.

I stopped, enjoyed the view for a few minutes, and headed back down.

If I hadn't seen the industrial-strength weaponry in the guard's shack before my climb I might not have been afraid of wolves, but had I not been afraid of wolves I might not have finished my walk either.

Little Mary Sunshine

April 23rd is National Sovereignty and Children's Day, a holiday commemorating the first meeting of Turkey's Grand National Assembly, the republican parliament, in 1920. Celebrations center around children, because they represent the future. Groups of kids from all over the world are invited to Turkey for fun, sightseeing, and shows. Among the best is the one in the Great Theater at Ephesus, where each group of kids gets a chance to perform a song or act to an audience of 25,000 parents and kids.

For those of us teaching at special high schools like İzmir Koleji, April 23rd meant a trip to Ankara for yet another conference, the purpose of which was to discuss ways to improve teaching and learning at our schools. We thought: let's go. This is gonna be rich.

When we got to Ankara, we discovered we were famous. News of the brouhaha over Dave had reverberated through the Peace Corps. Most of my colleagues thought we should abandon İzmir Koleji and teach somewhere else, but Peace Corps staff didn't agree, so we went back to our school and taught.

"We need a break," Rob said one day as we walked home from school. "I think we should do a play."

Here was a situation in the best tradition of Hollywood comedy potboilers, straight out of The Little Rascals: "Hey kids, let's put on a show!"

Rob had studied drama and acted in student productions in college. With his leading-man looks he had dreams of becoming a professional actor.

"I've talked to the director of the Turkish-American Association in İzmir. His building has a big auditorium and stage, and they'll cover some of our costs," he said.

The play he had in mind was "Little Mary Sunshine," an operetta that was a parody of operettas, a takeoff on "Rose Marie." Instead of the dashing Royal Canadian Mounted Police and hearty farm girls, "Little Mary Sunshine" had a corps of clueless forest rangers courting bored rich girls at a private school. It was a hoot, a light absurdity with immediate appeal given our own dismal career situation.

Rob told everyone in İzmir's foreign expatriate and Levantine communities about the play and enlisted their support as actors, stage hands, set and lighting designers, publicists, costume designers and make-up artists.

We rehearsed one night a week for three months. We assembled costumes from whatever we could cobble together. I was a forest ranger and needed some appropriately woodsy garb. The closest I could come was a khaki US Marine jacket, military surplus I had acquired during my high school years. Rob went to the bazaar in İzmir and found a guy to embroider circular patches, red with an evergreen at the center. Each of us forest rangers sewed a patch on the breast pocket of whatever khaki we could find and it became our uniform.

When opening night (May 16th) arrived we weren't ready, but then actors are never ready for opening night. Surprisingly, the tickets sold well enough that we weren't afraid of performing to an empty house.

When the curtain went up I scanned the audience. The first five rows were filled with our students, their parents and our fellow teachers from İzmir Koleji. Can you imagine? After all that tension and rancor at the school, they all turned out to support our play. They didn't have to. No one would've blamed them for not coming. They had lots of alternatives for an evening's entertainment, and we wouldn't have thought it disloyal for them to have chosen something else. But they didn't. They took the trouble to come out and pay money and sit patiently through an amateur production just in order to support us.

They applauded heartily. The seemed to enjoy themselves. They refrained from pointing out that in the big opening production number of the forest rangers marching in, I was the only one out of step.

Theresa

The play had brought together İzmir's expatriate and Levantine communities in a surprising way. We all got to know one another better, which led eventually to my encounter with Theresa.

Vurdumduymaz is one of my favorite Turkish words, signifying a stupefying combination of aloofness, insensitivity, dunce-hood and sheer raw stupidity. It translates as "I-hit-him-and-he-didn't-even-feel-it." No doubt there is also a Turkish word signifying a breathtaking inability to see and seize a patently golden opportunity presented to one in utterly unmistakable terms. If I knew what that word was, it would no doubt make me think of Theresa.

Franz introduced me to Theresa, a beautiful blonde of Italian Levantine heritage whose family were prosperous İzmir merchants. Theresa was about my age, gorgeous, winsome and rich. In a moment of ill-advised what-the-hell adventurousness, she took an interest in me.

Talk about *vurdumduymaz*. She invited me to join her for a day on her family's yacht. I assumed that it would be a normal Turkish/ Levantine outing with lots of friends, good food and conversation. I arrived at the dock in İzmir to find Theresa alone on the boat except for the captain.

"Where's everyone else?" I asked, surprised.

"Everyone else?" she exclaimed, a cloud racing across the brilliant solar glare of her visage. "I thought we'd just have a nice day sailing together." The sun came out again as she smiled. I still didn't get it.

The captain cast off, motored out of the harbor, and set sail. We glided across the bay, the sun bright and hot, the sky and sea two complimentary shades of brilliant blue. The captain, although he was also acting as chaperone to protect Theresa's reputation, was careful to leave us alone as much as possible. We didn't see much of him, and when we finally anchored in a quiet cove for a swim and a picnic, he went below into the crew's quarters "for a nap"—I assume on instructions from Theresa.

Theresa removed her slacks and top to reveal a skimpy bikini. She lay on the deck and spread cream on her long, slender sun-bronzed limbs. The sea slugs on the ocean floor beneath our keel got the message before I did, but finally it sunk in. I was being seduced.

She was beautiful, sultry, and eager to get to know me. Her English was good. We chatted. I gazed at her. What was not to like? But why was I being seduced? Was I that great a catch?

Even I could see that Theresa was not the kind of girl to go after a man just for sex. Even though she had been brought up in a strict convent school in İstanbul, and might therefore be on rebound out to have some fun, that wasn't enough to explain this situation we were in here, all alone on a yacht on the blue Aegean, she as close to naked as a girl could get and still act demure. It was clear, even to me, that she could have as much sex as she wanted, when she wanted, with whom she wanted. She had everything she needed to make it happen—if she wanted it to happen. Did she? What was in it for her?

Finally it hit me. Or, rather, *vurduduydum*, "It hit me and I felt it." The point was marriage. I was an eligible young American. Theresa already had Italian and Turkish passports. Adding an American one might open up all sorts of interesting possibilities. Marriage alliances had been made in the Old World for flimsier reasons. If sparks flew between us, it could turn out to be a union of love and convenience at the same time.

The problem was, I wasn't interested in marriage, at least not yet. Jane and I wrote long letters about our adventures, and discussed our relationship, but not in terms of marriage. What the alternative was we didn't know, but marriage, if it came to that, was a long way off. For both of us there were too many other things we wanted to do before settling down, travel being foremost.

For Theresa, marriage *was* travel. She had a cool set-up here in İzmir with lots of friends and a yacht and a summer house, but getting out of Turkey was difficult. The Turkish lira was soft money, strictly controlled by the government. Turks traveling out of the country were allowed to change only a very small amount of liras into foreign currency, and that at a very expensive rate of exchange. Unless they had friends abroad who would pick up tabs for them, most Turks—and Turkish Levantines like Theresa—were stuck in the country or forced to deal with the black market.

With an American husband, she and he could travel and live anywhere: America, Europe, Turkey. Winters at the apartment in New York or San Francisco, summers on the yacht in İzmir. Holy cow.

I looked at Theresa and sighed. What a sweet disposition! What a body! What possibilities!

What a disappointment the day must have been for her.

Theresa was quiet as we headed back to the dock. We had no more dates. A few years later on a visit to İzmir, Franz told me that Theresa had married an American civilian working for the US military in İzmir, and they planned to move to America.

If Theresa was my big chance, I had missed it. *Vurdugitti.* "It hit me and then it went away."

Speaking of going away, so was I. May was the last month of classes. I was on my way to İstanbul.

ᘺᘉᘻ

6

İSTANBUL

I can't tell you when I discovered the miracle of Ayasofya, but it was soon after I arrived in İstanbul to live there.

Ayasofya is the Turkish name for Hagia Sophia, the Church of the Holy Wisdom, built by order of the Byzantine emperor Justinian and finished in 537.

The architects, Anthemius of Tralles and Isidorus of Miletus, funded by their brilliant megalomaniacal emperor, were out to change the history of architecture, and they did. The great church, greatest in Christendom until the construction of St Peter's Basilica in Rome a thousand years later, is filled with innovations, chief among them its soaring dome. The dome was a daring achievement of engineering at the time—too daring, as proved by its partial collapse only 20 years later—but in one respect Anthemius and Isidorus were faithful to the traditional architecture of the Greek church: it is not static. You are not meant to stand and observe, but to move and experience. When you enter the church, you enter a sacred, magical, mysterious realm in which miracles are revealed.

If you stand in the church's outer door and peer into the darkness, far ahead of you in the shadowy apse on the eastern wall glows a gold mosaic of the Madonna and Child. On the winter solstice the sun streams directly through the windows beneath the mosaic just as the architects intended.

You walk into the church toward this golden vision and as you do the great mosaic of Christ Pantocrator, Ruler of All, slowly appears high above over the Imperial Door. At this point it's clear that the architects are controlling you the same way a cinema camera controls what you see on screen. To Anthemius and Isidorus, *you* are the camera, your eyes the lens, your imagination the film. They are presenting their powerful images to you just as surely as any movie director plays with your brain.

You approach the Imperial Door, the huge central entrance into the nave, and as you do so the dome rises above the Madonna and Child. But wait…that's not the dome at all, just a semi-dome supporting the great dome above. The dome begins to appear as you walk farther—or so it seems.

It is only when you reach the threshold of the Imperial Door that you realize you've been fooled again. Above the two semi-domes, the great dome begins truly to appear, incredibly high, unbelievably huge and broad, soaring above the vast nave of the church suspended, as one ancient writer put it, "by a golden chain from heaven."

Entering Ayasofya and experiencing its miracles never ceases to thrill me, partly because the magic of Anthemius and Isidorus is so effective, and partly because I am experiencing what the Emperor Justinian experienced on December 26, 537 as he entered the church for its dedication. It is a direct, experiential link between me and the Byzantine world of 1500 years ago. In Ayasofya, indeed in much of İstanbul, history is immediate, its ghosts alive and speaking to us whenever we stand quietly and listen.

İstanbul: this was the place for me!

By the end of May my travel guidebook proposal had ascended through the Ankara governmental hierarchy to the lofty office of the undersecretary of the Ministry of Tourism. He was the guy who actually ran the ministry. (The minister, a political appointee, took little part in day-to-day operations.) In early June I went to Ankara and presented my proposal to the undersecretary in person. He was polite and positive but non-commital. Betting that my pitch would be accepted, I hopped a bus to İstanbul and started searching for an apartment.

Transports of Delight

İstanbul is at the conjunction of two continents, Europe and Asia. The Bosphorus, a 20-mile-long strait that flows through the city's heart connecting the Black Sea with the Sea of Marmara, is the dividing line: its west bank is Europe, its east bank Asia.

In 1968 the best way to find an apartment in İstanbul was to go to the district where you wanted to live and walk the streets looking for *Kiralık Daire* (Apartment for Rent) signs in windows. Hah! Walking the streets of İstanbul is just what I wanted to do. I was in heaven.

Several people had mentioned Ayazpaşa and Cihangir, on the European side near the major hub of Taksim Square, as good neighborhoods, so I walked through them. The street signs alone provided sufficient entertainment: Güneşli ("Sunny"), Sormagir ("Don't Ask, Just Enter"), Tavuk Uçmaz ("Chickens Don't Fly"), Çifte Vav ("Double Double-U"), Arslan Yatağı ("Lion's Bed"), Saray Arkası ("Behind the Palace") and many more.

At Saray Arkası Sokak 29, in the Ayazpaşa ("Jack Frost") district just down the hill from Taksim Square and the huge old German imperial embassy (now the West German consulate), I found my place in a modest building owned by a widow. My apartment, No 5, was on the third floor looking east toward Asia.

By June 5th my project and my move to İstanbul were officially approved. Instead of a teacher's salary of $118 per month, I would receive the princely sum of $135, the extra few dollars to go toward travel expenses.

I returned to Bornova, packed my Peace Corps trunk, bookcase, typewriter, and suitcase, and shipped it to İstanbul by train. I then hopped on a bus to Ankara for the summer Peace Corps conference.

A week later, my baggage and I had both arrived in İstanbul but at different places. I slept the first night in my new apartment on the bare floor dreaming about how, the following morning, I would cross the Bosphorus to Haydarpaşa Station and retrieve my trunk, inside which was a *yorgan*, a thick cotton-filled Turkish quilt which I would spread on the floor to cushion my bones until such time as I could buy a bedstead and have a mattress made.

The next morning at Haydarpaşa I went to the baggage office and showed my receipt to a clerk. He gave it to a runner whom I followed into the huge, dark, musty depot in search of my stuff. We soon found it. The runner gave a holler, and I was immediately attacked by a dozen porters ferocious for my business.

İstanbul's porters, called *hamal*, were famous. They hung around the markets, stations and light industrial areas wearing big wood-strip baskets or triangular "saddles" on their backs, ready to carry anything anywhere. Their strength was legendary. No one looked twice as a skinny little old hamal humped a huge refrigerator across the Galata Bridge, up a steep hill, then up three flights of stairs to an apartment kitchen. Ten dozen pairs of shoes in boxes? A hundred tanned sheepskins? The rear axle of a Buick? Call a hamal and he'd move it for you quickly and efficiently.

Then came the little Japanese pickup trucks and three-wheelers, and the hamals slowly disappeared, out of work.

Hamals did their simple work well, but when it came to setting a price for their services the hassle factor was straight out of the Bible.

"How much to take my luggage down to the ferry dock?" I asked. The ferry dock is right in front of Haydarpaşa Station, about a three-minute stroll from the baggage depot.

"Whatever you want" came the inevitable reply. That didn't help because I knew that whatever I said and whatever I offered, there'd be a nasty fight over the amount at the end of the three-minute trip. We'd spend ten minutes hassling over a three-minute job.

We were already into it. The hamals jostled around me, picking up my stuff and starting to carry it away in order to force the issue. As often as they picked it up I'd order them to set it down until we had agreed on a price. I finally picked out the tallest and most aggressive hamal, the one with the two-wheeled cart, and said "twenty liras."

"Fifty," he answered.

"Twenty."

"Forty."

"Twenty."

"Thirty."

"Twenty or nothing."

"Okay, twenty," he said, and hefted my stuff onto his cart. He rolled it down a ramp to the ferry dock, fifty yards away, where the ferryboat was just arriving.

Straining against the weight of the heavy cart and its load, he stopped it just before it whacked into the ferry which thrashed and wallowed as it docked, washing up a wake of sea water laden with grapefruit peels, plastic bags, jellyfish and the occasional bottle. The ferry's mates cast hawsers onto bollards to lash the boat to the quay, but the ferry would not be tied up long, probably no more than two minutes, just long enough for passengers to get off and on.

Thus I had a new problem: my stuff was still on the hamal's cart, but the station porters and the ferry porters were different groups, and the one group would not do the work of the other. I now had to haggle over a price to hire ferry porters to lift my stuff off the station porter's cart, carry it ten feet, and put it on the ferryboat, where the mates were about to unwrap the hawsers from the bollards in preparation for departure. There wouldn't be another ferry for 40 minutes. I had less than two minutes to haggle with the ferry porters, which was actually secondary at that moment because the station porter, far more adept at haggling than hauling, had realized my predicament and decided to deep-six our earlier agreement and double his fee, which I was counting out to pay him. By reopening the haggling when every second was precious he hoped I'd just cave in and pay double. Howling recriminations, I shoved the original fee at him (exact change) with my left hand while I fought off the six ferry porters with my right as they all attempted to pick up my baggage from the cart, each one hefting at least some corner of it so they could all get in on a fee that would thus end up being so enormous that we'd have to exchange jobs for me ever to be able to pay it off.

The work of transferring my stuff from the cart to the ferry could have easily been done by one man in two minutes, or two men in one minute, but instead there were seven of them jostling me as the ferry prepared to pull away. At this point I had more than a lifetime's worth of porter aggravation but less than a minute to get my stuff on the ferry, so finally I pointed at two of them and they quickly and easily transferred the baggage from the cart to the ferry while the station porter loudly badmouthed me to everyone within earshot. He held out his hand with the fee I had paid him—the exact fee we had earlier agreed upon—and bellowed self-righteous rhetorical questions about how a man could ever live on such a paltry recompense and what was the country coming to when an honest worker couldn't earn an honest day's wage (for three minutes' work) and how was he going to feed himself let alone his family, let alone have a few liras for any of life's simplest, cheapest pleasures now and again, blah blah blah.

The passengers on the ferryboat stared at him, then glanced furtively at me, red-faced and sweaty, seated glumly atop my trunk in the ferryboat's breezeway in order to prevent its being moved, at huge cost per inch, by any of the several ferry porters who had climbed aboard the boat, bound for Karaköy, in the expectation that upon our arrival they could gouge me out of even more money. As the ferry departed and we drifted away from the dock and out of haggling range, the strident voice of the station porter was felicitously lost in the cries of the gulls, the low thrum of the powerful marine engines, and the swash of the wake against the quay.

Crossing the Bosphorus by ferry is one of İstanbul's many small but intense pleasures. Back in 1969, in the time before high-speed ring roads and soaring Bosphorus bridges, the ferries were the city's transportation lifelines, but riding them was always more than mere transportation. Sitting atop my baggage, red-faced, sweaty and grumpy, I was in fact on a scenic mini-cruise from Asia to Europe, drifting past the minarets of the Blue Mosque, the domes of Hagia Sophia and the turrets of Topkapı Palace, bound for the Golden Horn…which made it all the more distasteful that the ferry porters hassled me all the way to Karaköy.

It's not so much that I was the only game in town as that I was a foreigner, and to the porters all foreigners were rich. They were right, of course. In their terms I *was* rich. I had a college education, a monthly paycheck, and people at home who could lend me money if I got into a jam. To my way of thinking I still had to pay my bills on a Turkish junior teacher's salary, and I couldn't do that by paying five times what a Turk would pay every time one of these guys picked up my trunk and moved it ten feet.

The ferry docked at Karaköy and I glared at the posse of hamals as I tensed my muscles for the struggle to get my stuff off the boat in the midst of the flood of disembarking passengers before the mates would again cast off the lines and head out to sea.

Just then the captain came on the intercom and announced that the ferry would be out of service for a half hour.

I was saved! I needn't be in a hurry to get off the boat. I sat atop my pile of baggage until everyone was gone, even the ferry porters who eventually retired to the sidelines, glancing at me furtively but frequently in the vain hope of discerning an opening for another attack.

I dragged my things onto the dock and sat on them until the porters cleared out, their visions of fat fees from foreigners evaporating like a morning mist over the Bosphorus.

I looked down the dock to the street, over a hundred feet away, to which I must now somehow drag my stuff, and saw another human tsunami racing towards me. Taxi drivers! Oh Jesus.

The taxi drivers were a better-dressed lot, but just as pushy. The only good thing about them was that, as middle class businessmen, it was well beneath their dignity to soil their hands by carrying stuff. They wouldn't be jostling me to pick up my trunk and haul it away.

I formulated a plan, picked out the most prominent driver, looked him in the eye and spoke slowly and clearly.

"Look, I'm an English teacher, not a rich guy. I need to get this stuff to my new apartment in Ayazpaşa as cheaply as possible. What's your lowest rate?"

No Turkish taxi used a meter in those days. They all had them, but they didn't use them. The excuse was that the meter was broken, which it often was, but it didn't really matter. As with the hamals, you had to haggle. Smart people negotiated the fare at the beginning of the trip, clueless ones at the end.

"For all that heavy stuff? Three hundred liras," the driver said.

Three hundred liras: about a third of my monthly salary. The taxi drivers might be better dressed, but their perception of foreigners was identical to that of the porters.

"I can't afford it," I said. "That's more than I make in a month."

When you're haggling, there is no such thing as lying or dishonesty.

"Two hundred then, but somehow you've got to get it down to the end of the dock where the taxis are."

"I'll get it there," I said, but I can only afford fifty liras for the fare."

Fifty? They all looked at one another.

"Okay, one hundred," the driver said, "just as a favor. I've got a new car and all this heavy stuff is going to wear out my springs." As though I was moving a piano and five cases of barbells, or all the soufflés in a first-year cooking class.

"Sorry, fifty is my limit. That's all the money I have."

"Borrow the other fifty from a friend," the driver said, ever helpful.

"I don't have any friends here. I've just arrived. See? Here's my luggage." I was proud of myself. I don't usually think that quick.

The drivers mumbled together for awhile, then strolled away toward the street.

I knew they'd be back, because it was obvious that I needed a taxi, and obvious that one of them would earn some money by driving me to Ayazpaşa.

I turned away from them, took out my wallet from my back pocket, removed all but fifty liras, put the wallet back, and shoved the rest of the bills in a front pocket. The leader of the pack drifted back toward me.

"Seventy-five."

"I don't have it. I just don't have it," I said. I pulled out my wallet, opened it and showed him. His face fell.

"Listen," he said, "you've got to have a taxi, and I just can't do it for that. Wait here and I'll go see if I can find a guy with an old car who will do it for fifty."

A likely story. I figure he'd just wander away, have a tea and come back, hoping to find me impatient to go for seventy-five, at which time he'd raise the fare to a hundred.

I started to hump my baggage slowly down the dock, flopping my trunk end over end, then going back to get my bookcase, then my typewriter and my suitcase. Whatever was going to happen next, it wasn't going to happen from way out at the end of the ferry dock. I needed to get me and my stuff to the street. The hamals, who were still lurking nearby, charged toward me, but I hollered at them to get lost. When I was three-quarters of the way down the dock to the street, the taxi driver was back, followed by an older, bespectacled man with a handlebar mustache.

"He'll take you for fifty," the driver said.

I was mortified. He was telling the truth! I could have afforded TL75 and the fancier taxi—barely. I just hate to be cheated. This guy had gone out of his way to do me a favor. This was my first lesson about İstanbul taxi drivers. I had a lot more to learn.

Taking pity on my poverty, the two drivers helped me move my stuff down the dock to the street. Behind the first driver's five-year-old Chevy, resting on fat whitewall tires and polished to a reflector glare, was a maroon 1940s-vintage Chevy fastback. We put my trunk in the old Chevy's shallow trunk, and the other stuff in the back seat.

I shook the first driver's hand and thanked him for his help.

"Don't mention it. Sometime you can teach me a little English, eh?"

I got into the old Chevy. Handlebar turned the key, coaxed the clunker to life, crunched it into gear and we growled away. The noise from the engine was that of an immense coffee grinder with a full 200-pound sack of beans rammed down its throat. We ground and groaned up the hill to Taksim, then plummeted down behind the West German consulate into Ayazpaşa and pulled up in front of Saray Arkası Sokak 29. After unloading my stuff we looked around for a hamal. Handlebar found one. We started haggling, but Handlebar butted in.

"He can't afford that!" he hollered. "He's just a teacher! He's just arrived in İstanbul! Give him a break!"

The hamal, browbeaten and sullen, agreed to my first offer and carried my stuff up three flights to my apartment. I shook hands with Handlebar, and he slid onto the smooth Naugahyde of the Chevy's shiny front seat and rumbled away, grinding another sackful.

Saray Arkası Sokak 29/5

Even with my baggage, my new apartment was stark raving empty. My luggage was its only furniture. My trunk was my chair, dining table and writing desk. I slept on the bare floor, but at least now I had a quilt to sleep on. Talk about an uncluttered life.

The apartment had a fairly large balcony, and had once had a fine Bosphorus view, but several years before a big luxury apartment building had been constructed across the street, and now the view was completely blocked. Instead of the glistening Bosphorus with its white ships carrying the romance of world travel and the flags of a score of nations, I had a view of kitchens and maids' quarters in rich peoples' apartments. The rich people had "my" Bosphorus view.

My new home was fine for one person: from the main room, large glass doors opened onto the balcony. A curtained alcove to one side of the main room served as my bedroom. A short hallway led to the front door, the very small kitchen (fine for Peace Corps cuisine), and the tiny bathroom with a shower and bathtub and—miracle of miracles!—a gas-fired flash heater. I could have a hot bath anytime I wanted! No need to (1) buy a bag of kerosene-soaked wood chips at the grocer's, (2) put some in the bottom of a water heater, (3) add sticks and other fuel, (4) light the fire, (5) wait an hour until the water was hot. That had been the routine in my earlier apartments, except for Abdullah's.

The main reason I chose this particular apartment however, the reason I was willing to pay almost half my monthly salary for it, was the great copper-clad fireplace in the main room. A fireplace!

My childhood home in Pennsylvania had a fireplace. We collected wood from the trees in our back yard or cut it in the mountains, and often sat together by a cozy fire on cold winter days. Our house had central heating but wonderful as it is, it doesn't replace a real wood fire. The mind-numbing idiocy of television, the so-called "electronic hearth," doesn't even approach the soul-soothing satisfaction of sitting and watching the play of flame on logs.

My Ayazpaşa fireplace was a grand affair with a raised brick hearth and a chimney sheathed in an elaborately embossed copper shield. I never quite understood why such a modest apartment had such a grand fireplace.

It was early summer when I moved in; I waited impatiently for the nip of winter so I could light my fire. I thought of how great it would be if Jane were there to watch the flames with me.

In the meantime I sat on my balcony watching the shearwaters (Bosphorus gulls) wheeling above, wishing I could see what they were seeing.

Saray Arkası Sokak was convenient for my work, a ten-minute walk downhill from Taksim Square but, as I was soon to discover, a slow 15-minute slog uphill to the square. When I first looked at it, the street seemed quiet, with little traffic.

My landlady, Mrs Nacide Zincirkıran, was an agreeable widow of refined manners in late middle age who, in defiance of her fierce family name ("Chain-breaker"), was active in the Society for the Prevention of Cruelty to Animals. She also spoke a bit of French. I spoke it better. Between her halting French and my imperfect Turkish we managed to communicate pretty well. She told me where to go to buy furniture cheap and where to have a good mattress made with new cotton so I'd have no bedbugs.

Every İstanbul apartment building, however small, had a *kapıcı*, a combination doorman, porter and factotum. The kapıcı put out the trash, swept the steps, ran errands, and let visitors in the front door if they didn't have a key. Ours, a tall, stately octogenarian named Haydar, had white hair, white bushy eyebrows, and a luxuriant, flowing, well-combed white beard. He dressed in an old, much-mended black suit. From its frayed lapel dangled the Independence Medal, awarded to those who had fought in Turkey's War of Independence in 1921–22.

"Haydar Efendi is worthy of respect," Nacide Hanım would say. "You see his Independence Medal? You know what that means? Yes, worthy of respect. He has nowhere to go, so he serves as doorman for us." Haydar slept in a tiny closet beneath the main staircase, guarding the door, destitute but dignified.

Welcome to the Neighborhood

My new neighborhood had two shops. The nearest to my door was run by a nervous, bespectacled man named Cemil. His was the larger shop, with more selection but, as I was soon to discover, higher prices and, as prices were never marked, especially high prices for unwitting foreigners, of which there were several living nearby. The smaller shop around the corner was less fancy but Ahmet the shopkeeper charged the same fair prices to everyone.

In those days it was looked upon as proper to be a loyal customer of one shop, and not to shop at others unless absolutely necessary. In exchange for this loyalty, the shopkeeper willingly provided extra services like free delivery, special orders, or even selling on credit for a short time.

The rich people in the big apartment building that blocked my view sent their maids to Cemil who filled their orders nervously, quickly and expensively. A few foreigners shopped at Cemil's, so at first, so did I. I bought a big bottle of drinking water from Cemil, and paid him an enormous deposit of TL20 on the bottle until a friend told me that the customary deposit was TL2. I took back my last water bottle and demanded my deposit back. Cemil handed me two liras.

"I gave you TL20 as a deposit. I'd like the rest, please."

"The deposit is two liras, " he said.

I produced my deposit receipt for TL20, signed by Cemil. He frowned, grumbled, and gave me the other TL18. I took my valuable business to the shop of Ahmet from then on.

Ahmet's shop was tiny, but he had better vegetables. Not only that, Ahmet was always smiling. On one occasion I had to fight with him because he owed me five kurush in change—half a penny—and didn't have that small a coin.

"*Boş ver,*" I said. "It's not important."

"No, no, I insist!" Ahmet answered. "I must give you your change!"

He spent a full lira's worth of work-time searching for a five-kurush coin, failed to find one, then with a smile of resignation said "I'll give it to you next time you come in."

I don't remember what happened after that. Maybe he still owes me five kurush. If so, he's going to have an even harder time finding that coin now that one dollar equals well over a million old liras, which is to say 100 million kurush.

Cemil's shop disappeared after a few years. Ahmet's was still in business decades later, though Ahmet himself is long retired.

Besides the shops, there were the itinerant peddlers:

Balıkçı! Taze balık! (Fish! Fresh fish!)

Sütçü! Süüüüüüüt! (Milkman! Miiiiiiilllk!)

Gaz'teci! Gazete! Gazete! Gaz'teciiiiiiii! (Paper boy! Newspaper! Paaaaaper!)

Eskici! Şişe alıyorum! Eskiiiiiii! (Junkman! I buy bottles! Juuuuuuuuuunk!)

And, on winter evenings if we were lucky....

Bozaaaaaaa! Bozacı! Bozaaaaaaa! (Boza! Boza-man!)

...the call of the man bringing the tangy fermented millet drink that had been a favorite of the Janissaries, the sultan's standing army. The musical street calls were a part of İstanbul as much as Ayasofya and the Blue Mosque.

Five times a day (and on special religious holidays, even more) the call to prayer echoed from the minarets of the city's thousand mosques, including the Ayazpaşa Camii, our little neighborhood mosque just up the hill.

Throughout the night it was comforting to hear the trill of the night watchman's whistle as he patrolled the streets, a reminder of Ottoman times. In *Portrait of a Turkish Family*, İrfan Orga describes the pre-World War I scene: "*Bekçi Baba* ('Papa Watchman') was coming up the road, a fearsome-looking figure with his dark cloak flapping out behind him and his stick thumping the ringing stones."

The ribald chatter of the taxi drivers was a different kind of noise. The drivers gathered at the southern end of Saray Arkası Sokak to wait for the rich people in the neighborhood to hire them for fat fares. Owning a taxi was a big deal, a real business requiring substantial capital. The drivers were generally lazy jerks who'd rather gouge an old lady on one fare than work to get four fair ones.

Nacide Hanım complained bitterly about them. They hung around polishing their investments— heavy old Dodges, Chevrolets, Fords, much repaired—until they shone. They chatted, hollered, told jokes, gave one another wedgies and made rude noises until past midnight.

Dozens of cats wandered the streets day and night looking for free meals. The shopkeepers put out scraps. After dinner a few neighborhood residents filled plates with table leavings, set them at their doorsteps, and fled for cover as the hurricane of living fur and flashing teeth howled down the street toward them.

Some days heaven came to earth, in cat terms. Those were the days Nacide Hanım went to the butcher shop, bought huge chunks of bloody liver and lobbed them from her second-floor balcony onto the granite paving blocks below. In an instant, Liver Central was a roiling swarm of cats.

Plop! The roiling swarm leapt for the bloody blob. Two meters to the left... plop! The first were now last as the swarm rushed to the new goal. Plop! Plop! Plop! In cat heaven bloody meat rains down from the sky just like this.

Then—silence.

Silence? No more plops?!

A hundred feline eyes gaze heavenward, focused on Nacide Hanım's fingers still wet with crimson gore...but the liver was gone. Heaven retreated, earth was but earth again.

Licking the cobbles carefully, sniffing for an overlooked drop of blood or fragment of gristle, Nacide's cats returned reluctantly to Real Life: oily eggplant and cold noodles left from the neighborhood's dinner tables.

Dogs were another matter. They slept in the gutters, meek and apparently lifeless during the day, but woke at dusk and laid claim to the streets. Each dog had his turf. Growls, barks and occasional bites greeted anyone passing along "his" street. Adnan Menderes, Turkey's prime minister during the 1950s, had the city's stray dogs rounded up, shipped to an island in the Sea of Marmara and abandoned, but so had the Young Turks a half century before, and so had Abdülmecid a half century before that. Since the 1500s İstanbul's dogs have always been shipped away, and others have always moved in to take their places.

Having settled in, I began to explore İstanbul like a resident. I naturally gravitated to Sultanahmet, first to gawk at the great buildings like Ayasofya and the Blue Mosque, then to gawk at the hippies. The hippies led me to Yener.

King of the Hippies

In Sultanahmet the newly-arrived hippies ate cheaply at the Lale Pastanesi (now the Lale Restaurant—that's lah-LEH, "tulip"), which they called "the pudding shop" because one of the best food bargains in the old days was *sütlaç*, the rich milk-and-rice pudding sold in Turkish pastry shops. The Lale was the city's legendary hippie headquarters. After a few days in İstanbul and one too many puddings they'd discover they could eat beans and rice even cheaper at Yener, behind the Lale on Şeftali Sokak ("Peach Street"). The sign over the door read *Yener Lokantası, Sıtkı Oruç.*

Like the hippies, I discovered Yener soon after arriving in the city, and like the hippies I assumed that the owner's name was Yener and called him that. Yener means either "Victorious" or "Edible," or perhaps both. His name was actually Sıtkı Oruç, which is a howl in itself since *oruç* means "fasting," as when you don't eat anything.

Yener was a short, balding, ebullient man of middle age with huge mutton-chop side-whiskers. His restaurant was tiny, with room only for the cookstove and 3½ dining tables. Yener served standard Turkish soups, stews and grills. A plate of broad beans in tomato sauce, a plate of rice pilav, some big hunks of fresh bread and a bottle of water made a good lunch for 55¢ (TL5), right in line with my budget.

Yener delighted in hosting the hippies who passed through İstanbul on the route between Europe and India. The common stereotype of a hippy was a lazy, irresponsible, unclean, sex-crazed drug addict, which was silly. Most were simply young, adventurous foreign travelers, the vanguard of Baby Boom tourism that would arrive in Turkey and enrich its coffers two decades later. Being adventurous, they arrived first. They shared rooms and tents and minibuses and—yes—sometimes joints and sexual organs because society was changing and they were leading the change.

Most İstanbullus were ambivalent about the hippies. The merchants who ran the hotels, restaurants and shops around Sultanahmet welcomed them because they spent money. The police disliked them, suspecting them all of crime and drug abuse. Most people found them strange and disagreeable because of their weird clothes and unfamiliar habits. It was culture clash.

Yes, some of the hippies used drugs, mostly marijuana, and some abused drugs, just as people did in their home countries, but the hippy's true high was from the potent elixir of personal freedom and vagabond travel. As for Yener, occasionally in the evenings he'd also serve free beer, wine or rakı to his favorite customers, laughing and joking about drunkenness—but never actually getting drunk himself. His natural ebullience and *joie de vivre* had no need of stimulants.

"Drinking's fine!" he'd say. "Look, Atatürk died of cirrhosis."

I spent time in Yener's to break the loneliness of living and working alone. Jane and I had agreed to try to meet in Europe in August, but August was still months away and who knows? We might not get to meet in any case. There were always lots of girls passing through Yener's. I wouldn't have minded a little female companionship.

On one lunchtime visit to Yener's I chatted with an attractive young Danish woman. I asked her where she had traveled, and she rattled off an improbably long list of cities and countries.

"How long have you been on the road?" I asked.

"About four years now," she answered. These people were not on a vacation but a life quest, gathering pieces of the Big Puzzle.

The young travelers started out from home with their savings, and when money ran low they'd stop somewhere and work until they had enough money saved to move on. This sort of footloose vagabondage is now accepted as normal. Young people from Europe, America and even Turkey now do it without a second thought, and most of Australia does it all the time. But in 1968 it was revolutionary and highly suspect.

Two beautiful Swedish girls who came through Yener's got jobs as hostesses in a bar near Taksim. Their job was simply to welcome the male customers and make the place look sophisticated. I tried to chat them up, ever hopeful, but failed miserably. Yener taught me the Turkish word *züppe* (snooty) to describe them.

Some of the young male hippies would change into more conventional clothes and give English lessons to earn money. One I met stayed in İstanbul for several years and built up a list of high-profile clients, including the vice-president of a prominent bank. Another, from Germany, worked his way around the world repairing Volkswagen engines. Still others who owned minibuses would take on passengers and charge them enough to cover travel costs as well as their own personal expenses.

Besides being their commissary, the hippies used Yener's restaurant as a communications center, exchanging travel tips and the names and addresses of good, cheap lodgings and eateries in scores of countries. They'd advertise to mutual advantage: "Minibus in good condition bound for Kathmandu, needs two more people to share costs."

Yener bought a big bound notebook and set it on a table. While eating lunch or sipping tea, hippies wrote messages in the notebook for friends who might arrive later. They wrote messages of thanks to Yener for his friendship and support. They drew doodles, or wrote thoughts, dreams, travel stories, or poems. They drew maps of good routes to take, and left details of good places to stay.

The notebook filled up. Yener bought another. That one filled as well, and soon Yener had a shelf full of notebooks, a unique free-form history of the hippy Sixties, hand-illustrated by the original cast.

İstanbul newspapers loved Yener because he was always good for some colorful copy. I have a clipping from the front page of *Akşam* dated November 4, 1971, showing Yener, flanked by two blonde "hippies" (actually nicely dressed young women), reading the inscribed copy of *Turkey on $5 a Day* that I had sent to

Yener in exchange for his kindness. The headline says *Yener, "Aşk İmparatorluğu Dışişleri Bakanı" oldu!* ("Yener has been named 'Foreign Minister of the Empire of Love!'"), which is how I had inscribed the book.

Unfortunately, too many times the press coverage was of Yener in trouble. The police, suspecting that Yener's was a trading point for drugs, often harassed Yener, sometimes forcibly. The newspaper photos showed him with bruises, black eyes and bandages. The press coverage acted as insurance against repeated police abuse, however. The police didn't like to see evidence of "baton justice" printed in the newspapers, so their harassment of Yener was infrequent.

Touristic Non-Tsunami

Like the young hippies, the few older budget and middle-income tourists who came to Turkey in 1968 were of an uncommon type. Adventurous, eager to explore, ready to take this foreign country on its own terms, they were delighted with what they found. They gawked at the mosques and palaces of İstanbul, traipsed the marble streets of Ephesus, climbed to the top of the castle walls in Bodrum, basked on the beaches in Marmaris and Antalya, and dove into the rock-cut churches and underground cities of Cappadocia. They loved the country, the scenery, the history, the ruins, the people, the cuisine.

I can remember meeting only one tourist, a Frenchman, who didn't like Turkey, but it seemed to me that he was just being exceedingly French. Come to think of it, there was one other person, a woman I met at a friend's apartment in İzmir, who didn't like Turkey either. She was French, too, by coincidence. She said "Turkey has no art, no culture, no proper food." She was being extremely and extraordinarily French. What she meant was that Turkey was not France, and this state of affairs was entirely unacceptable. She got to İstanbul and didn't see the Louvre, so she determined that Turkey had no art. It never occurred to her that in a society that had been Islamic for 800 years there would be no tradition of sculpture and portraiture because these "idolatrous" arts were proscribed by Islam. The great arts of Islam are non-representational: architecture, textile design, faience (colored tiles), jewelry, marquetry and metal working.

She looked for the Comédie Française and didn't find it, so she was convinced Turkey had no culture. Had she looked beneath the surface she would have found a vibrant theater life, not to mention the living traditions of Karagöz, the Turkish shadow-puppet show, and bardic poetry recitals straight out of the Middle Ages still held annually.

How she could have disliked Turkish cuisine is entirely beyond me, but when you're French and the subject is food, anything's possible. Every place should be France, she thought. Napoleon was on the right track when he conquered most of Europe, he just didn't go far enough. He should have conquered the

Ottoman Empire too.

Every country has such narrow-minded people. Perhaps they stand out so much when they're French because France does indeed have such a marvelous culture, a culture which so many other countries have sought to emulate over the years—including the Ottoman Empire in its last century.

I shuddered to think what she'd say about the USA. Her attitude was surprising in part because young French travelers had been among the first Europeans to discover Turkey, and they had loved it.

I left her in her unhappy funk, so disappointed with everything around her, unable to find anything decent to eat, and went out and had a good meal at my favorite kebap grill on Anafartalar Caddesi.

Other than these two ultra-Gaullists, the feeling among the small number of foreign visitors was universal: Turkey is wonderful, so I thought it should be easy to write a good travel guidebook about it.

After living and traveling in Turkey and talking to other travelers for a year, I think I had a working definition of the people I would be writing for. So what should I write? I looked at the competition on the bookstore shelves.

There was an old Swiss-published Nagel guide in French, woefully out of date, and the Hachette Blue Guide in English, detailed but formal, stuffy, printed in tiny type, and also out of date.

The Fodor's guide was good for some historical and cultural background but the practical information was weak and aimed at the Hilton set. The 1969 edition had four pages on travel by car, and no information at all on travel by bus. Fodor's "Typical First-Class Budget for a Day" was TL179 (US$14.91, or UK£6/4s). At that rate, if I gave up my apartment and spent my entire salary on travel, I could afford to be on the road in Turkey for nine days, after which I would have no money, no food, no shelter, and no more bus fare. I was interested in showing people how to travel in Turkey for only a third of that: $5 a day—and even that was a budget for the well-off. After paying my rent and other monthly expenses, I could perhaps afford $50 to $60 per month for travel, which meant I'd need to travel for $2 per day or less. Surprisingly, and luckily for me, it was fairly easy to travel in Turkey then for that amount.

Speaking of the Hilton, Turkey's hotel situation was terrible even in the luxury class. İstanbul had the Hilton and the Divan Oteli, İzmir had the Grand Ephesus Hotel and Ankara the Grand Ankara Hotel, a few beach resorts had one or two new, modern hotels, but beyond these few the hotel situation was dire. Freya Stark, the great British traveler, put it this way in the 1950s:

> The Turks, with the most splendid, varied and interesting country in the world, are naturally anxious to obtain tourists, and their difficulties in this respect are caused chiefly by the quite phenomenal badness of their hotels. [Riding to the Tigris, p 11]

She goes on to say that this is all the more perplexing because "the Turks are perfectly able to organize a good hotel."

The sort of tourist I was interested in attracting and guiding around Turkey couldn't afford the Hilton, the Grand Ephesus or a beach resort. They wanted simple, cheap hotels that were clean, safe and welcoming. A lot of Turkey's cheap hotels were too basic for anybody but a hippie, with 50¢-a-night beds and flat "elephant's feet" *alaturka* toilets and very basic shared bathrooms. Simple, cheap, serviceable lodgings were difficult to find, which is why everybody needed a guidebook.

As I was soon to discover, the cheap lodgings outside the major cities were the *ev pansiyon* ("home pension"), the basic no-frills hotel, and the traditional caravanserai.

The ev pansiyons were simple but good, normal homes with a spare room or two for rent by the day, the Turkish equivalent of England's bed-and breakfast houses. The local Turkish women who rented their rooms rarely knew more than a few words of a foreign language, however, and they offered little privacy. The cheap hotels were utterly spartan with no décor, comforts or services beyond beds and cold showers (one needed an appointment for a hot shower). As for caravanserais, these traditional medieval travelers' inns still existed in most Turkish towns. They usually had only one cold water tap (and no showers) to serve the entire hotel. In the morning, men (including me) lined up at the tap for the chance to wash and shave in cold water. If you wanted a bath you went to the *hamam* (Turkish bath) for an hour or two.

So the situation was one of chicken-and-egg. Which comes first, the tourists who need hotels to stay in, or the hotels for the tourists to stay in?

Other travel services were better. The trains were adequate if slow. Buses were comfortable, cheap and convenient, but air travel was expensive and limited to a few routes with frequent cancellations "because of adverse weather" even on bright sunny windless days, which meant that not enough seats had been sold. Restaurants, at least, were good, cheap and everywhere. The delicious food and attentive service more than made up for the simple surroundings.

I would discover all of this as I worked and wrote, taking research trips from my little apartment on Saray Arkası Sokak. But in July 1968 I was thinking about more important things, namely girls.

∞

7

THE BLONDE AT THE
CIRCUMCISION PARTY

"I'm coming to İstanbul in July. Will you be around? Can we get together?" she asked in her letter, which I read with trembling hands. If I had occasionally been a lonely bachelor in college, I was five times as lonely in İstanbul all the time. Olivia, a Radcliffe girl I had dated a few times in college, was for me the Impossible Dream, a girl too beautiful, smart, well-bred and personable ever to fall into my arms. Would I get another chance?

Can we get together? By osmosis if you want.

Olivia was traveling with a friend, and asked if I could meet them at the airport.

"We hear all these stories of young women arriving at the airport in İstanbul and being abducted by local Romeos," she wrote. It hurt my pride that she wasn't afraid I'd abduct her. Was I not a Romeo? Apparently not, or at least not as titillatingly sinister as a Turkish Romeo.

She arrived on the daily Pan Am flight from New York on July 20th. I dutifully met her and her friend at the airport and escorted them to their hotel, leading them bravely through the surging crowds of Turkish Romeos who thronged the arrivals terminal in their imagination.

"Welcome to İstanbul," I said. "The university's closed due to riots. You're just in time for a huge anti-American demonstration to be staged tomorrow in protest of the Sixth Fleet's presence in the Bosphorus. Your tax dollars at work."

We went out for dinner. What a pleasure! Olivia was her sparkling self, asking probing questions about the current Turkish political scene and reducing me to a quivering mass with her smile when I tried to answer. I don't remember a thing about her friend. In fact, I don't remember anything about the evening except Olivia's smile. She was completely unaffected, no coy tossing of curls or squinting of eyes, no winking, or leaning over and hanging on my words with demonstrative intensity as though I were some oriental oracle. She didn't need tricks. She was honest, straightforward, self-confident and gorgeous, and I was utterly, completely captivated.

It was 3 am, back in the women's hotel room, by the time even I decided I'd better go home. The buses had long since stopped so I walked home to Ayazpaşa through the night-bound streets of İstanbul.

At 3 am on a summer night there were still people in the streets, particularly in places like Sirkeci, Eminönü and Karaköy, with their railway station and ferry docks, but there was little danger. To have walked across any American city of equal size at that hour would have been to assure theft of your money at least and of your life at worst, and maybe it wouldn't be wise to walk across İstanbul at night nowadays, but in the İstanbul of 1968 I feared only the dogs. The somnolent piles of dog-flesh littering the gutters during the day rose up as Cerberus at night. I found sticks and heavy litter—stones, roof tiles, bits of brick—to carry just in case, and used them more than once. Snarling dogs prowled the alleys, sometimes in packs, looking for infractors of dog-rule. A few times they decided I was it, but a few well-aimed bits of brick changed their minds.

The next evening Olivia and her friend came to my apartment. I served them drinks and a simple dinner, and we sat on my balcony, talked, laughed, and non-looked at my non-view of the Bosphorus. It was delightful, but her company only made me want more of her company. As they were getting ready to leave, her friend went off to the bathroom and I asked Olivia if she'd like to go to a party. Not just any party, a Turkish *sünnet* (circumcision) party. Not just anyone's circumcision party, Yener's son's circumcision party.

She loved the idea.

Despite his unconventional hippy sympathies, Yener was a good family man with a comely wife and stout nine-year-old son. Before Olivia arrived he had invited me to his son's *sünnet*, and I had accepted.

Circumcision? Let's Party!

Circumcision is minor surgery in which the foreskin covering the head of the penis is surgically removed. It's done on many male babies regardless of religion to enhance cleanliness and prevent infection, but it's a religious requirement for Jewish boys at birth, and Muslim boys of nine or ten as a right of passage into puberty.

For Muslims, it's a cause for great celebration similar to confirmation or first communion for Christians and bar mitzvah for Jews. Before the operation, the Muslim lad is dressed in a special fancy suit of white satin with red decorations and paraded around the town with all his friends and relatives to the strains of wild music often provided by a live band. After the operation, which only takes a few minutes, the proud parents host a big party for all their relatives and friends.

I had never been to a sünnet party so I wasn't sure what to expect, and I couldn't describe it to Olivia either, but I felt sure that whatever a sünnet party was it would be better—certainly no worse—with a gorgeous blonde on my arm. I took a bus to Sultanahmet, picked up Olivia from her hotel, and took her by taxi (damn the expense!) to Beyazıt Square.

The party was in a spacious function room at the Beyaz Saray, a big multi-purpose building facing the tall stone gates of İstanbul University. We entered the building, followed the music and found two bands, one Turkish, the other Western, tables laden with food and drink, and most surprising of all Yener the hippie cook-shack owner dressed in a suit. When he saw us he rushed over, his face split in a wide grin. He hugged us, shook our hands and pulled us into the room.

"Maşallah! Maşallah! Look, it's Tom Bey! And who's this? Olivia? Olivia Hanım! Hoş geldin! Hoş geldin! Come meet my wife! Meet my son! Come! Come! Eat! Drink! Dance!"

The high-ceilinged room was filled with Turkish men in conservative suits, Turkish women in stylish dresses, and a disreputable-looking handful of hippies, regular customers from Yener's restaurant dressed in tattered jeans, buckskins and beads. Yener had invited some hippy friends out of the goodness of his heart and the traditions of Turkish hospitality. They looked about as comfortable as transvestites at an army physical exam.

Olivia and I got in line and paid our respects to his son, a sweet boy who lay in a fancy brass bed under a satin coverlet on one side of the dance floor looking vaguely in pain, shyly happy and mostly bewildered—not all that bad for a nine-year-old who had just had the tip of his penis whacked off by a bearded old man muttering holy formulas.

Uh-oh. A table by his bed was cluttered with gifts. I was supposed to have brought a gift! How was I to know? I grabbed a gift off the table behind my back, whipped it out and showed it to him before placing it gently back on the table. He smiled. We moved on to the buffet and drinks tables laden with goodies.

None of Yener's beans-and-rice here! Dozens of Turkish delicacies covered the snow-white tablecloth: four kinds of olives, four cheeses (white, yellow, a crumbly-dry village goat cheese, string cheese), stuffed vine leaves, stuffed cabbage leaves, white beans and sweet onion slices vinaigrette, tangy pickled vegetables, creamy purées and vegetables in mayonnaise, little shish kebabs and tiny lamb chops, salads of Boston lettuce and arugula (rocket) and romaine, three kinds of bread. I took the opportunity to whisper their names softly in Olivia's shell-like ear curtained by blonde ringlets, my lips gently brushing her flesh now and then. My excuse for this intimacy was that the loud music made normal conversation impossible.

The Turkish band took a break; the Western band struck up a dance tune. Yener rushed over to us.

"Dance! Dance! You must dance!" he exulted, dragging us onto the floor and pushing us together. A few Turkish couples were dancing but the floor was mostly empty, a state of affairs which Yener obviously considered reprehensible. The band was playing! This was a party! Dance! Yener would have danced for us but I wanted to make my own moves on Olivia.

The foreign hippies in their weird clothes stood in a group off by themselves, their hands welded to beer bottles. These were unlikely Fred Astair and Ginger Rogers impersonators. They were looking at us. We were obviously the sole potential Terpsichorean representatives of the world's 168 non-Turkish nations. Somebody among the foreigners had to dance. We saw our duty and we did it.

Despite years of childhood lessons which I cordially hated, or perhaps because of them, I am a lousy dancer. My sense of rhythm is entirely intellectual, and it translates only awkwardly into physical motion. Luckily, Olivia didn't seem to mind. Actually, it was pretty nice holding her slender waist even while shuffling like a walrus in a swamp. In fact, I soon forgot I was a walrus. Nothing mattered except the feeling of her waist in my right hand and her fingers in my left, and the mysterious communication coming from deep within her eyes.

We danced. We ate and drank. We knew no one else at the party. Most of the others were from Yener's extended family, and spoke only Turkish. The hippies looked more lost than we did. So we chatted as best we could over the loud music, and I drank in as much as I could of Olivia.

She was a good sport about all this. After the first half hour and a good scoping of the scene it must have been flat-out boring for her, but she exhibited relaxed fortitude, which only made me want her more. She was patient, strong, serene. Actually, I was ready to leave too, breathless to find out what might happen between us after we left the party. The only thing holding us there was Yener and our debt of courtesy to him, but after a few hours had passed we decided the debt had been paid and it was time to go. We found Yener, thanked him, said our good-byes.

"No! No! You can't leave! The party's just starting! Eat! Drink! Dance! You can't go!"

We danced. Our feet got tired, then more tired, then turned to lumps of aching flesh. By now the walrus had cut a wide, ugly swath through the swamp and was ready to rest on his rock. It was getting late. It really was time to go.

"If we seriously wanna get outta here, we're gonna have to dance out the door," I whispered into Olivia's delicious ear.

We were, and when Yener wasn't looking, we did.

After the party nothing much happened. We walked from Beyazıt along the ancient Roman road through the salty night air of İstanbul back to her hotel, not saying much, just friends coming home from our first sünnet party, one of us with a broken heart.

The 5000-Mile Vacation

After Olivia left I did what every self-respecting broken-hearted lover does: I ran away to sea.

On July 26th I boarded the Turkish Maritime Lines ship m/v *Akdeniz* in Galata and handed over my deck-class ticket ($37.40) to the purser. A porter in a white naval uniform led me deep down into the bowels of the ship to a large dormitory next to the engine room. I put my shoulder bag on one of the steel bunks, went topside again, leaned on a railing, and gazed at İstanbul as the ship steamed out of the Golden Horn, around Seraglio Point, and into the Sea of Marmara bound for Barcelona.

Night had fallen by the time we traversed the Marmara and passed through the Dardanelles at Gallipoli. When I awoke the next day we were steaming through the Aegean headed for Piraeus. The day after that we crossed the mouth of the Adriatic, and on the evening of the 29th we approached Naples, Stromboli lighting up the dark sky with its volcanic grumbling. I thought of Jane who, her academic year over, was no longer in Naples but traveling around Italy. Alone? With a girlfriend? With a bunch of friends? With…with… I didn't want to think about it. We had tentatively agreed to meet in Venice in August. I thought of that. Soon I thought of little else.

On the 30th we stopped briefly at Marseilles, and on the last day of July we reached Barcelona. I left the ship and found a cheap place to sleep. Tomorrow my goal was Rabat, Morocco, where my sister Posie and her husband, an American diplomat, had recently moved. My parents were flying to Rabat for an August visit, and I wanted to join them and see Morocco, which I did.

Café Viennois

After Morocco I flew to Rome with my art-loving parents and we drove to Siena and Florence, living on their American Express card. I left them there, closely examining the great works of the Italian masters, and on August 15th took a train to Venice. If everything went according to plan I'd find Jane there.

We had exchanged letters for a year, but we had also been living in our own separate worlds, new and different and absorbing, far from the pleasure and convenience of sharing college classes, study periods, and weekend dates. The world and the succession of days, weeks and months apart was coming between us. Where was our relationship now? Would we still love one another? Would it be like the old days on campus? Or would we both be changed by our experiences abroad, out in the world, going our separate ways?

I hoped a few days in romantic Venice might light us up and show us the way.

We met in St Mark's Square, and within an hour, as we talked, I learned that she had just come from a week's vacation, not alone.

"I have lots of Italian friends," she said. "One of them went with me on vacation. Yes. A male friend. A man."

I was devastated, though of course I had no right to be. After all, I had just come from a date of sorts with an old Radcliffe flame. If things had gone well with Olivia, would I even be in Venice now? What was wrong with Jane dating other men? Nothing.

All the same I did something exceedingly male: I clammed up. I went incommunicado. I refused to talk beyond the bare housekeeping necessities.

Naturally, Jane was frustrated. She had no idea what was going on in my head. She wanted to know. I wouldn't let her see.

I wouldn't let her see because I was so wounded. That I had no right to feel wounded made it even worse and made me retreat even deeper into myself.

She gently coaxed and prodded, got very little, and grew frustrated. We had planned to go to Vienna together. It finally occurred to me that no self-respecting person would want to take a trip, romantic or unromantic, with someone in permanent pout and if I didn't come out of it pretty quick I could pout all by myself all the way to Vienna, or İstanbul, or Timbuktu, or wherever I wanted to go, and Jane would go out and find somebody to talk to. I eased up and said a few words, then a few more, and before long we were enjoying Venice together.

We took a train to Vienna and found a hotel. The next day I rented a small motorbike and we tore out into the countryside. It started to drizzle. Cars passed us and threw up a fine mist of mud. Drenched and composted, dissolving in laughter, we returned to the city, got rid of the motorcycle and rented a Volkswagen beetle.

Following our copy of Frommer's *Europe on $5 a Day* we headed for Gumpoldskirchen, a wine-making village on the edge of the Vienna woods, and checked in at a pension in a huge old mansion. Our room was an antique high-ceilinged salon overlooking the town square. It was perfect.

We pocketed our room key and went out for a walk. The little wineshops (*heuriges*) were all hung with evergreens, signifying the harvest and the arrival of the new wine. People began to gather in the town square around a platform decorated with bunting and flags. We had landed right in the middle of Gumpoldskirchen's annual new-wine festival.

The mayor, utterly authentic in Loden jacket and felt hat, introduced this year's wine princess, a rosy-cheeked *mädel* of generous proportions, her capacious bosom erupting from the bodice of a snowy dirndl. She took a healthy swig of new wine from a bucket-sized goblet, smacked her pillowy lips and pronounced it *gut*! The assembled burghers applauded heartily but hastily, cutting short the ovation to run off to the wine-tastings and heuriges. So did we.

After daintily tasting tiny glasses of several local vintages which we couldn't tell apart, we went to a heurige and ordered what everyone else was having: big chilled glass mugs brimming with new white wine.

"You know about new wine?" the waiter asked as he set down our mugs. "Watch it. Don't drink so fast, don't drink so much."

We finished our mugs all smiles, shared a second mug, staggered back to our pension and collapsed on the bed. He was right about the wine, but what a way to break the ice in a stalled relationship.

The next day we took off into the Austrian hinterland, intent on discovery: old monasteries, gilded palaces, glacial lakes, rustic villages that were perfect sets for *The Sound of Music*. We drove to Bad Ischl, where Franz Josef, Emperor of Austria and King of Hungary, had had a summer villa. We put on coveralls and took a little mining train down into a salt mine. When we got to the bottom there was an official photographer who took a picture of our group—very Austrian. We look surpassingly dorky in the photo, which I still have, but we were having fun. We discovered why we were attracted to one another in the first place. It was as sweet as in college.

After the sweet comes the bitter. By the end of the month we were back in Vienna. The newspapers were filled with bulletins about happenings in nearby Prague: the liberal "Prague Spring" government of Alexander Dubček and its "communism with a human face" had been overthrown by local hard-liners backed by the Soviets. Dubček was deposed and arrested.

Thousands of Czechs and Slovaks, in Austria on vacation outside their country for the first time since the advent of communism decades before, didn't know what to do. They gathered in little knots on Vienna's street corners to talk it over: do we go back and live under hard-line communism, or do we abandon everything at home and seek asylum in a free country, poor as beggars? Nearby their tinny little communist cars, piled high with stuff and kids, awaited their decision.

Jane left, a heart-wrenching goodbye, at least for me. I pleaded with her to come visit me in Turkey soon. She said she'd think about it.

I explored Vienna on my own, sipping coffee and eating crescent rolls at the Café Hawelka in the shadow of St Stephen's Cathedral, thinking about how in 1529 the armies of Süleyman the Magnificent had besieged Vienna unsuccessfully, leaving behind coffee and crescent rolls when they pulled out. Without the Turkish siege, the Vienna coffeehouse might never have come to be. No *kaffee mit schlag*, no *kleine braune*, nothing at all decent to sip with a slab of Sacher torte. Would Freud even have existed? Or, ultimately, Starbucks?

On September 6th I flew back to İstanbul, alone again, naturally.

On the 8th I took a bus to Ankara. The new 1968 PCV trainees had arrived, and I had been asked to play a Rob-type role and help introduce them to life in Turkey. The Peace Corps office organized a picnic. When we got to the picnic site we found a whole sheep roasting in a pit of hot coals. When we left the sheep was bones.

Among the new PCVs were a married couple named Joanie and Murray assigned to İzmir. I was required to return to İzmir Koleji to give make-up exams at the beginning of the new school year, so I went with them.

Murray, like I, was in the Ministry of Tourism program. He went to work in the İzmir Tourism Information Office and designed a program called "Meet the Turks" which brought foreign tourists and local Turkish families together. The local families, who were required to know a foreign language, volunteered to spend a bit of time with the tourists, perhaps inviting them to their home for a cup of coffee.

The program was an instant success because of the generosity of the Turkish families. Instead of a cup of coffee, they often took their foreign guests on sightseeing trips and invited them to stay for a huge Turkish dinner or even overnight. Murray's program was a fine example of a creative, valuable Peace Corps contribution. Unfortunately, it didn't last long after his departure. It needed his inspiration and direction to prosper, and no one else was there with that commitment to keep it going.

It was hard for me to leave the familiar scenes and scents of İzmir, to leave my new friends and return to my lonely writer's life, but İstanbul was waiting.

Divine Calculus

I returned to İstanbul, but I spent little time in my apartment. İstanbul to me was the Hippodrome, the historic center of the old city. I stopped in at the Blue Mosque, as I still do, just to sit for a few minutes in its sacred quietness.

The Mosque of Sultan Ahmet I (built 1606–1616) contains a visual tip-of-the-hat from its architect, Mimar Mehmet Ağa, to the architects of Ayasofya who worked their miracle a thousand years earlier. Few people realize this among the crowds of tourists who enter it once in their lives to marvel at its grandeur, or among the crowds of locals who pray there every day.

I discovered Mimar Mehmet Ağa's salute to Anthemius and Isidorus one day as I approached the mosque from the Hippodrome, walking slowly through the gate in the outer wall, complete with its hanging chains that forced horsemen to dismount when entering the holy precinct. I looked ahead and my eye rose up the broad staircase and penetrated the tall portal of the mosque courtyard. Through the portal in the center of the courtyard was the domed *şadırvan* (ablutions fountain). Above its dome rose another dome, the one atop the main portal into the mosque sanctuary.

I approached the steps and climbed them slowly, looking ahead, watching in amazement as dome after dome appeared above the two I had already noticed. A cascade of domes and semi-domes billowed heavenward until the mosque's great dome appeared triumphantly above all. As I entered the courtyard the two slender minarets flanking the mosque shot heavenward insistently: Up! Look up!

The two great buildings, Ayasofya and the Blue Mosque, stand beside one another on the Hippodrome, separated only by a small park. They are both entered from the west. In one, the visitor's eye is lifted heavenward inside, in the other, on the outside: master architects conversing across a millennium.

I walked across the courtyard and approached the west door of the mosque, which was reserved for Muslims (tourists then used the north door). An old man smiled and pointed toward the north door, but I said a few words in Turkish and he chuckled an excuse-me-I-didn't-know-you-were-a-Turk. (At that time it was accepted without question that no foreigner spoke Turkish, so I must be a Turk.)

It was not prayer time, so there were only a few people in the mosque performing their "catch-up" prayers for ones they had missed earlier. I carefully avoided walking in front of them. I had been taught that the strictest Muslims didn't like anyone walking in front of them at prayer because it might be misinterpreted that they were praying to the person in front of them instead of to God.

I found a quiet place near one of the massive marble pillars and sat down in the traditional position, legs folded beneath me. I closed my eyes and listened to the stillness, the soft padding of stockinged feet on rich carpets, hushed movement and rustle of garments as a few men performed their ritual genuflections. God-rays, colored by the stained glass windows above the *mihrab* (prayer niche), pierced the still air, illuminated floating motes of dust, then blazed on the floor.

After a few minutes I was conscious of someone approaching and sitting down near me. The mosque was nearly empty, so he must have approached on purpose. I looked his way. He nodded. I nodded back.

"*Merhaba*," he said.

"*Merhaba*."

He was young and relatively tall, with black hair and mustache, and a smiling, open face.

"You speak Turkish," he said in Turkish, half as an exclamation, half as a question. The old man must have told him. "Are you a Turk? Where are you from?"

"America."

"America! And you speak Turkish? Amazing," he said. "Good for you!" He was carrying the sort of big leather open-mouthed satchel that mailmen carry all over the world.

"You're a mailman?" I asked.

"Yes, yes. Are you a tourist? A soldier?" These were the two most likely possibilities.

"No, I'm a teacher," I said, choosing not to get involved in I'm-writing-a-guidebook-but-I've-just-started, etc. "I've been teaching at a school in İzmir."

"Very good! You have come to teach us? Very good!"

We sat in silence for a moment, enjoying the peace and vastness of the holy space.

"Uh,…." Pause. "Are you a Christian?" he asked hesitantly, approaching the topic as delicately as possible. He was embarrassed, and I was embarrassed by his embarrassment, by his having raised one of the three topics—politics, sex, religion—which must be approached delicately anywhere in the world. He might as well have asked "Was that fart yours?"

Now, any young person out in the world searching for the meaning of life is liable to have complicated religious loyalties, but it was easiest to give him the answer he expected, which was…

"Yes."

"Good, good." Pause. "Yes, Christianity. It is good. Judaism, too. All good." Pause. He pondered his strategy. "Do you know that the Prophet Abraham and the Prophet Jesus are sacred to Muslims? Mary, too. And Saint Peter. And Saint Paul. And the Jewish saints and lots of other saints. Of course the Prophet Muhammed is the last and greatest of the prophets. We have lots of saints in Islam, Muslim saints. We revere the Bible. It is a holy book, like the Holy Kur'an. And the Torah too. It is holy. But the Kur'an is the final book, the best of all."

He paused, gathering strength for The Pitch.

"Have you ever considered becoming a Muslim? It would be good. We would welcome you."

I was touched. The last time someone had tried to convert me was when a fiery southern preacher had visited our little neighborhood church in Pennsylvania and tried, his face suffused with passion and holy light, to get all the stiff, phlegmatic Pennsylvania Dutchmen in our congregation to come forward for Jesus, to walk up the aisle during the singing of the hymn, to weep and cry out and speak in tongues and sweat buckets and be reborn and accept Jesus as their living and personal lord and savior.

Nobody moved. We can do it from right here in the pews like we always do, the Dutchmen thought to themselves. Jesus is not a southerner, he's a Dutchman. He does it our way.

The preacher's face fell. Stiff-shirted northerners! Nice people, he thought, but they don't get it. Too bad they're gonna burn in hell. You gotta be *saved*! The light went out of his face, and at the end of the hymn he closed his Bible, gave a wan smile and strode slowly from the pulpit.

I looked at the mailman. Careful, careful. "Thanks. I'll think it over, but at the moment I'm fine being what I am."

"Yes! Fine!" he said. "Yes, of course! I just wanted you to know about Islam. Perhaps you will think it over, and you will see. Judaism came first, then Christianity, and finally Islam, the last and best. All the good things in those earlier religions are in Islam. Think about it: we have all your saints…and more!"

A quantitative approach to faith.

We shook hands. He got to his feet. "Enjoy your stay in Turkey," he said, smiling. "Thank you for coming to teach us. I wish you all the best."

He walked away to a quiet spot, raised his hands in supplication to heaven, and began his prayers.

∽∾

8

STARDOM!

"COME TO ANKARA OCT 19. BRING A BLONDE," the telegram read.

It followed by two days a letter that began "This may be the screwiest letter you'll ever receive from Peace Corps staff...."

I saw the letter when I came in from my balcony where I had just blown the minds of Ayazpaşa's neighborhood matrons by hanging out my freshly hand-laundered shirts. In Turkey men didn't do laundry even if, as they walked down the street in B.O.-redolent clothes, the paint peels from walls and dogs die in their tracks.

The letter explained that the Ministry of Tourism wanted to make a movie that would show people what tourism is and how Turks should behave toward tourists. The movie would be shown in city cinemas and village tea houses. It would help Turks to prepare themselves for the tourist onslaught that was going to begin Real Soon Now. Tourists would bring millions of dollars, pounds, marks, francs, lire and drachmae to Turkey and save the economy, so the bearers of this flood of lucre should be treated well.

Cheap Blond Foreigners

The crew shooting the film for the ministry had plenty of talented Turkish actors to use as stars, and therein lay the problem. They were Turks, not foreigners. They didn't look, or walk, or gesture, or laugh or grimace like foreigners. In the interest of verisimilitude, the stars had to be real honest-to-goodness foreigners. They also had to be blond, because as every Turk knows all foreign tourists are blond.

This caused some vexation to the director because, as everyone also knows, blond foreign actors are expensive, and he had a government budget, which is to say below-subsistence. He decided to look for a source of Cheap Blond Foreigners.

Did someone call me?

According to the conventional wisdom circulating through the Peace Corps office in Ankara, I was lounging in İstanbul, supposedly working on some hokey pie-in-the-sky guidebook project, but probably sleeping late, living in my PJs, and admiring my glorious Bosphorus view as I killed yet another bottle of cheap rakı with a blonde on either arm. I had no teaching schedule—indeed, as far as they could tell I had no schedule at all—and no obligations to anyone else. I was already receiving a munificent $135-a-month salary courtesy of the Peace Corps, so I was in effect a Cheap Blond Foreigner Already Paid For. All they need do was to send me a letter outlining the project and telling me to hop on a bus with one of my Cheap Blonde (ie, female) Foreigner pals who could be my co-star.

The letter arrived on October 17th. "Please telegraph your answer as soon as possible," it concluded. So I did:

"YES BUT NO BLONDE. SHALL I FIND?"

The answering telegram that you read above arrived a few hours later.

Fantasies immediately thronged my brain:

I'm out on the town in İstanbul, circulating through the bars and cafes. Sharp suit, cool shades. Easily I saunter up to a pair of gorgeous blondes just arrived from Sweden, Germany, Holland. Choosing the more gorgeous of the two I croon...

"Hey, babe, wanna be a star?"

The blonde not addressed looks up eagerly, her face alight, her mouth agape, and answers breathlessly "Yah! Yah!"

"Not you, pal," I hiss dismissively. "Your good–lookin' friend."

Slowly an enigmatic Mona Lisa smirk glows on the lips of the more gorgeous one. She rises, takes the arm I gallantly offer, and we glide off to...uh, well, the bus station, to catch a night coach to Ankara.

Or not. Most likely not.

In fact I went to Sultanahmet right away, looked around and even spoke in tentative tones to a few female tourists, some of them blonde. Most of them had boyfriends, all of them had reservations (not to Ankara, reservations about me), and none had anything to wear but old jeans, baggy sweaters, and other down-at-heels travel garb. Therefore they couldn't dress like a "real" tourist which, I soon learned, meant a tourist as seen through the film director's eyes: ultra-fashionable body sheaths ending somewhere high above the dimpled knee, preferably in that murky zone north of good taste but south of pornography.

I was an utter failure at getting girls even with the ultimate killer pickup line. I climbed on the bus to Ankara alone.

As it turned out, this was not a problem. The Peace Corps office had located a Cheap Blonde Foreigner right in Ankara, the twentysomething daughter of an American diplomatic couple of Scandinavian heritage, and she was ready to roll. She had a wardrobe full of fashionable body-sheath dresses and tiny skirts, none of which descended even within shouting distance of her beautifully dimpled knees. Not only that, besides being a certifiable Nordic blonde, she was truly gorgeous. My face might be made for radio but hers was designed with the camera in mind: full forehead, come-hither almond eyes, prominent cheekbones, Bardot-pout mouth.

Her name was Diana. We met on October 20th, the day after I arrived in Ankara. When I laid eyes on this woman, the shyness of my youth returned and clomped down on me like a letter from the IRS. I was knocked out. I had absolutely no clue what approach I should take with this gorgeous creature. Nonchalance? Genuflection? Heart attack?

The film director, Nurettin Tancı, saved me from my Diana dilemma by introducing himself. He had gone to film school in England and was now working for the Ministry of Education's Film, Radio and Television Educational Center in Ankara. He had assembled a crew which included a cameraman, an assistant, a gaffer and two drivers, one for the little Opel station wagon which was to be "The Tourists' Car" in the movie, and one for the crew's minibus. He explained the project.

"In the next few years many foreign tourists will arrive in Turkey. This is what we want. We want the tourists to enjoy themselves, to have good experiences. However, the Turkish people aren't used to tourists. Most of them have never seen a foreigner. They don't know how to act. They don't understand foreign customs or ways of behaving. We want to help them understand foreigners and welcome them properly. So we'll make a film and show it in local cinemas to teach the people how to welcome tourists. It will be called 'A Cup of Coffee: How Should We Act Toward Tourists?' We have a saying in Turkey: 'A cup of coffee gives memories for forty years.' You two will be 'the Farmers,' a foreign tourist couple traveling in Turkey. You will have coffee with Turks you meet, and have nice memories for a long time."

So I was going to get a free trip around Turkey with a glamorous companion and end up a movie star. Could this get any better?

It could. We were going to get paid! Turkish government wages of TL45 ($3.75) a day, plus expenses.

The need for a film such as this was real, I knew. Shortly after I first arrived in Turkey the *Ankara Daily News* reported that a female foreign tourist wearing a red dress had been killed on the Black Sea coast. At a rest stop she walked away from the bus and up to a nearby hilltop to take in the view. A hunter on the other side of the hill, who had never seen any woman like that before, took her for an apparition of the devil and shot her dead.

Life on Location

On October 21st we piled into the Opel and the ciné-minibus and headed west to Bursa, the first capital of the Ottoman sultanate. I got to know Diana a little bit as we drove. She was friendly but a bit distant.

"I'm living with my parents temporarily," she said. "I was in the States but…well, there were some problems, so I'm spending some time in Ankara with them."

So she had things on her mind. Career? Economic? Romantic? I couldn't tell, and she wasn't saying. The film project was a welcome distraction, she said. She was responsive to the director's wishes as we worked, but showed little emotion one way or another about it all. Notably—to me, at least—she also showed little emotion about me. Not that I expected anything different, especially if she was in a fragile emotional state, but after a year of living like a monk I must admit that my imagination blossomed with the unfolding possibilities.

We arrived in Bursa in the evening. Diana and I were given rooms in one of the better hotels. The director and crew bedded down in a much cheaper place.

The next morning we showed up at the Ulu Cami, Bursa's venerable Great Mosque (1396) to shoot The Tourist Couple Wandering Through The Venerable Mosque. Diana was wearing one of her body sheaths. The venerable old hajis (men whose white beards showed they had made the holy pilgrimage to Mecca), recoiled in shock and alarm.

Nurettin Bey had been careful to procure all the proper official permissions—from the Ministry of Tourism, the Ministry of Religious Affairs, the city government, the local mufti, the historical commission, probably even the chief astrologer and the head of the parking ticket office. He marched in waving a sheaf of papers blackened with rubber stamps and signatures, but that made no difference to the hajis. They had come to the mosque to pray and here were these weird-looking foreigners, one of them obviously—far too obviously—a woman, being chased around by klieg lights and a movie camera.

I don't blame them. What they didn't know, and what I didn't have the heart to tell them, is that we were the tip of the iceberg, nay, a mere blob of *sorbet*, compared to the tsunami of Sony-toting infidels who would soon crowd noisily into their sacred space.

The old men registered their protest with Nurettin Bey, then retired to pray, no doubt asking Allah to explain what the devil was going on in His house and had He had a change of heart and come out in favor of secularism, infidels and body sheaths, or what?

We shot the scene and were out of there, off to the Yeşil Cami (Green Mosque), where things went better because it's out of the city center, away from the bazaar, and more sparsely attended.

From Bursa we drove west along the Sea of Marmara coast to Erdek, a popular seaside resort, then south to İzmir and Ephesus, where we filmed The Happy Tourists Treading The Marble Streets. On the highway south of Ephesus we encountered a camel caravan, still used to transport common freight in the Aegean region in 1968. We drove up and down the highway trying to get some shots with the camels. (Alas, the camels didn't make the final cut.) I enjoyed driving a car, which I hadn't had the chance to do before in Turkey. Diana seemed to enjoy herself and carefully followed the director's instructions, which were to look out the window at the passing scenery and now and then to chat with me, the other half of the happy couple. We got it all on film, and came finally to the modest fishing village of Marmaris, where it promptly began to pelt hail.

At that time Marmaris was a mere village which made its living entirely from the bounty of land and sea instead of from imported bodies toting credit cards. Hearty fishermen still set out in their boats early each morning, and sinewy farmers with gnarled hands and toothy grins still tended their citrus orchards with ancient pruning hooks. The film shows it all quite clearly—the bollards for tying up boats along the treeless concrete quay, the black piles of fishing gear, the brawny mariners mending their nets or chatting in familiar groups. Looking at sleek Marmaris today, with its traffic-thronged corniche shaded by towering palms and crowded with trim yachts, our movie seems painfully antique.

In the Marmaris of 1968, the only affordable place to stay was an *ev pansiyon* ("home pension"). The only hotel worth the name was the Hotel Lidya, off by itself far around the bay, a favorite of the grafty political class and utterly out of our price range.

We drove to our pension, met the smiling proprietress, and were shown to our rooms. Of course I was shown to my room, and Diana was given a room by herself. The matron of the pension didn't know the situation between us except that we weren't married, and that was enough for her. She naturally assumed the role of mother-chaperone. Being a mother and having sons of her own, she could easily read my mind. After she had shown us to our rooms, she gave me a steely look that said, unmistakably, "I know what you're thinking, and it will happen over my dead body after a loud and unpleasant ruckus. P S: Take a gander at my biceps."

The next day we started shooting the Marmaris scenes. Diana and I sauntered along the quay, we "shopped for souvenirs" in the tiny market, we "went to the Tourist Office for brochures."

The Tourist Office then was in the same building as it is now, right down by the dock in the center of town. Nurettin Bey had chosen it because of its "color-ful director," Celal Bey. Diana and I walked in and "asked Celal Bey for tourist information," and the opening scene of the movie was in the can.

After the day's shooting, we returned to our pension. The matron gave us a warm welcome which included, for my benefit, an abbreviated but incontrovertibly authentic version of the steely look. I wasn't going to mess with her or her biceps. We retired to our separate bedrooms.

The Thumb in My Soup

The next day we took off again in the Opel and the minibus, heading northeast for Konya, the most religiously and morally conservative town in Turkey. One of the crew members had come from a village in Konya province, which would make it easy for us to shoot the Tourists Stranded in a Village scenes.

We drove to the main square in Konya and checked into the ambitiously-named Turist Oteli, on the south side of the square. Diana and I were assigned to separate but neighboring rooms, a situation which had distinct possibilities, although tonight we just collapsed into our respective rooms after the long drive.

The next day we went to a simple restaurant to shoot the Tourists Receiving Bad Service. We were welcomed warmly and graciously into the modest eatery by the proprietor and the sole waiter. Nurettin Bey had already explained the project to them, so we got to it. We sat at a table in the spartan dining room. The waiter filled our glasses with water from an uncapped, re-used rakı bottle, the implication being that it was not purified spring water as it should be, but plain old tap water in a bottle of suspect cleanliness. (In the Tourists Receiving Good Service scene we shot later, the water comes from sealed individual spring water bottles.)

While the camera rolled, the waiter brought us each a plate of soup. The waiter, though untrained, was experienced. He did it normally, naturally, and well. It was a simple act.

This presented a problem. If the film was to instruct the Turkish people in the right way to treat tourists, it should also show them the wrong way so they'd see the difference. Nurettin Bey instructed the waiter to serve us the soup again, and this time to be sure his thumb was in it. The waiter frowned and self-consciously obliged, looking grim, which suited Nurettin perfectly. Halit Oklan, the cameraman, moved in for a close-up of the soup-covered thumb. In full close-up, the waiter raised his thumb out of the gooey soup to let a few globules ooze off and strike the plate rim. It was perfect.

We didn't even get to eat the soup. That was the last scene for the day.

That Night in Konya

In holy Konya, "hot nightlife" is praying for long hours on a crowded mosque carpet. It wasn't what I had in mind, so after dinner in the Turist Oteli dining room which served excellent food (the *bamya*—okra—was particularly good, believe it or not), Diana and I retired to (ahem) her room for cards, chat and whatnot. I voted for whatnot, but Diana unfortunately showed an extraordinarily avid interest in gin rummy. At least it wasn't solitaire.

Shortly after shuffle and deal, there was a knock at the door. I opened it to find a bellboy.

"Yes?"

"Do you need anything?" he asked.

"No thank you," I answered.

"Are you sure I can't get you anything? Tea? Coke? A snack?"

"No, no, we're fine."

He looked furtively around the room, especially at Diana, then reluctantly withdrew.

I closed the door and we resumed our annoyingly endless card game. Though we got along fine, Diana and I didn't appear to have all that much in common. When it came to romantic notions, it looked as though we had nothing at all in common.

Another knock at the door. It was the same bellboy. He had a light bulb in his hand.

"Are all your lights working? No burnt out bulbs?" he asked.

"All our lights are working," I said. We both glanced around the room—he with an extraordinary eagerness to take in every detail, particularly of Diana and the state of her clothing. The room was, in fact, far too brightly lit for my liking, which is saying something in the Turkey of 1968 when a 25-watt bulb was equated with an interplanetary laser, a rank extravagance, a profligate waste of precious and frightfully expensive electrical current.

I slowly closed the door on the bellboy. Back to the cards.

About 20 minutes later, no doubt long enough for *it* to have happened in his fetid imagination, another knock. I opened the door.

It was a different co-conspirator this time. He was holding a scrap of paper.

"This message came for you," he said.

I looked at the scrap. It bore unintelligible scribbles. I tried to make out Turkish words, English words, French words. It was just gibberish, not even letters.

"What does this mean? Who called?" I asked.

"I don't know," said the bellboy. He looked in at Diana, who was fully clothed and concentrating on her cards. His face fell.

I thanked him and closed the door.

Diana and I talked, both bored by this time, but knowing that silence would be even more boring. Not only that, silence might so enflame the imaginations of the entire staff of bellboys now pressing their ears to our door that the weight of the press might bring down the door. I imagined 500 pounds' worth of bellboys, their trousers taut with sexual anticipation, cascading across Diana's threshold.

Their dream was my dream, but it wasn't happening and certainly looked like it wasn't going to. I said goodnight to Diana, unlocked the door, waited a respectable time for the sound of scattering feet to fade away, returned to my room, and fell asleep.

Two Sheep, Four Eyeballs

The next morning we started out early for the village. The crew member who came from there introduced us to the *muhtar* (village headman) and the men who headed the other prominent families. The muhtar invited us to his house for lunch. As we approached the house, I saw the skins of two sheep hanging on a line behind the house, ostensibly to dry but also to indicate to all and sundry the amount of honor being bestowed upon us visitors. Two whole sheep had been sacrificed for our lunch. We were pretty damned important.

The house was a simple one of concrete, but well-made and very clean, in the way of Turkish village houses. Diana and I removed our shoes, put on the slippers provided, and entered the central room. We were introduced to the muhtar's wife and daughters, after which we turned to the left and entered the Turkish equivalent of a parlor. We were shown to the seats of honor on the *sedir*, the broad bench built along the wall at the far end of the room. The sedir was covered in snowy-white embroidered cloth bordered in lace. It looked too good to sit on. I reluctantly sat down, afraid that I might soil its pristine purity. The muhtar, the village worthies and the film crew sat on the soft carpets, leaning their backs against the walls. The women of the household had retired to the kitchen to the right of the central room to cook our lunch.

We went through the formalities. Each of the village worthies rose, approached us, greeted us formally, shook our hands, and bade us welcome. We were offered lemon cologne to refresh our face and hands, which we accepted; cigarettes, which we declined; sweets, which we accepted just to be polite; and tea, which we accepted because Turkish tea is one of God's gifts to this world.

There was the usual small talk: how was your journey, how do you like Turkey, it must be pretty different from America, etc.

After a polite chitchat interval, we started filming. The cameraman shot us entering the room, sitting on the sedir, going through the same sequence of events that we had just gone through for real. After that scene was done, a villager appeared at the door with a saz. He approached us, shook our hands, welcomed us, then sat with us and played the saz while the camera rolled.

The story line had it that our car had broken down outside this village. The villagers towed it to the muhtar's house, and the muhtar offered us his hospitality overnight while we awaited the arrival of a repair part from a nearby city.

We shot the necessary scenes, including one in which Diana and I retire to the guest bedroom and begin to remove our clothes, which seemed to be about as close as I'd ever get to the real thing. Then it was time for lunch.

Ironically, lunch was the most enjoyable part of our village visit but it wasn't part of the story line so it wasn't filmed. We sat down—all the men and Diana—on chairs at a big table set up in the central room, a substantial concession to foreign-tourist customs as villagers would normally have sat on the soft carpets in the salon and dined from a low circular table covered by a large cloth which we would have drawn over our laps as a napkin as well. If Diana had been a Turkish woman she would have assisted the muhtar's womenfolk in the kitchen and dined with them there, but Turkish hospitality being what it is she was seated in a place of honor beside our host.

They served us a village feast of Turkish hors d'oeuvres, roast lamb, baked vegetables, fresh flat bread. It was delicious, and bounteous enough for a Hollywood-size cast.

The muhtar was served the sheep's head, as was his right as *paterfamilias*. He grasped it in one hand, ripped off a jawbone, and offered it to Diana as a token of favor. She accepted it demurely and placed it on the edge of her plate, never to be touched again. I declined the eyeballs proffered to me after inspecting them, shocked to see that they were inspecting me back.

How does one eat an eyeball? I didn't know. It brought to mind that time in a Chinese restaurant when I was served a duck's foot.

"How d'you eat a duck's foot?" I asked my Chinese-American friend.

"Like any other foot," he answered.

Our luncheon conversation was tedious because Diana spoke no Turkish, mine was halting when I got into the more complicated subjects, and our hosts knew no English, but we did what we could. As we rose from lunch, I turned to the muhtar's wife and daughters and thanked them profusely for the feast.

The muhtar ushered us out of the house and we went back to work, shooting the breakdown scene. We hopped into the Opel and drove out of the village to a country road. We backed the car into the ditch by the side of the road so it could play dead.

"Action!" Nurettin Bey shouted, and a villager carrying a huge rake came walking along the road. He stopped, and I engaged in picturesque pantomime to explain our dead car. He shrugged and walked off.

Cast into cinematic dejection by this apparent lack of sympathy, Diana and I sat down in the dirt by our "dead" car and waited for whatever Allah had in store for us. She took out a cigarette and I lit it for her, which shows you how long ago all of this happened.

After a few minutes (a few seconds in cinema time) lo and behold! The villager reappears with an *at arabası*, a village horse and cart. He ties a rope from the Opel's front axle to the axle of his cart, and we make our way into the village under one horsepower. In an interesting twist, I'm steering the car while Diana, body sheath and all, pushes from behind along with the muhtar who, by reason of a hilarious continuity lapse, has miraculously materialized out of nowhere. "The next day" (in the make-believe world of cinema), after our scripted night spent in the muhtar's house, a man arrives with the necessary repair part, installs it in our car, and we're off.

Off to İzmir, our last filming stop. We drove west all day from Konya, through Turkey's great lakes, past the snowy calcium waterfalls of Pamukkale, down the orchard-filled valley of the Meander River, finally reaching İzmir in the evening. The director had no friends here from whom we could sponge free digs, so we "stars" were given rooms in the Otel Babadan, a simple but comfortable hotel popular with US military personnel on leave. As in Konya, the director and film crew stayed in a much cheaper hotel nearby.

This was it! Diana and I were alone in a hotel accustomed to foreigners. Our rooms were only a hallway apart, and İzmir wasn't Konya: the bellboys here had seen enough foreign military couples passionately reunited that they didn't give a damn.

After dinner we took a walk and, at a respectable hour, returned to our rooms. I suggested that we do something together in her room, and she assented. I made my move. Our lips met. We talked about romantic encounters. Our lips explored a far country. Diana whispered that she wasn't ready for a romantic encounter, but would I like to play cards?

Suggesting strip poker would only have confirmed her in the belief that I was incapable of originality, and not much of a card player either, so sagely I restrained myself. Gin rummy it was.

The next day, after the filming, we said goodbye. She was sweet to me. I was hopelessly smitten with her, but I'd never see her again except in my dreams. She flew back to Ankara and was gone.

Andy Warhol said that in the future everyone would be famous for 15 minutes. I was a movie star for a week. I guess fifteen minutes in Manhattan is like a week in Turkey.

I boarded a bus for İstanbul. I had a book to write.

∽∞∾

9

TEA AND TURKISH
LESSONS

With my film career and all pending romances now just smoldering wreckage, it was time to get to work.

My goal in writing a guidebook was to introduce Turkey to American travelers, and to help them to have a smooth, enjoyable trip. Where to start?

I thought it over. When I had told friends and family that I was going to Turkey in the Peace Corps, they raised questions and made comments. I learned from this that among Americans Turkey was conceived in this way:

- A desert full of Arabs speaking Arabic
- Looks like the picture on a pack of Camel cigarettes—pyramids, sand dunes, palm-tree oases. Camel smokes were, after all, made from "Turkish and Domestic Tobaccos"
- Ruled by a sultan living in a palace with hundreds, perhaps thousands of female sex slaves
- Probably a rigid political dictatorship
- About to "go communist"

Troy, Ephesus, and all those other famous places with Greek and Roman names were in Greece, they thought. St Paul was born in Tarsus and that was probably in Israel, as was Cappadocia (both of which are actually in Turkey). In fact, anything mentioned in the Bible was probably in Israel except Egypt, and the way things were going at that time Egypt would soon be in Israel, too.

This was going to be a piece of work. I wasn't starting from zero, a state in which Americans knew nothing about Turkey, I was starting from less-than-zero, a state in which they knew something about Turkey and it was all, every bit of it, hilariously or on occasion tragically wrong.

My Turkish students at İzmir Koleji were studying all the countries of the world, learning about the history of Europe, the natural resources of Peru, the traditions of Japan. Meanwhile, American pupils were contemplating their geographical navels while their country's government bombed the shit out of a poor little country off in Asia somewhere. Near China, I think. Or India. Or Indochina, whatever that meant.

I had my work cut out for me.

Beyond the obvious duty to explain a foreign country, culture and language to my readers there was the question of practical information. Frommer guides provided detailed information on hotels, restaurants, transportation, entertainment, sightseeing and shopping. I studied Frommer's *Europe on $5 a Day* as a model. It described hundreds of hotels, hundreds of restaurants, and yet more hundreds of places to see and things to do. I'd have to go to each of these places and get all the relevant information: mailing address, phone number, prices, hours of operation, description of the place and its services, location…there were hundreds of discrete facts on every page of a Frommer's guide, literally hundreds of thousands of facts in every guidebook.

Having used Frommer's guide in Europe, I also knew that every fact had to be *correct*. Readers knew immediately when a fact was out of date, or missing, or just plain wrong. Sure, most travelers realized that guidebooks were not researched, written, edited, printed and distributed the day before they bought their copy and that some information was bound to be a bit out of date, but it was essential to keep the errors to a minimum.

How hard could it be? I wrote an outline of the project, bought a notebook, walked up to Taksim Square and began my research with precisely the wrong topic: restaurants, one of the more highly perishable types of information in a travel guide.

I strolled along İstiklal Caddesi, the main avenue in Beyoğlu, the more Europeanized section of İstanbul, taking notes. I ate *burma kadayıf* (a spiral roll of syrup-soaked shredded wheat stuffed with whole pistachios) at a grand pastry shop named Saray Muhallebicisi. I discovered the *kebap* (roast meat) grill named for Abdülvahid the Egyptian behind İstiklal's only mosque. I had dinner in the old Hacı Salih Restaurant on Sakızağacı Caddesi, and went again to the Fischer Restaurant across from the British Consulate-General, with its savory gulasch and sweet *palatschinken* crêpes. I ate like a king. PCV cuisine was a distant, unpleasant memory.

I reveled in the city, walking for hours through every historic district, visiting mosques grand and modest, peering into ancient caravanserais, getting lost in the labyrinthine Grand Bazaar and the colorful, un-grand markets of the Tahtakale district near the Galata Bridge on the Golden Horn. I took notes. I hopped on buses without looking at the destination, got off at the last stop, walked around and looked at everything, then rode the bus back. I took more notes. I was in heaven.

As I took my notes, I began to realize how slippery "facts" are. A hotel room has one price, right? Wrong! I discovered that the prices posted behind the reception desk were usually a total fiction. They were the maximum prices allowed by the Ministry of Tourism. The actual room price is the one you actually pay, the one quoted by the reception clerk, and that price, usually lower than the one on the wall, depends upon the season of the year, the number of tourists looking for hotel rooms on that particular day, the due date of the hotel owner's mortgage payment, the desk clerk's mood, who *you* are, etc. In short, there was no one simple immutable price, even though that's what I was required to put in my book.

Same with restaurants. Turkish restaurants were famous for not having menus or price lists. Turks didn't need them. Most customers were regulars. They knew what they liked and what it cost.

Turkey was in that blissful pre-tourism state in which there was little cheating because most people are honest and those who aren't didn't realize it was far easier to cheat a foreigner than a local.

Transportation—at least long-distance transportation—was a bit better. Because most transport companies were relatively large, they fixed their prices and printed them in tariffs. The bigger problem was that of giving recommendations for one mode of transport over another. In *Europe on $5 a Day*, Arthur Frommer told his readers how to get discounts, which particular trains and routes to take, and even what the meter should read at the end of a taxi ride. How was I going to do that in İstanbul where the taxis didn't use their meters? I didn't know. I just kept working, hoping I'd figure it all out.

Allah's Big Book

I gathered information on the Bosphorus and its historic buildings, cruising up and down the strait seated on the upper stern deck of a gleaming white ferryboat with a glass of hot tea in my hand. The fresh sea air, the bright sun, the strong tea, and the beautiful shoreline gave me a new İstanbul definition of *keyf*, the Turkish art of contented contemplation.

In these days before the Bosphorus bridges, the ferries went everywhere, crowding the lower Bosphorus, propellers churning the murky brine, sirens whooping, searchlights sweeping the dark waters at night on the lookout for fishing skiffs. The mouth of the Golden Horn was alive with ferries, a roiling maelstrom of white wakes as dozens of them arrived and departed carrying voyagers throughout the city.

I marveled at the skill of the captains who docked the ferries just right, easing into the wharves hundreds of times each day with no more than a gentle bump. Late at night, when an apprentice master was at the helm, I could tell the difference. Every now and then the ferry would bang into the dock hard, the dock creaking and groaning ominously, the vessel shuddering in complaint.

Before the Bosphorus bridges, the car ferry between Kabataş and Üsküdar was the lifeline of commerce between Europe and Asia. The trucks queued for the ferry, forming lines of parked vehicles several kilometers long. Some of the drivers camped in their trucks for days waiting to get across. Think of the bridges now, and weep for those poor guys trying to grab some sleep cramped in their truck cabs.

The ferries were also the city's air conditioners. İstanbul has dependable winds, and one look at any flag gives you a good idea of what the weather and temperature will be. The wind from the north is the cool, dry *poyraz* bringing clear skies and bracing air. From the south blows the warm, moist *lodos*, which can bring fog or rain. It's rare for the flags not to be waving, for the air to be still, but it does happen.

It happened one boiling hot day during my first summer in İstanbul. By mid-morning the sticky heat was on everyone's mind, and the entire city was anxiously watching the flags for any sign of relief. By noon people were getting frantic and those in command of their own schedules made their way to the ferry docks, boarded a boat—it didn't matter where it was going—and urgently sought a seat in the shade and the breeze generated by the boat's movement. This was a reversal of the norm. In fine weather the seats outside—in the bow, the stern and along the sides of the cabin—are the most sought after because they offer warm sun.

I got on one of the choicest runs, a boat going far up the Bosphorus, but by the time I boarded it the only empty seat was on the port side with the sun blazing down on it. Still, it was better than sweating in a stifling apartment, so I sat in the sun.

The man to my right shifted over to make room for me. He had a piece of newspaper about a foot square which he held atop his head as a shield against the fierce sunshine. I coveted his worthless scrap of newspaper with Biblical ferocity and cursed myself for not having brought something, anything, to use as a sunshade.

Without a word or even so much as a look in my direction he removed the square of newspaper from his head, folded it neatly in half, tore it lengthwise, and offered me half.

"*Teşekkür ederim,*" I said. Thank you. And so he knew I spoke at least a little Turkish.

"Are you German?" he asked automatically. Germans were the most frequent European visitors to Turkey so it was a logical assumption.

"I'm American," I answered.

"Welcome to Turkey! Are you a soldier?"

With 40,000 of my uniformed countrymen in Turkey, this was a logical assumption as well.

"No, I...." I decided to take the easy way out. "I'm a teacher. An English teacher."

"Ah, good, very good. How do you find Turkey? Do you like it here?"

"Very much, very much."

"How did you get here? By train? By ship?"

"I came by plane."

"Ah, yes. Hmmm. I don't like flying in airplanes," he said with a frown.

"Why not? Have you had a bad experience?"

"No, no, I've never been in an airplane."

"So why don't you like them?"

"Well, if the slightest little thing goes wrong, you fall out of the sky."

We pondered this for a moment, holding our shreds of newspaper on our heads, shifting hands occasionally when the blood had drained from the raised arm and the arm was about to go to sleep.

"Yes, but people say that driving in a car is much more dangerous," I answered, thinking of the statistics.

"Oh yes, there are lots of dangers. Lots of ways to die. It all depends on God. He has His big book, you know. Everyone's name is written in His book, and opposite each person's name is a number, the precise number of years, months, weeks, days, hours, minutes and even seconds that each person has to live. Why, you could be relaxing in your easy chair at home and if your time has come...pfffft! You've had it."

We sat in silence for a moment, pondering the immense gravitas of predestination. Then, unable to restrain myself, I asked him:

"So if that's the case, if you're going to die when your time comes no matter where you are, then why don't you like airplanes?"

"Well," he said, "it's obvious: the slightest little thing goes wrong and you fall out of the sky."

The ferryboat steamed northward through the blue water, its bow wave and wake rolling out behind it with a cooling splash. We sat in the sun, tempered at least some by the boat breeze and our squares of newspaper, gazing at the palaces and castles along the Bosphorus, pondering the immensity and immanence of death. I recalled the wise words of Ralph Waldo Emerson: "a foolish consistency is the hobgoblin of little minds."

Brewing Insomnia

I started the İstanbul period of my life with a sensible daily work routine, but it soon deteriorated to an absurdity. I started out waking at 7 am, going out to collect information, and returning after lunch to write. I set up a writing table in my main room and, as summer faded into autumn and the days grew shorter and colder, placed an Aladdin kerosene (paraffin) heater next to it. The heater not only chased the chill but also proved to be perfect for brewing tea samovar-style: I put a large water-filled kettle atop the heater, and a small pot full of strong tea atop the kettle. When my little gold-rimmed Turkish tea glass was empty, I'd refill it by pouring an inch of strong black tea and cutting it with hot water from the kettle.

The poet Stephen Spender once commented on his friend W H Auden that he drank endless cups of tea not just for the flavor and the caffeine but because the slight distraction of fussing over the pot and the cups provided a welcome, mindless catalyst to the heavy brainwork of poetic creation. For some people, 100% concentration is less productive than 95% concentration, which is to say concentration with frequent brief interruptions, as for a cup of tea.

Being exceedingly cheap, not to mention addicted to caffeine, I steeped the same tea leaves in the little pot all day, extracting every molecule of flavor and caffeine. By the afternoon the brew was so full of tannin it puckered my mouth, and so full of caffeine that I glimpsed the key to world peace. Zooming on the jolt I stayed alert long into the night, collapsing into bed near daybreak and sleeping until noon or even later. I was well along the slippery slope to nocturnalism, turning into a marsupial like the koala, who lives on eucalyptus leaves, only I'd live on tea leaves—the same leaves stewed all day until, at midnight, they were a fetid, disgusting mush.

My odd nocturnal schedule began to interfere with my work. I'd arise at two or three o'clock in the afternoon, eat some "breakfast," and go out to collect information only to find that many of the museums were just about to close, the restaurants were done with lunch but not yet geared up for dinner, and the hotels couldn't show me any vacant rooms because they were all occupied.

I had to get myself back on a sensible schedule, but how?

Turkish lessons!

At İzmir Koleji I had no time for language lessons. Because it was a dual language school, the administrators, many of the faculty, and (eventually) the students all spoke English. Few of the citizens of Bornova spoke English, but many people in İzmir did because of the American military presence. Unfortunately, the ease with which Bornova PCVs could get around speaking English kept us from improving our Turkish language skills, which was one of the most important goals of the Peace Corps, the "Handsome Americans."

Living alone in İstanbul was different. Many educated people spoke English or French, and *gastarbeiters* returning from Germany spoke German, but people on the street and in shops spoke only Turkish. Hotel staff might know a few words of English, but the staff in restaurants, shops and museums spoke only Turkish. I'd be interacting with them all the time. I needed to speak and understand Turkish better.

The Peace Corps office would pay for private lessons. They told me to make arrangements at the US Consulate-General on Meşrutiyet Caddesi in Tepebaşı. I walked to the consulate, showed my US passport to the Marine guard and strolled inside.

At that time the consulate was housed in the Palazzo Corpi (1880), the sumptuous villa built for Italian shipping magnate Ignazio Corpi, who imported Piedmont rosewood for its doors and windows, Cararra marble for its floors and facings, and Italian painters to execute fine frescoes for its ceilings. After a decade of work it was finished. Corpi and his young mistress who was also his cousin moved in, and Corpi promptly died.

As a travel writer I've learned that no legend is complete without either a distressed damsel or a ghost, or preferably both, so the Palazzo Corpi is, according to legend, still haunted by the ghost of the young damsel, Corpi's cousin-mistress.

Probably because of the ghost legend, the US government rented the palazzo on the cheap from Corpi's heirs. US Ambassador Leishmann bought it with his own money for a fraction of its construction value, then got Congress to buy it from him by beating the leaders of Congress at cards. In effect, the Palazzo Corpi is the only US diplomatic mission to be won in a hand of poker.

I explained to the receptionist that, ghost or no ghost, I was a PCV who wanted to take Turkish lessons. She picked up the phone, spoke a few words, and in a few minutes a big, friendly consular officer appeared and introduced himself.

"I'm Richard Brown. I'm taking lessons myself," he said. "You can have private lessons with one of our teachers. Come back tomorrow morning at 9 am to meet them."

I made a point of getting to bed at a decent hour and returned to the consulate the next morning precisely at 9 am.

"This is Can (pronounced "jahn") Hanım," Richard said, introducing me to an attractive, petite brunette with a broad, open forehead, fine features and a warm smile. "And this is Işık Hanım," indicating a tall blondish young woman with huge glittering eyes, pouty lips and creamy skin. The prospect of improving my Turkish took on a whole new dimension.

We discussed schedules. I wanted to have my lessons early in the morning to get me up and out. Işık Hanım's early schedule was full; Can had a free hour at 9 am, so she would be my tutor.

The lessons went well. Can, who had studied English at İstanbul University, was intelligent, personable, pleasant and patient. We shared a love of poetry. I started memorizing poems by Orhan Veli Kanık, the most popular poet of the early republican period, just to learn vocabulary, and because I like memorizing poems. Can was studying obscure English poets like Congreve. She helped me to interpret Orhan Veli, and I convinced her to forget about Congreve and read T S Eliot and Dylan Thomas.

Of course Can already had a boyfriend, handsome and personable, who soon became her fiancé, then her husband. My romantic hopes were dashed yet again, but my Turkish improved considerably.

The consular personnel were kind to me, inviting me to the less formal consulate social functions and sometimes to their homes for dinner. Richard and his wife were especially hospitable. Going to their posh apartment was a kick because they lived on Tavuk Uçmaz Sokak ("Chickens-Don't-Fly Street"). In the 1970s, its sense of humor in terminal retreat, the city government changed the street's name to Akyol ("White Way"), an incalculable loss to jocular municipal nomenclature.

Kerosene Sucks

Autumn turned to winter and the weather turned unpleasant. Although the winter in İzmir had been chill, sometimes briskly cold with flurries of snow, it was not as bad as the İstanbul winter of 1968-69, which was extraordinarily bitter. Nacide Hanım's little apartment building had no central heat, so I had two kerosene heaters in my apartment, a big one with a stovepipe into the wall, and the portable flue-less Aladdin heater upon which I brewed my tea. They were efficient and easy to use, and they kept me warm if I could find fuel for them, which was not always easy. Demand was high because of the severe cold, so supplies were scarce.

Apartment buildings with central heating had coal delivered to them by the truckload. For the rest of us, dealers in each neighborhood stockpiled firewood, coal, charcoal and kerosene in dingy lots and makeshift shelters. I bought two large plastic containers and walked the streets in search of kerosene. I always found some eventually, but I wasted a lot of time walking and looking, often in freezing rain. As the winter ground to its depth the shortage got worse, and my dismal walks got longer.

Nacide Hanım had a 55-gallon oil drum full of kerosene on her balcony to fuel the heaters in her apartment. Every now and then she'd call a tank truck, haul the hose up to her balcony on a rope, and pump the drum full. I asked her about it, and she helped me to get a drum.

Nacide Hanım's drum had a small spigot at the bottom to let the fuel out. Unfortunately mine did not, so I had to extract the fuel by inserting a plastic hose and sucking on it until I got a siphon flow running, from which I filled my plastic containers.

Sucking sucked, however, especially sucking foul-smelling, poisonous kerosene, so I found a better way. Once I had filled my containers, instead of emptying the hose and breaking the siphon flow, I plugged the loose end of the hose with a plastic Turkish champagne-bottle cork, of which I had a growing collection, and which fit exactly. The siphon was preserved. All I had to do was remove the cork and kerosene would flow again. I left the hose and cork dangling at the side of the drum, ready whenever I needed fuel.

Kerosene was a relatively clean-burning fuel compared to lignite, the soft brown coal that was the principal heating fuel in İstanbul, and indeed in all Turkish cities, in those days. On October 15th, the officially-declared start of the winter heating season, landlords in centrally-heated buildings were required to start their furnaces. The acrid-sweet smell of burning lignite suffused the city on that day, and increased in strength as the cool days of October faded into the chill days of November and the cold, damp, raw days of December, January and February.

Lignite burns dirty and the chimneys of the city's big buildings shot tons of black dust and soot into the air. When I washed my shirts and hung them to dry on my balcony clothesline in winter, I'd carefully blow off the big flakes of soot before bringing them in. If I touched one of the flakes it would make a black spot and the shirt would have to go right back into the wash.

Forget lignite! Forget kerosene! I had my *fireplace*. Up the street on Ayazpaşa Camii Sokak, between the Park Oteli and the West German consulate, was a guy who sold coal, kerosene (when he could get it) and also firewood. I bought an armful of sticks, lugged them up the stairs to my apartment, and lit a fire.

Within five minutes my entire apartment was filled with smoke. There was no damper, nothing to open or adjust. I opened a window to increase the draft. I built up more flame to increase the draft. All it did was produce more smoke. My fireplace suffered from bad engineering and worse construction. It would not draw air properly. Soon my apartment and my entire modest wardrobe were suffused with the acrid stink of smoke. For two weeks afterward I went around smelling like a 170-pound walking baloney. My romantic fireplace visions were shattered forever. I went back to kerosene.

Merry Mr Molotov

Work went on. I researched and wrote. One day a friend introduced me to an American teacher at the American College for Girls in Üsküdar. I asked her out to dinner. She took the ferry over from Üsküdar to Kabataş, just down the hill from Ayazpaşa, and we took a taxi to the Fischer Restaurant, one of my favorites. With Frau Fischer presiding over the dining room, it was one of the best restaurants in the city, but less expensive than most.

We enjoyed a good dinner and conversation. As we were ordering dessert we heard fire engines roar past on Meşrutiyet Caddesi, sirens wailing.

"Hah, some poor guy's in trouble tonight," I said. Chuckle chuckle.

We finished our dinner and took a taxi to Saray Arkası Sokak for an after-dinner drink and who-knows-what, but the taxi couldn't get all the way to my apartment because the street was filled with fire equipment.

We got out and walked to the scene of the action. It was Nacide's apartment building. It was my apartment! Kerosene was cascading down the front of the building. A dozen firefighters had their hoses trained on the façade, ready to drench it if it caught fire. They stood there nervously, wondering exactly how bad this evening's duty could possibly be.

Nacide Hanım had assured my privacy by entrusting me with the only two keys to my apartment. She had no spare. I ran up the steps three at a time with four firemen close behind me and opened the door. We rushed out on the balcony. The cold weather had shrunk the plastic champagne cork at the end of the siphon hose a fraction of a millimeter and the pressure behind it had popped it out. The siphon worked fine, flooding the balcony with kerosene which then flowed through runoff pipes down the façade to the street. Nacide Hanım's apartment building was now an enormous Molotov cocktail ready to blow.

We took out the hose. No more siphon. The firemen hauled up a hose and flushed my balcony and the street with water, asked me politely to make some other arrangement for extracting my kerosene, and went away. They seemed unperturbed by the whole business, surprisingly tolerant of the genius who had thought up the siphon idea and almost incinerated half of Saray Arkası Sokak. My date, by contrast, had had enough. I escorted her down to the ferry for her voyage back to Üsküdar. All in all, the evening was pretty much a disaster.

Not only that, there was lots of winter left but barely any kerosene.

Introducing "The Brick"

It was November, I had been living in expensive İstanbul for four months, and I was in debt. I earned TL1500 (US$135) a month, almost half of which went for rent, another TL500 for my new heater and drum of kerosene. That left me less than TL500, but after paying my debt of TL200, I had TL300 (US$27) to pay for all my expenses for a month. This was bad, but hardly as bad as it was about to get. How bad could that be? Allow me two words: Richard Nixon.

Nixon, the anti-John Kennedy, had just won the American presidential election and along with him Spiro Agnew, an American of Greek ancestry, had become vice-president. The Turks were mortified. Kennedy had been a hero to every Turk, standing up to the communists, standing by America's allies (like Turkey). Jacqueline Kennedy provided the twist of the knife by marrying Aristotle Onassis, an old Greek who had started in business as a tobacco smuggler. The Turkish newspaper headlines shrieked "John Kennedy dies again!"

As for me, I had more immediate problems to deal with, and they had at least a peripheral connection to death. I thought I was going to die when I woke up on November 16th with a splitting headache and ferocious pains in my gut, then violent chills, then a high fever near delirium. The biological demons within me sought release through every bodily orifice for hours, enough suffering to convince me that I needed to take action if I were to live. Hans the Dutch Boy may have held back the Zuider Zee by plugging a hole in the dike with his finger, but I needed something more for the holes in my body. I needed The Brick.

The Brick was the sophisticated pharmaceutical term used by PCVs to designate a combination of tetracycline, a powerful wide-spectrum antibiotic, and Lomotil, a synthetic opiate which benumbed the musculature of the lower bowel. If you got diarrhea, as every PCV did from time to time, you swallowed The Brick and it stopped.

In my case, hosting the more sophisticated and virulent intestinal flora of cosmopolitan İstanbul, it took a bit longer but finally The Brick displayed its impressive gastrointestinal obstructive properties and I fell asleep. After 12 hours I awoke bathed in cold sweat, and it was over.

This was my inauguration into the guild of travel writers. Food poisoning is an occupational hazard. Any guidebook writer worth his tripe soup gets TD (Travelers' Diarrhea) early and often, and protects his esteemed readers by not mentioning the restaurants in which he contracts gut-busting bugs. You only hear about the ones with wimpy bugs virtually unnoticeable to your sissy pink innards, bugs which pass through you on vacation, barely causing a ripple in the daily efflux. Over the years I have hosted monster bugs in İstanbul, Jerusalem, Mexico City, Montréal, Paris and even my hometown of Boston, not to mention scores of lesser cities.

When I wasn't hosting amoebae, salmonella, rubella and Barbarella for lunch and dinner, I was reading and writing background material for the history and culture portions of my guide. I read books on Byzantine and Ottoman history and architecture, Anatolian archaeology, Turkish literature, Islamic thought and practice. It dawned on me that guidebook authors are supposed to know everything about everything, or at least appear to. Luckily for me, American higher education, like American commercial marketing, is deftly tuned to the cadences of refined narrative bullshit. I was learning a lot, but I had already learned how to make it look like a whole lot more.

Thanksgiving Bread

Late in November I came in the front door of Nacide's apartment building. Haydar Efendi stopped me and said "There's a message for you." He produced a square white envelope.

"A uniformed man in a black car brought it," he said.

The paper of the envelope was impressively heavy and it bore the Great

Seal of the United States embossed on its flap. I opened it. It was an invitation to Thanksgiving dinner with the American Consul-General at his villa on the Bosphorus. Thanksgiving was only a few days away. I anticipated that this would be the biggest, best and cheapest meal of the year.

As luck would have it, it was Ramazan. Many İstanbullus were fasting all day and feasting all night, which fit right in.

On Thanksgiving day I worked as usual, running around the city gathering data until late afternoon. I was striding purposefully along İstiklal Caddesi on my way home to get ready for the big dinner. As I walked I noticed lines forming in front of the bakeries: people were buying freshly-baked *pide*, the special flat bread sprinkled with sesame and fennel seeds that's customarily eaten at *iftar*, the breaking of the fast.

The smell of the fresh bread reached the street and I was sunk. Just one bite, I thought to myself as I got in line. I had been working hard. I was hungry. Just a bite of fresh pide to tide me over until Thanksgiving dinner, which would not be served for several hours.

When my turn came the baker handed me a big loaf of flat bread straight from the oven, so hot that he wrapped it in newspaper so it didn't burn my hand. I left the bakery. The pide cooled readily in the chill November air. I took a bite, then another. Then another, and a few more. Soon the loaf was gone.

Thanksgiving dinner was all I imagined it would be: two turkeys, stuffing, mashed potatoes, puréed squash, green beans, and several pumpkin pies for dessert. Too bad I had no appetite. So what? I've had lots of good thanksgivings since then, but never a better pide.

Whirling in Konya

A week after Thanksgiving, December clomped down on me. I decided to get out of town, so I caught a bus to Konya, the scene of my recent cinematic stardom, for the festivities commemorating the 695th anniversary of the death of Jelaleddin Rumi, called Mevlana, the great mystic philosopher and poet, and founder of the whirling dervishes. Although world famous today and especially popular in the USA, in 1968 Rumi was known only in the Islamic world.

On December 9th, the dervishes whirled in a modern sports hall. It was hardly the proper venue for a religious exercise, but the worshippers made up for it in grace and *gravitas*.

The *sema*, or whirling ceremony, began with the chanting of Kur'anic passages by a *hafiz*, a man who has memorized the entire Kur'an. He was, like many *hafiz*, blind at this point from squinting at all that Arabic squiggle, but the Holy Book having been memorized, he figured he no longer needed his eyes. Dark glasses covered them. He had an excellent voice and chanted with captivating passion and authority.

When the hafiz was finished the dozen-piece dervish orchestra and equally large chorus struck up a slow, stately, lugubrious hymn in a minor key. The dervishes lined up in a rank on the floor. They wore long black cloaks and tall brick-red sugarloaf felt caps meant to symbolize their tombstones. They shed their cloaks, symbolically casting off the cares and thoughts of this world, and revealed white costumes, long-sleeved and close-fitting above the waist, but with long full skirts below. The white cloth was a symbol of their purity and holy desire to commune with the Divine.

As the music intensified, the dervishes approached their sheikh one by one, bowed to him and began to whirl counter-clockwise, right arm extended palm-up to receive the blessings of heaven, left arm palm-down to pass them on to earth. As they spun out onto the empty floor they formed a constellation of moving whirlers. The constellation itself revolved slowly, an imitation of heavenly bodies in the cosmos.

The worshippers whirled for 10 or 15 minutes, stopped, rested a few minutes, then whirled again and again, four times in all. To end the sema, the hafiz chanted more wisdom from the Kur'an, then a short prayer, his heart and voice filling the spacious hall with exultant expressions of faith.

Atatürk had closed all the dervish lodges and disbanded the orders in 1925 because many were politically reactionary, but the Mevlevi have always been given special consideration. Officially, the sema is permitted as a cultural tradition, nothing more than a folk dance, but it was clear to me as I listened to the hafiz sing his heart out and as I witnessed the Sufi adepts whirling and whirling, growing ever closer to ecstatic union with the Divine, that this was no folk dance. It was a living tradition, a mystic path to knowledge of the universe.

Hotel Month

After the restaurant-and-food-poisoning months of November and December, January (1969) was hotel month. I decided to inspect 100 İstanbul hotels in order to find the 60 best to include in my book. (The final tally was actually 62.)

Sixty hotels sounds like a lot, but it's not, at least not for a guidebook. A single tourist may stay in only one hotel, but ten thousand tourists will stay in a range of hotels: spartan but cheap, moderately priced, comfortable but expensive; close to shops, close to the railroad station, close to sightseeing; with Bosphorus views, or with enclosed parking; big, modern and anonymous or small, atmospheric and family-run. Hotels highly recommended by guidebooks tend to fill up with readers of that guidebook, so the author also has to recommend secondary and tertiary choices just so his readers aren't left without a place to sleep.

January was a lousy time to be checking hotels. I slogged through the cold rain and entered the hotels looking like a refugee with a bad attitude. Most of the hotels were dead empty, which at least made it easy to check out the guest rooms. I'd ask to see a room and the reception clerk, who was more often than not holding down the fort all alone because there were few customers, would simply pass me a key and tell me to go take a look.

In one or two hotels, then, I was surprised to be told the place was fully booked. Why this hotel and none of the others? The "full" hotels were nothing special, not particularly clean, or fancy, or in convenient high-traffic locations. In fact, more often than not they were on back streets away from the tourist sights. In fact, they were usually in the low-rent districts. What made them so appealing that they were full when the others were empty?

"Merhaba! I'd like to look at a room, please."

"Sorry, we're full up."

"Full up? Okay, that's fine. I don't need a room for tonight. I'll be coming back to İstanbul later. But could I just see a room?"

Normally in this situation the clerk would ponder his key rack to see who was in or out of their rooms, choose a key, apologize for the fact that it was occupied with suitcases and stuff strewn all over, give the key to a bellboy, and he would open it for me.

In a few cases, though, the clerk would ponder his key-rack and repeat. "Sorry, all the rooms are occupied."

"But the keys are all there," I'd say. "Some of the guests must be out."

"No, the rooms are all occupied. Sorry."

All occupied. I figured it out: you could rent the room for an hour and play fleshy games with its female occupant, but if you actually slept in the bed you were wasting your money.

Obviously, I still had a lot to learn about writing a travel guide. In future years I would happily wander into fun houses in a dozen cities on four continents (most unexpected: Tel Aviv) in search of good cheap rooms for my readers only to find all the rooms already occupied by at least one female apparently quite eager to get to know me in all sorts of interesting ways. The real shocker—think this over—is that some of the rooms really were dirt cheap even with this special extra service.

ʂʘʗ

10

FRIENDS AND LOVERS

February in İstanbul was difficult and dreary, so it fit right in when I met Robert Komer, the head of the CIA's "pacification" program in Vietnam. At that point Komer was no longer involved in southeast Asia. He had leapt from the frying pan into the fire, from "pacifying" Vietnamese villagers to being a target of violent protests in Turkey.

News of his appointment as US ambassador roared through the radicalized halls of Turkish academe like a village bus through a flock of chickens. Turkish students already hated the naked exercise of US military power in Vietnam. Now one of its foremost gymnasts had landed in Ankara. He was forced to descend from his airliner at the end of the runway because the terminal was packed with howling protesters ready to string him up.

On January 6th, Ambassador Komer paid a courtesy call on the rector of Ankara's Middle East Technical University, which had been founded with US financial and administrative support, and which received millions of dollars in aid from the US Agency for International Development. While the ambassador and the rector lunched, a group of radicals chased away his chauffeur, overturned his huge black Cadillac limo and set it on fire.

The ambassador was miffed but undaunted. He continued his official duties.

The İstanbul PCV contingent had been invited to meet the ambassador at a consulate staffer's villa in Emirgan, on the Bosphorus. He was gracious to us, he seemed interested in our work, and he served great food and free booze.

Despite his recent pyrotechnical vehicular misfortune, there was even a cheery fire in the villa's fireplace. It smoked as badly as my fireplace did. The US government must have paid a king's ransom to rent the villa, yet the fireplace smoked. Suddenly I didn't feel so bad about my own. It hit me that European-American-style fireplaces were never really a big thing in Turkey.

The Ottomans had traditionally used charcoal braziers for heating, even in the palace. Turkish builders apparently never got the knack for making a fireplace with proper draft.

I came away from the evening with grudging admiration for the ambassador's diplomatic and people skills, and, from the smoky fireplace, another dose of cheap-suit baloney-smell.

There Actually IS a Free Lunch

A few days later I received a note from the director of the American Research Institute in Turkey. The Institute was a place where American scholars could stay while doing historical research. It was housed in a *yalı*, a large Ottoman seaside villa built into the Byzantine city walls overlooking the southern mouth of the Bosphorus. The villa had been built by the Köprülüs, scions of the illustrious family which had provided the Ottoman Empire with a long string of competent grand vezirs (prime ministers). Besides simple guest rooms for visiting scholars, the Institute had a kitchen to sustain them, a library for their work, and a small budget for social events. When the director discovered there were a number of travel writers working in İstanbul, he decided to throw a lunch and bring them together.

Lunch was served in the villa's central salon. The guest of honor was Professor George Bean, an Englishman who had taught at İstanbul University for many years. Professor Bean was a pioneer in seeking out Turkey's ancient cities, many of which had not been located, identified or properly explored. He researched the cities through readings of classic literature, then hired jeeps and donkeys and local guides and tramped through trackless mountains in search of archeological sites. He identified a surprising number, collected inscriptions, and literally put many of these ancient places on the map. His four books describing his explorations are classics in the literature of archeology and cultural travel.

Also lunching was John Freely, a physics teacher at Robert College whose hobby was writing about İstanbul. Freely bore a striking resemblance to Ernest Hemingway and cultivated it with a well-trimmed salt-and-pepper beard. He had lived in İstanbul most of his life, having moved to the city to take up a teaching position decades ago. His first book, *Stamboul Sketches*, established his reputation.

Another guest was Dux Schneider, who held both American and Swiss citizenship but had grown up mostly in England and spoke like a Brit. Tall and vaguely Central European-looking, he had a bowl-on-the-head haircut and an extraordinary amount of energy and joie de vivre. His knowledge of the world was deep and insightful, his conversation lively. He was writing a guidebook for a prominent British publisher.

As we lunched and chatted, it became apparent that most of us lived in the same neighborhood. The institute director, his wife and son lived on Rıza Bey Yokuşu, just around the corner from Saray Arkası Sokak. I had seen them walking up and down the hill to Taksim Square, but had not known who they were. Dux Schneider lived two blocks downhill from my apartment on Beşaret Sokak. As lunch was ending, he offered me a ride home in his well-traveled Land Rover, and invited me to dinner later in the week. This was great! The pall of loneliness seemed to lift.

Dux lived with his wife Monique and infant daughter Tamara in a spacious, light apartment with a long terrace balcony that had a panoramic view of the Bosphorus. The apartment was stark. "We're going to be here for less than a year, we don't want to spend money on decorating or furnishings, so we've hung our mountain-climbing equipment on the walls," he told me.

Dux's personal history was anything but conventional. Born in the USA of a Swiss father and a German mother, he had been educated at St Paul's School in London before enlisting in the US Army during World War II. He served in the Normandy landings and the Ardennes campaign, then went to Swarthmore College near Philadelphia on the GI Bill. He moved to New York City where he met and married Monique. I recognized Monique as the petite, long-haired blonde I had seen walking and shopping in the neighborhood several times. While Dux worked on his guidebook, Monique was caring for Tamara and writing novels under the pseudonym "Frances Oliver."

Monique came from a well-to-do family as well. Her parents were both prominent Viennese psychoanalysts who had studied with Freud himself. Fleeing Hitler, they settled in Grosse Pointe, Michigan, and developed a prominent psychoanalytical practice.

Dinner was simple but delicious and took full advantage of Turkey's excellent fruits, vegetables and spices. Dux enjoyed being an epicure, though it was difficult to live the good life on the meager advance he had been paid to write his guidebook.

As dinner progressed I learned more about them. In the early 1960s they had moved from New York to London where Dux got a job with a publishing company but he, like me, couldn't stand office work. Job stress built up, and he and Monique decided to leave it all behind, bought a Land Rover and set out to go mountain-climbing in eastern Turkey. The following year they contracted hepatitis in Hakkâri, then collapsed into hospital in Antalya. The doctor told them to rest for several months so they rented a house in Side (SEE-deh), then a tiny fishing village on Turkey's Mediterranean shore. They fell in love with Turkey and decided to stay awhile.

January in İstanbul might be bleak, but now I had more friends close by.

On the 27th, as if to celebrate the exit of the month, I woke to a rare delight: İstanbul under several inches of snow unsullied yet by morning traffic or lignite soot. It was bitter cold. I took a walk and enjoyed the vision of the great mosques wrapped in white, and the tessellation of roofs cascading down to the Bosphorus, their red-tile color now smothered in shimmering whiteness. Then I went back home to my Turkish sentence structures.

I was making progress. I could now skim a newspaper and understand the gist of an article without a dictionary. This was something of an accomplishment. I had been taught polite conversational Turkish, and had mostly taught myself street Turkish, but literary Turkish, even journalistic Turkish, is far more complex. Dependent and subordinate clauses fly out of every sentence like subscription cards out of a magazine. My job, as reader, was to examine each clause, sub-clause and dangling participle and figure out how to put them all back together into a sentence that made sense.

My friendship with the Schneiders deepened as we found more and more things in common. They seemed to enjoy my scintillating conversation, although later in an unguarded moment they admitted that what they really found interesting was the possibility that I might be available as a babysitter.

Liquid Orchids by the Bridge

"Do you know that the Galata Bridge opens every night to let ships in and out of the Golden Horn?" Dux asked me one day. The Golden Horn is the fresh water estuary that separates the old and new parts of European İstanbul. The Galata Bridge was the century-old pontoon bridge that connected old to new. "I'm going down there tomorrow morning," he said. "Want to come?"

We got up at 3 am and walked to Galata (Karaköy), arriving at 3:45. Just before 4 am the barriers at the ends of the bridge came down and the few vehicles in motion at that hour stopped behind them. Precisely at four the bridge engineers kicked over marine engines that propelled the middle section of the pontoon bridge out and swung it away, leaving a gap for ships to pass through.

The night air was chilly. A vendor of *sahlep*, a hot drink of milk mixed with pulverized orchid root and topped with a shake of cinnamon, posted himself at the bridge to serve the few pedestrians who were waiting to cross. I bought a steaming hot cup. It warmed my hands. The orchid-root powder made the milk glutinous, thick and sweet.

I have had sahlep before and since, but that cup from the vendor by the bridge is how I judge all others. I can taste it now, the scalding, thick sweet creamy liquid stinging my lips as I sip it gingerly, letting the cool night air tame its heat, the cinnamon teasing my nostrils.

I sip and it oozes slowly down my throat spreading a bloom of latent warmth through my chest, defeating the night's chill as the motors chug away, slowly opening the bridge.

For 30 minutes ships glided out of the Golden Horn, and from 4:30 to 5 am ships glided in. At 5 am the engineers swung the center section of the bridge back in place, raised the barriers at the ends of the bridge, and the few waiting cars (mostly taxis) started their engines and trundled across the bridge, this minor İstanbul drama finished for another day.

We walked uphill on Yüksekkaldırım past the medieval Galata Tower to Tünel Square and along nearly-deserted İstiklal Caddesi as the sky lightened toward dawn.

Don't Touch That Fish!

I ran into Monique at Ahmet's shop one day and she asked me if I'd like to come to dinner at some friends'. We went. Peter and Ella Wallenberg lived in an old apartment building down the hill from Galatasaray Square. Peter had been born and raised in the Free City of Danzig, now Gdansk in Poland. As a Jew, he had fled Hitler's capture of the city and had come to İstanbul where he found tolerance and plenty of work. He was a skillful, even brilliant designer, architect and interior decorator, mostly self-taught. His clients included many of İstanbul's most prominent families. He and Ella lived modestly, but knew good food and ate well.

As we sat at dinner, Peter retold a story of the old days in İstanbul, about the "gypsy palamut" and the umbrella. Gypsy palamut was a medium-sized bonito fish about eighteen inches that ran in schools.

"I was walking home along the Bosphorus near Tophane when I saw everyone rush to the water's edge. 'Gypsy palamut! Gypsy palamut!' they were shouting. I went to see what was happening. Huge schools of fish were roiling around in the water, masses of fish! It looked as though the Bosphorus was boiling with bonito. Everyone was grabbing fish with anything they had: nets, bags, pots, hats, whatever. I had only my umbrella. I opened it, scooped a huge mass of fish into it and carried it home for dinner."

"I don't know much about fish," I said to the Schneiders as we drove home to Ayazpaşa. Having been raised inland in America during the 1950s, I knew almost nothing about good fish. Though I acquired a taste for lobster during college in Boston, I had never really gotten into fish.

"I'll teach you," Dux said, ready at any time to talk about the finer things in life. He suggested I go shopping with him to Beyoğlu's Balık Pazarı (Fish Market), just off Galatasaray Square, the next day.

Like good İstanbullus, Dux and Monique went to the markets almost daily. In America, one goes to the supermarket once or twice a week and stores the food in a refrigerator. In the İstanbul of 1968, refrigerators were rare, just then appearing in butcher shops and only much later in private homes.

Among the first Turkish phrases I learned after moving to İstanbul was *Etlerimiz buzdolabındadır* ("Our meats are in the refrigerator") posted at the front of many butcher shops. Customers were used to seeing slabs of meat hanging in front of the shops, which is how butchers advertised their goods. With the meat in a refrigerator inside the shop, customers passing by might assume the butcher had no meat. Hence the sign.

We walked along İstiklal Caddesi to Galatasaray, turned right onto Sahne Sokak and penetrated the bazaar. With butchers, kitchen supply shops and a dozen delicatessen-like shops, the Balık Pazarı is really European İstanbul's gourmet shopping center.

What a delight! Cobbled streets, vendors selling roasted sheeps' guts and steamed mussels, shops piled with bright citrus, greengrocers stocked with winter vegetables, and of course the fishmongers.

Dux led me to his fishmonger, down Sahne Sokak past the Armenian Church of Three Altars, on by Nevizade Sokak with its rowdy tavernas. The owner was a tall black-mustashio'd Turkish Greek, his assistant an Armenian.

We looked at the fish. Dux showed me how to check the eyes for shine (no cloudiness) and the gills for deep red color. He pressed his finger down on the flesh and showed me how it was supposed to rebound. His finger left no impression in the bright scales. The owner approached us. Dux ordered the day's fish, paid, and carried it away.

A few days later I came to the same shop by myself. I began to inspect a *palamut* (bonito), prodding the flesh, peering at the gills and the eyes. The owner, seeing me inspecting his fish suspiciously, turned in a huff and refused to serve me. His assistant came out, took me aside and whispered "If the fish isn't fresh, the owner doesn't open the shop. He's miffed that you feel you need to check it." I bought the palamut from the assistant (500 grams, 10¢), took it home, fried it in a pan with butter, and was hooked for life on İstanbul fish.

The next time I went there I simply pointed to a fish and bought it.

I never got a bad fish. I came to the market almost daily. If his shop was closed, I'd know that either the fish wasn't fresh, the owner was ill, or it was a Greek Orthodox holiday. Other shops would be open and selling fish—tuna, bluefish, sea bass, turbot—but not his.

When I returned to America in 1970 I took with me my newly-acquired love of good fish, but I discovered I couldn't order fish in a restaurant. I only knew the Turkish names.

After getting acquainted for a few months, Monique had a proposal."Why don't you two travel together in the summer?" she asked. She was eager for Dux not to travel alone.

Dux's book would cover all of Turkey, whereas mine would include only the more popular tourist regions, most of which Dux had already researched. No matter. This was my chance to get off the beaten track for my own enjoyment and to see parts of the country rarely visited. We sketched out two long trips for the summer.

How Does It Feel to be Terminated?

February in İstanbul is a better month than January not because it is any less dreary, which it isn't, but because it is shorter. The 17th was a spring-like day, however, and given Turkey's volatile political climate at the time, it was just right for a riot.

A big leftist political rally was scheduled to be held in Taksim Square. It was not particularly anti-American, just pro-socialist. As the rally got going, right-wing thugs with clubs and uniformed police wielding truncheons waded into the crowd and flailed away. The crowd broke into a panic and flooded out of the square in all directions, some even fleeing the melée along Saray Arkası Sokak, blood dripping from bash-marks in their skulls.

Having been thus inspired by the bright promise of spring, I went to Ankara for the Turkey 15 "Termination Conference." We PCVs were debriefed by Peace Corps staff: what did we find good about our experience, what bad? Had we accomplished what we set out to do?

The general feeling among PCVs is that we had not. Peace Corps Turkey was not achieving its stated goals, and should be discontinued. Partly this was because of the difficult situation caused by the Vietnam war, and partly because we weren't sure our efforts were really necessary.

In many schools, PCVs were actually taking the places of Turkish teachers of English. After receiving a government-supported education in teacher training academies, these Turkish teachers were obliged to pay back the nation by serving for several years in government schools, but they could buy their way out of this obligation for $650. Many of these bright young teachers, fluent in English upon graduation, borrowed the money, got free of the national education system, took high-paying jobs in the private sector (where fluency in English was like money in the bank), and easily paid back their loans.

Although we didn't think much of our contribution to Turkey's development, ironically we felt that we ourselves had benefited greatly from Peace Corps service. The knowledge, insight and experience we had gained from living in Turkey was changing our lives. We cherished many of the friendships we had made. We felt fulfilled.

Most of us would later change our opinion of our contribution to Turkey. We would see many of our students go on to make valuable contributions to Turkey's development, in part because of the language training we provided.

As for me, I returned to İstanbul by night bus on March 1, arriving the next morning, and wrote in a letter,

All my friends are getting ready to leave in a few months. It's sort of sad. But this second year has been, in most respects, much better than the first. I've found how to live in a foreign country (it took a year, despite all that training) and I won't feel lonely because my American friends are not around. If I stay a third year (if I'm able to), I think the insights I have gained into international problems and inter-cultural relations will be expanded and clarified. An understanding of these aspects of today's history does much to expose the causes of conflict between cultures, which produces wars, misunderstandings, and general bad relations. It is very valuable experience indeed.

The letter went on: "If my project works out successfully, it will be the most valuable product a single volunteer has put out in a long time, and the most valuable ever in tourism."

Tourism was, in fact, developing in Turkey, albeit slowly. The *Daily News* reported:

Tourism Brought in 31 Million Dollars Last Year [1968]

[Minister of Tourism Nihat Kürşat reports that his ministry] ...began construction of yacht harbours, increased propaganda, established a tourist exchange, started selling high octane gasoline and opened Antalya and Çiğli-İzmir airports to charter flights.... At the end of this year [1969] the number of touristic beds will rise to over 39 thousand, an increase of more than three times in four years.

The radicalization of Turkish youth which had been fostered in part by the Vietnam War was no help, though. With admirable idealism but woeful short-sightedness they protested just about everything that had anything to do with the USA, or seemed to. For example, the project to build a bridge across the Bosphorus was roundly condemned as a US plot. They called it the "Morrison Bridge" after the director of the US Agency for International Development (AID) mission to Turkey, but in fact AID had no connection to the financing, planning, or construction of the bridge. Apparently they felt that the USA was somehow pushing this bridge on the Turkish government and its people. A huge mural painted by the leftists showed the completed bridge spanning the Bosphorus with the Sixth Fleet anchored beneath to protect it.

In fact, the Bosphorus Bridge project was a sacred-cow project to the Turkish government, which saw it as a visible symbol of the country's march toward economic development. After millennia of division, Europe and Asia would be physically united at İstanbul. This had been Atatürk's vision for Turkey: to be the country linking Europe and Asia physically, economically and culturally.

The students, however, were caught up in Cold War radicalism. As for me, I would have asked the truck drivers who waited for days, sleeping in the cabs of their trucks waiting for a place on one of the overburdened Bosphorus vehicle ferries, what they thought of the bridge project.

But really, the only legitimate question about the bridge was that of payback: would it earn enough in tolls to pay for its hugely expensive construction? No one would know until twenty years later, in the 1980s.

My Second Movie Career

The chill of winter dragged on forever. April finally brought some warmth, a pleasure for my bodily exterior. The weather in my interior was still roiled by food poisoning and, for exotic interest, an ear infection. Yet more exotic was nocturnal dyspnea, which means that I'd wake up in the middle of the night and not be breathing. I would not be able to move, not even to open my eyes. I'd lie there, thinking it was all over, when all of a sudden I'd start breathing again, and could finally open my eyes. I'd try to move. Still nothing yet, but after what seemed like several minutes (but was probably less) my limbs would respond and I'd budge. There was some serious medical stuff going on but I had no idea what it was.

Things weren't much better in the Turkish body politic. On April 5th, having had enough of a bad reception, Ambassador Komer resigned his post and returned to Washington with his family. A week later İstanbul's students signified their happiness at his departure by rioting on another theme entirely.

The most fun I had was singing music by Leonardo Leo and Pachelbel during Easter week in the choir of the Dutch Chapel, İstanbul's non-denominational Protestant church.

With the emerging spring came another shot at cinematic stardom.

"Columbia Pictures will shoot a film in Turkey this summer," said the article in the newspaper. "Tony Curtis will play the male lead."

The same Turkish newspaper carried a casting-call ad in English for movie extras.

"Must be foreigners. Must be able to ride a horse," it read.

I was still a Cheap Blond Foreigner so I went to see Maisie, the attractive young Turkish lady who was interviewing the extras.

"How'd you get the name Maisie?" I asked, that being anything but a typical Turkish name.

"My parents liked that old song....dum de dum dum Maisie," she sang, "so they called me Maisie. Any film experience?"

I told her proudly of my career as the male lead in *A Cup of Coffee*.

"Can you ride a horse?" she asked.

"Yes, of course," I said, which was mostly true. I had ridden horses growing up, though not very far nor very fast. My sister Posie was a hippomane. She bought her first horse at the age of 14 and has owned and trained horses ever since. She once bought a horse bred for the king of Morocco, planning to turn it into the perfect dressage mount. She has a horse farm in horse country in Virginia. She works in a horse veterinarian's office. One time I telephoned her:

"How are you?"

"Fine, I'm fine."

"How's everybody?"

"Everybody's fine." Pause. "The kids are fine too."

"Who's 'everybody,' then?"

"The horses, silly."

To grow up with Posie was to get it 24/7 about horses. It may well be said that I had opportunities to ride, though my riding ability was at present indeterminate.

Maisie gave me the eye for about ten seconds, sizing me up.

"Don't call us, we'll call you," she said.

In other words, my movie career was over for good.

A View of the Parthenon

I needed a vacation. I had written a number of chapters and could spend time correcting and revising them while I traveled. I decided to go to the isle of Rhodes.

I bought a deck-class ticket for $10 on Turkish Maritime Lines' m/s *Samsun*. It departed the Golden Horn on the afternoon of April 17th, arriving in Piraeus the next day. By the 20th I had stepped off an inter-island ferryboat along with a small crowd of other foreign tourists onto the stone-paved streets of Mykonos, where I planned to spend a night on my way to Rhodes.

We were met by a posse of pension owners, mostly women. "Two dollars for bed and breakfast," they said. I followed a woman up a frighteningly clean, narrow street between freshly whitewashed sugar-cube houses to her pension. It was bare, basic, almost too clean, and entirely suitable for my purposes. I dropped my bag and was home.

Mykonos was a revelation: the Greeks had tourism pegged. The town was spotless, full of character, and cheap. The people were relaxed, friendly, self-confident and welcoming. I sat at a cafe in the *plateia* (main square) drinking Nescafé (unavailable in Turkey), correcting my manuscript, chatting with locals and tourists.

"Where are you from?" a grizzled old fisherman asked as he nursed his tiny thimbleful of dense Turkish—…uh, pardon me, *Greek*—coffee.

"I'm American, but I'm living in İstanbul right now," I answered.

"Stamboul?" he asked. "Constantinopolis. In Turkis? Ah, Turkis! A rich country! If only we had that...."

Here it was in raw form: the *Megali Idea* (Great Plan), which had gotten the Greeks into such trouble ever since they declared independence from the Ottomans in 1822. The Great Plan was the Greek dream of taking back the core lands of the Byzantine Empire, and especially the noble city of Constantinople. Considering that there are under 12 million Greeks and over 70 million Turks, at least 20 million of whom have military training, this is equivalent to a skinny kid taking on a sumo wrestler. Greece had attacked Turkey in 1854, 1866, 1878, 1896, 1912, 1913 and 1919 to pursue the Megali Idea, usually with disastrous results. The latest iteration was the Cyprus crisis of 1967. The Megali Idea refused to die, and kept the political pot boiling.

It was early in the tourism season and, as I was later to see, early in Mykonos' evolution from idyllic cheapo Greek isle to overwrought, self-absorbed international glitterati swamp. The town was far from full, just comfortably populated with foreigners, enough to make it interesting. We heard stories of the nude beaches on the other side of the island, and of the sterling efforts of the local constabulary who patrolled them by boat, binoculars in hand, eager to find infractors of the island's decency laws though apparently in much less of a hurry to make them put their clothes back on.

I never made it to Rhodes. Mykonos was too perfect: peaceful and beautiful, with the occasional roaring night in a taverna.

On the 24th, however, my time was up and I climbed back on the ferryboat for Athens. During the voyage I chatted with the other foreign passengers, including a young woman named Tina. She was from an old New England family which had once been wealthy and powerful—with the emphasis on 'once.' Tina had curly hair, girlish features, and a sombre *weltschmerzlich* aura as though she bore on her slender shoulders the entire weighty world of French existentialist philosophy. She was, as a matter of fact, living and studying in France, so maybe she did, though if she did, I have no idea what French philosophy was up to while she was away in the Greek islands. Nothing simple, that's for sure.

Life was Serious Business to Tina. She was reading Norman O Brown's *Love's Body*, a "meditation on the condition of humanity and its long fall from the grace of a natural, instinctual innocence" and other current *weltschmerzlich* titles. When the ferry arrived in Piraeus we took a bus together to the Plaka. We took a room together in a cheap hotel with a vestigial view of the Parthenon. We took solace in the activities learned by Adam and Eve in the fall from grace. Greece, it was apparent, had certain advantages over Turkey for young men at the height of their lifetime libidinal surge.

A few more ecstatically gloomy Greek spring days and we went our separate ways, she toward Spain, I to the Athens airport at which—blessings on my student card and the liberal, youth-friendly policies of Turkish Airlines!—I bought a ticket on a nonstop flight to İzmir for $10.

What? That's It?

I stayed in İzmir for a few days, visiting friends and pondering love, life and fate. I thought of Tina constantly. She was cute, smart and serious. She was worldly, adventurous, experienced in bed and on the way to being cosmopolitan. And yet she was not self-sufficient. She needed others. She was searching for answers in love, as was I.

It had all happened so fast. Where was she? We had promised to write, and in fact we did exchange letters for a few months, curious what might happen next, if anything. But at the moment I missed her terribly. Soon I was thinking of her constantly, obsessively. Anything else I did was merely a distraction from thinking about Tina.

That evening I was in Konak, İzmir's main square, on my way to visit my friends Joanie and Murray. I looked for a minibus up the long, steep hill toward their apartment in Eşrefpaşa. None came by. I felt an intense agitation, an urgency to move. I started walking. This longing, this anxiety, this passion was unbearable. I started to run. I ran to the switchback road that meanders up the steep slope.

My Tina-obsession only grew worse. I ran faster, hoping to exhaust myself, but the passion only increased. I wanted to be tired, worn out, so tired that I would think of nothing but sleep and oblivion.

Finally I felt winded. I couldn't last much longer. The hill was steep and I was not used to running. But I couldn't stop. I didn't stop. I reached the top of the slope, turned right and ran along İnönü Caddesi. I had run a mile uphill by this time. My heart was pounding dangerously, my lungs frantically expanding and collapsing, trying to keep up with my insatiable need for oxygen. My throat burned from the rasp of air. I was drenched in sweat.

I reached my friends' apartment building and sat down, exhausted. My heart thundered in my chest. The gasp of my lungs turned to wracking sobs. I sat on a step and the pain of lost love drowned me. It was worse—physically worse—than any purely physical illness I had ever experienced.

Was I punishing my heart for being so susceptible, so vulnerable to capture? If I forced it to pound right out of my chest or utterly to exhaust itself and stop, would that solve my problem?

I was a physical wreck, my clothes rumpled and soaked with sweat, my face a spent battlefield of emotion. My legs ached, my lungs burned. I couldn't visit my friends like this. I dragged myself slowly downhill to my cheap hotel and collapsed.

The next day, April 27th, was my 24th birthday.

I tried again on my birthday to visit my friends and succeeded. Soon I was back in İstanbul, where I made an appointment with the doctor for a nagging medical problem. My romp with Tina was still in my mind, and apparently not only in my mind.

"Nothing a hefty shot of penicillin won't cure," the doctor said. ∞

11

THE EAST IS FLAMING RED

In May, Anatolia is perfect, its broad vistas of rolling steppe swathed in wildflower color: here a stretch of brilliant purple a kilometer long, there a howling streak of yellow boosted by the brown earth beneath as it challenges the blue of the sky. Fruit orchards send cascades of pink blossom petal-snow blowing across the roads. Tender shoots spring up in the rough-plowed fields, first inklings of the lush green carpet to come.

For someone accustomed to the dense enveloping forests, ever-flowing mountain streams and fragrant leaf-mold underfoot in Pennsylvania, I surprised myself with how quickly I came to appreciate the spectacular beauties of Turkey's far sparer landscape.

May 1969 was a perfect time to go running around the countryside in a Land Rover looking for interesting things to write about. We would not be disappointed.

Dux needed to tour the entire country for his book, and he wanted someone to talk with and to share the cost of gas. His itinerary went far off the beaten track to places I wouldn't be covering in my book, but that was the trip's attraction: I'd visit places I wouldn't otherwise get to see.

We packed our bags, numbered our notebooks, bid farewell to Ayazpaşa, coasted downhill to the Kabataş car ferry and floated across the Bosphorus to Asia. After a day's drive we were east of Ankara, in Hittite country.

Where the Hittites Sit Tight

The Hittites are mentioned in the Bible as inhabitants of the Promised Land before the Israelites arrived, but until the 1800s nobody knew anything more about them. I still knew nothing about them, so Dux filled me in as we drove.

By 1375 BC the Hittites had become a force in the Middle East, and until

1200 BC they were among its great powers, challenging the might of the Egyptian pharaohs and battling them for control of Syria, Judaea and Samaria. With the rise of the Phrygians around 1250 BC, and later the Assyrians, Hittite power collapsed and their civilization vanished. In a very real sense the Hittites went underground, not to reappear for over three thousand years.

So how did we finally find out about them? We invented the science of archeology.

Here's an amazing fact: until the 1800s, nobody cared much about old stuff like ruined cities, temples or pyramids. They just sat there in the desert collecting dust or in the jungle getting overgrown by trees and creepers. Jackals bore litters of whelps in the pharaoh's tomb-chamber, monkeys set up housekeeping in Mayan temples, and nobody gave a damn. Then, in 1799, Napoleon sent a few inquisitive French professors along with his military expedition to Egypt. Within decades the rage for old stones spread across the globe and intrepid travelers were turning up forgotten civilizations everywhere. Europeans were all over the Middle East, John Lloyd Stephens discovered the ancient Mayan cities of Central America, and the science of archeology was born.

In the case of the Hittites, a French traveler named Charles Texier stumbled upon some old ruins at a place called Boğazköy in 1839 and wrote about them. In 1907 excavations began and turned up exquisite works of art: effigies of big-antlered deer, delicate sun symbols, and graceful clay vessels and figurines. They also found the Hittite government archives written in cuneiform on little clay tablets. Boğazköy, it appeared, had been Hattusha, the capital city of the Hittites some 3500 years ago.

Dux and I had Boğazköy—or Boğazkale, as it's now called—to ourselves. Its situation is striking: a sprawling city built on an easily-defended hillside surrounded by dramatic mountain crags. The stark hillside site, the stream filled with a spring torrent carving its way among the hills, the severe, treeless landscape, and the incredibly ancient stone foundations combine to make a powerful impression.

On the opposite side of the stream gorge we found Yazılıkaya ("Inscribed Rocks"), the Hittites' open-air temple. The vertical walls of a dramatic cleft in the rock were carved with reliefs of gods, goddesses and religious processions. The inscriptions suffered sun, rain, dust and frost for three thousand years, but were still plainly visible. Dux took photos and notes, and we pushed on to Çorum, the nearest city.

Chewin' Chalk

Çorum is a farming town famous for its *leblebi* (roasted chick peas). Atatürk loved to munch roasted chick peas while sipping rakı, and the great leader's affection for the little dried pulses has given Çorum a warm glow ever since.

We tried some. Munching a dried chick pea is similar to sucking a stick of chalk, though a good belt of rakı ends the otherwise forlorn exercise with a positive gustatory and spiritual return. Historians gently suggest that Atatürk's affection for *leblebi* might not have been merely gustatory but political as well. Leblebi was everyman's snack, plain, simple, cheap, healthful and eminently Turkish, in stark contrast to the exotic, expensive and usually imported delicacies that all too easily tickled the palates and slid down the noble throats of the imperial class he sought to discredit and depose.

Chick pea roasters' shops (*leblebiciler*) line İnönü Caddesi, Çorum's main drag. There seems to be a roasters' hierarchy, with each shop selling peas of lesser or greater quality, in this or that style of roasting, as though chick peas were coffee beans. Rash innovators of the chalk-plus school add sugar or clove or hot pepper to their products in a mostly-futile effort to make them more palatable and thus to rise in the hierarchy. To us, the huge sacks of roasted chick peas held about as much gustatory attraction as volcanic ash, which is even cheaper than chick peas in this part of the world, but almost as palatable. We tried a few sample leblebi, but as we were not yet at that point in the day when a belt of rakı made sense, we hauled it out of Çorum and hurried northward, heading for the Black Sea littoral and the mountain town of Amasya.

Counting Blue Seminaries

Amasya is far more beautiful and interesting, a city set in a dramatic steep-walled canyon through which flows the swift Yeşilırmak ("Green River"). Besides the beauty of its setting, it has fine Seljuk and Ottoman mosques, a Mongol madhouse, and an outstanding collection of graceful Ottoman houses.

We cruised into town at dusk. As we rounded a curve and headed east, Dux pointed out an aqueduct carved into the vertical rock face on our right.

"Probably from the Pontic kingdom," he said. Amasya had been a Hittite town. It was later conquered by Alexander the Great, then by the Persians. By the third century BC, its king, Mithridates II, ruled a substantial portion of Anatolia, and tax revenues flooded into his capital to build things like aqueducts and the striking rock-hewn royal tombs that look down on the town from the dramatic cliffs to the north.

"There's the Gök Medrese Camii," Dux said and pulled to the side of the road, stopping in front of an old stone building, the Sky (Blue) Seminary Mosque. In the failing light we saw a few small rectangles of blue tilework on its weathered façade and dome, all that was left of the rich decorative patterns that had earned it its name. It had been built for a Seljuk Turkish grand vezir named Seyfettin Torumtay in 1267, just after the Crusades. The donor's elaborate mausoleum stood in front of the mosque. The dressed stone bordering the doors and windows was elaborately carved, but in some places the borders were plain, uncarved. I wondered why, then it hit me: Torumtay had been an important guy in 1267, but except for Elvis a guy's importance is apt to fade pretty quickly once he's dead. Once he was stiff inside it, the people responsible for finishing his tomb probably just walked off with whatever was left of the project budget.

We decided to come back and have a closer look the next morning in daylight. Right now our goal was to find a place to sleep, which we did at the deceptively-named Konfor Palas Oteli (Comfort Palace Hotel) which was in fact a miserable hovel, but concomitantly cheap.

Our next concern was food and drink, perhaps a belt of rakı (but hold the leblebi). Most local restaurants in places like Amasya and Tokat open early for breakfast, bustle with workers and market-goers at lunch, close by early evening, and serve no alcoholic beverages. We wanted just the opposite: a place that stayed open late for dinner and served any sort of fluid poison a thirsty travel writer might want. We wandered from the hotel along the river to the main square where we accosted a local for a dining recommendation.

"Şehir Kulübü (City Club)," he said, pointing across the bridge to a simple modern building perched strategically above the river and the bridge so as to enjoy fine views of both. We went there, climbed a flight of stairs, ignored a sign reading "No Admittance to Non-members" and asked if we could have dinner. Admission was apparently limited to high municipal, provincial and commercial officials. The waiter called the maître d' who, noticing our weird traveling clothes and foreign accents, immediately ranked us as honorary local notables, swept us into the dining room and seated us at a choice table. We ordered dinner and rakı and were then left to ourselves, which suited us perfectly.

The Amasya City Club was our first clue that in every Anatolian town of any size there is one place at which the local *ayan* (notables), the movers and shakers of government, business and industry, gather each evening to eat well and to drink in peace. They come for long social evenings with sumptuous multi-course Turkish dinners accompanied by plenteous portions of rakı, beer or wine, all served by nervously obsequious waiters. To achieve this they either appoint the best restaurant in town as their social club or, if there's no restaurant good enough, establish one of their own, preferably with municipal funds. In Amasya it was the City Club.

Well fed and watered, and assured of a bed, we wandered north along the banks of the Yeşilırmak admiring Amasya's fine Ottoman houses all the way to the Bimarhane, the Mongol madhouse. The Bimarhane (Insane Asylum) was endowed by İlduş Hanım, wife of the Mongol Ilkhanid Sultan Oljaytu, in 1309. All that's left of it are its grand doorway and parts of four walls, but we could see that it was an interesting blend of grand Seljuk Turkish design spiced up with bits of other architectures picked up by the Mongols on their rampage westward out of the depths of Asia.

After a sound sleep in the dismal non-Comfort of the non-Palace Hotel we visited the rest of Amasya's fine buildings. The Burmalı Minare Camii, or Mosque of the Spiral Minaret, has just that: a huge minaret which spirals upward toward heaven. It's not unique—there are several other mosques in Turkey with spiral minarets, such as in Edirne west of İstanbul—but there are few enough spiral minarets that you don't think "Seen one spiral minaret, seen 'em all."

The Büyük Ağa Medresesi (Great Chief Seminary) was even better, an octagonal stone theological school constructed on the order of Hüseyin Ağa, chief white eunuch to the Ottoman sultan Beyazıt II, in 1488. The students' tiny rooms surrounded an architecturally elegant octagonal courtyard which would have been used in ancient times for classes but was now the scene of a furious soccer match among the young Islamic scholars.

The seminary was the last significant building up the river, so we turned around and walked back to our hotel, packed up the Land Rover, and toiled up the steep track that leads to the citadel crowning a rock outcrop high above the town. The morning air was fine and cool, the sky blue, the wind surprisingly brisk and no doubt accelerated by the great gorge yawning below us.

We climbed the citadel wall and looked down: far below us the river meandered gently through the town which clung to its narrow banks hemmed in by the vertical rock walls of the canyon.

The citadel was the highest point around. From it the land sloped steeply downward for a hundred yards or so to the edge of the precipice, where we noticed a little roofed shelter. We scrambled down to it and discovered an ancient imperial Russian field piece used as a "Ramazan cannon" to announce to the faithful below that the sun had set, the daily fast was over, and people should eat. The firing of a cannon was a common practice in the days before municipal public address systems, cheap watches, radios and TVs, and must have been particularly useful in Amasya as its rock walls would certainly have obscured the exact moment of sunset.

We drove southeast to Turhal, then Tokat.

Belediye Everything

Turhal and Tokat were nowhere on my touristic radar, but Dux wanted to see them. He ended up describing Turhal in just over four lines in his book, Tokat in under two pages. I feel certain that the two of us constituted nearly 50% of the entire tourist traffic to Tokat during that decade.

Interestingly, it was from Zile, about 22 km southwest of Turhal, that Julius Caesar sent his famous one-liner to Rome: *Veni, vidi vici* (I came, I saw, I conquered) after defeating Pharnaces, king of Pontus, who had defied Roman rule from his base in Amasya. It occurred to me that Caesar's clever pronouncement may be the earliest known sound-bite.

We rolled into Tokat late in the afternoon, found a cheap room at the spartan Belediye Oteli (Municipal Hotel), and walked to the Belediye Sarayı (Municipal Palace). In the shady garden to its right was the Belediye Lokantası (Municipal Restaurant), Tokat's answer to Amasya's Şehir Kulübü. Obviously municipal funds had played a large part in the establishment of Tokat's fundamental tourism infrastructure. The *ayan* of Tokat had gone their Amasyan neighbors one better by providing both a hotel and a restaurant for local and visiting notables.

The late afternoon air was warm and mild, so we took an open-air table near a circular three-tiered fountain. The sound of its water added a delightful aural dimension to dinner. Its top two shallow basins held a dozen heads of crisp romaine lettuce. Diners were invited to pluck a head from the chill water and use the leaves to scoop up the various creamy vegetable purées which are important ingredients on the *rakı sofrası* ("rakı table") the varied progression of hot and cold hors d'oeuvres which accompany a serious rakı-drinking session. We plucked, we supped, we drank, and after an hour or two Tokat's touristic potential loomed large in our eyes.

Tokat has its own Gök Medrese (Blue Seminary) next to the Belediye Oteli. Though built as a seminary in 1277 under Seljuk-Mongol rule, it was used as the town hospital until 1811, but by the time we arrived it had been converted to be the Belediye Müzesi (Municipal Museum), a much better use for it. It still has a few of the old Seljuk blue tiles in its courtyard, which is how it got its name. It also has twenty tombs which probably hold the remains of the seminary's founder, Pervane Muhineddin Süleyman, and his family, but which, according to local legend, are occupied by forty girls. Why forty girls in twenty tombs? Legends usually hang together a bit more than this one, if only because legends, when found to be unbelievable, are easy to fix: you just change or embellish them until they make enough sense to invoke everybody's romantic imagination.

It seems to me that the local authorities could put somebody on this, call him the Belediye Misalcı (Municipal Legend-Guy), have him do a little clever editing and guerilla marketing and whip the local girl-legend into shape to actually produce some tourism numbers for the town.

Perhaps the girls in the tombs have been ignored because of Christina, an early Christian maiden from Tokat martyred by the Roman emperor Diocletian. A macabre wax effigy of the saint is among the museum's proudest exhibits. It hints that Tokat was not always solidly Muslim as it is today. Obviously, the lifelike wax Christina was once the prime exhibit in a local orthodox church, now long since disbanded. I can't help thinking that she is on display to show local Muslims the depths to which Christians will go in effigy-worship, which is forbidden in Islam.

After an okay night in the Belediye Oteli—we slept nearly as well as Christina—we drove south, up over the Çamlıbel Pass (6500 ft, 1981 m) and down into Sivas.

The Nervous Quotient

Called Sebastea by the Romans, Sivas seemed an unfriendly town to us, and it has mostly seemed that way to me ever since, though I admit I don't have much evidence to go on. It's ironic because Sivas has a large population of *Alevi* (Alawites), heterodox Muslims known for their more liberal attitudes toward traditional Islamic worship: men and women pray together, and music and dance, frowned upon in orthodox Islam, play a greater role in Alevi worship. Like most minorities the Alevi are widely misunderstood and therefore persecuted, which leads them to be secretive, which only increases the misunderstanding.

Maybe they suspect everyone of being out to get them. Judging by the famous incident in 1995 in which Sivas's Hotel Madımak was torched by a crowd of zealots, they might have a point. The hotel was full of Turkish writers here for a conference, among them a few who had spoken positively about Salman Rushdie's book *The Satanic Verses*.

Dux and I drove along Atatürk Caddesi, Sivas' main street, and couldn't help but notice the brand-new Hotel Köşk. This was an unexpected treat: three-star comforts such as a restaurant, elevator, reading lights, and hot showers here in the wilds of eastern Anatolia. We approached the reception desk and asked the young clerk how much a room might cost.

Normally Turks, and especially hotel reception clerks, are welcoming to a fault, smiling eagerly and honestly at the appearance of foreign visitors. They can't do enough for you. They demonstrate their eagerness to please by a burst of nervous energy directed, theoretically, at the satisfaction of your every desire. When you walk into a hotel, a posse of bellboys will race toward you and seize your luggage like bump-and-grab robbers. Desk clerks will dive into their room records and hold long, earnest discussions with one another on the suitability of this room over that one, and is any of them good enough for our Honored Guests? I have had housekeeping staff literally bow and scrape to me in an effort to be accommodating.

Note that I say "to be accommodating," because Turks are justifiably proud people. Atatürk taught them that they need not bow and scrape out of feelings of inferiority to foreigners, and then proved it by thumbing his nose at all the Great Powers of Europe, winning the War of Independence, chucking out the sultan, and establishing the Turkish Republic—and living to talk about it.

Rather, this bowing and scraping, this burst of nervous energy to satisfy your every desire, is an elaborate vestigial ritual from the Ottoman Empire, when in fact it mattered a lot. If the sultan or some other high official suddenly appeared, it was your job to figure out what was going on in his brain and do whatever was necessary to make the guy happy or, in a brief and mostly boring ceremony, your head might be parted permanently from your shoulders. At the least you might suffer the *falaka*, whereby the soles of your feet would be beaten to a bloody pulp with a willow switch.

These drastic measures were seldom necessary because everyone knew the drill:

1. Important Person (IP) sighted
2. Commence mind-reading
3. If IP's desires known, bustle about nervously performing whatever action is necessary to fulfill them. If desires unknown, exhibit nervousness as sign that you are aware of IP's power and status, and that you are eager to please: wring hands, bow and scrape, etc.

Mind-reading (Step 2) was the hard part.

Often, however, it was pretty clear what the IP might want, and when it was, the degree of haste with which you jumped to it was important. You were supposed to regard the IP's every whim as a life-or-death necessity, as indeed, in some cases, it was, the life and/or death being your own. To appear leisurely in your pursuit of the IP's gratification was to denigrate the IP's status, a big Ottoman no-no.

The power to disrupt other people's composure and poise wholesale was an important status symbol. The sultan could make everybody in the empire nervous, and in fact just about everybody all the way to Vienna and beyond, but below that in the Ottoman pecking order the situation was less clear cut. For example, if two pashas entered the room, you could usually tell who was the more powerful and important by the way the servants behaved. If more servants rushed to Pasha A and nervously helped him off with his cloak, then guided his well-padded posterior to the cloth-of-gold cushions on the divan, and fussed over him like a big-city gangster in a small-town whorehouse, then he was obviously more important than Pasha B. His status was higher. He won.

This is why it was good to have your own servants. The lighting of *çubuks* (those yard-long tobacco pipes you've seen in old engravings) could then be turned into a critical status battle: your eight servants could bang into one another in their haste to fill the bowl, attach the amber mouthpiece, position the pipe just right, light it, test the draw, and hand it to you. They should do all this fast, well, and in the highest possible state of nervous tension. Another man's servants might do it all in the same amount of time, but if they didn't suffer at least one concussion in their haste, they obviously didn't really think their boss was all that important, and you won.

The Ottoman Empire, with all its class divisions, is long gone, but the custom of nervous accommodation survives—except in the lobby of the Hotel Köşk in

Sivas in May of 1969. Our appearance made nobody nervous. The desk clerk didn't answer our question immediately because he was not entirely sure that we were in fact acceptable as guests at all. His answer to our question about the price of a room might well have to be "Too much for you, buddy."

This was, after all, not just a brand-new hotel but The Best Hotel in Sivas. Visiting governors and generals stayed here. Well, actually, the hotel was so new that almost nobody had stayed here yet but the young clerk felt certain that when the time came virtually every Important Person who passed through Sivas would stay here, and he was not at all certain that these two scruffy travel writers who pulled up in a mud-spattered Land Rover would pass muster. We refused to bow and scrape or otherwise to signal our acceptance of his status as Lord High Minion You Encounter First at The Best Hotel in Sivas, so he was left to wing it.

We indulged in a few minutes of verbal spar-and-parry, after which he reluctantly awarded us a status classification of Indeterminate and decided that as he had several—actually quite a number—of vacant rooms, we could have one for the night. His renting us a room was a foregone conclusion of course, but it was important to go through the status pantomime. He was learning the ropes.

We thanked him with a cold shoulder and went to our room which, to our surprise and dismay, was no great shakes. The water in the shower was cold because there were so few guests they hadn't turned on the furnace to heat it. We traipsed back down to the lobby and complained to the desk clerk, but after a lengthy and complicated discussion it somehow turned out that the cold water was our fault.

Desk clerks aside, Sivas lived up to its billing as one of the most important cities in the Seljuk Turkish Empire of Rum. It had the historic buildings to prove it. We walked to its magnificent old theological seminaries, the Bürüciye, the Şifaiye, and the Çifte Minare medreses, with towering minarets and elaborate green and blue tilework on their facades. The sprawling Ulu Cami (Great Mosque), dating from 1197, impressed us by its early Seljuk *gravitas*, but my favorite building was the bold, exuberant Gök Medrese, of which thusly-named buildings, it appeared, we were making a collection.

The Frogs of Divriği

After a one-star night in the nominally three-star Hotel Köşk, Dux and I arose to a day of heavy rain. We packed up, bid a welcome farewell to the desk clerk, and headed for the village of Divriği deep in a mountain valley southeast of Sivas.

We drove south to Kangal, near which there is a spa, the Balıklı Kaplıca ("Hot Spring with Fish") famous among psoriasis sufferers: you relax in pools of warm mineral water and little fish nibble all the scaly psoriasis skin off you.

You think I'm kidding, but I'm not.

As far as Kangal the road was of macadam, but shortly after turning east toward Divriği the macadam disappeared and the unpaved road deteriorated. The farther beyond Kangal we went, the worse the mud sucked at the tires. Finally Dux stopped, set the wheel hubs, and engaged the Land Rover's four-wheel-drive transmission. We drove carefully down into the valley, every now and then passing a vehicle mired to its axles and immobilized in the muck. When we reached Divriği we searched for the teahouse, had ourselves a few bracing glasses, then pushed on up the slope to the Ulu Cami (Great Mosque). A few minutes later the caretaker came slogging up the sodden mud track with the keys.

The portal of Divriği's Ulu Cami (Great Mosque, 1228) left me dumbstruck. It is so bombastic, so pretentious, so beautifully done, it exhibits perfectly the exuberant megalomania of Ahmet Şah and his wife Fatma Turan Melik, the Mengücek emirs of this godforsaken valley. They were not particularly powerful except in the realm of blow-your-mind portal decoration, but in that they were peerless.

As with most great Seljuk-style buildings, the doorway is the important element, the building itself just a big square afterthought. The mosque interior is quite plain, which is fine since after passing through the doorway you don't want to look at another decorative element for at least 24 hours.

If the portal of the Ulu Cami is beautifully bombastic, the design of the adjoining Şifaiye (or Darüşşifa, "House of Health," a hospital) is sublime. A lofty, harmonious hall built for care of the ill, it has a central pool with a spiral drain designed to lend the gentle music of running water to the room and soothe the suffering of the patients.

We wandered around in the drizzle for a half hour taking notes, then we returned to the portal of the Ulu Cami so Dux could take a photo of it. Conditions were miserable. I held an umbrella over him while he set up his Leica on a tripod and snapped a few black-and-whites.

Wet and chilled by this time, we drove down to the village teahouse again to slurp a few hot ones and chat with the locals. We were into our third round when a big Citroën with Paris plates rolled into the main square and its weird, complicated hydraulic suspension system eased its butt down into the frog-like Citroën Squat. The teahouse emptied, as it had for us, as everyone went out to partake of this new diversion. Nobody in Divriği spoke French, and we figured the French couple probably spoke no Turkish, so we walked over to translate.

The French couple weren't sure where they were. I assume they had come to see the Ulu Cami (they had a French guidebook), but they asked only about a road eastward to Erzincan, which was shown clearly on their road map. We asked the teahouse men about it. They said there was no road eastward despite the map's authoritative-looking yellow line. The way to get to Erzincan was to return to Sivas and take the highway from there.

We had come to trust the locals when it came to roads. They knew the good and the bad. The French couple weren't so sure.

"You could take the train," one man said in an attempt to be helpful. "It comes through here in the middle of the night. You could have your car put on the train. That'll take you to Erzincan." The French couple seemed intrigued by this suggestion, there being no other apparent solution to their dilemma beyond the most sensible one, that is, of going back the way they came. Putting their frogmobile into gear, they lumbered off in the direction of the station to explain to the stationmaster in elaborate pantomime that they wished him to levitate their weird *voiture* onto a midnight flatcar bound for Erzincan.

So far as I know, they never saw the sights in Divriği. They just made their way into this remote valley with difficulty and then made their way out in the most difficult way possible. I give them credit for being intrepid—there weren't very many Europeans tooling around Turkey in their own cars in 1968. In fact, there were damn few Europeans tooling around Turkey at all. But why they had come was as much a mystery to us as the non-existent road east from Divriği was a mystery to them.

We bade our Divriği teahouse friends goodbye and started back toward Kangal. The road was even worse having absorbed a few more hours' rain, and we had to drive carefully. Plowing through the muck in low gear we passed a man on a horse, rifle at the ready, both man and beast soaking wet. He cast us a fierce, angry, embittered look. He was obviously miserable, but not as miserable as his wife who was slogging along behind the horse on foot through the sucking mud.

Anyplace But

After the French couple's experience with maps in Divriği we should perhaps have been wary of local maps, but of course we weren't. The day, not to mention the light, was fading fast as we continued from Kangal south toward Gürün, where we would turn west for Kayseri where we expected to find a hot meal, a cold beer and a warm bed.

The road swooped down into a shallow valley and up the other side, then down into an identical valley and up the other side, then down and up again, down and up, over and over. It soon became apparent that the entire central section of our map was drawn wrong. The actual kilometer distances on the ground were far longer than those given on the map, and we were much farther from Kayseri than the map had led us to believe. We drove on through the rain in grumpy silence, passing only the occasional miserable fieldstone or mud-brick peasant hovel on the godforsaken steppe.

Silently, we cursed the cartographers. I would later learn how inexact a craft cartography is, and how much there is of fantasy about it.

Cartographers sit at desks, drafting boards and computers and draw minia-ture simulacra of the world. They don't go out into the world to get their evidence of what the world, and in our case its roads, actually looks like. That's far too much work. Instead they…uh, rely on the expertise of other cartographers! They procure what is called in the trade by the delicate name of "source material," that is, other maps drawn by other cartographers.

Fine! Nobody wants to reinvent the wheel. Every American lexicographer since Webster has cribbed from Webster's original dictionary, so why can't cartographers crib from the work of earlier cartographers? But if we follow the cartographic family tree back to the first "source material," what do we find? "Here be dragons" and the like, North and South America misshapen like failed omelettes or homemade pizza.

In the case of our map, I can't blame the cartographers for not wanting to traipse back and forth through this blasted countryside measuring off kilometers and getting all the turns and curves just right, but that *is* their job after all, and if they didn't want to do it right they should have told us so. Had they simply left this part of the map blank and written "Here be dragons" in it, at least we would have known that we didn't know. With luck, we might even have spot-ted a dragon.

Instead we found ourselves not in Kayseri but in the small town of Gürün at nightfall. It had grown up here because two roads and a river met at this point, and the cities of Malatya, Sivas and Kayseri were all more or less equally far away. I imagined that we were only the latest in a long line of forlorn wanderers who had ended up in Gürün at nightfall without the energy or daylight to go on to a city with real services for travelers.

Despite its location at a crossroads, Gürün had precious little to offer the traveler—and, from what I could see, not much more for the locals. To our surprise and delight we located a room above a store rentable for the night. It had twin beds, and there was a cold-water sink down the hall. We bought some bread and cheese and ate it, then took a stroll through the town drawing stares from all, and greetings from some. We were obviously the first foreigners that any Gürünlü had ever seen and, as foreigners also probably *gavurs* (infidels), if not outright communists.

That was it for Gürün. We collapsed into bed exhausted. Our plan was to get up at dawn, slurp some tea and hit the road.

The sky was still pitch dark when I awoke to noise, shouts and the bright yellow flash of flame pouring in through our window. I leapt out of bed, looked out and saw to my alarm that the building adjoining ours was burning dramatically. Smoke and flames poured from it. Men shouted and ran around chaotically in front of it.

The building housed a shop. The shop sold, among other things, steel tanks filled with propane gas. However the fire may have started, it had progressed to the point that it was heating up the tanks which were now exploding, sending blankets of flame out the doors and windows.

Dux's Land Rover was directly in front of the shop, getting a flame-bath with each explosion.

"Dux! Wake up! The building's on fire!" I shouted.

He slept.

I shouted again. No response. I shook him by the shoulder. No response. I beat him on the back. He was either stone dead or in a catatonic slumber.

It took physical abuse to wake him, but finally I did. There was no need for me to point to the problem. He leapt into his trousers, shot down the stairs, dashed for the land Rover and moved it to safety. I gathered up our stuff, fled the room and jammed it into the back of the car.

Although the entire town was awake, afoot and milling about, there was no organized attempt to put out the fire. The shop-owner had arrived and was distracted with grief. With his whole stock in trade going up in flames, his neighbors had to restrain him from charging into the flames in a futile attempt to save his livelihood. The river was right on the other side of the highway, but this town apparently had no history of bucket brigades, no firefighting plan or equipment of any kind.

As we stood watching the building burn, a young man shimmied up a utility pole near the burning building. What was he doing? Other men shouted for him to come down. Apparently he thought the fire had been caused by electricity, a nefarious innovation no doubt introduced into Gürün at great expense within the last ten years by hard-working government engineers. The guy looked as though he was going to try to disconnect the wires in a hideously ill-informed attempt to put out the fire. The men finally prevailed upon him to come down before he became a burnt offering to the very demon he sought to subdue.

He climbed down from the pole and approached us.

"*Toz olur!*" he shouted. "*Toz olur!*"

We didn't know what it meant so we didn't react, but it was clear to us that he blamed us for the fire. Others guys were giving us wary glances. He didn't seem like the kind of guy who would listen in calm absorption to an explanation of the *post hoc ergo propter hoc* logical fallacy, so we decided to bid a hasty farewell to picturesque Gürün and its midnight pyrotechnical gaiety.

Toz olur, we later discovered, means "Beat it!" which, at the moment, sounded like a capital idea. As we set off for Kayseri the dawn was just beginning to lighten the eastern sky behind us.

12
SELJUKS ON THE
SILK ROAD

As we drove west with the sun rising at our backs, we were following the ancient Silk Road, one of the earliest great "tourism" routes. Driven out of our doss-beds by a conflagration, we might as well go to work. Maybe we could get a lot done by getting an early start. Our immediate goal was thus no longer a hotel in Kayseri but rather the small village of Karadayı, where we expected to find the Karatay Han, a famous Seljuk caravanserai. Actually, our immediate goal—remember, it was 5:30 am and we had already been up for a while—was strong tea, two or three glasses each, but there was none in evidence, just rolling steppe-land, so we drove west past Pınarbaşı and turned south for Karadayı. Visions of rich camel caravans plodding along the well-worn track between Europe and China began to light up the main screen in our sleep-benumbed brains.

The Silk Road weaved its way through the Seljuk empire bringing luxury goods, scientific and cultural advances, and new military techniques. The Karatay Han is among the finest examples of the Seljuk caravanserai, or caravan way-station. It was my first caravanserai and is still my favorite. Although it was right on the Silk Road in the old days, eight hundred years later the highways had been routed elsewhere so we had to drive over an unpaved track for nearly half an hour to reach the building. It stood majestically in the middle of nowhere, a humble village clustered at its feet.

As soon as the Land Rover stopped in front of the caravanserai's portal a villager materialized beside the car, peering expectantly through the driver's window. We got out.

"*Hoş geldiniz!*"(Welcome!) said the one-man welcoming committee.

"*Hoş bulduk!*" (We are welcomed) we answered. "We've come to look at the caravanserai."

"Good, good," the man said. "But first, come have some tea."

In Turkey dreams come true, especially if they involve a glass of tea. He led the way to the village tea house. We entered the bare, simple low-roofed room in a mud brick building and saw that the tables were filled: all of the village's farmers were having a few hot ones before heading out into the fields.

As we entered, all eyes turned our way. Mouths gaped. We might as well have been Elvis in drag—and in duplicate. With a ferocious scraping of crude chair legs on rough board floor, the occupants instantly rearranged themselves so that a prime table near the stove was perfectly available. We sat. With all eyes on us, the drama of Dux and Tom in the Village Tea House commenced.

"So, where're ya from? Lebanon?" our host asked, looking at me.

Lebanon? I hardly looked Arab.

"I'm from America," I said. "What made you think I was from Lebanon?"

"Your jacket," he said, pointing to the red Little Merry Sunshine patch with evergreen on the breast pocket of my US Marine Corps jacket. He logically assumed, this being the Middle East, that the evergreen was a cedar of Lebanon.

"Are you a soldier?" he asked. The Marine Corps crest was on the other pocket. I suddenly realized some of the weird signals I had been communicating to everyone I approached during my travels.

"No. We're writing travel guidebooks about Turkey. For tourists." He accepted this with the equanimity of a Turkish countryman who has seen and heard many things, some of which simply do not add up no matter how you rearrange them.

"For tourists," our host repeated, musing. "Good, good. It'll be good to have tourists come to our village."

"Do many tourists come here now?" Dux asked.

"No. Nobody comes."

The conversation died. The village men stared at us like sailors at a peep show. Staring is not considered impolite in Turkey. Otherwise, they could not have been more considerate. We sipped our tea, which tasted great. When our glasses neared empty they were instantly whisked away and replaced with fresh ones. We knew that any offer of payment would be met with effusive rejections followed by affirmations of lifelong friendship.

"So…" Dux said into the deafening silence. "How're the crops?"

The silence was shattered by spirited disputes over the winter-wheat harvest and how it compared with previous years, the April rains and spring planting, elaborate grumbling about the government-controlled grain markets, the virtues of this or that fertilizer, Mehmet's new tractor. Dux had hit a vein.

With a lifetime supply of information on the agricultural situation of Central Anatolia and enough caffeine in our veins to power an interplanetary rocket, we took our leave and returned to the caravanserai. The caretaker appeared and unlocked the steel gates.

Food and Lodging 20 Km

Camel caravans carried valuable cargoes between China and Europe, bringing wealth to the countries through which they passed. The Seljuk nobility encouraged the rich trade by building these huge fortress-like caravanserais about every 20 km along the major trade routes. These were works of charity, and so the nobles, both men and women, provided each caravanserai with an endowment, the income from which provided free services for travelers. Caravaners could stay at any caravanserai for up to three nights free of charge, and receive food for the drovers, fodder for the animals, secure storage of goods and valuables, medical care and even a good Turkish bath, all courtesy of the founder, in this case Jelaleddin Karatay, grand vezir to Alaettin Keykubat, Seljuk Sultan of Rum.

When the workmen began cutting the stone for the Karatay Han in 1219, builders in England were just about to begin work on Salisbury Cathedral. The caravanserai, being a lot simpler project, was completed in 1236, the cathedral in 1258. The great cathedral at Rheims had been started only eight years before, but took a century to complete. During construction of the caravanserai, Constantinople was in the hands of the Crusaders; England's Magna Carta was issued for the third time, in definitive form; Guillaume de Lorris wrote *Le Roman de la Rose*; the Japanese potter Toshiro returned from China and introduced the making of pottery into his homeland; Holy Roman Emperor Frederick II led the Sixth Crusade to Egypt; Saint Francis of Assisi and Saint Anthony of Padua were canonized; Berlin was founded; coal was first mined at Newcastle; and the Mayan cities of Chichén-Itzá and Uxmal flourished in Yucatán.

This was not Salisbury Cathedral, a Gothic simulacrum of heaven on earth with enough fussy detail to amuse even the most jaded parishioner through even the longest litany and most boring sermon. The Karatay Han was a medieval truck stop. Form followed function.

I love Seljuk architecture because of the striking contrast between its simple, elemental geometric forms and its lavish decoration. The walls of the Karatay Han, and indeed of most Seljuk buildings, are severely plain, with precious few decorative elements. The main portal, in contrast, is a blow-out of geometric detail. This fits a caravanserai perfectly. Imagine having walked your 12 to 15 miles for the day, coming over a rise and seeing the rectangular bulk of the caravanserai on the next horizon. No need for fussy architectural detail in this long view. When you arrive, all the detail is in the doorway, which is a happy sight indeed because within it wait rest, comfort, safety, a hot bath, a good dinner, a mosque for sunset prayers, and—of all things the most important—steaming tea. (No coffee until the 15th century).

We mused on all this as we stood there in the Karatay Han's courtyard, then we wrote some notes, took some photos, thanked our hosts, climbed back into the Land Rover, and headed for the Sultan Han near Tuzla, 45 km northeast of Kayseri. Somewhat grander than the Karatay Han, the Sultan Han was built just after it, endowed by Sultan Alaettin Keykubat I (1220–1237), Karatay's boss.

From the Sultan Han we set off in search of the Haydar Bey Kiosk, reputedly the only extant example of Anatolian Seljuk domestic architecture. Sacred buildings such as temples, churches and mosques are often protected against the ravages of time because people tend to preserve sacred space no matter what their beliefs. Temples become churches and churches become mosques more often than they become ruins. Likewise, government and military buildings tend to be recycled over the centuries, but domestic architecture changes. Yesterday's lavish country house doesn't suit today's lifestyle and so becomes a livestock barn or—worse—a stone quarry to provide materials for an entirely different building. That there was a Seljuk nobleman's house still in existence was therefore a bit of amazing luck. We wanted to see it.

"It's supposed to be northeast of Kayseri," Dux said. Its location was described in one of the old guidebooks he used for reference, but the roads and the countryside had changed substantially since those books were researched, and the landmarks described in the guides were not easy to find. We drove around on back roads for an hour or so, found nothing, and decided to seek guidance from the tourist office in Kayseri.

Ushered Into the Presence

If our welcome in Sivas was reticent, in Kayseri it was aggressive and overtly promotional. The Kayserili (citizen of Kayseri) has a long-standing reputation as a sharp trader. The most popular local legend is of the boy who borrowed his father's donkey, painted it, and sold it back to him, which makes you think the boy must have gone on to become a supplier to the US government.

It's no wonder that Kayserilis should be traders. Twenty kilometers northeast of the city at Kültepe are the ruins of Kanesh-Karum, a 6000-year-old settlement that grew rich from its position at the nexus of natural trade routes (among them the Silk Road) joining east with west and north with south. Six thousand years of buying and selling is a lot of frequent flyer miles.

Due south of Kayseri looms Erciyes Dağı (Mount Aergius, 3000 feet), an extinct volcano with a snow-covered summit that's become something of a symbol for the city. We drove to the city center, which is around the *kale*, or castle. Near it are the great mosques and medreses, a famous Seljuk medical center, and the tourist office. We entered the office to ask for directions to the Haydar Bey Kiosk.

Tourist offices, especially in places like Kayseri that had zero tourists in 1969, were lonely places where nothing ever happened. The staff were happy enough to be there, reading the morning's newspapers, sipping endless glasses of tea, speculating on the fortunes of Kayseri Spor, the local soccer team, in the upcoming match, and arranging the stacks of colorful tourist brochures so that the edges were perfectly parallel. If the long-promised tsunami of tourists should sweep over them today, the staff members of the Kayseri tourist office were ready.

When we walked in, it was as though we had been beamed down by Scotty from the *Enterprise*. The entire staff jostled at the counter to help us and to answer our questions until one man collected his wits enough to suggest that the advent of actual tourists, and foreign ones at that, was a matter of import great enough to require the attention of the Director himself. There was instant and unanimous agreement and the crowd of clerks rushed around the counter, seized us by the elbows and rushed us into the Director's office. In his anarchic enthusiasm, one clerk bumped against the counter and knocked a pile of brochures seriously out of parallel.

The Director welcomed us incredulously, then enthusiastically. It dawned on him at once that our appearance could validate the importance of his position, not to mention his budget, and might even raise his status among the town worthies who ate and drank together nightly at the Hotel Turan. Tea was offered, accepted, brought, slurped. He excused himself for a moment, lifted the handset of his telephone, asked his secretary to place a call, then gently returned the handset to its cradle.

We chatted pleasantly about this and that. He asked about our work and we explained it, mentioning that our time in Kayseri was short and his prompt assistance would therefore be all the more appreciated because it would aid us in completing our research as quickly as possible. He received this intelligence with a placid, benignant smile, followed by a question: would we like another glass of tea? Of course we would! The order was given, the tea brought. We fidgeted and exchanged alarmed glances. Would this guy eat our day?

The telephone rang. The Director raised the handset, spoke, listened, spoke, and replaced it in its cradle.

"We will go to see the Vali now," he said. The Vali is the provincial governor, the biggest big shot in the province.

"Why are we visiting the Vali?" Dux asked.

"He would like to meet you," the Director replied.

"How does he know we're here?" Dux asked.

"I told him," the Director answered.

Dux was starting to get nervous. He saw his workday disappearing down a bureaucratic black hole. When Dux got nervous I got nervous because the downside of Dux's admirable energy and joie de vivre was a ferocious temper. If someone or something irritated him enough, he could go postal and become a raving maniac, his face contorted into a grotesque mask of threat and anger, his voice the clarion of doom blasting the irritator in any of four languages along with generous sloshes of spit. It was not pretty to watch but it was always utterly effective: the irritator would vanish, the police would arrive.

The Director rose from his chair and swept his arm grandly toward the door, signaling us to pass through. Then, thinking better of this rash gesture and the effect on office morale if mere tourists were given precedence, he passed through it first himself, leaving us to bring up the rear. The office clerks nervously rearranged themselves into different backfields during his passage through the outer office, just in case something should be expected of them.

The Director had left the building. Dux followed close behind. I brought up the rear, and as I pulled the door closed I saw a clerk carefully square the violated pile of brochures until it was perfectly parallel.

As we drove to the Vilayet (the provincial government headquarters), Dux quashed his irritation and tried to put a good face on what was turning out to be a blasted morning. "Maybe it's good to have the top man in the province know about us. If we run into trouble, perhaps we could call him."

With the Director grandly leading the way, we entered the Vilayet building, ascended the stairs and were shown into an outer office. We warmed our butts there for a few minutes, after which we were ushered into the gubernatorial presence.

The Vali's office was a huge room, the center of it empty, the periphery surrounded by chairs. It was the stage set for a *meclis*, or traditional assembly, in which all the provincial notables would attend on the Vali as his courtiers. The Vali sat at a large desk at the far end of the room. Behind him on the wall was a framed square of red velvet gathered and pleated every few inches. The purpose of the velvet was to frame the Vali as he sat at his desk and thus to act as a proper backdrop for his august person. Visitors would see him set against the velvet in the frame; visitors with cameras and permission to photograph would capture and immortalize him, framed in red velvet forever. The velvet frame behind the Big Guy's desk was a common item of Turkish office furniture at the time.

The great desk bore a thick cushioned leather blotter, a small Turkish flag, several expensive-looking pens, and the Vali's nameplate on a block of wood, helpfully provided for the totally clueless. Not one leaf of paper blotted the gleam on the desk's highly polished surface. The Vali's job was to sign off on papers, not to worry over them. If a paper needed signing, it was carried in by a lackey, skimmed for a second, placed on the cushy blotter, signed with a flourish, blotted with an old-fashioned roll-it-back-and-forth blotter, and returned to the hand of the lackey, who carried it away. There was no need for papers to clutter the gleaming real estate of the Vali's mighty desk.

The Vali rose from his chair and welcomed us with a warm smile and a formal handshake, after which he acknowledged the Director's presence with a brief glance. I instantly understood. The Director did not even rate a grasp of the gubernatorial hand. To the Director, then, we were the means by which he might jump six seats nearer to the Vali at the nightly drinks-and-dinner table of the ayan at the Hotel Turan. We were the blue-ribbon bantam, the prize bull, the hog with a pedigree.

The Vali waved us into the seats of honor on the supplicants' side of the desk and, following the gracious formalities of traditional Turkish hospitality, offered us cigarettes from a silver box. He then asked for our preference: tea, coffee, something else? Figuring that the Vali's coffee would be good, we went for that. A lackey, waiting anxiously, sped away to fill our order.

The initial pleasantries successfully accomplished, the Vali turned his regard to the Director and raised his eyebrows in serene inquiry as if to ask "So…what have we here?"

The Director explained. By the time he was done the Vali had been given to understand that we two scruffy, unshaven, unkempt foreigners, fresh from a night in blazing Gürün, were in fact lords of the entire mighty publishing apparatus of Western Europe and North America. We were here, like the angel Gabriel, to announce Kayseri's pre-eminence to the world, which would initiate a flood of touristic visitors such as Kayseri had not seen in its entire 6000-year history as a crossroads of commerce. Marco Polo and Ibn Battuta were scruffy hippie vagabonds compared to us, Indiana Jones a mere meddler. We were the Real Article.

While explaining this the Director addressed the Vali as *zat-i âliniz* ("your exalted personage"), a grandiloquent form of address that had supposedly died with the Ottoman Empire but to which the Director had resorted in frustration after finding no word in the egalitarian republican lexicon worthy of, well, the Vali's exalted personage. He was laying it on with a trowel.

The Vali, no doubt having discounted the Director's praise of us by about 95%, then turned his gubernatorial regard in our direction and asked in minimal but useful French what he could do to help us in our work.

Dux, being the senior member of the team, answered that we merely wanted to visit Kayseri's historic buildings. In other words, we wanted nothing special, the implication being that while we were honored to be allowed to besmirch the Vali's spotless agenda, the interview wasn't really our idea. The Vali looked back at the Director as if to say, "So what are we all doing here?"

The Director backed and filled, reiterating our gigantic importance in the realm of tourism media. The Vali got the picture. Maybe as a token—just to offset the stories of the publicity coup that the Director was sure to circulate—he would jump the Director up one chair closer to his dinner table throne, but that was it.

We finished our coffee. The Vali offered us his calling card, which was an unofficial *laissez-passer* throughout the province: we could show it to anyone and they'd know we knew the Top Dude, the nervousness quotient would immediately increase by orders of magnitude, and our wishes would instantly be fulfilled. We thanked the Vali and took our leave.

The quasi-papal audience over, it was now possible to extricate ourselves from the Director's death-grip before our work-day was entirely gone. He was as sorry to see us go as we were happy to escape.

Which One's the Volcano?

We walked around the major Seljuk monuments of the city center, of which there are many. They are built of dark volcanic stone which gives them all a sombre, heavy appearance despite the artistry used in their design and construction. When you compare a dark-stone Kayseri building with one from Cappadocia, the land of sunny sandstone just over the hill, it's like comparing a black helicopter gunship to a yellow hot-air balloon.

The comparison was not helped by the carpet touts, who are more famous even than Kayseri's Seljuk monuments. They hang around the great buildings waiting for the rare tourist to approach and gawk. Just as you're beginning to appreciate the marvelous architecture of a 700-year-old Seljuk mosque, a carpet tout will sidle up to you and in vaguely Brooklyn-accented English say "Hey! You like this mosque? It was built a long time ago. Wanna buy a carpet? Come see my shop." Road-kill carrion never attracted vultures more quickly or certainly than a tourist attracts Kayseri carpet touts.

It's not the first tout that bothers you, it's the fourth, fifth, sixth, and later. Or the one who won't let go, who dogs your steps all over the city, following you through hours of walking, reminding you every five or ten minutes that he's got a shop with really nice carpets, most tourists love them and buy one from him, and by the way he has now invested *an awful lot of time* in you, so you'd better come buy something quick or things might get nasty.

Dux and I stayed the night at the Hotel Turan, the best and nearly the only decent hotel in Kayseri at the time. The food in the rooftop restaurant was quite good, as it should be in the locus of the Vali's nightly court.

The next day we did find the Haydar Bey Kiosk, a small two-story stone house standing alone in the midst of a field. Its design was simple compared to the elaborate public buildings we were used to seeing from the Seljuks, the vast mosques, medreses, hospitals and caravanserais. Its very simplicity and human, domestic scale lent it charm.

When, many years later, I sought to revisit the kiosk on my own, I couldn't find it again. It seems simply to have vanished, like Brigadoon.

Going Underground

Leaving Kayseri we headed west over the mountains into the biblical region called Cappadocia. I recalled a conversation I had had at the Peace Corps office in Ankara the previous year.

"Have you heard about this 'underground city' near Nevsehir?" asked a Peace Corps staff officer. I was in Ankara at yet another Peace Corps conference.

"I think I've heard something" I answered, lying. I hadn't heard a thing, but it was my job to know all about the touristic sights in Turkey. The PC officer was not easily fooled so he went on to explain.

"Apparently there are hundreds of rooms dug in the ground. Early Christians excavated these places to hide from raiders," he said.

I put "underground city" on my list of places to visit and, in May of 1969, Dux and I did.

We rolled into the little farming town of Ürgüp on the 16th of May, dropped our stuff in a pension and went off to see the painted cave-churches.

The landscape, sometimes called moonscape, of Cappadocia was formed by Mount Erciyes, the volcano northwest of Kayseri. It erupted millennia ago and spread a thick blanket of volcanic ash over the land. The ash turned to a soft volcanic rock called tuff. Wind and water eroded the tuff leaving a surreal topography: sinuous folds of rock looking like the skirts of a satin gown; absurd cones and pinnacles of rock topped by flat boulders; vast cliffs striped with bands of tawny color from minerals in the tuff. Erosion by rain and wind filled the valleys with mineral-rich soil which, combined with Cappadocia's abundant summer sunshine, makes them perfect for orchards, vineyards and garden plots.

Enterprising humans discovered the valleys, probably in Hittite times if not earlier. They planted vegetables and vineyards, fermented some of the grape harvest into wine, knocked back a few earthen cupfuls of their first vintage and thereupon decided to stay. Besides the fertile soil they liked the cheap housing: it was easy to gouge comfy caves out of the soft tuff. When babies came along and more room was needed, they'd just get out the axe and carve out another room to serve as a nursery.

In the Christian era, these troglodytes (cave-dwellers) built churches the same way they built houses and stables: by a process of subtraction, taking away the tuff they didn't want and leaving a cave room that fit their needs. Some Cappadocia country bumpkin went off to the big city and saw that "real" Byzantine churches had barrel vaults and columns and other traditional architectural elements, so the Christians of Cappadocia made their churches look the same way: when they carved out their churches they gave them barrel vaults and columns, etc., even though you don't need those things to hold up the roof of a cave.

The Göreme Valley is filled with cave churches, many of them decorated with quite wonderful frescoes. It is now a UNESCO World Heritage Site but in 1969 it was little more than a rural curiosity guarded by a solitary caretaker/ticket-seller. We climbed and crawled around the churches as we wished, took photos, got lost, found our way out, and went on to the nearby Zelve valley which didn't even rate a ticket-seller. Then we asked about the Underground Cities.

"Derinkuyu and Kaymaklı, south of Nevşehir," the locals said. We drove there.

We arrived in Derinkuyu and asked at a tea house for the underground city. The men pointed the way to a doorway in a small hill. The doorway was sealed with an iron gate. The gate was locked.

By the time we got to the doorway, flashlights in hand, a caretaker had appeared. He had a flashlight as well. He led us down the stone passageway into the earth. The first thing we saw, not far into the passageway, was a huge Jesus's tomb-style stone wheel-door set in a groove. From the interior of the cave the ponderous wheel could easily be rolled across the passage to close it off, blocking intruders. Anatolia, the land bridge between Europe and Asia, has a long history of armies marching back and forth across it. Keeping out intruders was no doubt an important thing to be able to do if you lived here for very long.

Down and down we went, the guide pointing out rock-hewn cave-rooms to this side and that, above and below. Dux and the guide went ahead. I took a slightly different track. Soon I was lost. I could hear the guide chattering but couldn't figure out how to get to them. I felt as though I was in a huge sponge made of stone, with cavities all around me but no clear path out. Visions of labyrinths and minotaurs crowded my consciousness, and I cursed myself for not having unraveled string or scattered bread crumbs or whatnot as I went down. Finally, after a lot of hollering back and forth, I made my way back to the others, and was very glad to be able to see them again.

The guide continued the tour.

"This was the kitchen" he said. "You can tell because of the ceiling, blackened by smoke. This was a wine press. The grapes were stomped here and the juice flowed down the groove into this reservoir. Here's a press for olives, with the oil reservoir below. This flat rock with the little cup-like depressions was for grinding salt."

He pointed to a cavity in the wall of a room.

"This is an air shaft and a well," he said. "Put your head in there and look up. You'll see the sky."

I did, and I did. The vent was a surprisingly symmetrical rectangular shaft several feet on each side, carved from the soft tuff.

"Now look down" he said as he took out a half sheet of newspaper he'd brought along. He lit it with a match and let it drop down the shaft, which was as straight and well-made below as it was above. The flame roared down…down…

down, finally bottoming with a plop. From its light as it flew I saw toeholds dug into the sheer, straight sides of the well.

"The well is filled with rubble now," he said, to explain why there was no water. "It used to be deeper."

We went even deeper into the cave complex, sometimes hunching over to crouch through a low passage. At the bottom of the complex we entered a large barrel-vaulted room.

"This was the big church," the guide said. "There were others. And this isn't really the bottom. It goes deeper but we don't have the money yet to dig it out. Also, the archeologists say there's a tunnel connecting this underground city with the one at Kaymaklı, ten kilometers away."

This seemed an incredible claim, but at this point I wasn't going to put it past them. Apparently these labyrinths were first excavated in Hittite times, about three thousand years ago, and expanded during the first millennium AD when the Arab armies invaded Anatolia on their way to besiege Constantinople.

It was cool—about 55°F—and utterly quiet in the big church. I imagined it crowded with long unwashed residents pressed against one another, fervently praying for salvation as a foreign army beat at the stone wheel-door seven levels above.

Enough of that. We returned to the surface and headed for the Ihlara valley.

When we got there, Dux took out one of his old guidebooks to read about it. Ihlara is a dramatic gorge framed by vertical rock walls. Along the course of a stream which wanders through it are sixty small churches and hermits' cells dating from the 11th to 13th centuries, roughly the time of the Seljuk Sultanate of Rum.

Dux looked at a map in his old guidebook, and something didn't seem right. The map didn't seem to match the text. He couldn't figure out quite where he was supposed to start the walking tour described in the guidebook. Wherever he started, he was going to start alone because I was feeling under the weather from another bout of food poisoning. He walked away, down into the gorge.

When Dux came back a few hours later he was laughing.

"They've never been here," he said, waving the old guidebook.

"Who? Who's never been here?" I asked.

"The people who wrote this guide. Their text description starts at the south end of the gorge, but the churches are numbered from the north. They just cribbed everything, including the map, from some earlier guidebooks, and got it all wrong."

Who do they think they are, cartographers?

This was our first example of travel writing without traveling. We were such innocents! After our books were published we discovered how the system really works: a conscientious author spends a lot of time and money traveling to every single place described in his book, and after it's published a dozen epigoni rip it off, rephrase it and sell it as their own without ever having to go there. This is not illegal, unfortunately, and often it's only the original author who can even spot the crib, although the reader usually finds out by following the cribber's work and being led astray, as Dux was at Ihlara.

From Ihlara we set out westward for Konya, site of my recent stardom, and took a room at the Turist Oteli, where the bellboys remembered me but now couldn't care less. Two foreign guys sharing a hotel room? They knew all about that stuff you did with your buddies. It was girls who were the mystery.

The next day we reached Ankara, then back to İstanbul, where my standard of living was about to get a huge boost.

ɷ

13

PERILS OF THE
TURKISH BATH

I didn't actually pour the champagne down her cleavage. It was an accident, as you'll see. But there it was, the dark stain spreading outward across the sequin-clad white satin bodice of her evening gown. This was going to get sticky.

It was a soft early June evening in İstanbul, and the great gilded throne room of Dolmabahçe Palace was crowded with fat capitalists. Not just any fat capitalists: the most powerful fat capitalists in the world.

Not since the throne room was inaugurated on July 13, 1856, nearly 113 years before, had it seen such a powerful assemblage of potentates. On that occasion it hosted the Ottoman sultan, the Grand Vezir, a posse of pashas, the ambassadors of the European empires, and the generals, both Ottoman and European, recently victorious in the Crimean War against Tsarist Russia.

In 1969, the men standing in small groups chatting, drinks in hand, were the leaders of the world's richest and most powerful multinational holding companies. Many were foreign, some were Turkish. Their wives were dressed in expensive designer fashions.

Their host was the President of the Turkish Republic, successor to the sultan, who provided his distinguished guests with drinks and delicate hors d'oeuvres. The favored beverage in 1969 as in 1856 was champagne, served by waiters in white linen jackets gliding smoothly through the crowd with trays aloft.

Despite its vastness the throne room was crowded, the guests inattentive to the waiters' movements. Someone stepped back and bumped a waiter passing behind. Thrown off balance, the waiter crashed into me, lost control of his tray and a glass tottered, spilling a cascade of Moët et Chandon Brut La Française (NV) down the décolletage of an elegant lady's *poitrine*. Horrified at the accident but unwilling to shoulder the blame for a social disaster that was not his fault, the waiter regained his balance and rocketed off to refuge in the butler's pantry.

I pulled out a white cotton handkerchief from the pocket of my cheap, ill-fitting grey suit and offered it to the lady, who dabbed delicately and ineffectively at the spreading stain. With a furtive glance, an apologetic half-smile and a whisper of thanks, holding the now-sodden lump of cloth by the tail like a dead rat, she handed it back to me. Thus was the mess—or at least some of it—gallantly transferred from her décolletage to my pocket.

Even I realized that striking up a conversation with this attractive lady about bodice-drenching was probably not going to have a happy ending, so I drifted away in silence and pondered the strange succession of events—accidents?—that brought me to the throne room of the sultan's palace to drink champagne and dab décolletages with the world's richest capitalists.

Sure, I was supposed to be writing a travel guidebook, and I didn't seriously think that sipping free champagne in a gilded palace was what you'd call "research," but I figured a few glasses couldn't hurt and besides the price was right. Close-up cleavage was just a bonus.

What happened to the capitalists during the next few days was either tragic or hilarious depending on your point of view, but equally surprising, perhaps, was what I was doing in the palace in the first place.

Where Fat Capitalists Convene

"Ever heard of the ICC? The International Chamber of Commerce?"

I had not. I was sitting with Richard Brown in his office at the Palazzo Corpi (US consulate) in İstanbul. It was April of 1969. Richard had asked me to come see him after my morning Turkish lesson.

"It's a worldwide organization. Many of the world's biggest companies are members," he explained. "İstanbul is going to host their annual convention, and the organizers want our help. They need people to help the delegates, to interpret for them. We're going to be extra busy just handling what we do, so we thought we'd ask you to help with translation. I've talked to the Peace Corps office and they've agreed to lend you to us during the convention."

Sure, I thought, why not? At the time I never dreamed I'd end up sipping champagne in Dolmabahçe and then participating in what might best be described as a hilarious disaster involving a Turkish bath.

"Actually, I won't even be here," Richard continued. "I'll be on home leave starting a few weeks before the convention. I was wondering if you'd be interested in house-sitting for us while we're away."

Richard and his wife lived in a spacious modern apartment on Tavuk Uçmaz Sokak (Chickens-Don't-Fly Street) in Cihangir, the next district over from Ayazpaşa. The apartment had a spectacular Bosphorus view, 24-hour hot water, a refrigerator, and even a maid. My assent was a mere formality, and he knew it.

When I returned from my first trip with Dux in late May I settled in at Tavuk Uçmaz Sokak 12. My duties were light: water the plants and live there so that potential burglars wouldn't find it empty. Everything else was done by Hatice Hanım, the energetic grey-haired housecleaner who came daily to keep the apartment tidy and to straighten up the kitchen.

Of course, there was the inconvenience of having to find another neighborhood grocery shop, but luckily there was a good one right across the street. Because I was the Brown's "guest" the grocer conferred upon me the distinction of Honorary Old Customer. I dropped in each morning to buy my breakfast eggs and the half-dozen Turkish newspapers I read daily to improve my Turkish and to keep from doing the really hard work of writing a guidebook.

In late May the newspapers were full of pictures of rioting university students. On May 31st İstanbul University was closed because of the riots which were scripted, as usual, to the merry theme of Yankee Go Home. It was not a super-great time for fat imperialist-capitalists to be pouring into İstanbul, but what the hell. June arrived, and with it the ICC delegates.

The convention would be held in the brand-new Atatürk Cultural Centre in Taksim Square. Atatürk had been an opera lover, and no doubt the first plans for an İstanbul opera house had been drafted during the later years of his presidency. After 29 years of construction the building was still not done, but with the ICC convention coming it had to be, so it was rushed to completion.

İstanbul's Big Chance

For Turkey, and particularly for İstanbul, the convention was a priceless opportunity to introduce itself to the world. Because of its neutrality during World War II and its policy of economic and military self-sufficiency, Turkey was somewhat isolated in world affairs and needed a publicity coup to raise its profile. The ICC convention might just be it. The Olympic Games would've been better, but even the most ardent patriots wouldn't allow themselves to dream of that. The ICC convention, on the other hand, was just barely possible.

And it was indeed important. Delegates included people like Arthur K Watson, president of the ICC and chairman of IBM World Trade Corporation, a director of Pan American World Airways, and later American ambassador to France. Many other delegates were of a similar caliber. Many delegates were Americans because the ICC was based in New York and American companies included most of the world's largest and richest at that time, but in fact the list of delegates included important people from all over the world.

On June 2nd, the day before the convention began, I got a phone call from the consulate asking me to go out to the airport and meet a man named Mike Moynihan, a public relations expert working for Arthur K Watson. Moynihan had contacted the consulate and asked to be briefed on the current situation in

İstanbul. The consulate sent me to do the job, which showed either an ignorant confidence in my competence or an unwarranted disregard for Moynihan's importance. An official consulate car picked me up and took me out to the airport. I was delighted with this simple perk, like a novice screenwriter being offered a percentage of net.

I found Mike Moynihan, who had just arrived, drinking coffee in the terminal restaurant while he waited for his clients, Mr and Mrs Watson, to arrive on a later flight.

Mike, who turned out to be the brother of the Honorable Daniel Patrick Moynihan, US senator from New York, was looking for trouble spots, things that could embarrass the Watsons or make them look bad. I soon caught on that important people can't just trust to common courtesy or civility to keep their reputations intact. They need professional help. Even if they are utterly blameless in all things (and what famous person, with the possible exception of Mother Theresa, could be?), their enemies, adversaries, challengers and of course the ubiquitous press will all work hard to find flaws or screw-ups and trumpet them to the world. You don't have to be Princess Di to know that fame and fortune are double-edged swords.

Given the current tense climate in Turkish-American relations and the activities of anti-American leftist groups, Moynihan's job was like a square dance in a minefield. You've got to remember that the ideal of a socialist welfare state was still an appealing possibility to many people at that time despite the awful but mostly secret reality in socialist countries. The sins of capitalism were well known and repeatedly exposed by the free press in democratic capitalist countries. The outrages of self-proclaimed socialist saviors were barely suspected, and kept carefully under wraps.

Russia had a huge number of big rockets with scary nukes on the tips, they had beaten the US into orbit with Sputnik and Yuri Gagarin and so, the world thought, socialism must have something going for it. The fact that they could make a 50-megaton bomb but not a decent hamburger seems to have escaped everyone's notice.

Meanwhile, the world's mightiest superpower was making the rubble jump in a dirt-poor, already-flattened southeast Asian country, terrified that California would soon be invaded by skinny rice-eating peasants in lampshade hats.

About this time Orhan Tahsin, a columnist for the daily *Tercuman* newspaper, did an informal survey of Turkish graffiti. After WWII, he wrote, Turkish students scrawled ugly caricatures of the Russian bear on walls because of the Soviets' demands that Turkey give them the northeastern Turkish towns of Kars and Ardahan which could later serve as advance posts for a Russian invasion of Turkey. In the 1950s it was "Ass Makarios" who had taken control of Cyprus.

Now it was the "American dog," which Tahsin thinks a poor choice, a disservice to the noble dog. "The dog is a faithful animal which occasionally bites," Tahsin wrote. "He leaves the exploiting to his master." A better symbol of American power, Tahsin thinks, would be the elephant, galumphing through the savannah, too big and clumsy to realize how much damage it's doing.

In the days leading up to the ICC convention, most İstanbul newspapers were full of reports on the "big capitalists" arriving in İstanbul. Cartoons showed fat guys in top hats and three-piece suits huffing huge black cigars, palming sackfuls of dollars and being nasty to the working class. The city awaited the opening of the convention with a weird mixture of pride and embarrassment, elation and anxiety, amusement and apprehension.

I told all this to Moynihan. When I was out of words about politics, which didn't take long, we talked about horrible car accidents we had seen, a topic which, come to think of it, had a certain current-events interest in İstanbul.

A deafening announcement on the loudspeaker heralded the arrival of the Watsons' flight. He went off to meet them, and I faked a diplomatic mein as I rode back into the city in the consulate car.

Fat Capitalist Central

The headquarters hotel for the convention was the İstanbul Hilton, which at that time was the city's only luxury hotel of an international standard. It had been fully booked for the convention months ago. In fact it had been overbooked. Delegates who couldn't get rooms there—including quite a number who thought they had rooms but arrived to find their rooms already occupied—were lodged in the best other hotels available, which were mostly far from the center, up the Bosphorus in Tarabya, or in Yeşilköy out by the airport.

From meeting Moynihan at the airport I went to the Cultural Centre where an orientation session was being held for us consular factotums. There were lots of junior people from a dozen consulates and embassies, all appointed to translate and do other dog's-body work for the delegates. We were told to wait in a designated dog's-body kennel-room until we were needed.

We sat there and chatted for a few minutes. After the initial round of introductions the conversation died. Someone said "Screw this!" into the silence and we all got up and walked out to see what was going on.

One of the convention's chief organizers caught sight of me and called me over. She was standing with a dark-skinned delegate who apparently owned, or at least controlled, about half of India. His room at the Hilton had been double-booked, and he needed a place to stay.

"Tom is writing a travel guide to Turkey," the organizer said to the Indian magnate. "He knows all the hotels. He'll find find you a room."

I knew all the hotels alright, the ones that charged $4 to $6 a night. The Indian guy, I heard later, owned an international chain of five-star hotels. He was ready to pay the astounding rates charged at the Hilton—$25 or $30 a night!—only because there wasn't time for him to buy some other hotel and have it converted for his private use.

I took him to the Hotel Santral just out of Taksim Square, where I had stayed on my first visit to İstanbul a year before. It was clean, quiet and cheap, and even closer to the Cultural Centre than the Hilton.

The desk clerk led us upstairs to a vacant guest room, opened the door, and we looked in. The delegate's face collapsed: sombre dark green walls unrelieved by even a cheap calendar, and threadbare furnishings—bed, chair, table, lamp (with 15-watt light bulb)—that had been in poor taste even when new during the reign of Abdülhamid II.

He thanked me for my time and fled.

I saw him a few days later. He told me he had found a five-star room at the Hotel Çınar near the airport, 20 km away. I congratulated him and secretly totted up the cost in my head: *amour propre* and status preserved vs hours lost waiting in traffic. How did he get to be so rich anyway?

I was kept busy running small errands for the American delegates. Adolph A Berle, a famous name among President Franklin D Roosevelt's Brain Trust, asked me to take a sheaf of papers to Mr Watson in his suite. The head of a huge holding company asked me where he could get little cigars. What he had in mind, I knew, were creamy, fragrant Dutch Schimmelpennincks. Dux had introduced me to them, and I liked them myself. I described for him the only thing available in the Tekel shop in Taksim Square: rough little numbers called Marmara. Turkey grows some of the world's finest tobaccos, but it doesn't put them in cigars, big or little. Turks don't smoke cigars. A pipe is a European affectation. Turks smoke cigarettes, so that's where the good tobacco goes, at least what's left after the export buyers have placed their bids at the auction.

"Get me all of them," he said. "One of everything."

I ran to the Tekel shop in Taksim and bought Marmara cigarillos, fragrant oval-shaped Jockey Club cigarettes, Yeni Harman, Bafra, a pack of each. He began smoking his way through the entire Tekel *nicotiana tabacum* product line.

Inconvenient to Grand Central

I met the ICC's executive director and staff. They were New Yorkers, friendly, pleasant, blunt, highly competent, always in a hurry and, like all New Yorkers of that era, utterly convinced that anyplace outside New York was inferior and barbaric with the possible exceptions of Paris and Hollywood, but only on certain days.

On second thought, only Hollywood. Paris was off the list because Parisians pretended not to understand perfectly simple statements in plain Noo Yawk English. Not only that, it was impossible to figure out how to flush a Parisian toilet. Every single one had some odd unique flusher-gizmo found nowhere else. And the snooty Parisian waiters refused categorically to serve you your coffee with your dessert. No matter how many times you said you wanted it right now, when your dessert was sitting there warm in front of you, they insisted on serving the coffee afterwards. What's with these people?

To the New Yorkers, İstanbul was the Hilton and the Cultural Centre. The rest of İstanbul was Someplace You Drove Through.

On the ICC staff was a pleasant, attractive, tall brown-haired woman in her 20s named Julie. She was delighted to be away from her desk, out of her office and on the other side of the world in exotic İstanbul, even though İstanbul was coterminous with the Hilton.

Julie had a mannerism that was cute and alluring in New York but which caused a good deal of confusion and inconvenience in İstanbul. When asked a question she invariably smiled and arched her eyebrows for a few seconds before answering. In New York, a dashing young man might ask "How'd you like to take a drive in my Porsche out to the ol' beach house in the Hamptons?" Instead of blurting out "Zowie!" Julie would launch a Mona Lisa smile and arch her eyebrows ever so fetchingly, hinting perhaps that the young man might just be in for more good times than he could imagine. It was not a bad way to start a relationship—if you were a New Yorker.

In İstanbul Julie's fetching mannerism sent an entirely different message. Arched eyebrows means "no" in Turkish, so when a Hilton waiter approached her and asked if she'd like some tea, her arched eyebrows sent him away before she had time to say "Yes." She was having a damnably difficult time getting a cup of tea and had no idea why.

I explained it to her, which helped a bit, but it's difficult to stop a mannerism particularly when it's been carefully developed over a number of years to elicit appreciative smiles from eligible New York bachelors—or non-bachelors, for all I know. However, if she didn't want to die of thirst she was going to have to fix it because to my knowledge not one single waiter in the entire İstanbul Hilton was a New Yorker. It was the cute arched-eyebrow mannerism or the tortures of dehydration. She could take her pick.

On the morning of June 3rd the ICC convention was officially opened by the prime minister of the Turkish Republic in the main auditorium of the Atatürk Cultural Centre, and Turkey's dream came true. Here were the kings and princes of capitalist commerce enjoying lavish traditional Turkish hospitality in an up-to-the-minute facility.

The next day the convention began in earnest, with business meetings organized around topics of importance to the leaders of great companies, almost all of whom were men. Many of the delegates were accompanied by their wives, for whom sightseeing activities had been arranged: a tour of Topkapı Palace, Ayasofya and the Blue Mosque; a shopping trip to the Grand Bazaar; a visit to a traditional Turkish bath, etc. These people would all go home with a fine impression of the richness of Turkish cultural, artistic and commercial life.

After decades of relative obscurity, İstanbul and Turkey had finally walked confidently, chin up, onto the world stage.

Champagne at the Palace

"There's a reception tonight in someplace called...what is it? Doll-muh-base? Is it some palace?" Julie asked. It was June 4th, the second day of the convention.

"Dolmabahçe (DOHL-mah-bah-cheh)," I answered, "and yes, it's a palace, a big palace. A r-e-a-l-l-y b-i-g palace. It's that one down there." We were in the Hilton coffee shop. I pointed through the plate glass downhill toward the Bosphorus, where the massive marble bulk of Dolmabahçe hunkered on the shore.

"The president of Turkey's giving it. I've got a few spare invitations. Want one?"

Want one? Was the Bosphorus wet? Maybe one more cocktail reception meant little to a New Yorker, but to me the heavens had just opened and the angelic choirs had struck up a rousing gospel number complete with Grand Wurlitzer. Yesterday I had gotten emotionally exercised over a ride in a five-year-old consular Chevy, and this woman is asking me if I'd like to see the inside of the gigantic gilded throne room of Dolmabahçe Palace ablaze with lights and busy with liveried waiters passing out free food and booze.

She handed me an engraved invitation.

That evening I dressed in my best cheap factory-seconds suit and 1950s tie and walked from Richard's apartment to Dolmabahçe. I flashed my invitation to the guards and strolled serenely into the throne room, blazing with a thousand lights, grander and brighter than I had ever imagined on that chilly, rainswept night over a year before.

The brilliance of the great hall, the glitter of the tons of gold-leaf decoration, the chic beauty of the expensively-dressed guests—it was a dream. This was the Peace Corps? What would my friend Dan think?

The waiter spilled that glass of champagne, I proffered my handkerchief to the drenched damsel, and the rest you know.

The reception lasted an hour or so, after which the delegates went off to a delegates-only banquet at the Hilton. No Peace Corps scum need apply.

The Daily Newsprint

I walked uphill to Taksim. It was getting late and the next day's early editions of the İstanbul dailies were coming onto the newsstands. I bought my normal allotment. I read *Milliyet* every day, *Cumhuriyet* and *Hürriyet* sometimes, the expensive International Herald-Tribune when I was feeling flush, and usually *Le Journal d'Orient* for a laugh.

Le Journal was a funky relic from İstanbul's cosmopolitan past, a crudely printed single sheet, folded once. Written in French and printed on ancient noisy cold-type presses crammed into a greasy room on Jurnal (or Curnal) Sokak near Tünel Square, it carried the dolorous news of the city's rapidly dwindling 19th-century expatriate community. The large obituary section was the paper's healthiest and most avidly read feature among its ever-shrinking subscriber base.

My favorite part, however, was the small box at the bottom of the front-page center column. Here, limned with admirable brevity, was the daily *betise*, some signal outrage or horrid blasphemy of 19th-century European social convention designed to initiate a stimulating *frisson d'horreur* in the wizened, rapidly cooling hearts of the aged crones whose Franco-Ottoman world had long since disappeared and for whom such a frisson was, with the possible exception of a day-old *petit-four* cadged from the *patisserie* of the Park Oteli, the day's only thrill.

The editors seemed to delight in betises that purported to show the inferiority of vibrant, progressive modern Turkish society to the graceful, calcified ceremonial of the Ottoman era, and particularly in the ones that demonstrated the obvious superiority of Constantinopolitan sophistication over the rude manners of Anatolian country bumpkins. My favorite was the one about a *delikanlı* ("crazy blood," a teenager) in a remote Anatolian village who decided that electricity, which had just been brought into his village at great expense and with much fanfare, was the work of the devil and must be forced out. He shimmied up one of the new utility poles intent on cutting the wires, but when he touched them he was, in the unforgettable words of *Le Journal's* dedicated *rédacteur des betises, carbonisé instamment* (instantly burnt to a crisp).

Now that would have made our visit to Gürün worthwhile.

Fortified with my daily load of newsprint, and with the sultan's share of Dolmabahçe canapés and champagne sloshing merrily in my gut, I made my way slowly, with great self-satisfaction, to Richard's luxury apartment for a sound night's sleep.

Flash in the Bath

A few days into the convention I awoke to an unseasonably overcast sky and sprinkles of rain. I crossed the street to the grocer's to buy my breakfast eggs, glanced at the morning's fresh stock of newspapers on the marble counter, and instantly went into shock. I bought two copies of each paper, ran back to the apartment and called Mike Moynihan at the Hilton.

"Have you seen today's Turkish newspapers?" I asked guardedly.

"No," he answered cheerfully. "Why? What's up?"

"You'd better take a look," I said. "Every paper is filled with photos of delegates' wives naked in the hamam—that's the Turkish bath. Front page, back page, inside pages. Every paper. Some are more discreet than others, but every paper has them."

"Naked?" he blurted. "D'you mean naked? Buck naked? Nothing on at all?"

"Nothing on at all," I answered as gently as I could. "Mrs Watson is dressed. She's in an Ottoman outfit, holding an antique pitcher. She looks great. She was smart. But all the others are buck naked."

"Get up here right away," he said. "Bring the papers."

I raced to the Hilton and went to the delegates' lounge. It was pandemonium, with delegates shaking in impotent rage as they surveyed the wreckage of their wives' modesty.

"You can read Turkish, can't you?" one man growled at me. He was the CEO of an immense corporation. "Come with me," he said, dragging me onto the balcony and slamming the plate glass slider closed.

"What does it say here, under this picture of my wife?" he asked, barely suppressing his fury.

"It says she's doing the belly dance, sir."

"I can't believe this! I just can't believe this!"

Mike Moynihan arrived and asked me to follow him. We made our way to the Watsons' suite for a crisis meeting: Watson, Moynihan, a staff member from the ICC, and me. Mike asked me to tell the story as I knew it, which meant what I had read in the newspapers.

Yesterday the wives' touring program took them to a historic Turkish bath accompanied by several young local women as guides. The ladies entered the bath, undressed, and were relaxing in the steam when their guides took out small flash cameras and started shooting away. Several of the women asked them what they were doing. The guides said they were taking souvenir photos that would be for sale to the ladies later on. Many of the women—buck naked as the cameras flashed—weren't at all sure they liked this, but the guides reassured them. For most of the ladies this was their first visit to a Turkish bath. Maybe photos were part of the ritual. In Japan men and women take hot baths together naked, so who knows? In any case, it was inconceivable that the photos would be made public.

Mrs Watson, more savvy than the rest, was taking no chances. She ignored the bath, changed into a traditional Ottoman costume and posed for photos holding an antique pitcher.

The guides had obviously been paid big money by the newspapers for the negatives. My guess is that the newspapers provided the cameras, not to mention getaway cars, new identities, and 100-year leases on hideaway villas in Bulgaria.

"So what do we do?" asked Watson. He was upset that this public relations disaster had happened on his watch as ICC president.

No one had any brilliant ideas. The damage was done. Punishing the guides—assuming they could be tracked to their hideaways, which was unlikely—would change nothing.

Delegates' wives disappeared into their rooms and ordered meals from room service.

Turkey's press was not completely free, but what the newspapers had done was apparently not illegal. Besides, the government probably didn't want to be seen prosecuting its own citizens merely because they had embarrassed foreign fat cats who were despised by many people on the left of the political spectrum in any case.

İstanbul's radical leftists were ecstatic. We showed 'em! Even the non-leftist newspapers couldn't resist. *Cumhuriyet*, the self-important left-of-center "newspaper of record," found itself torn between its leftist impulses and its sense of gravitas and decorum. The left won, not to mention the profit motive. It printed only the more tasteful and less revealing photos, but print them it did.

Several ICC delegates who controlled international newspapers and newsmagazines threatened to run savage articles on "the press in the developing world," but this, they soon realized, would only guarantee that every single newspaper in the world would pick up the photos.

One wonders if it ever occurred to them that people like Jackie Kennedy were persecuted by their photographers virtually every day of their lives.

The convention's Turkish organizers were speechless with embarrassment. Turkey's glorious advent onto the world stage had been vaporized in the flash of a camera.

In his closing remarks on the last day of the convention, the head of the Turkish host committee did his best to put a good face on the disaster: Turkey was a democracy with a free press, he said, and although we might not always like what the press does—and in fact might hate it—the price must be paid in the name of democracy, and so forth.

The convention was over. The delegates and their wives boarded their flights, took their seats in first class, accepted the glasses of champagne proffered them, and flew away. Moynihan and a few intrepid ICC staffers boarded the *Orient Express* bound for Paris. Life returned to normal. I went back to writing.

A few months later, fire broke out in the Cultural Centre, heavily damaging the brand-new building. Rumor had it that the administrators had taken their time in signing the insurance documents, perhaps so that certain not-publicly-announced monetary considerations could be paid in cash in exchange for the award of the insurance contract. When the tragedy occurred, therefore, the building was uninsured.

Aladdin's Lamp Shop

Speaking of fire, I was about to discover an odd and wonderful purveyor of antique lamps. It happened during my research explorations of the Grand Bazaar.

No guidebook to Turkey contained a map of the huge labyrinthine market, said to hold 4000 shops. It would certainly be helpful for American visitors, most of whom were avid shoppers, to have a map. It might be a good selling point for the book as well. I went to the bazaar and walked around in search of maps. I finally found one in the phone-booth-sized office of the guy who kept tabs on rents and tenants.

"It's old," he said, "and not up to date, I'm afraid." It was a hand-drawn map. Photocopiers were not common then, especially not in the Grand Bazaar. How could I get a copy?

"I know a guy with a blueprint machine," he said. The guy copied the map as a blueprint for me.

I walked every street and alley of the bazaar, noting the changes. Here three small shops had been converted into one big one. There a street had been closed off and turned into one big shop. When my book was published, it bore the only up-to-date map of the bazaar commonly available. I think I may say with confidence that nearly all of the Grand Bazaar maps in guidebooks today are descended from my original work. Why doesn't that make me feel good?

I took notes on some of the best shops and prices in the bazaar. Tourists seemed mostly interested in the center of the market, the Old Bazaar, or Bedesten. It was in fact the oldest part, a square building with its own massive ironclad doors. It may well date from Byzantine times.

The entire sprawling bazaar complex, a warren of narrow streets that had once been open to the sky but progressively enclosed as the city and its bazaar grew, was sealed off each evening by doors at every possible entry point. Because the Old Bazaar had its own extra set of doors, it was the most secure part of the bazaar and perhaps because of that it was the preferred location for shops selling antiques and old jewelry. I looked at the grand old copper Russian samovars. In my caffeinist phase, a decorative yet usable tea-making machine had a lot of appeal. I had studied a lot of Russian history in college. Some of the samovars even bore the imperial crest of the Romanovs. I wanted one.

Rents in the Old Bazaar were high and so were prices, so I ranged farther, strolling the streets outside the bazaar. Çadırcılar Caddesi, running along the outer wall of the bazaar to the west, had a few old ironmongers' and junk shops.

Most of these carried only scrap iron—nails, spikes, keys, broken pots and small machines—but one, at No. 3, down at the far end of the street near İstanbul University, looked as though it might have some old copper vessels.

The grimy shop window was filled with old stuff: bowls, trays, pots, ewers, powder horns, coins, Ottoman police badges...and samovars. I peered in the door. The shop was the size of a large shower stall. Sitting on a low wooden three-legged stool was a portly troll-like man of middle age, prematurely grey. He was dressed in standard Turkish-male street clothes: a dark-colored suit and white shirt without tie.

"*Buyurun!*" he said, which is the all-purpose Turkish word for "Come in! Have some! Help yourself! Whatever!" (It's quite a useful word.)

There wasn't much space to enter into, what with the troll-shopkeeper and all the copper and brass, but I stepped inside. In front of the shopkeeper was a large tinned copper tray, and on the tray was food. It was lunchtime.

"Buyurun!" the shopkeeper said again, sweeping his arm over the food. "Have you had lunch yet?" he asked in Turkish. "Have some!"

"Thank you, I just had lunch," I said, which I had.

"Some tea then. At least you'll have some tea?"

"Tea. Yes, thank you."

The shopkeeper raised his head from his food, looked around and bellowed "*Çavuş!*" A boy appeared out of nowhere.

"Two teas," the shopkeeper said. "How do you like it? Strong? Weak?"

"Strong, please," I said.

"Strong! One strong, one normal!"

The boy vanished.

The shopkeeper applied himself to his food, apparently ignoring me as I inspected his wares.

"Whatcha lookim fob?" he asked in Turkish with his mouth full.

"Oh, nothing. Just looking." I had learned that to show enthusiasm for an item was to immediately drive up its price.

I picked up a few things, acted as though I was ever so mildly interested, and put them down again. I had never seen such a variety of old copper and brass things, all of them dusty and tarnished with age, but some in good condition. Fine pieces. He even had several heavy old bronze wick lamps, "Aladdin lamps." They were real and had been used by the Ottomans. Judging from the generously wide looping handles, they were probably carried from room to room in a large residence, a mansion or palace.

My nonchalance was part of the customary, elaborate shopping ritual and we both knew it, the shopkeeper and I, but we also knew that we had no choice. We had to go through the ritual to work up to a fair price.

"How 'bout those samovars," I said finally.

Two boys appeared in the shop. The first cleared the tinned tray of lunch leavings, the other set down two glasses of tea, one dark.

The shopkeeper handed me my tea, picked up his own, tipped up the tray, rolled it away, and gestured for me to sit on the other three-legged stool which had been holding up his luncheon table. I did, ending up about eight inches off the floor. That was okay. There was precious little headroom in any case because the ceiling was hung with pots, kettles, pitchers, ewers, buckets and lamps, all of copper or brass. The probability of head injury was up there with the odds for a devaluation of the lira.

"Çavuş!" the shopkeeper said, barely raising his voice. The boy appeared out of nowhere. The shopkeeper indicated a samovar. The boy took it down carefully from its shelf, brought it over and set it on the floor between us. I looked it over. The boy brought another, and another. I liked what I saw.

"What about price?" I asked.

The shopkeeper ignored me, directing the boy to run to a neighboring shop and bring another samovar.

"What do you like?" the shopkeeper asked. "Old? New? The best ones are complete and have handles with hinges."

"What about this one?" I asked, pointing to a medium-sized one bearing the Russian imperial crest.

"Ah, that came from Russia. We get those over the border. They need the money in Russia."

"So what's it cost?" I asked.

"Çavuş!"

The boy appeared.

"More tea?" the shopkeeper asked.

"Yes, please."

"Another dark one and a normal" the shopkeeper commanded. The boy disappeared.

"What do you want a samovar for?" the shopkeeper asked.

"To make tea," I said.

"Three hundred liras" (US$25).

It seemed like a pretty good price. I said nothing. I examined the samovar more closely. I looked at the others, which I didn't care about in the least.

"For you, two seventy-five."

We sat in silence. The tea came. We sipped.

"Why isn't your shop in the bazaar?"

"I like it here. It's too expensive in the bazaar. Too many people want shops in the bazaar, so the rents are too high. Besides, I get sun here." The afternoon sun was pouring through the dirty shop window, but only illuminated the front of the shop. The back, though not far away, was so packed with stuff that light would never penetrate, and would probably suffer some weird refraction if it ever did.

"Two hundred fifty," I said.

"I like being an antique dealer," he said.

The boy came into the shop and mumbled a few words to the shopkeeper, who mumbled back. The shopkeeper rummaged in the pocket of his trousers, extracted a slip of paper, handed it to the boy and the boy vanished.

I got up and stepped toward the door.

"Two fifty," the shopkeeper said.

"Good," I answered. I took out my wallet and counted out the lira notes.

He accepted them without counting and put them in the drawer of a tiny old wooden chest to one side.

"*Bereket versin.* May Allah give you bounty. Çavuş!" The boy appeared. "Wrap this in paper and string. Make a handle so it's easy to carry."

"Alaettin Yanık," the shopkeeper said, offering his hand. We shook, then he stood, walked to the door of the shop and pointed to the standard small red shop sign with white lettering hanging above the door. It read "Abdullahoğlu [Son of Abdullah]. Alaettin Yanık."

Alaettin. Turkish for Aladdin. The troll with the lamps and samovars was Aladdin.

ΩΩ

14

HOTTER THAN NORMAL

If May was the perfect time to tour central Anatolia, July 1969 was the perfect time to stay away from the torrid southeast down near the Syrian border, but Dux and I didn't have the luxury of waiting for cooler weather. It was my first lesson in the perils of guidebook deadlines and printing schedules: because of plans beyond your control, sometimes you had to research destinations at exactly the wrong time, like Montréal in February or Egypt in September or Adana in July, all of which I ended up doing.

I Don't Know How the Locals Stand It

Imagine a gigantic Turkish bath with an ambient temperature of 100 degrees Fahrenheit (40° C) and humidity near 100%. Imagine every molecule of air being so hot and charged with moisture that only some measly law of physics keeps it from exploding into steam.

Now imagine a six-lane Formula 1 speedway running through the center of this Turkish bath, right across the slick marble floor, plowing through the *göbektaşı*, the central raised platform where you lie to receive your massage. Along the speedway roars an endless Indie 500 of turbocharged Mercedes sedans, giant Japanese Neoplan buses, dinosaur-sized diesel trucks spewing black exhaust, and the occasional suicidal motorcyclist. This stuff rockets through the Turkish bath 24 hours a day.

Imagine yourself standing in bewildered, acute heat discomfort in this diesel-fume-filled Turkish bath with the six-lane speedway running through it and you will know what it's like to stand on a street corner in the southeastern Turkish city of Adana on any summer afternoon.

This must be what it's like to be in Mississippi in August, which is interesting because both Mississippi and Adana have perfect climates for growing cotton, undoubtedly one of God's gifts to humankind. If today cotton is taken for granted and looked upon as the cheap and common cloth, I suppose we have in part the Adanalıs (citizens of Adana) to thank for it.

Before the American revolution, cotton was in fact the world's most expensive thread, more than twice as expensive as silk, because it took so much work to grow, clean and spin it. You had to pick out all those annoying little cottonseeds, and then when you spun it the fibers were weak. People did it, of course, because cotton cloth was valuable, and it was valuable because it was cool and clean. Wool, no matter how much 18th-century laundresses washed it, always seemed to retain some animal grease, but cotton came clean.

Then in 1767 James Hargreaves patented the spinning jenny, which could spin cotton thread strong enough to use as the weft (the cross-wise threads) in cloth. Two years later Richard Arkwright patented his waterframe, which produced a thread strong enough for the warp. When James Watt refined his steam engine in the 1780s and '90s, cotton thread could be spun and woven efficiently by machine rather than by hand, and the price began to drop like a dot.com stock. When, in 1794, Eli Whitney patented the cotton gin to comb the little seeds out automatically, the cotton boom really took off. Britain spun 79 million pounds of raw cotton into thread in 1810. By 1860 the figure was over a billion pounds. Millions of people benefited from having cheap, clean, cool cotton for clothes, bed sheets, mattress ticking, handkerchiefs, Turkish towels and bandages.

In the 1700s cotton came largely from Egypt, and in the 1800s from the American south. In the 1900s cotton was king in Adana. So at least the humid heat is good for something.

Not, however, for travel writing. Pounding the searing pavement for hours to inspect hotels and restaurants, to review the museums and peek into the few historic mosques, to check the bus station and the train station, is how otherwise indifferent travel writers come to hate Adana.

In the evening, when the sun goes down and the heat (but not the humidity) abates ever so slightly, what do Adanalıs do? They go to restaurants and eat Adana kebap, ground mutton laced with flaming hot pepper. They don't have to pine for the noonday sun at all. They can swallow it and feel it cauterize their esophagi, and during the next two days it does the same thing to the rest of their digestive tract all the way to the end.

Hot as it is, Adana is not the hottest place I've been in Turkey. That would be Harran, which I'll get to in a minute. First we must go nuts in Gaziantep.

Nut of Choice

Happy to haul out of Adana, we got back into Dux's Land Rover and continued eastward to Gaziantep, a small city built, as so many Anatolian towns are, around an astoundingly old citadel on a hill.

Gaziantep is famous for its pistachios (*Şam fıstığı* they're called in Turkish, "Damascus peanuts"). We ate some. They were good.

Baklava is made with pistachios or walnuts, depending upon your local nut supply. Walnuts are more common west of the Bosphorus, but in southeastern Turkey the Nut of Choice is the pistachio.

Besides growing pistachios early and often, the Gazianteplis specialize in baklava made with pistachios. It's quite wonderful. We ate some of that, drank some tea, checked out the citadel, the museum, and a few other spots and would have blown this burg, having enjoyed virtually all of Gaziantep's limited tick-list of touristic pleasures, except that it was nightfall. We found a hotel, dropped our bags, and went out to find dinner.

As always, the best restaurant in town is the one where the governor, the mayor, the police chief and the major pistachio nut growers go to dine and drink each evening. This proved to be a spacious, light second-story dining room in the town center decorated in a style that looked to me like Second Empire French Whorehouse. The frilly gauze curtains, repro Queen Anne chairs and mod-odd chandeliers were a striking departure from the normal spartan Turkish masculine eatery ambience, which says in effect "We are the décor. We don't need stuff on the walls and we don't care if the fluorescent tubes turn us green. Better the lights do it than the food."

Could it be worse? Yes! There was a tremulous electric organ, complete with leisure-suited organist who cranked the tremolo to warp speed and played without break for hours, making us long for the artistic elegance of Muzak, silence obviously being out of the question. The food was excellent, however, as it usually is in Turkey, and the drink cheap and plentiful. Did we enjoy our evening? Yes. Were we ready to return? No, at least not until after the organist is assassinated.

During the decades-long war between the Turkish armed forces and Abdullah Öcalan's PKK Kurdish terrorists, Turkey's southeast provinces emptied out as people fled the fighting or were pushed out by one side or the other. Many—and certainly those with any capital—fled to the first town that was safely away from the fighting. That happened to be Gaziantep. With lots of people and money flowing in, Antep grew like a nut in full sun.

Today Gaziantep is the financial center of the southeast. Tall office buildings punch the sky in the city center, and hundreds of high-rise apartment blocks throng the outskirts to house its surging population. The marvelous mosaics salvaged from Zeugma, the ancient city now sunk at the bottom of a huge man-made lake to the north, draw visitors from around the world. It's pleasant enough (if you like dry heat), a great place to grow if you're a pistachio, and Turkey's best city for trading nuts, eating baklava, or listening to organ music with microwave tremolo, if that's what you're into.

The Hotseat of Nimrod

We drove east, blasting down the rough macadam which now covers the ancient Silk Road as fast as possible in order to maximize air flow through the Land Rover. Dux's was not one of those LRs with the clever false roof above to repel the sun and allow air to cruise through below, thereby keeping the real roof cool. No, this was your basic British version unadapted for extremes of climate, which meant that it was exquisitely attuned to the ambient temperature. If it was freezing outside then your flesh stuck to the metal, and if it was roasting outside you ended up *à point*. In fact, it's possible to imagine the Land Rover on the Şanlıurfa road as a rolling oven with the speedometer being a sort of crude inverse thermostat: the higher the mph, the cooler we felt.

Be that as it may, we still met, and even surpassed, the fussy EU requirements for certification as beef jerky when we finally turned off the Silk Road into Şanlıurfa (called Edessa in Crusader times) and made our way to the shady pool at the foot of the Throne of Nimrod, the craggy limestone butte at the city's historic center. It's easy to understand why the ancients came to consider the spring and pool, called Ayn-i Zeliha, to be sacred. In the midst of this dry, blazing country, the tinkling water, cooled by the shade of huge old eucalyptus trees, is a vision of heaven. The legends of the patriarch Abraham's birth in a nearby cave just add to the fun.

We sat in the shade, drank a half dozen small bottles of mineral water and a similar number of teas, then braced ourselves for the ascent to the citadel, King Nimrod's "throne." The view from the top was, as usual, worth the climb. We took some notes and went back down to discover our bodily moisture-content meters on empty again, so we sat back down in the tea house by Ayn-i Zeliha and had ourselves a couple dozen more drinks.

Urfa, as it's often called, has now sprawled far, far beyond the boundaries it had during our visit in 1969 when it was a small Turco-Kurdo-Arab city of 100,000 souls. Ayn-i Zeliha has been furiously developed into Dergâh ("prayer-place"), a pilgrimage center for Muslims coming to visit Abraham's birth-cave and lesser religious sites nearby.

We took a room at a small, hot hotel in the commercial center. The next day, in the cool of morning, we headed south to Harran.

Biblical Beehives

Harran you won't believe. On the baking pancake-flat Syrian plain you come upon a large cluster of huge mud beehives, or anthills, or dung mounds, but they're too perfect to have been made by insects or animals, and there's laundry hanging beside one and a TV antenna jutting from another so you assume that unless the presence of the antenna is a wry comment on the quality of the Syrian TV programming it was intended to receive, it's not a dunghill. Could it be a house?

It could be and is, as are all the others. Harran's houses look ancient, like something out of the Old Testament, which in fact they are.

"And Terah took Abram his son..." it says in the Book of Genesis, "...and they went forth with them from Ur of the Chaldees...and they came unto Harran, and dwelt there."

That was in 1900 BC, long before my guidebook was published, so no one can accuse me of spoiling Harran by luring tourists. Abe was not one of my readers, he found it on his own. His book, as you well know, is the best-seller of all time without ever having needed a boost from Amazon.com, so don't blame me.

Dux and I found it on a pleasant July morning. It was pleasant because it was still early, before the heat of the day. We were, or rather Dux was, looking for the ruins of the Fatimid citadel on the mound next to the beehive houses. The mound is probably a tumulus composed of the detritus of a dozen civilizations which now lies waiting for the archeologists, but most of what's on the surface is from around a thousand years ago, which is to say almost brand-new by Anatolian standards. The ruins of Harran's Umayyad Great Mosque on the tumulus are perhaps a century or two older.

We crawled around the ruins for an hour fending off curious kids ritually importuning us for candy, pens, cigarettes and coins, but they were good kids, mostly just curious, and we apparently provided a decent return to them on their investment of time and eye-wear merely by being weird foreigners who exhibited a remarkable ability to walk upright unaided. When we returned to the Land Rover we gave them our empty water bottles and they beamed and thanked us as though the bottles had been filled with Veuve Cliquot Ponsardin (Gold Label). Harran, for all its curiosity value, was miserably poor, which made it all the more remarkable that all of the people we met seemed happy. Lesson?

We wandered about among the beehive houses in the village, which is to say we led a cortège of maybe three dozen curious kids, teens, dogs and at least one goat until an adult noticed us and graciously invited us into his mud-domed home. It was simple to the point of primitive (think "Biblical standard of living"), but tidy, homey and surprisingly cool. We were treated to tea, we took some photos and promised to send our host copies (which we did), thanked our host and the other villagers for their warm hospitality, and returned to the Land Rover which was now surrounded by kids peering through the windows. Having identified the precise sort of wealth which we had brought in from the outside world, they were raking the car seats and floor with laser-like gaze in the hope of sighting another free empty water bottle.

I've returned to Harran numerous times over the years, and the experience is pretty much the same each time although the kids grow less curious and importunate with each visit, as Harran is now more frequently visited by weird foreigners capable of unassisted bipedal locomotion. And what the kids ask for is more likely to be Britney Spears' latest CD or, even better, a full-size color photo or inflatable doll.

While researching the second edition of my Lonely Planet guide in 1986, I made my third visit to Harran. I saw three girls in colorful traditional dress glancing at me, the unusual foreigner taking photographs of their strikingly photogenic beehive houses. I looked their way, smiled, said *Merhaba!* and asked if I could take their picture.

"*Evet!*" (yes) they answered, and they lit up with smiles as though I had just offered them a one-month all-expense-paid luxury trip to Paris, wherever that might be. I squeezed off a few frames.

The oldest girl, probably in her late teens, looked very Turkish or Kurdish with her jet black hair, prominent black eyebrows and high cheekbones. She was wearing a bright orange dress with multicolored floral patterns over blue-and-white polka dot *şalvar* (Turkish bloomers). She had on a plain white headscarf, a sleeved overwrap with shiny rick-rack trim, and an army-type canvas belt with one of those brass buckles where you slide the little rod sideways to cinch it. (I had a belt like that when I was a Cub Scout.) She had her left arm through the handle of a big woven split-reed basket.

The second girl had on a long blue dress, white headscarf, sleeved overwrap, a thick men's leather belt riding low on her hips, and a large blue plastic basin in her left hand. Her hair was lighter, her features more Caucasian, and her smile even more brilliant than her friend's.

The third girl, in a green dress with a pinky-red headscarf, was much younger, with blonde-tipped curls and a tiny infant in her arms. Even the infant was colorfully dressed in blue-and-yellow baby top and head covering.

They all had perfect teeth.

All together they were a concerto of colors and smiles too good to pass up. Their considerable delight at being photographed, at having this extraordinary little moment of unexpected and exotic pleasure interpellated into an otherwise routine, familiar day, came through in their simply brilliant smiles. The photo even caught the gleam in the second girl's eyes.

Catching that moment and their pure innocent joy and pleasure is what photography is all about. I loved them and I still love that picture.

I submitted the photo along with hundreds of others when I sent in my manuscript in mid-1987, and the photo editor chose it for the book's front cover. I thought it an excellent choice: eye-catching, colorful, exotic, it offered the allure of mystery and the ease of friendly welcome all at once.

When the book appeared early in 1988, the cover photo caused a furor.

Diplomatic Disapproval

Cut to the Turkish Embassy in Washington DC, a sumptuous mansion finished in 1914 for Edward H Everett of Cleveland, inventor of the crimped metal bottlecap with cork insert and owner of the fortune derived therefrom. Everett must have been fascinated by "oriental" (that is, Middle Eastern) culture because several rooms are decorated *alla Turca*, which makes the mansion a happily appropriate choice for a Turkish diplomatic mission, which it became in 1932 a few years after Everett's death.

Pass through the metal detector, show your photo ID, get frisked by the security guards, approach the grand staircase but instead of climbing it turn to the right and knock on the big, dark solid wood door before you. An electronic latch buzzes and you enter the huge wood-paneled chamber decorated in classical style which was, in 1988, the office of His Excellency Dr Şükrü Elekdağ, Ambassador of the Turkish Republic to the United States of America.

As you enter, Dr Elekdağ, a tall, handsome man with jet black hair and craggy features, rises from his desk and, when he has confirmed visually the identity of his visitor, comes out from behind it to greet you. I feel pretty sure that there is a loaded pistol ready to hand in the desk, and that the desk itself may be bullet- and bomb-proof, which is why Dr Elekdağ stays near it until he knows for sure who you are. (He has already been alerted by security about your visit, which is by appointment in any case.)

On the landing halfway up the grand staircase is a memorial plaque to several dozen Turkish diplomats, their spouses, children, staff and clueless bystanders assassinated by Armenian terrorists during the 1970s and '80s. Dr Elekdağ is merely taking prudent precautions for someone in his position at this time.

For a number of years during the 1980s I worked as a consultant in public relations for Dr Elekdağ. On most visits to his office, we discussed ways to educate Americans about the Turkish Republic, its history, culture and people, like informing them that the sultan was long gone and Turks weren't Arabs. Most Americans hadn't had a data refresh in nearly a century.

This visit, however, was different. Dr Elekdağ wanted to discuss the cover photo on my recently published Lonely Planet guide. He was, as always, reserved, polite and formal, but obviously displeased with the choice. Probably 'furious' would be a more accurate way to phrase it, but he was far too well-mannered, gentlemanly and, well, *diplomatic* to expose me to unvarnished wrath.

"These village girls do not project an accurate picture of our country," is all he said.

He was not the only one to think this way. Bookshop owners in İstanbul were refusing to stock or sell the book because of what they called "those gypsies" on the cover. My Turkish friends were all, 100%, upset at the choice. Turkey had struggled so mightily over more than half a century to modernize, secularize and democratize. It was on its way to becoming the economic powerhouse of the eastern Mediterranean, and now the best-selling guidebook to the country comes out bearing a photo of country bumpkins. The picture, they thought, sent exactly the wrong message: Turkey is poor and backward.

I understood why they disapproved, but suggested they look at it as a tourist might: unfamiliar with Turkey, the prospective visitor would see color, tradition, innocence, happiness, and a transparently heartfelt welcome. The photo was perfectly suited for its task of enticing people to buy the book and to visit Turkey. Besides, visitors would see the 'real' Turkey once they arrived, and would realize that the Harran girls were only one small aspect of it.

That's how Lonely Planet and I learned why most guidebook covers are relatively boring photos of famous and easily identifiable buildings: these types of photos can't blow up on you.

For later editions I and other LP authors were shown the cover photo choice and asked to comment on it. For the cover of the fourth edition, the photo editors had chosen a close-up of a section of colorful Turkish carpet. I thought it an excellent choice, and told them so.

"Can it blow up on us in any way?" they asked. "Could this carpet design be some traditional pattern, say a Kurdish or Armenian or Iranian or Chechen one, which could somehow have political overtones? Do the motifs have secret meanings?"

No, it was fine. Everyone thought it was great. It delighted a lot of travelers and sold a lot of books.

Even so, the photo of the girls in Harran is still one of my fondest visions of the friendliness one encounters so easily and so often in Turkey.

Hotter Than Normal

One of my subsequent visits to Harran was, like my first one, in high summer—that is, in high heat. (It took me a surprisingly long time to catch on and schedule my visits to blazing southeastern Turkey in the winter months when temperatures are nearly perfect.) As I was driving north from Harran back to my hotel in Şanlıurfa, I picked up a hitchhiker, a Turkish man in late middle age. He was dressed in a suit, white shirt and brimmed cap like most male Turks, no matter what their occupation.

"I'm a long-distance truck driver," he said. "I don't have a rig of my own. I drive other people's. I'm going to Şanlıurfa to renew my license."

We were speeding between fields of tall tawny grain, whipping up a breeze.

"I'm surprised the crops don't wilt in this heat," I said.

"The crops? They love the heat," he answered. "Can't get enough of it. The hotter it is, the bigger the harvest."

"I read in the paper that this year is hotter than normal."

"Brother," he said with an ironic smirk, "in this part of the country it's always hotter than normal."

Not too far south of Urfa I noticed a small hill off to the east. It rose alone from the otherwise pancake-flat plain. Later, at a conference in Washington, I attended a lecture by an American archeologist who had also driven this road and noticed the hill. To her it was obviously a tumulus. She hiked over to it and found a bulldozer gouging an irrigation ditch right through it. She asked the bulldozer to stop and within ten minutes had located several artifacts three thousand years old. She sped off to Urfa, alerted the museum, and the bulldozer was soon replaced by a swarm of archeologists digging with teaspoons and toothbrushes. The American archeologist herself was handing out the tools.

This is typical of Turkey: cruise around for awhile and you find some ancient layer of civilization, or a Biblical village like Harran.

Harran now has a *Kültür Evi* (Culture House), a model beehive house that visitors can enter and examine upon payment of an admission fee. When Dux and I first visited it, foreign visitors were a rarity and local folk were happy to invite you in for free. Harran must get thousands of visitors each year now, and having them tramp through your living room would get old real fast, so I guess the Culture House is a good thing despite the inevitable whiff of Disneyfication.

In any case, do your best to visit Harran as soon as possible. So far as I know no one has yet opened Patriarch Abraham's Original Beehive Mud House and Chaldean Lounge, complete with air-conditioned gift shoppe (souvenir Genesis booklets *autographed by the author* a mainstay), but it's only a matter of time.

Walk upright when you go. Give the kids a treat.

ΩΩ

15

INDIANA JONES WAS HERE

The black volcanic stone walls of Diyarbakır bode ill. Dux and I had driven here from Urfa, the countryside becoming ever more deserted and hot as we rolled.

We penetrated the black walls at the Harput Gate (Dağ Kapısı), found a small hotel just inside, and strolled out to see the sights. The city has a number of interesting, unusual mosques because of its long and tumultuous history, and Dux wanted to see them all for his book.

Despite boding ill, Diyarbakır also holds promise. The Tigris, which flows right past the city, provides the region's most precious commodity: water. For centuries Diyarbakırlıs have cultivated the rich, damp alluvial soil of the river-bed which slashes a deep green gash through the arid, dusty countryside. With proper management, the water can make the desert bloom.

Old Diyarbakır within the walls has a Roman street plan, which means that straight avenues laid out by Roman city planners run north-south and east-west, forming a cross, but within the "quarters" of the city, there is no plan, only chaos. We walked ever deeper into the labyrinthine maze. The farther we got from the main avenues, the more likely it was that street children would throw stones at us. They had never seen a foreigner before, let alone a *gavur* (infidel). To them we were barely a notch up from the devil.

Just as surely as a kid threw a stone, an old man sitting nearby would burst into fist-shaking animation, admonishing the kid for a gross breach of hospitality. The old guy would apologize to us on the kid's behalf. We'd smile at the kid who would then, we hoped, be inoculated against throwing stones at gavurs, at least this month.

Both the kid and the old man were Kurds, of course, as was just about everyone else in town. Despite its Arabic-root name, Diyarbakır was and is the ethnic center of Turkey's Kurdish citizenry.

A Matter of Kurdisy

Kurds speak an Indo-European language and may be ethnically related to the Persians. They are believed to have migrated to eastern Anatolia, Syria and Iraq centuries before Christ. Turkey's population of 70 million may include as many as 10 million Kurds. Some four million are dispersed throughout the country (with a million in İstanbul alone), the other six million live in eastern and southeastern Anatolia, constituting a majority in some places, such as Diyarbakır.

In 1969 the citizens of Diyarbakır had a gripe: in a democratic country where speech is supposedly free, it was against the law for Kurds to publish books, study in school, or broadcast radio and TV shows in their own language. The laws were passed in the early days of the republic to discourage ethnocentrism which threatened to tear apart the new state in civil war. Kurds argued, with some reason, that such strict measures were no longer necessary, and should be abolished (which, 30-some years later, they were).

Kurds have never had a nation-state based on their ethnicity. Periodically over the millennia they've rebelled against their non-Kurdish rulers, sometimes with the stated purpose of setting up their own Kurdish country. Frequently they've been used as pawns in the game of international politics: if Syria wants to pressure Turkey because Turkey has dammed the Euphrates and now controls Syria's water supply, Syria might fund, train and shelter Kurdish guerillas as a tool in case the Turks get stingy with the water.

Enter Abdullah Öcalan and his PKK (Kurdistan Workers Party), a nasty terrorist organization supported by Hafez el-Assad's Syria and the PLO. In the 1980s, the PKK staged hundreds of guerilla raids into southeastern Turkey and terrorist outrages in cities throughout Turkey, killing thousands of Turks—officials, troops, civilians and the occasional clueless foreigner—as well as Kurds who were not seen as sufficiently pro-PKK. The government reacted strongly to what was in fact a threat to the country's very existence. As is usual in such situations, extremists on both sides drove out the moderates, and the scars from the conflict will take at least a generation to heal.

On one revision visit to Diyarbakır I dropped into the tourist office to see what useful info I could pick up. After he had handed me the latest poor excuse for a city map, I chatted with the clerk.

"Too bad you missed the watermelon festival," he said.

Is that the most fun a person can have in Diyarbakır all year?" I asked.

"Pretty much," he conceded. "Actually, it wasn't all that great this year. The largest watermelon weighed only 22 kilos (49 pounds). It's been a bad year. No rain."

"What's normal? Or, rather, what's the biggest watermelon that's ever been grown here?"

"40 to 60 kilos these days, up to 100 (220 pounds) in the old days."

Diyarbakır's answer to the big cardboard box turned into a kids' playhouse is the 60-kilo watermelon hollowed out. You can see a picture of one, complete with happy kid in it, on any postcard rack in town.

My fondest memory of Diyarbakır, though, is of the time I collapsed in the Turist Oteli. I had driven here from Urfa. The Southeast Anatolia Project (called GAP in Turkish) had recently changed the landscape and put huge previously desert tracts under cultivation. As with other huge change-the-ecology projects such as the Aswan High Dam in Egypt, GAP had many unforeseen and unintended consequences. With irrigation, plants sprang out of the ground and bacteria, viruses and parasites came from miles around to get in on the feast. They traveled quickly and comfortably by water.

A few made their way to my table, my plate, my food and my gut, where they apparently discovered Nirvana. In an instant they wanted to populate my whole body, which they proceeded to do.

I was first aware of their presence when fever and diarrhea hit as I was driving through the arid, treeless, mountainous wilderness which separates Urfa and Diyarbakır. The road was littered with army checkpoints. Military vehicles traveled only in convoy along this PKK-infested road, with hyper-alert gunners manning jeep-mounted heavy calibre machine guns at the convoy's front and rear.

This was not a great place to stop and look for a toilet. Or to find one. I can't imagine an outhouse out here being anything other than a jocund target for a rocket-propelled grenade.

By the time I pulled into Diyarbakır I was really, truly sick. All I could think of was a quiet room, clean sheets, a spotless bathroom and plenty of liquids for rehydration.

I went straight to the creatively-named Turist Oteli, which was both the oldest and the most expensive hotel in town. It had been opened years before in anticipation of the tourist boom which never arrived. It was where government bigshots stayed, and also the occasional busload of Germans. It was a few decades old by now, and out of style, but well-maintained. The price didn't bother me because, the way I felt, any money I didn't spend today would only end up as part of my estate, so why scrimp?

I managed a wan smile for the reception desk clerk and a word or two of conversation for the chatty bellboy, then locked my room door, collapsed, and slept for 14 hours.

When I awoke the next day the sun was streaming into the room, cutting through the gauze curtains on the single window. I took a shower, drank a bottle of juice from the minibar and, my entire fund of energy exhausted, collapsed back in bed for a few more hours' sleep.

The room was quiet. The bathroom was clean and the water hot. The sheets were snowy-white and scented with wintergreen. The minibar contained a careful selection which included just the rehydration beverages I'd need. It's funny thinking of a hotel room as heaven. Is a simple, clean, quiet, pleasant hotel room where travel writers go when they die?

Parlez-vous Aramaic?

From Diyarbakır, Dux and I headed south to Mardin, just north of the Syrian frontier. Mardin is perched on the edge of the Anatolian plateau overlooking the pancake-flat Syrian plain which broils in the sun below.

It was approaching mid-day and hot as hell when we pulled into town, so we made a beeline for a shady little restaurant with a view of the baking plain.

"I can't stand the idea of eating anything hot or heavy," Dux said.

"Me neither."

Dux asked the waiter what they had that was good to eat in the heat of the day.

"*Cacık*," the waiter said. It turned out to be cool yogurt beaten with grated cucumber, a bit of garlic and salt, and a dash of olive oil and parsley sprinkles for garnish. You eat it with a soup spoon. It was perfect. I've eaten *cacık* hundreds of times since but none has tasted so good as that plateful in Mardin. It was the culinary equivalent of a cool cloth on a fevered forehead.

The Greeks have it too. They call it *tsatsiki*, the Greekified form of cacık, but it's a thick yogurt paste loaded with garlic and spread on bread. It's hot rather than cool.

After refreshment it was into the oven for us, walking Mardin's sun-broiled streets to find the Iraqi-Seljuk Great Mosque, the medieval Sultan İsa Medresesi, and the later Kasım Padişah Medresesi. Dux took notes.

"Now we need to find Deyrul Zafaran," he said. "It's a Syriac monastery. They still use Aramaic in their services. Aramaic is the language Jesus spoke."

The monastery was six km east of Mardin, set on a rocky hillside. We rolled up to the front gate and were met by a bearded, black-robed priest who spoke Aramaic, Arabic, Turkish, French and English. He turned us over to a teenaged boy, one of the orphans who lived there, who would be our guide.

"This is the oldest part of the monastery," our guide said as he showed us a claustrophobically small room formed of huge ashlars. "It was a pagan sun-temple."

The monastery church was astounding for its age. The doors and wooden patriarchal throne were a mere 300 years old, the floor mosaic more than 1500. It was a reminder that the monastery has been here since 495 AD. The Monophysites started worshipping here a millennium and a half ago in Aramaic, and never stopped.

Monophysite: shortly after the monastery's founding, Jacobus Baradeus, bishop of Edessa (now Şanlıurfa), put forth his theory that although Christ was both human and divine, he had only one (mono) "nature" (*physis*), and that was divine. This was not the church's party line, however, so Jacobus ran afoul of the patriarch in Constantinople, who said that Jesus had both human and divine natures. The patriarch excommunicated Jacobus, who thumbed his nose at the boss and set up his own church, called Jacobite or Syrian Orthodox by historians. The Armenian Orthodox Church, Egypt's Coptic Church, and the Ethiopian Church all split from the patriarch's church about the same time for about the same reason.

Think this over: here are holy men yelling and screaming at one another and causing wars over abstruse, inscrutable, unprovable mystic theories. It sounds utterly ridiculous, these clueless old guys fussing at one another 1500 years ago, until you think about Hitler's master-race bullshit, or communism's historical-imperative nonsense, or the expressed reasoning of the September 11th terrorists, or the outrages perpetrated by believers in any number of doctrines current in any of today's world-class faiths. Along with religion's sublime truths wc always sccm to gct this off-thc-wall fantasy claptrap, most of it thought up by old guys and forced on us by young zealots while the few real saints—think Mother Theresa—are out actually getting the work done.

The monastery has survived, or at least been resurrected, after the devastations wreaked by the Persian army in 607 AD, and by Tamerlane in the 1200s, but the recent Kurdish troubles had again seriously threatened its existence.

We thanked our guide and headed off into the sunset. Mardin was our turn-around point on this trip. We headed north, back to Diyarbakır, and the next day west, then south. When we reached Urfa, Dux decided to take a shortcut to Antakya by way of Aleppo in Syria. He wanted to see Aleppo, he owned the car and he had a Swiss passport (besides his American one), so it would be easy for him. The Syrians welcomed Swiss visitors. As for me, with only an American passport, entering Syria at that time required a visa, a month's wait to get it, and a big payment of money, so on his way to Aleppo he dropped me at Urfa's bus station and I boarded a bus bound for Gaziantep and Adana.

The Fatal Bus Ride

The bus ride started out alright, or at least as well as could be expected. Turkey had no air-conditioned buses back then so the trip was bound to be hot, but in the broiling southeast the passengers made at least some concession to the necessity for fresh air. Abandoning the traditional Turkish fear of drafts, a few windows were opened a crack to keep us all from becoming kebap.

We pulled out of Urfa's bus station. My seat mate was a carpenter, a friendly, heavy-set middle-aged guy who introduced himself politely then took out an enormous cucumber and a knife. He peeled the cucumber carefully, sliced it into pieces and offered me one. I took it, ate it, and discovered that chance had awarded me the bitter end. No spitting it out, though. I simply couldn't bring myself to offend his generosity. I sat there with the bitterness filling my mouth, suffusing my being as though I had slurped acorn soup laced with quinine and bile.

About an hour out of Urfa the highway's macadam top disappeared, torn off in preparation for laying down a new and better one. The roadbed was dusty and rough, and the roughness increased the noise level as well as the jostling. After a few hours, when the driver finally took pity on us and stopped for tea, toilet and smokes, we passengers were a dispirited bunch. I understood where the Turks got the custom of wishing one another *geçmiş olsun* at the end of a bus journey. *Geçmiş olsun* means "May it be in your past." It's the ritual formula you say to anyone who is ill or who has a vexing problem.

Fourteen hours after leaving Urfa we pulled into Adana all but dead. Well—I hate to tell you this—one old guy actually *was* dead. I don't know how or when he died, but they brought a stretcher up to the bus, put his carcass on it and hauled him away.

Imagine dying on a bus trip! We all fear dying in a plane crash or a train wreck or an auto accident. According to ancient legends, your last trip is supposed to be by boat: off to the horizon (Egyptians) or across the River Styx (Romans). But a bus trip? I think of what bus travel is like today in Turkey and I weep for the old guy. Instead of dust, bumps and noise, he could've gone out in air-conditioned comfort, with a jolly video dancing before his eyes, lemon cologne refreshing his face and neck, and a hot glass of tea at his lips. At least he wasn't in Adana when he copped it, but for all I know it may have been the prospect of arriving there that did him in.

After such a trip it was exciting for me (at least) to arrive in Adana, because that was where I could hop onto another bus that soon roared away and headed south into Hatay, land of *Indiana Jones and the Last Crusade*.

What's in a Name?

I love that part of *Indiana Jones and the Last Crusade* where Indie appears in the "Republic of Hatay" between World Wars I and II. Approximately one one-thousandth of one percent of the people who see that movie might have any clue at all as to the whereabouts of the "Republic of Hatay," or its capital city of Alexandretta. Therein lies its charm.

Hatay is the modern name for the historic Sanjak of Alexandretta, at the eastern end of Turkey's Mediterranean coast. The city of Alexandretta was founded by Alexander the Great around 330 BC. Just under a thousand years later the

Arabs conquered it and translated its name to İskenderun (İskender means Alexander in Arabic and Turkish). Almost 1400 years after the Arab conquest people in Europe and America were still calling the city by its old name and marking the old name on maps. So for almost a millennium and a half we've refused to recognize the name change. Talk about crusader mentality! We did the same thing with Constantinople, which became Kostantiniyye shortly after 1453, and eventually İstanbul. Although Atatürk insisted that everybody call Angora Ankara and Constantinople İstanbul and Smyrna İzmir and Antioch Antakya, the Greeks still use the old names to this day and entertain fantasies of getting them back.

Hatay was not precisely a republic between the world wars. It was a *sanjak*. A sanjak was an Ottoman territorial unit similar to a county in size. The Sanjak of Alexandretta—or Republic of Hatay—included the cities of İskenderun (Alexandretta) and Antakya (Antioch). After the Ottoman defeat in World War I, the sultan's lands in the Middle East were claimed by the victorious powers and governed by "mandate:" the British got Egypt and Palestine, and the French got Syria and Lebanon. Curiously, the Sanjak of Alexandretta was designated an autonomous district attached to Syria rather than part of Mandate Syria itself.

Atatürk recognized Hatay's strategic importance: a foreign army based there could threaten the Cilician Gates, the mountain pass north of Adana which leads directly to the Anatolian heartland, and which has been the entry point for conquering armies for millennia. He decided that Turkey had to have Hatay to remain secure. The French seemed about to make it part of Syria, so in 1937 Atatürk put pressure on the French to establish the "Independent State of Hatay" in place of the "Sanjak of Alexandretta." A plebiscite was organized soon thereafter, the vote went in favor of Turkey, and the quasi-autonomous "state" became the Turkish province of Hatay in 1939—just in time to help Turkey preserve its neutrality during World War II.

So Hatay is no longer independent but, historically speaking, for a single New York minute it sort of was, and the Hollywood people seized upon this fact for a clever bit of historico-political engineering.

Most of the time, movie people don't want to tick off potential viewers so they try hard not to alienate anyone except perhaps those with no money for movie tickets. They particularly dislike ticking off whole countries because some of the citizens are bound to have the price of a ticket so they need to be clever about where the action is located, especially if the plot is Standard Hollywood Plot No 1, which is that there are lots of baddies trying to do nasty to the hero. Nazis are the convenient bad guys because most people hate them and the real ones are long dead and therefore incapable of filing nettlesome lawsuits, but what to do about the location? What if you want some of the movie action to take place in a picturesque desert? There are no deserts in Germany, picturesque or otherwise, or in Austria for that matter, so you've got to look elsewhere.

North Africa is the obvious place to locate your movie Nazis because during World War II there were in fact Nazis there; but the countryside is mostly boring desert, not picturesque desert. You can't put them in other countries of the region because there were no German troops there during World War II. Spies yes, troops no. You can shoot lots of desert scenes for your movie in these places, and in fact some of the most beautiful and exciting scenes in Last Crusade were shot at Petra in Jordan; but you can't *locate* your movie there.

So what do you do? Make up an imaginary country to locate your movie in? Well, you could, but that sacrifices a significant amount of verisimilitude, and in an Indiana Jones-type movie most of the verisimilitude has already been sacrificed so you want to hold onto whatever's left.

Ironically, with so little left, every tiny bit of actual truth takes on huge importance. People come out of Indiana Jones movies saying "You know that part about the Rolls Royce Phantom II, 4.3 liter, 30 horsepower, six cylinder engine, with Stromberg downdraft carburetor? It really *can* go from zero to 100 kilometers an hour in 12.5 seconds," etc. If there were only one actual atom of truth in such a movie, that atom would be talked to death.

In short, there've got to be at least some fragments of truth in an Action/ Crowd-Pleaser movie, just as in advertising and government, or the whole ridiculous suspension-of-disbelief structure crumbles and you're left with no paying customers.

That's why, as a movie-making person, you love Hatay.

It is at least believable, if not completely accurate, that there was a pasha in charge of Hatay, and that the Nazis bribed him with a Rolls Royce so they could go get the Holy Grail, etc. Even if it's not strictly true, it's so obscure that, as noted above, only one one-thousandth of one percent of your paying customers will notice, and even fewer—perhaps only two, namely Steven Spielberg and Yours Truly—will give a damn.

Speaking of accuracy, movie people like to be able to say that such and such a movie is "based on a true story." This always kills me. "Based on a true story," in Hollywood parlance, means "we've changed this sucker around so much that it's a bigger myth than corporate accounting, but now it fulfills our ego, box office and political-correctness requirements, and it's important to our *amour propre* to appear ethical, so sit back, relax, and, against your better instincts, believe that this is true." If you need convincing on this point, I refer you to *Midnight Express*, which was "based on a true story" in which a two-bit convicted drug smuggler is miraculously transmuted into a suffering hero while the Turkish authorities who are trying to protect American youth from the scourge of illegal drugs become the heavies, and Hollywood cashes in at the Turks' expense. But more of that later.

The Bile Green Color Wasn't Even the Worst of It

My bus south from Adana into Hatay passed right by İskenderun, formerly Alexandretta. I didn't stop to see it. I came back a few years later the historic, romantic way: by ship.

So imagine this: I get off a comfortable Turkish steamer at İskenderun, which is even more southerly and humid than Adana. I'm a young, underpaid travel writer looking for a cheap—and I mean *cheap*—hotel room. I look through the dismal collection of dives squatting miserably on the waterfront. Only one of them has a vacant room.

"I'm afraid it's our worst room," the desk clerk says. He shows it to me and my heart sinks: it's a box 12 feet square with glossy bile-green walls and no window. No window?

No window!

I didn't expect a window to help much in the heat—a fan would be the thing—but this room in which I spent the night—oh yes I did—was to teach me a lesson about windows, which is that you need at least one. It can be small, but you need it.

Jail cells have windows. Hospital rooms have windows. Principals' offices have windows. Even dungeons have windows. They may be small, and barred, and high on the wall above where the neck irons are attached, but they're there. They may look out onto vacant lots, or next-door walls, or pig farms—on second thought let's not think about pig farms, they stink and this is a book about a Muslim country—but there's got to be a window.

Only here there wasn't.

Lest you jump to the conclusion that my problem is claustrophobia, let me assure you that my work has taken me to the center of the Great Pyramid at Giza, to the secret priestly tunnels beneath the Temple of Horus at Edfu on the Nile, to the windowless tomb of King Tut in the Valley of the Kings, to the stifling center of the Pyramid of Kukulcán at Chichén-Itzá at noonday, and I have not suffered unduly from claustrophobia. In fact I did not suffer as much claustrophobia in these places as I do in your normal 32-inch-pitch economy-class airplane seat. I have noted the absence of windows in the pyramids and temples, but it did not bother me much, probably because I was not about to sit down and try to sleep in any of those places.

This cheap hotel room on the waterfront in İskenderun was certainly not the pharaoh's burial chamber. For one thing, there was no thoroughly-trained, attentive team of svelte royal virgins standing by with heaven knows what spicy unguents—in the history books that stuff is usually referred to coyly as "unguents"—to rub all over me. Had the pharaoh's girls been there in the guts of the pyramid or down in the subterranean tunnels in Edfu I might have, ah, toughed it out and even, eventually, gotten some sleep. However, there were no lissome Egyptian maidens in this cheap hotel room in İskenderun either, and I would've settled for a window.

Why should lack of a window matter when I'm asleep anyway?

I leave it at this: it does.

Look, I regularly stay in cave rooms in Cappadocia. In a Cappadocian cave room you are relentlessly surrounded by bedrock. The floor is rock, the ceiling is rock, the walls are rock, everything is rock. But every cave room has at least one tiny window, which transforms it from a tomb into a sanctuary. I love my customary cave room at the Esbelli Evi, a charming inn in Ürgüp because, besides a brass bed, it has a tiny window.

I don't want to leave you with the impression that İskenderun is one big windowless room. On the contrary, it is now a pleasant, modern city, clean and well kept, with friendly people and an impressive amount of maritime trade. On a later visit I stayed at the modern Hataylı Oteli just off the waterfront, in a room with three-star comforts and a particularly good Turkish breakfast included in the rate. But that one night in a windowless bile-green room in old Alexandretta will, I fear, never leave me completely in peace about bile green hotel rooms, or windows, ever again.

I'll Have That, Whatever It Is

Talk about hot, Antakya, biblically known as Antioch, is hot as hell in summer. But it's the dry heat of Syria rather than the wet heat of Adana and İskenderun. It's not particularly pleasant, this dry heat, but somehow it feels as though it should be good for you, like eating bran flakes or drinking six glasses of water a day (a very good idea in Antakya), or not sleeping in drafts.

Even the locals sleep in drafts here, and feel lucky to have them. In July of 1969, when Dux and I first came here, people built little wood-stick shelters on the roofs of their houses and covered them with palm fronds. They'd sit there during the day catching the breeze—the draft, if you will—and sleep there at night, camping with all the comforts. Sleeping without a window can be hell, sleeping without walls can be heaven.

Antakya has several interesting things to see, including a grotto in which, legend has it, St Peter preached, so the locals refer to the cave as "the oldest Christian church." Antakya also has, on its outskirts, the ruins of the Roman resort town of Daphne. Most interestingly, it has a lot of mosaics recovered from the ruins of Daphne, and they are truly beautiful mosaics. The Antakya Museum, filled with Roman mosaics, is the reason most people come to Antakya.

That's why Dux and I came, and the mosaics alone were worth the trip. Antakya has few other sights, so we didn't stay long even though it was a pleasant enough town if you sat in the shade with a drink during the hottest part of the day, which is what most of the locals did.

I've gone back to Antakya many times since. I've found that one visit per decade to the Cave-Church of St Peter is enough, even though the view over the city is nice from there. However, I visit the mosaics every time I'm in town.

On one visit to Antakya I noticed a huge new hotel right on the riverbank in the town center, the Büyük Antakya Oteli. I went inside to check it out and was hit by a blast of arctic air-conditioned air, always a good sign. I asked about prices, and for a bellboy to show me a room.

Surprise! Even the guest rooms are air conditioned. I don't always feel rich enough to stay at the "Great Antioch" (as its name translates), but I like knowing it's there just in case I'm feeling flush.

When I return to Antakya now, however, driving up and up into the chill air of the Belen Pass and down the other side onto the searing plain, I am on a quest for *künefe*. I discovered it here, and here is where it must be eaten if you want the fully authentic experience.

One day long ago, my travel writer's workday ended in Antakya, I repaired to the Han Restaurant on Hürriyet Caddesi. It was a simple but agreeable eatery with a second-floor open-air dining terrace. The air, if not exactly cool, was pleasant the way dry air can be after the sun goes down. I took a table and ordered soup, salad, kebap, and a cold Efes lager.

"Pardon me, but will you be wanting künefe for dessert?" the waiter asked. "If so, I need to tell the kitchen now so they can start preparing it. It takes awhile."

"What's künefe?" I asked.

"It's a traditional Antakya sweet made of shredded wheat, cheese and walnuts."

Shredded wheat, cheese and walnuts didn't sound particularly sweet to me, but with Turkish cuisine you never can tell. One of my all-time favorite desserts, called *kazandibi* ("bottom of the pot," because it's ever so lightly scorched brown in the making), includes pounded chicken. Chicken! You don't notice it unless you know it's there. There's also a dessert made with eggplant, of all things. So if this guy says it's made with shredded wheat and cheese and walnuts and is sweet, I figure it is.

"Sure, let's try it," I said.

It's part of a travel writer's job to be a guinea pig, to experiment with foods and report to readers. I have done this many times. As you already know if you've read this far, I'm not squeamish. Aside from roasted eyeballs and syrupy Moroccan mint tea, I'll ingest almost anything. For my first guidebook I steeled myself, strode purposefully into an *işkembeci* (tripe soup restaurant) on İstiklal Caddesi in İstanbul, and sat down to a bowl of stewed cow's stomach. My first bowl was also my last, but I ate it, slimy squares of squishy stomach lining and all. Turks believe işkembe (tripe soup) is a specific against hangover, and I can see why they think this. Tripe soup makes you forget everything else, even throbbing head pain, and I don't mean this as a compliment.

Sometimes taking a fling into the culinary unknown results in delightful surprises, sometimes in forgettable novelties, but if it's forgettable it couldn't have been all that bad. Tripe soup, for the record, is unforgettable.

In Tunis, where most menus are in French, I once took a fling and ordered *clémentine* for dessert. This was before anyone outside North Africa knew what a clementine was, before those cute little wooden crates full of clementines appeared in supermarkets to cheer the chill days of winter in New England.

Clémentine! Its musical name conjured up visions of a traditional rich French concoction created by some long-ago chef for his mistress and named in her honor, something like *pêche Melba*. Could it have been created for Winston Churchill's wife and presented to her at a state dinner (white tie, medals, long gowns, cavernous décolletage) at which the presiding monarch, enchanted at the chef's genius, called him out of the kitchen to receive the approbation of the dignitaries assembled? My imagination grew fertile and my mouth moist.

Clémentine! I saw a vision of fluffy *gateau* suffused with Benedictine liqueur, eased into a pool of crème-fraîche drizzled with raspberry reduction, the whole then sprinkled with shaved chocolate and powdered sugar. *Clémentine?* Yes, let's have clémentine for sure.

The Tunisian waiter set down in front of me a plain white plate. On it was a tangerine.

"What's this?" I demanded. "I ordered clémentine!"

I was certain there had been a colossal mistake and that my dessert, a triumph of Gallic postprandial gastronomic confection, had been delivered to some other table while I ended up with somebody else's dietetic piece of fruit. I wanted my clémantine, and I wanted it now.

"*Mais monsieur,*" the waiter spluttered in confusion, "*c'est ça qui arrive!*"

"It is that which arrives." So I got a vocabulary lesson for dessert: a clémentine is a tangerine without seeds. I hoped the same wouldn't happen with my künefe.

I needn't have worried.

My *pièce de résistance* having been dispached to my nether regions, the waiter served me my künefe. It was a circular disc about six inches in diameter and half an inch thick made of finely shredded wheat, golden brown and hot from the oven. I needed a knife and fork to cut into it because shredded wheat strengthens wonderfully when folded around sweet cheese and chopped walnuts, then soaked in sugar and honey, then baked. I was doubtful, but not beyond the first taste. Willfully ignoring what must have been enough calories to get a sumo wrestler through a limbo competition, I enjoyed every bite.

So Antakya, for me, despite its other attractions, means künefe. I'll bet the

Roman swells lounging on the mosaics at Daphne didn't have künefe, so I'm one up on them in that department.

ಜೆ

16
HEAVEN, HELL & EDEN

Turkey is a Biblical place—Abraham lived in Harran, St Paul of Tarsus was born here, he preached in that cave-church in Antakya and wrote his Letter to the Ephesians, all sorts of biblical types cycled through Cappadocia and all that—but never did I expect my guidebook research to turn up Heaven, Hell and the Garden of Eden, which is actually what happened. Sort of.

Leaving Hatay, Dux and I drove north from Antakya, up over Belen and down to Adana, then west through Tarsus and Mersin. We kept driving.

No town west of Adana all the way to Alanya had a decent hotel in 1969, and by decent I don't mean the Hilton, I mean something minimally—minimally!—acceptable to me, and my standards are very low indeed, rejection of windowless bile-green cell-block quarters to the contrary notwithstanding. Actually I'd venture to say that in 1969 there wasn't a decent hotel between Alanya and Diyarbakır, Adana especially included.

The night was so hot and muggy, and decent hotel rooms so blatantly non-existent, that we decided to camp, lying atop our sleeping bags on the beach. We spread them out, lay down, and were immediately attacked by mosquitoes, swarms of them, galaxies of them. Imagine Nacide Hanım's street cats attacking a liver the size of an ocean liner. The mosquitoes were the cats and we were the liver.

We crawled inside our bags and began to dissolve in sweat. That wasn't going to work either.

We fled to the Land Rover, but we had to keep the windows open to catch whatever breeze might blow or we'd putrefy. The flying monsters came right in the windows and resumed drilling.

We gave up and took a walk along the beach. Dux was a few feet ahead of me. Suddenly he stopped and pointed at a loggerhead turtle that had emerged from the water and was crawling slowly up the beach.

"I wonder if it's a female, and if she's going to lay her eggs," he mused.

The turtle eyed us warily. I eyed the turtle's thick mosquito-proof shell enviously. She paused for a moment, stared in our direction, thought the better of her ovine excursion, slowly turned and crawled back to the safety of the sea. She'd lay her eggs another time when there were no potentially ovophaginous intruders, hairy with flying blood-suckers, hanging around on the beach.

We decided to follow her example and take a swim. We waded into the clear water, only slightly cooler than a bath but refreshing compared to the muggy air. Our legs and arms moved slowly in the water, enjoying the coolness. They glowed.

Glowed?

It's called *yakamoz* in Turkish (the word comes from Greek), and is caused by phosphorescent plankton. Disturbed by our limbs, the microscopic beasties set up an eerie glow in the swirling water. From being fricasséed travel writers we were transformed by yakamoz into magical sea creatures surrounded by 10-watt haloes.

We stayed in the water quite awhile. We were dead tired, but the coolish water, with its magical phosphorescence, was so much better than the air that we were loath to leave it. Finally we emerged, dried off, got into the car and drove, found another beach with fewer mosquitoes, and collapsed into sleep for a few hours before dawn woke us.

As we breakfasted in a little lokanta in the next town reading the morning's newspaper, we noticed an item about two men who had taken a room in a small hotel on the Mediterranean coast a few days previously. They had emptied an aerosol can of insecticide into the room just before going to bed. The poison gas killed all the mosquitoes and, by dawn, them as well.

After breakfast Dux said "I think today we'll go to Hell."

Last night wasn't bad enough? I thought to myself. We got into the Land Rover and I concentrated on his driving. What was this about hell? What did he know that I didn't?

What he knew is that *Cennet* (Heaven) and *Cehennem* (Hell) as they are called in Turkish, lie east of Silifke in the hills just over a mile north of the coastal town of Narlıkuyu. Heaven is the 250-meter-deep cave called Korykos by the ancients. According to legend Typhon, a half-man, half-monster, did battle with Zeus, king of the gods, in the depths of Korykos in a trial of Good versus Evil. Zeus won, his Olympic ratings being too high for the myth-makers to sacrifice even to the high production values of a man-monster like Typhon. Typhon was but an episode. Zeus was the star of the series.

Whatever Zeus actually did in this cave, the local people seem to think it was pretty cool. They come to the cave and tie scraps of paper and strips of their clothing inscribed with their names and desires to the scrubby tree near its mouth in hopes that the powerful spirits of the cave will help them out. This fun-fair of pagan superstition must drive the local mufti nuts.

Even so, the superstitious locals are in historic good company as demonstrated by the ruins of a little fifth-century Byzantine church dedicated to the Virgin Mary perched smack in the yawning mouth of the Heaven cave itself. "*Gavurler!*" ("Infidels!") I can hear the mufti swear under his breath.

Inside, the cave is a cave. We went down about as deep as we could go with a flashlight (and since then they've installed un-spiritual electric lighting to a depth of a hundred yards). We saw stalactites (which always get mentioned first because they're the ones up top, and the word is lighter-sounding), and stalagmites (that 'g' makes it heavier-sounding—don't you hear it?), and pools of mud, and thousands upon thousands of bats. For the bats it may be heaven, but for the rest of us spending even a day here—no! an hour!—let alone eternity, would not be bliss. In fact, spending an hour in Heaven's cold, gloomy dankness would in no way compensate for even the first time that we, keeping our eyes and hearts fixed on eternal bliss, decided to be good and not get drunk, or get laid, or get unethically rich just so we wouldn't sink our chances of getting in here. This is just not the place to bet your hopes on, believe me.

Hell, the cave nearby, is much the same although—and I love the irony of this—it's not as deep.

Bear with me as I jump ahead a few years, to a time after my guidebook had actually been published. I received a letter from one of my readers, a dear lady in Rhode Island:

"I was on a flight from Ankara to Tel Aviv," the letter began. "As we were flying over the Mediterranean coast I looked down and saw the Garden of Eden. You've traveled all over Turkey. You've traveled all along that coast. I looked in your guidebook and didn't find any description of the Garden of Eden. Have you seen it? Can I visit it?"

This is not as silly as it sounds. You can actually visit Armageddon (it's in Israel) and Troy (in Turkey) and Solomon's Temple (Israel again). You can go to Tarsus, where St Paul was born, on this selfsame Turkish Mediterranean coast, and to Karain, the cave near Antalya that has been inhabited for 25,000 years. Archeologists have even identified fabled Xanadu (Shangdu in Inner Mongolia). So wanting to visit the Garden of Eden isn't quite so nutty as it may seem at first.

I wrote back to her: well, I've been to Heaven and Hell along the Turkish Mediterranean coast, but no, I haven't seen the Garden of Eden. If I run across it, however, you'll be the first to know.

My first guide to Turkey didn't cover any place on the coast east of Alanya for the simple reason that few tourists went there. Guidebooks are ever and always an exercise in preaching to the converted. Though we guidebook writers pose as intrepid explorers, in fact we write mostly about places where others have already been and, more importantly, places where lots of people are planning to go. That's why they buy our books, and that's how we make our money.

So Dux and I didn't stumble across the Garden of Eden that day, but we did visit Heaven and Hell, which is not such a bad score where places of biblical significance are concerned. I'd say Heaven and Hell trump the Garden of Eden any day. Even by cheating you can't beat Heaven and Hell, although by cheating you may affect your odds of ending up in the one rather than the other.

Maybe the Heaven and Hell we saw were the same place as the Garden of Eden the letter-writing lady saw. It's in the spot she described. If it is, Adam and Eve cleared out long ago, probably because of the mosquitoes, so perhaps they were not as foolish as the Bible makes them out to be. As for the Tree of Temptation, it is now covered in strips of cloth and little scribbled notes, the mufti wants very badly to touch a match to it, and the locals have swiped all its apples.

Ottoman Playboys

We continued our research along the coast, checking out Silifke and Anamur and Alanya, all of which were just small towns. Alanya is now a big fancy resort full of British and German vacationers, but in 1969 it was quiet and sleepy, and didn't detain us long. We were headed for Side.

Side (SEE-deh), the historic village west of Alanya on the way to Antalya, was a dusty little place dominated by a huge Hellenistic theater. Extensive ruins of a great ancient city, one of the richest in the ancient region called Pamphylia, were spread over a large area, and included a marble temple right at seaside that was said to be the place where Antony once met Cleopatra for a romantic interlude. The contrast of past glory and present modesty couldn't have been more pronounced. The village had a small, bare main square with a sleepy Jandarma (gendarme, paramilitary police) post, a post office, a little *köfte* (meatball) grill run by Tek Gözlü Ali (One-Eyed Ali), and a little electric generator which was switched off at 10 pm. The running water was inclined to stop often and without warning throughout the day. On either side of the village was a one kilometer swath of pure unspoiled white sand beach.

Side was familiar territory to Dux because he and Monique had chosen it for their recuperation after a bout of hepatitis. They picked up the bug in Hakkâri on a mountain-climbing trip. They collapsed into a hospital in Antalya. After a week or two of stabilization, the doctor told them to "go somewhere nice, take a rest, eat lightly and don't drink alcohol for six months." They had already stayed in Side for a time, so they returned there and followed doctor's orders. For all I know they were the first non-resident Europeans to stay in the village overnight since Alexander the Great.

Side's primitive charm was irresistible. Word got out, and they were soon joined in Side residency by the wealthy American newspaper editor Alfred Friendly and his wife. The Friendlys bought an old village house, restored it, added all the mod-cons, and used it as a vacation retreat.

The other non-villagers in town were Dux's old friends Suat Şakir, scion of a prominent Ottoman family, and his wife Mizou, daughter of an Ottoman diplomat and a French lady. They had built a modern pension—actually a simple hotel—facing the eastern beach. Suat Bey was the *patron*, Mizou Hanim the *chef de cuisine*, of the Pansiyon Pamfilya. Dux and I called on Suat and Mizou, hoping for some good conversation over a great, preferably free meal with drinks. We were not disappointed.

Suat Bey welcomed us as though we were the Prodigal Sons. We sat down to a sunset dinner of sweet greens with bitter herbs, poached sea bass, and crème caramel. We drank good Turkish white wine with dinner, followed by shot after shot of rakı to warm the cooling night.

The Şakirs, Suat's family, were of the Ottoman nobility. Originally from Afyonkarahisar, Şakir Paşa (1855–1914) was a general, ambassador, and the brother of a grand vezir. Several of his six children (four girls and two boys) distinguished themselves, but not in ways completely agreeable to the pasha. At the tender age of 21, his youngest daughter Aliye (1903–1974) had a scandalous affair with Charles Berger, the family violin teacher. She later married him and went on to become one of İstanbul's most famous—perhaps controversial would be a better word—bohemian artists. Fahrelnissa (1901–1991), the second youngest daughter, married Emir Zeid al-Hussein of the Iraqi royal family (yes, the Zeid who had fought with Lawrence of Arabia) and joined the diplomatic whirl.

Cevat (1890–1973) was sent off to Oxford where, by all accounts, he absorbed precious little of the pricey education his autocratic father had sent him to obtain, but picked up all available bad habits of English upper class youth. These included wining, dining, wenching, riding to hounds and running up awesome bills with local merchants, bills which eventually made their way to his father's desk in İstanbul. After numerous unheeded warnings, strait-laced Şakir Paşa recalled Cevat from Oxford.

Instead of returning to İstanbul, however, the twenty-year-old Cevat escaped to Rome, enrolled in the Academy of Fine Arts, and promptly fell madly in love with one of the life-drawing models. They got married, had a baby, and moved to İstanbul. Cevat continued to paint. Şakir Paşa continued to pay the bills for his son and young family, but was not at all happy about it.

In 1914, when Cevat was 24, the poisonous relationship with his father reached a crisis. Under circumstances that have never been fully explained, late one night during a bitter argument Cevat shot and killed the pasha.

Convicted of manslaughter, Cevat was sent to prison, then exiled to Bodrum, the tiny, primitive fishing village called Halicarnassus in ancient times. Today Bodrum is a flashy international resort, but in the years following World War I it may as well have been the moon as far as a cosmopolitan sophisticate such as Cevat was concerned.

Cevat made the best of it, painting primitive village scenes and describing them in stories. He signed himself the "Halicarnassus Fisherman" (*Halikarnas Balıkçısı*). He was a sort of Henry David Thoreau manqué, writing about the simple life and folk in the fishing village and about the "blue voyages" (*mavi yolculuk*) he took in his little boat along the unspoiled Mediterranean coast.

As for Cevat's brother Suat, he was married four times, once to a wealthy, divorced Egyptian-American heiress, once to someone else, and twice to Mizou. The sons of Şakir Paşa, and especially Cevat and Suat, seemed to have a knack for spending money but not for earning it, which might be why, at the age of 70, Suat was running the Pansiyon Pamfilya for amusement and pin money.

Besides Turkish, Suat Bey spoke perfect, upper-class British English and several other languages. He enjoyed intelligent, sophisticated conversation, of which he got very little in Side, so he was glad to see Dux, and apparently didn't mind meeting me.

It's a Sin to Eat That! Give It to Me.

Suat Bey loved to tell stories about village life and his estimable neighbors. We were willing listeners.

"One day a local fisherman brought me a lobster (*istakoz* in Turkish)," Suat Bey said. "'Beyefendi,' the villager asked me. 'We've heard that *istakoz* is *haram* [forbidden by Islamic dietary law] and, like other shellfish, we should not eat it. You're an educated man from İstanbul. You would know whether or not this is true. Please tell us.'"

"Well," Suat Bey went on, "I assumed my sagest expression and congratulated the fisherman on his religious fidelity. I advised him that lobster, as a shellfish, was indeed *haram*, and that to preserve the purity of the village and to keep his fellow villagers far from temptation, all *istakoz* which happened to become entangled in the fishermen's nets should henceforth be brought directly to me for proper disposal." Suat Bey sat back in his seat and paused for effect.

"Soon thereafter *Homard sautée au beurre* appeared regularly on the evening menu *chez Mizou*," he said with a broad grin, "and it was surprisingly afford-able, too."

The Pansiyon Pamfilya was a new, modern concrete building that did not really fit in with the traditional fieldstone village architecture. At the time, noises were being made in government circles that Side would be preserved intact in traditional style in the interests of tourism, and all non-traditional buildings would be razed. I brought the subject up with Suat Bey at dinner one evening.

"They say they're going to pull down all of the modern buildings in the village and keep it 'traditional.' What do you think?" I asked.

"I hope they do!" he replied. "I'd like nothing more than to have this village preserved. This modern pension is ugly! But until they tear it down, I'm going to live here."

Unfortunately, that would not be for long.

No *Piknik* Need Apply

Dux and I left Side and continued our work, but I returned to the village over the years and saw it change. The first and biggest change was Suat Bey's death three years later in 1972. The Pansiyon Pamfilya was sold so I looked for another, cheaper place to stay whenever I came to town. Luckily, I found Ayşe.

Ayşe Güzel's family had emigrated from Crete to Side when the Ottomans lost control of the island in 1898. Ayşe Hanım, a cheerful dynamo of a woman in late middle age when I met her, opened the Hermes Pansiyon just a block off the main square. It was a simple village house like all the others, but Ayşe kept it and its shady garden courtyard spotless and rented her snowy beds cheap. Ayşe planted a jasmine vine in the garden to shade several tables where guests could take their breakfast, write postcards, or make tea and sip it in the afternoon. Sitting under that jasmine vine, sipping tea and writing up travel notes was as close to ideal travel-writer working conditions as I ever expect to find.

"Yes, you can stay here," Ayşe said to me in Turkish the first time I arrived, "because you're not *piknik*." (*Piknik* was Ayşe's term of contempt for hippies.) "I don't want Turks and I don't want piknik because they make a mess. I want Germans. Americans are alright. No French."

So I passed muster, and settled in at Ayşe's whenever I was in Side.

One year I chose it for my mid-trajectory break. Taking to heart the rising chorus of stress Cassandras, I included three days of R&R in Side in the middle of my breakneck guidebook revision schedule.

"Three days?" I asked myself on the day I arrived. "What am I gonna do here for three whole days? I should get back on the road tomorrow. This town'll only take a few hours to research."

On Day Two, after breakfast under the jasmine vine, sipping my third glass of tea, I thought "This is okay. It's probably good to take a break, bring down my blood pressure. Maybe I'll get back on the road tomorrow."

On Day Three, in the evening sitting under the jasmine vine sipping wine and chatting lazily with Ayşe's other guests—not one of them piknik, mind you—I thought "Why do I hafta go back to work?"

Ayşe Hanım had two sons, and strapping lads they were—though, come to think of it, I never saw either of them actually strap anything. Not once.

Her favorite son was Hüseyin, a handsome, engaging fair-haired young man with an easy, confident manner and a ready smile. "*Tıpkı Alman gibi!*" she'd say of him. "He looks just like a German!" which in Ayşe's case implied a compliment.

Hüseyin helped out at the pension. One spring he bought lumber, nails and varnish and built an extra guest room onto the pension. It came out looking like an alpine hunting lodge, scroll-carved bargeboards and all. There was definitely something to this German thing with him.

With the burgeoning tourist trade, Hüseyin decided to open a carpet shop. He bought a storefront right on the main square, opened his shop, and, industrious like his mother, made it a successful business.

"You've got a camera," Ayşe said to me during one of my visits. "Take my picture. I want to give it to my strapping sons so they can remember me after I'm gone."

"Let's take the picture at Hüseyin's shop," I suggested. I wanted the rich carpets for a backdrop. We walked to the shop and I shot a roll of film with Ayşe in various poses: seated in an easy chair surrounded by lush carpets, the epitome of the Turkish matriarch; standing in front of the shop admiring the goods, the proud mother.

The pictures turned out pretty well. I had some good enlargements made and sent them to Ayşe. "Perfect!" she told me later. "Now they'll have something to remember me."

"They won't have a chance," I said. "You're too energetic to go easily. You'll outlive us all." She gave a hearty, energetic laugh.

Anything With Wheels

Dux and I returned to İstanbul and Ayazpaşa. By now it was midsummer. I had been working on my book for over a year, and I still had a lot of work to do. I had kept the Aegean, Turkey's most popular tourist region, for last so I could check out the hotels, try out the restaurants, take down the bus fares and schedules, and sketch out the maps during the summer months when the resorts were busy with tourists. I also wanted the most popular region to be the last one I researched so that the information on it was the most up-to-date.

I came smack up against the challenge of transportation. I had no problems in İstanbul, and none when traveling with Dux, but now I was on my own out in the countryside. It was a problem.

Transportation has always been pretty good in Turkey given its level of economic development, but transportation follows crowds: if a bunch of people want to go somewhere regularly, the means will spring up to serve them, whether it be commuters taking a minibus to an office building, or migrant workers taking a bus to the fields, or *haj* pilgrims taking a charter flight to Mecca.

Conversely, and obviously, if there are no people wanting to travel, there will be no way to go.

My problem was this: I was writing a guidebook for travelers, thousands of travelers, who would want to take public transportation to tourist sights off the beaten path. But the travelers had not yet arrived, and so transportation to the many things to see outside the towns was still difficult.

Basically, you took pot luck.

For example, I left Çanakkale, the town on the Dardanelles across from Gallipoli, on an İzmir-bound bus and hopped off at the junction with the road to Troy. I waited there for about fifteen minutes, at which time a farmer came trundling along on a tractor. I flagged him down, asked for a lift, and climbed aboard, sitting on the big right fender. It's traditional in Turkey to offer bus fare for any hitched ride, so when we reached Troy, I offered to pay. The farmer would accept nothing.

"It's enough to meet a foreigner who speaks Turkish," he said.

I poked around in Troy—I was the only person there—then set out to walk the several miles back to the highway. About 10 minutes into the walk I heard a heavy vehicle growling up behind me. It was a soda truck. I flagged it down and hopped into the cab.

Sind sie Deutsch? asked the driver. Among the few travelers who ever made it to the ruins in Turkey, Germans seemed to be the majority.

"I'm American," I answered in Turkish.

"American?! Yes, yes. So you're a soldier, then."

"No, I came as an English teacher. Now I'm writing a travel guidebook. For tourists."

"A teacher, eh? Good! A pleasure to meet you, hocam. You speak good Turkish."

I didn't. What he meant was that he was surprised I spoke Turkish at all.

We reached the highway junction. He stopped the truck, set the brakes, and we both got down from the cab. He grabbed two bottles of soda from the back of the truck, popped them open, handed one to me, and said "Happy travels!"

Later in the month I was trying to get to Aphrodisias, the cult city of Aphrodite, in the Meander River valley. It was simple enough to get to Nazilli, a town right on the İzmir-Denizli highway from which I caught a minibus to the village of Karacasu, but from there I still had 12 km (7.5 miles) to go to get to Aphrodisias.

"Is there a minibus to Aphrodisias?" I asked at the small Karacasu bus station, which was really just a vacant lot with one minibus parked in it.

"You speak good Turkish" came the reply. "Are you German?"

"American," I answered.

"Bravo, bravo!" they said. "Are you a soldier?"

By this time I had come to think of this back-and-forth as Conversation 1-A. It was what happened automatically whenever I opened my mouth and spoke Turkish. I can't blame people. Few had ever met a foreigner before, and very few indeed had met a foreigner who knew more than "Hello," "Thank you," and "How much?" in Turkish, if that.

I was urged to sit, have tea and chat. I did, but I had work to do: how would I get to Aphrodisias?

"So…about that minibus to Aphrodisias…." I asked again.

"There's no regular service. A minibus will take you on a special trip for TL40."

"I can't afford that."

"Well…look, there's a government official in town. He's got an official car. He'll probably be leaving by the Aphrodisias road, and give you a ride."

Two carloads of French tourists bumped over the cobblestones and onward toward Aphrodisias, followed by the town's only taxi, a jeep. It was now noon. No official, no car.

A boy, about 11 years old, approached.

"Please excuse me, sir, but aren't you one of the teachers from İzmir Koleji?"

I was astounded. How did this boy know, and why was his English so good? I asked.

"I'm a student at İzmir Koleji. Mr Dave was one of my teachers. You know Mr Dave, I think. He's an American teacher, too. My name is Ahmet. Will you come and talk?"

Ahmet led me along the street to a simple tailor's shop, its ceiling hung with half-finished men's suits, the seams marked with white thread and chalk. Lining the walls were narrow shelves jammed with bolts of fabric. Three low stools were on the floor next to a higher stool next to the cutting table where the tailor was at work sewing a sleeve. The tailor rose from his work when he saw his son coming with a foreigner in tow. Ahmet introduced us, and the tailor, his father, offered me his high stool. He was much older than I, so I politely declined.

"But it is an honor to have one of my son's teachers in my shop!" he said in Turkish.

Ahmet was a scholarship student, getting a high-powered education his father never could have afforded on a tailor's income. The boy brought tea, and listened to our conversation. We chatted until we reached the end of my Turkish conversational ability, at which time Ahmet knew I needed a ride to

Aphrodisias. He disappeared, and a few minutes later came running back with the news that an oil tank truck was coming and would give me a ride, at least in part because I was a teacher. Within a minute I was sitting in the cab in front of several tons of fuel oil on my way to Aphrodisias.

Aphrodisias, the city of Aphrodite, goddess of love. As the oil tanker trundled along I thought of Jane and wondered what she was up to. After her year in Italy she had moved to London and enrolled at the London School of Economics to get a master's degree. I was never able to convince her to come visit me in Turkey. It would have been fun to visit the City of Love with her. The truck stopped, I got out and walked to the ruins.

Aphrodisias was first settled about five thousand years ago. By the eighth century BC its temple to the goddess of love was a place of pilgrimage. The Byzantines put a stop to the naughty Aphrodite-worship, tearing down the temple and building a chaste church on the site. Tamerlane roared through in 1402, pillaged the city, and it never recovered. The small Turkish village of Geyre occupied the site until 1956 when it was flattened by an earthquake. Finding some sliver of good in the tragedy, the government took the opportunity to resettle the surviving villagers about a kilometer away so that the ruins of Aphrodisias could be excavated.

Professor Kenan Erim, a Turkish-born archeologist from New York University, began the excavations in 1961 and revealed a wondrous city grown rich from the fruits of love-pilgrimage: a gleaming white marble theater, an exquisite small odeon, and a stadium in such good condition it could still easily be used immediately for races and shows.

It was late in the afternoon when I had finished touring the ruins and taking notes. I hit the road again, and I was concerned that I might get no ride at all. Aphrodisias had no services—no food, no beds, no telephones, no nothing—so I really wanted to get at least to Karacasu or Nazilli. I started walking, and wondered if I'd have to walk the entire 12 kilometers.

After a half mile or so I heard a car coming from behind me. I flagged it down. It was a Jeep jammed with empty beer bottles and village women—and I mean jammed. The cases of Tekel bottles *filled* the entire back and went up to the canvas roof. The three women filled the one passenger seat. Their crowded position and Turkish gender protocol forced the driver to be ever so delicate when he manipulated the long gearshift lever.

"Sit here!" the driver said, indicating the air to the left of the driver's seat.

"Where?" I asked, puzzled. There was no place to sit, just air.

The driver shifted to his right, exposing a six-inch section of the driver's seat and pointing to it with glee.

"Here!" he said.

A grappling hook welded to my right buttock would have been a useful bodily appendage at that moment, but as I didn't have one, I hooked onto the six-inch section of seat with the power of my imagination. I gripped the back of the driver's seat with my right arm, and the canvas top of the Jeep with my left hand. The canvas door of the Jeep banged against my knees.

"You speak good Turkish!" the driver shouted happily as he delicately shifted the Jeep into gear and roared off. "Are you German?"

Fish With a Stogie

I made it back to the Aegean coast at Kuşadası, and used that as my base for day-trips to the many other archeological sites in the region. On my third day in Kuşadası I was finishing up. I hitched a ride as far as the great theater at Miletus, walked around the site, took my notes, then looked for a ride south. There was nothing, so I headed out on foot. I had on a T-shirt, shorts and sneakers. My only impediment was a small Pan Am flight bag which contained an alternate set of underwear, a few toiletries, a bottle of sunblock, a spare notebook and a pen. I didn't even need a change of clothes. When I washed out my T-shirt and shorts the hot, dry Aegean summer air would render them as dry as a Balkan cabinet meeting in under 20 minutes.

I walked south from the huge theater of Miletus toward the colossal temple of Didyma. The sun was bright, the country road bordered by a riot of wildflower color and framed by fields of ripening grain. Birds chirped and flitted among the branches in the fruit orchards near the road. I had work to do and discoveries to make, but I could do the work and make the discoveries on my own schedule, in my own way. This was the direct opposite of office work! I was ignorant of it at the time, but years later it became clear to me that at that time, on that day, walking along that road, with a minimum of possessions, attachments or worries, I was as free and careless as I would ever be in my life.

At the end of the day I was back in Kuşadası, tired but satisfied. I washed up and went out for dinner, intent on treating myself to fish and wine as a reward for a few days' hard work well done. Though it would end up costing me three dollars—more than I could really afford—I decided on the *Toros Canlı Balık* ("Taurus Live Fish") Restaurant right on the water by the ferry dock. My rationalization for blowing my budget was that I had to try out the Canlı Balık in order to properly describe it to my readers.

The maitre d', a short, mustachioed, balding man who was also the restaurant's owner, showed me to a waterfront table and summoned a waiter. We discussed the available courses and I decided on *sigara böreği* (cylindrical pastry fritters stuffed with white cheese), a mixed salad, a small one-person fish, and a half-bottle of white wine. The waiter went away briefly, put in the order at the kitchen, and returned with my wine.

The evening air was warm and light, the sound of the sea water restful as it lapped the shore. I took a sip of wine. Every table at the Toros was furnished with a miniature basil bush planted in a whitewashed olive oil can. You brushed your fingers among the leaves, lifted your fingertips to your nose, and took in the scent of the spice. I took another sip of wine, sniffed the fragrant basil, and enjoyed the feeling of relaxation seeping into muscles and flesh tired from the day's exertions.

The waiter returned with my appetizer and salad, and I eased into them, bite by leisurely bite. The evening was too perfect to rush.

After a respectable time and the credible consumption of the plates before me, the waiter brought my fish. He was about to set it down on my table when the maitre d' came running over, his face contorted in alarm.

"What are you *doing?*" the maitre d' asked the waiter, his eyes huge with apprehension, his eyebrows rammed up to his hairline.

"I-I-I'm serving the gentleman his fish," the waiter replied, confused.

"Like *that??*" the maitre d' asked, his voice shrill.

All three of us looked at the fish. It was your standard ten-inch fish, silvery, nicely grilled and set in the middle of a white oval plate. A wedge of lemon and a sprig of parsley had been added for color. It looked good. I wanted to eat it.

"No, no, no, no, *no!*" the exasperated maitre d' cried. " Come with me!" he said and dragged the waiter, still holding the fish, off toward the kitchen.

A few minutes later they were back, moving slowly in solemn, self-satisfied procession. The fish was on the same plate, but otherwise it had been utterly transformed. A half-dozen thin slices of lemon were artfully arranged like scales along its back. Around its sides were green and black olives, radishes carved into roses, a peacock-fan of arugula leaves, and a veritable banzai forest of parsley. At the far end by the tail was half a lemon wrapped in cheesecloth so that when I squeezed lemon juice onto my fish no pesky seeds would fall.

"Almost ready," the maitre d' said. He was holding a small square of paper, a glass of amber liquid and a box of matches. He took the paper, rolled it into a tube, dipped it into the liquid (which proved to be brandy), stuck it into the fish's mouth, struck a match and lit the tube. The fish-cigar burned gently with a cool blue brandy glow.

"Now," the maitre d' said to the waiter, breaking into a wide grin, "*now* you may serve the gentleman his fish."

ૹ

17

MIDNIGHT EXPRESS

She was a PCV teaching English in Ankara. I'll call her Mary. She would have been quite attractive if there'd been somewhat less of her, but it was a Peace Corps commonplace that when volunteers got lonely the men lost weight and the women put it on.

I was in Ankara for the September Peace Corps conference. August had raced by in a flurry of bus trips and note-taking, and here I was one evening with a few other PCVs sitting in Mary's apartment. She took out a guitar, gave it a tune, and played the old Peter, Paul & Mary ballad *I'm Leavin' on a Jet Plane*, singing it sweetly.

Mary had a boyfriend called Moe, an African-American vagabond out to see the world. Hippies were commonplace in İstanbul but rare in Ankara, and a black hippy was rare anywhere. Moe was exotic and charming, a good talker, and Mary fell for him. He gave her attention, sex, excitement and a whiff of devil-may-care freedom, and she gave him food, sex, love, and a place to stay.

Moe wasn't in Ankara for the sightseeing, or even for Mary. He was there because he was a convicted drug smuggler. He had been caught with a wholesale quantity, hauled into court, found guilty, and sentenced to a long vacation in a Turkish slammer. As was customary at the time, his case was automatically sent up for appeal. The Turkish authorities gave him back all of his possessions except his passport—or the drugs—and released him on his own recognizance. In theory he was supposed to appear at his appeal hearings.

What? A convicted drug smuggler walking the streets?

Sure. While he waited for Turkish justice to grind along, he dossed with Mary and enjoyed life. It was part of the system.

The system was this: in certain parts of the country, Turkish farmers grew a lot of opium. They had grown opium for centuries. Their pastoral life was built on the cultivation of the opium poppy. They ate the tender leaves of the opium plant in their salads. They fed the harvested plants, deprived of their precious opium gum, to their cattle. The only thing they didn't use from the plant was the drug. They sold the raw gum to the government, as required by law, for use in making morphine-based pharmaceuticals.

The problem was, illegal traders paid far more for the gum than the government's low fixed price, so many farmers sold only part of their crop to the government and the rest to the traders because that's where their real profit was. The traders turned the gum into heroin, increasing its market value a thousandfold, and sold it to European and American drug dealers, who passed it on at a princely price to addicts.

What's the Problem?

Drugs were a pestilence in American society, causing not only the illness and death of countless Americans, many of them young, but also increasing all the other crimes related to the drug trade: robbery, burglary, fraud, racketeering, blackmail, assault, murder.

"First-world" countries needed to do something about their drug problem. What they did was to blame the Turks for "being the suppliers," choosing to ignore the real problem, which was the demand for drugs. Without demand, supply would dry up. With demand, closing down supply in one country would only cause it to pop up in another. But it was much easier and politically expedient to use Turkey as a whipping-boy than to solve the problem at home in the USA.

President Nixon and the Congress put heavy pressure on the Turkish government to solve the western world's drug problem. To pay for the fix, the USA gave Turkey $40 million. The money was for increased surveillance, arrests, prosecutions and convictions, and to smooth the transition to the "poppy straw" process whereby the poppy plants are harvested before they mature and the sap (prelude to gum) forms. Opium can be extracted from poppy straw only in an elaborate factory, and the factory would be run by the government. With no sap and no gum there could be no heroin.

Turkey had gotten a reputation as an easy place to buy drugs which, for awhile, it may have been. Few Turks used drugs but supply met demand: if foreigners came asking for drugs, the market would meet their needs. In a way, foreigners probably invented the modern Turkish drug market, or at least the export department.

With the pressure on from the American government, the Turkish police were ordered to cut down on the trade and arrest drug smugglers, which they did. The foreign traders were the easiest because they didn't know the territory as well as the local talent. Most of them were rank amateurs, easy to pick up, charge and convict.

Due to that jolly absurdity which infuses so much of modern life, arresting foreign drug smugglers earned the Turks no praise from the people who were demanding that they do it. In one memorable incident, a British woman put her 10-year-old son, his luggage packed with illegal drugs, on a plane from India to London by way of İstanbul. The Turkish authorities discovered the drugs, took the boy into custody and his mother too when she arrived on a later flight. The British tabloids crucified the Turks for persecuting a child and demanded his immediate release. The tabloids apparently thought nothing of the mother's sending her child off by himself on a halfway-round-the-world plane trip along with enough illicit drugs to earn him the death penalty. The boy was released, with no thanks to the Turks for interdicting a shipment of poison meant for British youth.

When a foreign smuggler was convicted, the Turkish government had a different problem: it had to imprison the criminal. This was expensive because foreign prisoners were held in special prisons that were more modern and comfortable than the spartan traditional Turkish lock-ups. Foreign prisoners had to be treated better or there would be even greater howling from the media in their home countries. As the Turkish police acceded to American pressure and arrested more and more foreign drug smugglers, the problem of room and board for picky foreign crooks got ever more expensive for the Turks.

What to do? Somebody came up with a creative plan. They'd release the convicted smugglers pending appeal. This cut the incarceration expense right away. As the convict was being released, someone would casually whisper that a train ran from İstanbul to Edirne through Greece...slowly. It was true.

After the collapse of the Ottoman Empire, when the new border was drawn between Greece and Turkey, the old railway line ended up partly in Turkey and partly in Greece. Until the 1970s when a new line was built entirely on the Turkish side of the border, a slow train departed İstanbul each evening at 10:10 pm bound for Uzunköprü, near the Greco-Turkish frontier. After leaving Uzunköprü it headed north toward Edirne, crossing the frontier into Greece at Pythion (Pithio). It stopped there to take on Greek border guards who rode the train until it crossed back into Turkey, reaching Edirne at 8:01 am.

Because it was a Turkish train going from one place in Turkey to another place in Turkey with no stops in Greece (except for the border guards), this "corridor train" was officially a domestic run, and no passport was needed to board it.

Although drug smugglers called it the Midnight Express, it was not an express at all but a *yolcu* (passenger) train, Turkey's slowest kind, trundling along at a pace just above a run. If you had a good reason to get off in Greece, you could work up the courage to jump.

After a convict jumped off the Midnight Express he'd call the American consulate in Thessaloniki, claim that he had lost his passport, apply for and receive a new one, and be on his way. If the border guards saw him jump, they'd jail him for a night, consult with the US consulate, get him a new passport, and send him on his way.

Mary Takes the Train

Mary showed up on my doorstep in İstanbul one day and asked a favor.

"We're leaving," she said. "Moe and I." She told me about the train.

"We're going to meet in Thessaloniki. Moe left last night, without his backpack of course, so he could jump. It's in our hotel room with mine. I was wondering if you'd help me get our stuff down to the station."

"Sure," I said, "but no drugs. No drugs! I suppose Moe has learned his lesson, but just in case, I want you to go through his stuff and make sure there are no drugs."

"There aren't any drugs," she said, "but I'll check again just to be sure."

I hesitated, then asked, "Are you really doing the right thing? I mean, with Moe. Do you really think he's good for you?"

"I love him," she said. "Yes, I'm doing the right thing."

"I'll meet you at your hotel an hour before train time," I said.

When I got to her room in Sultanahmet, she was tying up the top of Moe's backpack.

"I checked," she said. "It's clean."

"Okay." I lifted the pack and strapped it on. It was heavy. Mary strapped on hers and we hiked down to Sirkeci Station. We climbed aboard the train, found an empty compartment and stowed the packs.

"Good luck," I said, giving her a hug. "I hope it works out. Mary, stay away from drugs. It's a dirty business and everybody in it knows more than you do. The winners are the people at the top. The little people at the bottom are expendable, and everybody except the little people knows it."

"Thanks," she said. "I've got my head screwed on right this time."

It was a beautiful system. American politicians were happy: Turkish arrest and conviction statistics were up. Turkish politicians were happy: they were saved the expense and media headache of incarcerating the foreign criminals. The criminals were happy: they were back on the road. Drug users were happy: when it got tough to trade in Turkey, they looked to Thailand and found a new, abundant source of supply.

Hollywood was happy: it got together a group of Turkish-speaking actors with Greek and Armenian surnames, cast them as "Turks" to Oliver Stone's racist anti-Turkish screenplay, and produced a movie that magically transmuted the Turkish police—who had acted in response to, and for the good of, the

American public—into perverts, and a convicted American drug smuggler into a suffering hero.

The movie was a box office hit, and no one who saw it ever wanted to set foot in Turkey. For helping to curb America's drug problem, Turkey lost millions of dollars in tourism revenue.

Several months later I got a thank-you letter from Mary. She wrote that she met Moe as planned and they hit the road. A few weeks later he dumped her for another girl and she was alone.

"By the way, when you carried it to the station, his backpack had two kilos of drugs in it," she wrote.

Of course it did. I felt exceedingly stupid, but not compared to Mary.

High Tension

Autumn, 1969. Normally my two-year Peace Corps tour of duty would have been over by September and I would have been on my way home, but my book wasn't done. While I was in Ankara I signed the papers for another year of Peace Corps service, did some research for the Ankara section of my book, and had a medical exam.

"Your blood pressure is high," the doctor said, "very high. Unusually high for a person of your age. We need to get you thoroughly checked out to see if we can find the cause. We don't have the facilities here. We'll send you to an air base in Germany for a complete work-up."

I didn't want to stop writing and go to Germany for a complete work-up.

"I've got home leave coming. I'm going to fly to the States for Christmas. Couldn't it wait till then?"

The doctor wanted me to go to Germany before October. I later learned that his vacation began in October and he wanted my case off his agenda before he left. It was his agenda or mine. I pressed the point and won. I'd go by my agenda, which was probably stupid because high blood pressure is a serious illness.

In November the Schneiders left for the warmer climate of Crete and I inherited their apartment on Beşaret Sokak. The landlord reduced the rent for a few months, but the idea was that I'd find a roommate pretty soon and pay the normal rent. I rattled around in the huge four-bedroom, 1½ bath apartment, and wrote.

I got up in the morning, wrote all day, then went to bed. I wrote sitting at my work table. I put my typewriter atop a cabinet and wrote standing up, as Hemingway sometimes did. The grocer's boy brought me a daily order of food. I wrote until I couldn't write anymore because I felt like St Simeon Stylites, the famous Byzantine ascetic who perched on a pillar near Antakya for 40 years.

I couldn't stand my isolation any longer but all my friends had left and I really wanted to finish my manuscript before I left on home leave in December. I had written to Jane in London, asking if she'd meet me in Paris for a romantic weekend on my way home, but I had no idea what she'd say. For all I knew she could be engaged to some charming Brit by this time. This is not the sort of fact she was likely to reveal to me in one of her infrequent letters.

Actually, I believe I was lonelier than St Sim. After a couple of years he had crowds of acolytes and admirers gathered at the base of his pillar shouting encouragement and tossing up tidbits. I was about to go stir crazy for lack of human society. What to do?

Go shopping, of course.

Works Like Magic So Aladdin Wants It

If I was going to be home for Christmas, I'd better take some gifts for my family. It was time to consult Aladdin. I went to Çadırcılar Caddesi No 3.

Aladdin was sitting on his stool by a dented bucket filled with glowing coals, his version of the charcoal brazier with which Ottoman hovels, houses, mansions and palaces were all heated before the advent of kerosene and central heating.

"Merhaba!" I said as I entered.

"Ooooh Merhaba!" he said as he rose from his stool with a smile, extended his hand and shook mine. We both sat down.

We chatted for awhile. Çavuş materialized out of nowhere, carried off our order to the teahouse, and I selected a few things which might make good gifts.

"How much?" I asked. He ignored me.

"I've seen something," he said. "On an American, like you. For keys."

"A key ring?" I asked.

"You put it on your belt. A little circular thing, metal I think. You attach your keys to it. When you want to open a door, you reach for your keys and pull them and they're on a string and after you're done unlocking the door you just let go and the string goes back into the circular thing and your keys are back on your belt." He pantomimed the miraculous key ring, finishing up with a look of delight.

"Oh, sure, yeah, it's got a spring in it. Retractable key ring. Yes. I can get you one."

"Good, good. Get two. Three, get three. Are they expensive?"

"For you, anything," I said, having been in Turkey long enough to have learned at least this much of the script.

"You are a friend," he said with a wide grin. "Is this all you want today?" he asked, sweeping his hand over my few selections.

"Yes, that's all. How much?" I figured about 100 liras.

Aladdin pondered for two seconds, looked me straight in the eye and said "Fifty liras."

I got the point. I made a mental note to buy four retractable key rings before returning to İstanbul. I owed him.

Paris for Lovers

I finished the book. The first draft had been 30 pages, the seventh and last 800, almost a quarter of a million words. It was just over two years since the idea had first occurred to me.

On December 3rd I flew from İstanbul to Frankfurt, then on to Paris. Jane had written to say that yes, she would meet me there.

We stayed at a little Left Bank hotel and breakfasted on *café au lait* and croissants (*veritable croissants* made by hand the old-fashioned way, not the *croissants industriels* served today). We browsed through the book stalls along the Seine, penetrated the murky, sacred darkness of Notre Dame and Sacré Coeur, sat over coffee in café-bars along the Boul'Mich, and ran laughing and gasping along the Champs-Elysées. It seemed to be the culmination of our romance of nearly five years.

And yet...we were still not ready for forever. I don't know if it was sagacity beyond our years or simply the wisdom of the heart, but somehow we knew that, rich as our love was, it was not the love of a lifetime.

We had a great deal in common, which we both felt was essential to any relationship, yet we were far from identical, which was also important. When two people with identical views of the world get together the result is one duplicate soul; when two people with similar but differing views fall in love, the result is a double soul, a new, larger, better creation.

I can't tell you how we parted, how we brought ourselves to part, how it was physically or emotionally possible to part. We had to and we did. Jane went back to London and I flew to America, until next time.

I arrived in Washington on December 9th, and the next day I was thrown out of the Peace Corps.

"You're an insurance risk," the PC officer said.

I had spent the morning at an internist's office getting a thorough exam. The result was that my mysterious rise in blood pressure exposed the government to insurance liability and raised its premiums, so I was—as the bureaucratic phrase so delicately put it—"terminated."

Merry Christmas!

My friend Dan and his girlfriend Jane were living in Washington. They invited me to dinner. Always ready to have dinner with Dan—not to mention any girl named Jane—I did just that. The next day I flew home to Allentown-Bethlehem-Easton Airport in Pennsylvania, where my parents met me and drove me home.

I had no job. I had a serious, mysterious medical condition.

I had an 800-page manuscript in my suitcase.

ॐ

18
AUTHOR MEETS ARTHUR

There was only one typographical error in my 800-page manuscript, and I corrected it so carefully that you had to turn the page over and hold it up to the light to see that there had been an erasure and retype.

Reflecting upon it now, I think that is sick. But so it was.

On a bitterly cold January day I took the bus from Bethlehem, Pennsylvania to New York City, then the unaccustomed luxury of a taxi ride to 70 Fifth Avenue and the offices of the Frommer-Pasmantier Publishing Company.

This was the moment! I was about to meet the most famous travel writer in the world, the head of the country's most prominent budget travel guidebook publishing company. I would shake his hand, submit my first manuscript, and officially become a writer. It was a turning-point in my life, and I knew it.

I took the rattly old elevator up to the top floor. The doors opened and I stepped out. In front of me were the transparent glass doors of Frommer-Pasmantier. On the other side of the doors was a receptionist's desk, complete with receptionist. The young woman was wrapped in overcoat, scarf and gloves, but was shivering violently all the same.

This didn't look like my conception of a Manhattan publisher's office. I had imagined a posh lobby; gleaming, swift, silent elevators; a designer reception area. In my conception, the offices had central heat. I figured this one must be like the Hotel Yılmaz in Kars where—if the reception desk clerk is to be believed—the central heating works perfectly until just before you arrive, when it mysteriously and irreparably breaks down. It's as though the furnace saw you march in the front door, then died laughing.

I pulled open the door and stood in front of her desk.

"I'm here to see Mr Frommer." I said.

"Do you have an appointment?" she asked, her teeth chattering. "The heat's off," she added, exhibiting her acute grasp of the obvious.

"No, but I have a manuscript for him."

No reaction apart from another shiver, which I chose to assume was not a comment on the arrival of my manuscript, nor the idiocy of coming all the way to New York without an appointment.

"He's expecting it," I added hopefully.

"He's not here right now," she said. "You can give it to me and I'll give it to him."

I hesitated, then handed over my treasure, my baby, the product of more than two years' work, wrapped neatly in brown paper, to a person I didn't know—a cold, shivering person at that, indistinguishable in aspect from the thousands of unfortunate homeless wanderers shivering, even as we spoke, on Manhattan's winter streets. And that shivering person seemed to accord no importance at all to my brown paper package. What if it disappeared?

I had a carbon copy at home, but the brown paper package contained the one and only original, typed on the cheap-but-good Smith-Corona portable typewriter that I had received as a high-school graduation present, and which had gone to college and to Turkey (and back) with me. If the manuscript was lost I would have to type the 800 pages again, and not make an error. (Well, maybe just one.)

I left the office, and New York City, and went home, having seen the inside of a Manhattan publisher's office but not having made it an inch past the freeze-dried receptionist's desk.

The bus ride home provided a new and vivid writerly experience, however. I had focused on this book for nearly two years. Starting from nothing—no experience, no information and no talent—I had accomplished my goal of writing a travel guide to Turkey and having it considered by a major publisher.

So…now what?

Writing a book and submitting a manuscript is like pushing on a locked door and then having someone unlock it from the other side. The door opens and you fall flat on your face. There's nothing gradual about it. You'd think that the post-book, postpartum depression would actually start when a writer finishes a manuscript, but the joke here is that a manuscript is never finished until it is submitted. Before it's actually out of the writer's hands, the writer can change it, and will change it, even sometimes in the rattly elevator on the way up to the receptionist who's playing the percussion part to Ravel's *Bolero* on her teeth. Like a bullet, a book is not gone until you can't get it back again.

Mine was now gone and I had to decide what to do next.

What Now?

I no longer had a job nor a draft deferment, but I did have an appointment with a posse of doctors in a hospital who were going to poke, prod, cut and stitch until they found out why my blood pressure was about to blow my head off.

I also had an apartment in İstanbul with the lights still on and the clocks still ticking and the plants by this time badly in need of water.

The doctors poked and prodded for a week, and were still perplexed. They told me that I had to go into the hospital in April for an operation. I had no idea what the world would look like when (or even if) I came out, so I decided to go back to İstanbul and have fun doing it.

I bought a cheap JFK-to-Luxembourg ticket on Icelandic Airways, departing on February 17th. On the 18th, in Luxembourg, I hopped on a train, and by the 20th I was in Grindelwald in the Swiss Alps. I stayed there for three days doing nothing in particular. I sat in my room and looked out the window at the snow-covered mountains. I skated on the little ice rink in the town square. I drank good coffee and hot chocolate. I thought about the meaning of life, which looked a lot different with a mysterious, serious illness.

By the 23rd I was in Athens, then I was off to Rhodes, where I took a bus to the village of Lindos. Dux and Monique had some friends there, the novelist Willard Manus and his wife Mavis who had invited me to stay with them if I was ever passing through. The weather was lousy, rainy and chill, but I didn't care. Mavis introduced me to all their friends and gave me my first glass of retsina which, despite that it is awful stuff, I liked, and I still like. It tastes like turpentine smells. You think turpentine-flavored wine is bad? I later discovered that in Turkey you could get turpentine-flavored chewing gum and even ice cream. There are reasons why this is so but I'll spare you the details.

My few days in Lindos flew by and then it was on to İstanbul.

My first stop was at Çadırcılar Caddesi No 3. Aladdin was sitting in his shop. He lit up like his fabled lamp when I entered.

"Oooooooh Merhaba! Merhaba!" he exclaimed, rising and extending his hand. A handshake wasn't enough. He gave me a Turkish bear hug and kisses on both cheeks.

"You came back! How are you? ÇAVUŞ!"

The boy appeared out of nowhere, as usual.

"Tea!" Aladdin bellowed. The boy vanished.

We exchanged pleasantries, news of the weather, my trip. After a decent few minutes had passed I hauled out the four retractable key rings I had brought for him. They were gift wrapped, that being the Turkish custom.

It is also Turkish custom not to open a gift in front of the giver lest the receiver's face betray disappointment. Override by the giver is permissible, however, so I overrode and urged him to open it.

He did. His face broke into a wide smile, showing crooked teeth.

"*Evet, eveeeeet!*" he said. "*Yes, yeeessssss!* This is it exactly!"

He took one of the key rings out of its package, extracted his dozen-piece key ring from his pocket, attached it to the clip, and mounted the assemblage on his belt. He grabbed the keys, jerked them out in front of him, swiveled his wrist as though opening a door, and let them drop. They flew back to home base on his belt with a quick whirrrruuup!

He looked at me and smiled even wider.

The boy brought tea.

"Çavuş!" Aladdin said. "Look at this!" He replayed the demo for the boy, who smiled. Aladdin gave him a knowing look. We are now the cat's meow, it said.

"Thank you for the others," he said. With them he was going to get big points with a few carefully chosen power-brokers in the bazaar.

"What are you looking for today?" he asked.

"Nothing," I said. "I don't have room in my baggage to carry much."

"What about this?" he asked, picking up a small heavy copper plate about six inches in diameter. It was plain and uninscribed, but probably a few centuries old. He handed it to me with a look that said "It's a gift."

Back at my apartment, I packed up my stuff, including Aladdin's little plate, and sent it off. I gave away my plants, turned out the lights, said goodbye to all my friends, and took the train west to Thessaloniki where I met up with Dux and Monique. They were driving to their summer quarters in the Austrian Salzkammergut, a huge, historic lakeside villa owned by Monique's parents.

We drove from the Aegean's balmy shores into the frigid winter of central Europe: Niš, Belgrade, Maribor, Vienna, and finally the beautiful little town of Gmunden on the Traunsee lake. When we finally crossed into Austria from the communist Balkans and could buy a newspaper in a language we could read, we learned there had been renewed student demonstrations in İstanbul. No surprise.

I spent a pleasant few days with my friends, then began the long journey homeward. By March 27th I was home, and ready—or at least resigned—to go under the knife.

You Don't Really Need It So We Carved It Out and Threw It Away

"We don't know what it is, but we think it's worth taking out," the doctor said. "Something on your adrenal glands." He was an internist, a heart specialist.

I had been in the hospital in Bethlehem for over a week and they had found nothing. Now this, the result of yet another x-ray. Pretty soon they wouldn't need the x-ray machine. I'd glow in the dark and they could just look at me like a TV.

They assigned the head of surgery to the operation, so I felt I was getting the best. For him, my blood pressure problem was no doubt a welcome relief from the daily grind of extracting cancerous prostate glands, of which he did a half dozen before breakfast.

I woke up after the operation, woozy but in great pain, with a foot-long gash around my midriff on the right side. "Holy cow," I thought, "they must've removed something the size of a Buick."

"Nah," the surgeon said. "It's actually easier and better if we make a big cut."

Easier for whom? For him, or the Buick? Not for me.

"So what'd you find?" I asked, since he didn't volunteer the information. I did have some curiosity about the outcome.

"Ectopic tissue," he said and, observing my glassine expression, went on to explain. "Nothing. Just a glob of stuff on your adrenals. Not cancerous, not infected. Just superfluous. We took it out."

Unused spare parts floating around in my gut. What a concept.

It took awhile to recover. The prognosis didn't help much.

"Take these pills," the internist said as I left the hospital. "They'll bring your blood pressure down. Let me know if you have any trouble with the side effects."

"What side effects?"

"Dizziness, dry mouth, sexual dysfunction. The usual."

"How long do I have to take them?"

"The rest of your life."

The doctors weren't done with me yet. I had received a notice to report for my army physical to the US Army's regional induction center in Wilkes-Barre, up in the Pennsylvania coal country.

The night before I took the bus to the induction center, I went to the movies. I saw *Alice's Restaurant*, with Arlo Guthrie, an anti-war flick that included a hilarious army physical scene. It was hilarious sitting in my hometown's only cinema (named, creatively, "The Movies"), and it may have been hilarious if you were Arlo Guthrie going through the script on a movie set and getting paid big bucks to bend over and spread 'em, but as it turned out it wasn't hilarious the next day in Wilkes-Barre, Pa. It wasn't scary either. It was boring. It took most of the day because of all the waiting—a good introduction to army life, from what I hear.

"You're rejected," the guy in the uniform said. "Your blood pressure's too high."

Duh. That's what I had told them at the beginning. That's what half the doctors in Bethlehem had told me, not to mention doctors in Ankara and Washington. In any case, that was that. My Selective Service classification was changed to 1-Y, which means that if the Huns are at the White House I might get a call.

I went home. On April 27th I celebrated my 25th birthday.

A few years later I learned that my internist had died of a heart attack and my surgeon of prostate cancer. Physician, heal thyself!

Too late.

Who Did You Say You Were?

"Hello?" my father said, picking up the phone. "Tom, it's for you. He says he's Arthur Frommer. He wants to talk about your book."

I took the phone.

"Mr Brosnahan?" asked a deep, sonorous voice. "This is Arthur Frommer. I've read your manuscript, and I think it's marvelous. I'd like to publish it."

I thanked him. I was thrilled. Actually stunned first, thrilled later.

"By the way," Frommer continued, "that's the cleanest manuscript I've ever seen."

Heh. No wry comments about anal retention.

He's going to publish my book! I'm an author!

"When did you finish your research?" Frommer asked. I admitted it had been almost a year ago.

"Well, we'd like the information to be as up-to-date as possible. Could I ask you to go back to Turkey, check all the facts and make sure everything is up to date? As soon as you get the refreshed manuscript back to us we'll put it into our publishing schedule. In the meantime, let's make an appointment to sign the contract."

We did. Shortly thereafter I took the bus back to Manhattan, and another bus south to 70 Fifth Avenue. It was warm in the Frommer-Pasmantier office this time, but then again it was May, not January.

I sat and waited well past the hour of our appointment. Mr Frommer finally came out to the reception area to greet me and usher me into his office, where he asked me to be patient a little longer while he finished some urgent business.

Frommer's office was large and light, though hardly fancy, with evidence of serious work: piles of manuscripts, empty coffee pots, crumpled balls of paper in the corners of the room.

Finally he hung up the phone and turned my way with a broad smile. We chatted amiably for a few minutes, a secretary brought in the contract, and Frommer looked it over.

"I'm terribly sorry," he said. "This just isn't the right text. Could I possibly ask you to take a walk in Washington Square Park for another ten or fifteen minutes while my secretary retypes it?"

I was beginning to get the picture: Arthur Frommer works precisely twice as hard as any other human being on the planet.

"I only take four hours of sleep a night," he said after my walk, which I had knowingly stretched to a half hour and I'd still arrived back in the office before the contract was ready. "There's so much to do."

We signed the contract.

"Now let me write you a check," he said, assuming that I'd concur. He rummaged in his desk drawer, took out a checkbook, and wrote me one for $750, half of the $1500 advance against royalties.

Let me tell you, it's a magical moment when you get that first check for your writing.

Bulgarian Delicacies

The sooner I refreshed my manuscript, the sooner it would be published and earn royalties for me. No time to lose! On June 15th, martial law was imposed in Turkey because of violent protests by workers' groups. On the 19th I got on another Icelandic plane at JFK and flew to Luxembourg, took a train to Munich, then another to Gmunden, Austria. Dux, Monique and Tamara were heading back to Turkey, and I was tagging along. Zagreb, Belgrade, Niš, and finally on the 13th, Edirne, the westernmost town in Turkey. It was great to be back, especially after the privations of traveling through communist Yugoslavia and Bulgaria.

Typical scene: at the end of a long day's drive through commie-land we find the best hotel in town, which isn't saying much. Let's call it the "Distinguished Unique Mansion of the People," or DUMP for short. We enter the spacious dining room lit extravagantly by a pair of 25-watt bulbs and attended by one comatose 15-watt waiter. He sees us coming, scrambles to hide but is prevented from doing so by our laser-like glares.

There being no maitre d', we show ourselves to a table and sit down. It's easy for us but impossible for Tamara, who is three years old and can't even see the table top when sitting in your standard-issue Bulgarian dining room chair designed for a sausage-fed party apparatchik. The waiter approaches, ready to do battle.

"Do you have a child seat?" Dux asks.

We ask it in German, English, French and Turkish because the only word of Serbo-Croat or Bulgarian we know is pivo, the word for beer. We learned *pivo* in Ljubljana after having scoured every shop on every street, circulating like town criers chanting "Beer! Beer! Beer!" but no one responded until finally we spotted a half-dozen bottles sitting in a plastic tub filled with luke-cool water behind the counter in a shop. We pointed to them excitedly. "Pivo," the shopkeeper said. "Bingo!" we cried.

No child seat, though.

"Do you have anything else the child could sit on?" Dux asked. "Telephone books? A pillow?"

"*Nyet!* Children shouldn't even be in a fancy place like this," the waiter said. So Tamara sat there, her eyes barely able to see the top of the seriously spotted tablecloth, which wasn't so bad after all, come to think of it.

We asked for menus. The waiter produced one that looked as old as the Magna Carta, but far less detailed.

"I'd like the steak," Dux said.

"Nyet! No steak."

"The chicken, then."

"Nyet! No chicken."

"Well, what do you have?"

"Local specialties."

There was this mystery item on the menu: local specialties.

"May I order the local specialty?" Dux asked, the waiter missing the irony entirely.

The local specialty was chicken, which meant we could at least boast we had had a fowl dinner. The price was even fouler: because of the manipulated exchange rates on the soft commie currencies, the bill for dinner came to an enormous $12.

Envision now, if you will, our arrival in Edirne, the first town over the border in Turkey. After border formalities we head for the Kervan Oteli right in the center, the best in town, charging a substantial TL75 (US$5) per night for a double room with bath, breakfast included. After washing the dust of the communist Balkans from face and hands we found a table on the pleasant open-air terrace. A young waiter approached.

"We'll need something for the child to sit on," Dux said. The words were barely out of his mouth when the waiter shot off, casting back a vigorous "*Hay hay!*" ("By all means!") He quickly rifled a bedroom of its pillows and in seconds Tamara was sitting on a cloud.

The customary Turkish five-minute discussion of culinary possibilities ensued. We asked if the kitchen had such and such a dish, and the waiter said yes, yes and yes. We ordered too much, ate too much, and enjoyed it all. The bill was under $5, including *bira*.

We were definitely back in Turkey.

The Place for Me

The next day we rolled into İstanbul and right back to Ayazpaşa, our old neighborhood. The Schneiders had arranged to sublet the tiny top-floor apartment on Rıza Bey Yokuşu while the director of the American Research Institute and his family were away on vacation. I had arranged to stay with Mary Lou and Jim Johnson at Robert College.

Mary Lou and Jim were salt-of-the-earth Midwesterners who had come to

Turkey as missionary teachers years before, and eventually ended up in the village of Rumelihisar on the Bosphorus next to the huge castle built by Mehmet the Conqueror. Jim had a job at Robert College, the American university founded a century before by New England missionaries, which was also right next to the castle. Mary Lou raised their three children, kept house in a big New England duplex that had been built as faculty housing, and provided free bed and board for an astoundingly long, varied and motley procession of guests, students, way-farers, freeloaders, troubled youth, up-and-coming stars, artists and runaways of a dozen nationalities, of which I was merely the most recent.

When I moved in it was mid-July, and hot as hell even in İstanbul, and all the worse because Turkey was under martial law. The political tension between Left and Right had gotten so explosive that the military had taken over in one of its every decade "gentlemen's coups."

Atatürk had charged the armed forces with the protection of Turkish democracy. If the political parties were heading out of control, the army was supposed to bring them back into line. This sounds crazy, but in Turkey it worked. The armed forces, steeped in the legacy of Atatürk's reforms, are by far the most respected institution in the country, and have been ever since Atatürk established the republican army during the War of Independence.

In 1960, when Adnan Menderes, the popular Perón-style prime minister, was leading the country toward rightist one-party rule, the army sent tanks down Ankara's boulevards and the government fell. Now, in 1971, tanks were no longer necessary. The generals read a short message on the radio about the need for a strong government to fight anarchy, to establish fiscal responsibility, and to carry out social reforms. The government folded, martial law was proclaimed, and the generals set up a new non-political interim government to sort everything out.

As a foreigner, martial law wasn't too bad. I just had to produce my passport whenever a pair of the ubiquitous military police requested it. But there were soldiers everywhere and people were tense and unhappy not so much because the soldiers were there but because the soldiers were necessary.

I hit the road. Ankara, Konya, Bursa, Ayvalık, İzmir. I raced around the country by bus updating my manuscript. Enough had changed that I easily saw the wisdom of Frommer's request.

"I may have a place for you to stay," Mary Lou said when I returned to her house from a lightning excursion to crash in one of her spare beds yet again. I hadn't worn out my welcome, she said. She just needed my bed for the next vagabond arrival.

The place to stay was another faculty apartment nearby. The family was on vacation and I was welcome to stay there. I moved in. It was perfect for writing. I stripped to my shorts, brewed tea, concocted huge salads, cooked the occasional gigantic bowl of pasta, and wrote. I carefully retyped the entire manuscript, chapter by chapter as I completed them, putting in the latest prices in both Turkish liras and US dollars, following the Frommer style.

On August 9th, with most of the manuscript retyped, the government devalued the Turkish lira from 12 to 15 per dollar, which meant that all of my carefully-typed dollar prices were now obsolete. With the surge of inflation that followed, all of the carefully-typed Turkish lira prices would soon be wrong as well.

I began again and retyped it all.

The owners of my borrowed apartment returned from vacation and I had to move out.

"I have another place for you," Mary Lou said.

It was the *konak* (mansion) of the pasha who had been in charge of İstanbul's water supply during the last years of the Ottoman Empire, a fine big hilltop house with spectacular views of the Bosphorus and the Rumelihisar castle.

"Not only that," Mary Lou went on with a knowing gleam in her eye, "they've got sweet corn in their garden."

Corn (maize) is the staple grain of the Americas, like wheat to Europeans or rice to Asians. The great Aztec, Maya and Inca civilizations were built on corn. Any true American's heart leaps up with gladness at the thought of good, authentic sweet corn, and August is the month to eat it.

American sweet corn was unknown in Turkey at the time. To the Turks, corn-on-the-cob (*mısır*) was a street food, a cheap gastronomic amusement: ears of coarse corn roasted on charcoal or boiled for hours in mobile cookpots. The current residents of the "water pasha's" mansion were real Americans. They had imported sweet corn seeds and planted a patch. It was mid-August and the corn was just about ripe.

"I know," they said. "We'll miss it, but we want to take our vacation now. Help yourself. Enjoy it. Just remember to feed the dogs, please."

I moved in. This was even better!

"Oh," the owners said as they were leaving, "it looks as though Missy may be going into heat." Missy was the smaller of the dogs, a gigantic German shepherd. "She's been fixed so she can't get pregnant, though. You can let her out."

Hot Dog!

When Missy went into heat, all of canine İstanbul found out about it. Word went out on the barking chain and they appeared from every district and quarter: finely-groomed standard poodles from Nişantaşı, mangy curs from Kasımpaşa, borzois left over from the sultan's kennels at Dolmabahçe, bloodhounds from police headquarters in Fatih, hunting dogs from the Belgrade Forest. Champion swimmers leapt into the Bosphorus with a yelp and doggie-paddled over from Üsküdar and Beylerbeyi. I swear I even saw a strange breed bearing the double-headed-eagle livery of imperial Byzantium.

Missy scratched at the door, rolled on the floor and whined and howled to get out. Writing in the midst of this racket was clearly impossible. I let her out straight into the middle of a surging maelstrom of sex-crazed male dogflesh. The noise got worse, then far worse, finally rising to crescendo after crescendo as each dog hammered it home. Unable to work while surrounded by a scene out of Stephen King, I watched from a window.

Suddenly the howling died and the pack drew back, revealing Missy and another German shepherd connected rear-end to rear-end, unable to pull apart, locked in Penile Prison. Missy's tongue lolled juicily around in her open jaws, covering her face with splashed drool, as she performed the Kegel of the Century. The male was whimpering, whining and redefining the term "hang-dog." He'd pull away and when the pain became excruciating he'd ease back. Finally they just stood there looking anatomically ridiculous.

What was I, as a responsible house- and dog-sitter, to do?

Check the corn. I wandered down to the garden, unbothered by dogs, and shucked the top of an ear. It was still slightly immature, not quite ready yet. A few more days. Ah, but it was a fine stand of sweet corn! This was gonna be great. The price was right, too.

I walked back to the house. Missy had finally allowed the male to withdraw. He dragged his sorry arse and now-footlong dog-dick back to Beşiktaş, where he's still thinking that one over. Missy ran toward me, obviously having had enough for one day, or at least for the next fifteen minutes. With stealth and art I contrived to let her—and only her—into the house. After an hour or two of frenzied sniffing and barking at the door, her army of canine admirers dispersed only to reappear in full trumpet next morning at first light.

Okay, so I had to monitor this dog situation, too. I caught the rhythm for letting Missy out and then saving her—not to mention half the canine penises in İstanbul— from herself after a few hours. I stuffed cotton in my ears and wrote. And checked the corn.

"Tomorrow," I said to myself. "Corn for dinner tomorrow."

I knew it'd be a good day when I awoke at 7 am to a sunbeam in my eyes rather than being awakened before dawn by Missy's scratching and the chorus of canine Sinatras in the garden. İstanbul's favorite doggy odalisque was finally through her nymphomaniac stage, or so it seemed. I looked out the window: no male harem in sight. This was going to be a good day.

I wrote hard and well, and late in the afternoon went down to get the corn.

It was all gone. All of it. Not an ear left. The night before, the village kids of Rumelihisar, who had been surreptitiously monitoring the progress of the ripening corn even more closely than I, became connoisseurs of fine American sweet corn, picked just before it's to be eaten (no doubt mere seconds before my arrival), boiled lightly for a few minutes, dressed with butter and salt.

I ate pasta instead, and two days later the house's residents returned, rested and relaxed from their vacation, delighted to see that all was tranquil at the water pasha's mansion.

I went back to the Johnsons'. Mary Lou gave me a look and she didn't even need to say it: I have another place for you.

More Dangerous Than a Scorpion

It was another New England-style duplex. A Turkish professor and his family lived downstairs, and I could live upstairs, at least for a week or two, which was probably all I'd need because the manuscript was almost done. "If you need anything, ask the people downstairs," Mary Lou said. "I've told them about you." The people downstairs were a Turkish professor and his family.

The third morning of my stay, I went to the kitchen to make breakfast and noticed a big bug in the sink. Oops. It's a scorpion.

I hadn't had much experience with scorpions. I know they're common in the American southwest but we don't have them in Pennsylvania or New England. How does one, uh, dispose of a scorpion? I figured this was the time to consult the folks downstairs. I knocked on their door.

"*Evet?*" said the pretty young woman who answered their door. They had a daughter of dating age? This was a surprise.

"There's a...a...a"—I didn't know the Turkish word for scorpion—"a bug in my sink," I said, pantomiming a scorpion's sting.

The young woman was looking at me with an intense curiosity that appeared to go beyond scorpions. She wasn't concentrating on what I was trying to say.

"Let's go look," she said with a bit more enthusiasm than the occasion seemed to warrant. She led the way upstairs to my apartment. I went to the sink and pointed to the scorpion. She took a quick look, got a spatula, flattened the bug, dropped the spatula in the sink, and looked up at me again. I was pinned between the sink and the girl, and this was rapidly becoming a Situation.

We had been warned in Peace Corps training against getting into Situations. In the Turkey of the 1960s, we had been told, post-pubescent single people of opposite genders were never left alone together. It was up to society, in the form of chaperones, appointed or voluntary, to keep them from doing what comes naturally. If there was no parent or relative around, any citizen was expected to step into this role. It was absolutely essential because young people—at least the males—were *delikanlı* (crazy-blooded) and could not be expected to control their passions. Not only that, it was the parents' prerogative to select the proper mate for their child. Even the best love-match required the parents' blessing.

The results of an unsupervised tête-à-tête could be disastrous. Premarital sex was simply not permitted for girls, and pregnancy out of wedlock was a capital insult to a family's honor. In the more traditional regions of the countryside it was deemed reason enough by the girl's family (though not by the law) for both girl and boy to be put to death.

Needless to say, the strict rules made flirting and kissing a hundred times more thrilling in Turkey than in places like America where foreplay delights such as necking and petting (though not intercourse, at least not yet) were commonplace among teens and college students. Every Turkish girl and boy with a normal libido wanted to try foreplay, but rarely got the opportunity.

So here I am standing between a dead scorpion and a juiced-up Turkish girl, wondering which one is going to get me into more trouble. The girl was very attractive. Her parents were not at home, and besides we were alone in my apartment.

Travel writing is lonely work. You travel alone, sleep and eat and work alone. Why so? Travel writers go to all those fleshpot seaside resorts, cruise the topless beaches, check out the nightclubs and bars, don't they? True enough. But we do it at a hundred miles an hour. There's not enough time to talk to ourselves let alone get to know an eligible person of the opposite gender. Here was a Situation that solved that problem—Instant Intimate Acquaintance—if I wanted it.

I wanted it, but I'm not stupid. I sighed, eased away from the sink and around the girl, and strode purposefully through the front door. The girl followed, seething. She stalked past me, down the stairs, into her apartment and slammed the door. Damn!

I went back to work.

It Was Like One of Those Dreams Where You Can't Move Fast

Chatting with some friends I learned that the Peace Corps program in Turkey was being closed down. The threats from leftist radicals were simply too serious and frightening to ignore. The Peace Corps officers didn't want anyone to get hurt, so after eight years of relative success they decided to shut down and pull out.

It didn't directly affect me, a former PCV sitting in İstanbul furiously working to finish my book, but of course it made me sad to see a noble experiment end ignominiously in accusations, threats and rancor.

Speaking of my book, I was almost done with the update. The only remaining research trip was to Antalya, Side and Alanya on Turkey's Mediterranean coast. It was the one I dreaded. Mid-August was hot in İstanbul, but down south it was simply unbearable, at least for a northeasterner like me. Any town along the Gulf of Antalya would be like an open-air Turkish bath, and I would have to walk for hours at a lively pace in the heat of the day to do my work. Not only that, I was now taking a diuretic medicine to help control my blood pressure.

The sole purpose of a diuretic is to get water out of your body. The more water I drank to dispel the heat, the more water came flying out of me.

Okay, I thought. This is it, the last trip. I'll splurge and fly. If I'm lucky I can get it all done in one day. I was getting the hang of guidebook writing: work fast.

There was only one İstanbul-Antalya flight per day, in the evening. There was also only one Antalya-İstanbul flight per day, which was when the İstanbul-Antalya evening flight that had just arrived turned around and flew back. If I didn't get my work all done in one day, I'd have to endure another 24 hours in the heat and humidity, either that or take a 12-hour ride in an un-air-conditioned bus. Not a happy prospect.

I flew on down to Antalya with the clothes on my back, my notebook, a toothbrush, and my blood pressure pills. I found a cheap hotel and took a room for one night. I ran around checking prices in restaurants, then went to bed. Next morning I was up early and out at the bus station checking prices and schedules, then inspecting hotels, banks and the boat docks. By mid-morning I was on a bus bound for Alanya.

Alanya was a small town then, not the sprawling resort it is today, so checking out its tourist places was pretty easy. It was also hot, hot, hot! Sweat was flooding out of me, rolling down my face in sheets, getting in my eyes. I bought a cheap handkerchief and tied it against my forehead so the sweat wouldn't blind me. I sucked down bottle after bottle of mineral water. I left a damp trail through Alanya, then hopped on a bus to Side.

It was late afternoon by the time I arrived. I ran through the village, checking all the little pensions and the few restaurants, then caught a taxi out to the highway where I waited for an Antalya-bound bus to take me back to the airport.

"You'll get something pretty soon," the taxi driver said. "There's lots of traffic. You'll get something."

I had a comfortable amount of time to make my flight if I caught something pretty soon.

But there were no seats on the buses. The few that passed were completely full and wouldn't stop for me. I tried hitchhiking with private cars, but no one stopped. Time was passing and I was getting concerned.

Across the highway was a fuel station with a bus parked outside. I walked over.

"Whose bus is this?" I asked the attendant. "Is it going to Antalya? If not, is it for rent? Could it take me to Antalya?" It seemed a bit nuts to rent a whole 40-passenger bus for one guy, but the one guy was sweating heavily and about to miss his flight to coolth, not to mention the money he had paid for the plane ticket.

"It's broken," the attendant said. "Bad axle. It won't be going anywhere for awhile."

I went back to the highway.

Finally a bus stopped. It was packed, standing room only. I didn't care. It would be like a hamam inside, but hey, it was like a hamam outside, and at least the bus was a rolling hamam, rolling west toward Antalya airport and freedom. If it rolled fast and steadily, I'd make my flight.

I got in and stood, just another mass of simmering protein, fat and liquids, only damper than most. Of course there were no drafts, no ventilation. The driver crunched it into gear and the bus groaned into motion, straining under its protoplasmic load.

Halfway to Antalya the bus broke down. The driver lifted some floorboards in the middle of the bus and started tinkering with the transmission.

"Dunno folks," he said. "Doesn't look good."

I leapt out and flagged down everything westbound. Finally I caught a minibus driver returning home for the night.

"How much to Antalya airport?"

He told me how much.

"Step on it!" I shouted. The driver nodded, took off, slowed down, eased into a fuel station, and stopped.

Among many minibus and taxi drivers, a vehicle's fuel tank was not something you filled up periodically but something that was handy for holding just enough fuel to get you through your current job. If it took one liter of gas to get you through the day's routes, then you bought one liter in the morning and it was gone by evening. No point in tying up capital long term (ie, overnight) in a fuel tank.

The driver chatted amiably with the station attendant as he pumped several cupfuls of gas into the minibus. He chatted some more as he slowly pulled out his wallet, selected a few bills, and paid. He chatted in a friendly manner as the attendant made change. Meanwhile, my fingernails were being ground to powder between my teeth.

Finally he took off and we sped toward the airport. I tried not to look at my watch. It was going to be very, very close. Minutes mattered, even seconds.

I saw the lights of the terminal and the runway, counted out the fee we had agreed on, and thrust it at the driver as we were pulling up to the terminal. Before the wheels stopped I bounded out of the minibus and shot into the terminal. I ran up to the check-in desk, but the agents gestured frantically toward the boarding gate. I raced out onto the tarmac—no tedious security then!—and up to the Boeing 727 sitting there with all its lights on and its engines roaring. Two flight attendants, male and female, stood at either side of the rear drop-down stairway as though waiting just for me. The woman grabbed my ticket as I went by and I bounded up the steps with the stairway rising behind me.

The plane took off. Collapsed into a rear seat, I burst into tears.

I was done.

19

OTTOMANIA

The full moon glowed on the marble terrace as the musicians eased into a dreamy waltz. We put down our champagne glasses, held each other close and glided off across the smooth marble by ourselves, away from the others. To one side was the wine-dark water of the Bosphorus, to the other a stately Ottoman mansion built for the sultan's grand vezir.

"Let's not fall in," I joked.

"Fall in what? In love? Or in the Bosphorus?" She gave a tipsy chuckle, tipsy as much from the setting and the music as from the wine.

We were already in love. The setting just made it more vividly real.

We were at a wedding, though not ours. Actually, we didn't know whose wedding it was, just that the food and drink and music were good, and that the setting was incomparable: the new Hotel Carlton in Yeniköy on the Bosphorus, just north of the Sait Halim Paşa Kiosk, the Ottoman mansion.

We were staying at the Carlton. That afternoon we had taken a swim in the pool, then waited for the elevator to take us up to our room. When the doors opened we, dripping wet in our bathing suits, came face to face with a bride and groom in full nuptial regalia. They were having their wedding portraits made in advance of the reception, which would start in about an hour. We let them out before we sloshed in.

We changed into our best clothes and descended to see what was going on. Turkish weddings are for everybody, and having unknown foreign guests wander in seemed to delight the happy couple. They beckoned us to join them on the terrace, take a glass, wade into the buffet tables. We did. Then the moon came up, washed the marble quay with silver, and we glided off to be alone.

Not bad for the price, which had been a few hours' writing. We, my fiancée Jane and I, were in İstanbul on a free trip. I had won it in an essay contest. But I'm getting ahead of myself as usual.

Now I Really Am an Author

In early September 1970, Mr Frommer accepted my book for publication. I bummed around Turkey that month and then, leaving most of my travel gear in İstanbul, I boarded a Turkish ship bound for Rhodes, where I visited friends in Lindos for a few weeks. Soon after I arrived cholera was discovered in İstanbul, and on October 22nd the Greek government closed the border between Greece and Turkey. The official reason was so travelers from Turkey wouldn't bring cholera into Greece, but the Greek government was not even allowing travelers to go from Greece to Turkey, which revealed the real reason.

During the past few years, more and more tourists had been making excursions from the Greek islands to Turkey despite the dire warnings of the Greeks that Turkey was unfriendly, expensive and dangerous. Travelers who spent a day or two in Turkey discovered just the opposite: friendly people, great food, safety, low prices, and lots to see and do. They came back to Greece saying "Turkey is my next vacation destination." Naturally, the Greek government wanted these travelers to spend their money in Greece, not in some other country.

By now tourism was a mainstay of the Greek economy, so the Greek government made it difficult for travelers to cross into Turkey. By law, any boat sailing from a Greek island to Turkey could only be advertised using one small sign at the office where the tickets were actually sold. No other advertising or publicity was permitted. Anyone wanting to buy a ticket had to search and ask, and islanders were rarely forthcoming about the boats. By contrast, in every port town on the Turkish side of the water there were large signs shouting "BOATS TO GREECE!" The Turkish boat owners wanted the business.

With the border closed, I couldn't get back to İstanbul, where most of my traveling stuff was. I hung around Lindos for awhile and then, borrowing some winter clothes from friends, took trains through Europe to France. By December I was in Provence, where I was engaged as a house-sitter by Stephen (later Sir Stephen) Spender, the renowned British poet, and his concert-pianist wife Natasha Litvin. Their beautiful Provençal retreat had been broken into and trashed the year before, and the squatters had burned the books of Mr Spender's library to keep warm, so the Spenders offered the house to me rent-free if I'd just live there and keep the bad guys out. When spring came so did the Spenders, so I cleared out, moved on to their house in St John's Wood, London, never too shy or polite to turn down free digs.

I returned to Lindos for July and August, where I rented a primitive village house with no utilities for $10 a month. I borrowed a gas ring for cooking, collected water in a big clay *pythos* for washing, used the tourist toilets in the main square, and lived on $1 a day while earning $3 a day by translating Turkish poetry into English. No electricity, no phone, no furniture, no refrigerator, no radio or television, no bills, no worries. I worked at the translations in the morning, took a swim in the refreshing Mediterranean, and ate a simple lunch with a cold bottle of Amstel beer bought in a shop (my single luxury), worked another hour, then indulged in the Greek luxury of a four-hour siesta before dinner. As a poverty-stricken bachelor I was never expected to entertain. I was always invited to dinner at someone else's house.

I saved my daily Amstel bottles and experimented with them, filling each with a different amount of water until each played a different note when I blew across the top, and all together their notes made a complex chord: an Amstel aeolian harp! I set the bottles in a window and when the brisk *Meltemi* wind blew across them they played gentle background music.

Maltese? Serbo-Croat?

In September, 1971, my vagabond year over, I was back in Boston, having been accepted into the doctoral program at Tufts University, my alma mater, for a PhD in history. The US government was kind enough to grant me a full scholarship. The Feds appeared to believe that the world needed a few more Ottoman historians. I rented an apartment in The Waverly on Mount Auburn Street in Cambridge, Massachusetts, and moved in.

Much as I loved history, and Turkey, studying Ottoman history was like climbing Everest. The language requirements alone were almost insurmount-able. The perfect Ottoman historian should be able at least to read all the major languages of the empire in which documents and/or scholarly articles might be written: Arabic, Armenian, Bulgarian, Dutch, English, Farsi, French, German, Greek, Hebrew, Hungarian, Italian, Kurdish, Maltese, Rumanian, Russian, Serbo-Croat and Turkish. I could do English and French alright, and struggle through German, Spanish and Italian with a dictionary. (I even once got through a scholarly article in Rumanian with a dictionary, but it was like laying brick with a tongue depressor.) The absolute essential was of course *Osmanlıca* (Ottoman Turkish). For my Osmanlıca classes I was the only student, something that should have clued me in but didn't because I was *vurdumduymaz*.

Ottoman Turkish was written in the Arabic alphabet and contained lots of loan words and grammatical constructions from Arabic and Persian, the languages of classical Islamic civilization.

In his passion to build a modern nation-state, Atatürk had decreed that starting in 1928 Turkish would be written only in the Latin alphabet, the alphabet of Europe and America, the alphabet of the future, not of the past. He also encouraged scholars to "purify" the Turkish language, chucking out Arabic and Persian loan-words and replacing them with pure Turkish words, either old words resurrected for new service or rank neologisms. The result was that by the 1960s the living language of the Turkish Republic was as different from the language of the Ottoman Empire as modern English is from the language of

Chaucer. Turks who had grown up in the Republic needed training and a dictionary to read Ottoman Turkish, which was exactly Atatürk's goal: to cut off the younger generation from the imperial, monarchical, medieval Islamic past.

It's hardly surprising that I was the only student of Osmanlıca. This was a dead language from a dead empire. No one spoke it anymore, although a hilarious simulacrum of it showed up in Turkish historical-romance movies. When I told friends what I was studying, I got this slack-jawed blank look.

Speaking of friends, I was making new ones, having been away from Tufts for five years. One new friend invited me to a cocktail party in Cambridge, where I met a lively young medical technician. She was slender, athletic, vivacious and adventurous, of medium height with brown hair. Her name was Jane so of course I asked her out on a date. Not all that surprisingly, we fell in love.

Jane—the third of that name in my romantic life—was very different from me. In the astrological language popular at the time, I was a Taurus (bull, which I am), and she a Capricorn (goat). The bull pushes straight onward, moving steadily toward the goal, shouldering the weight. The goat cavorts and gambols, is easily distracted, and gets into all sorts of situations because of its energy, liveliness and curiosity. We thought of ourselves as complementary: she brought a welcome liveliness and spirit to our common activities, and I added a useful probity and gravity which kept her from getting into sticky situations. Ours was not the sort of relationship that always went smoothly, we had our ups and downs, but certainly there was never a dull moment.

Better Than Box Tops

Around this time I received a notice mailed from the Turkish tourism office, 500 Fifth Avenue, New York. It announced a writing and photography contest open to all former Turkey PCVs. The writer of the best essay or story about Turkey, and the photographer who submitted the best picture, would win free trips to Turkey in July, 1973. The judge for the writing contest was Talat Halman, a distinguished professor of Turkish language and literature at New York University.

I submitted an essay, and won.

I went to New York and met with the director of the Turkish Tourism Office.

"The contest was our way of keeping the former PCVs interested in Turkey," the director said. "PCVs are our best ambassadors. They can spread the word and help us educate Americans about Turkey."

I asked Jane if she was interested in a trip to Turkey. We were having a bit of a down in our relationship at that moment, and I wasn't sure what she'd say, but what she said was yes. Yes, she was ready for an adventure, and would give it a try. Maybe a trip together, being together 24 hours a day every day and confronting the challenges of travel would help us better to understand one another. She dove right in, reading books (starting with mine) and learning as much as she could about the place. In no time we were flying toward Turkey.

In İstanbul we were met at the airport by a Ministry of Tourism car and driver and whisked away to the Carlton, a new modern hotel right on the Bosphorus shore in Yeniköy. I was disappointed to be so far north of the city center, but the Ministry put the car and driver at our disposal, so transportation was not a problem. Besides, the spectacular view of the new Bosphorus Bridge, opened in 1973, made the ride worthwhile.

The day after the wedding reception and our waltz by the Bosphorus we climbed into the car and I directed the driver to Aladdin's shop on Çadırcılar Caddesi. Jane loved him. We ended up buying some old brass cups and also a *rahle*, an intricately carved Kur'an stand of dark wood inlaid with ivory, ebony and mother-of-pearl.

"Where are you staying?" Aladdin asked. I told him.

"I'll come for dinner," he said. "Tomorrow. Alright?" I was supposed to have invited him but I didn't, so he invited himself.

The next day we sat somewhat apprehensively in the Carlton's posh dining room. I wondered how the staff, used to hosting İstanbul's rich and famous, would react to a troll from the bazaar.

"A shopkeeper will be joining us tonight for dinner," I told the maitre d'.

"Very good, sir. I'll show him to your table."

Aladdin marched in dressed in a suit and tie, looked around at the posh room, and was pleased. He expanded like a pasha in his palace, sat down, tucked his napkin under his chin, and called the waiter over. He ordered elaborately but not especially expensively, and we had an excellent dinner.

He was, no doubt, merely observing that old Ottoman saying, *Tebdil-i mekanda ferahlık vardır*, "There is felicity in a change of venue." Or, in modern Turkish, "It's fun to see new places."

The Ottoman sage who made that one up should have been a travel writer.

Your Tax Dollars at Work

Jane and I continued to date, deepened in love, and were married in the spring of 1974.

June arrived, and with it my PhD examinations. I had been studying for this three-day exam for the past six months. I was a nervous wreck. I finished the written portions of the exam. The final portion of the exam was oral. I sat at a large table in the conference room of the Department of History with all my professors. They asked probing questions.

Finally the chairman of the department declared the exam over and asked me to leave the room. Five minutes later my favorite professor, George Marcopoulos, emerged with his hand extended to take mine.

"Congratulations!" he said. I had passed my doctoral exams. Now all I had to do was to write a doctoral dissertation—a task of, oh, ten years at most—and submit it to be minutely examined and critiqued.

Professor Marcopoulos added surprising good news: the department had received word from Washington that my application for a Fulbright Dissertation Fellowship had been approved.

I was exhilarated and exhausted. My new wife and I would be going to Turkey in September to take up the Fulbright so that I could do historical research in the Ottoman government archives.

In the meantime, Arthur Frommer had offered me a job revising *Mexico on $5 a Day*. Seeing as how I was in between government grants, I took the job. Jane and I drove from Boston to Mexico, Belize and Guatemala revising that guidebook.

In September we moved to İstanbul and house-sat a friend's apartment on the Robert College campus while searching for an apartment of our own.

I immediately went to Ayazpaşa, the district I knew best, and walked the streets looking for *Kiralık Daire* signs. I stopped at the apartment building where the American Research Institute director had lived and asked the landlord if he had an apartment available, or knew of one in the neighborhood.

The landlord was Mr Hasan Tugay, a handsome, dignified grey-haired man with a white mustache. Hasan Bey's wife, Güzel Hanım, was equally distinguished, with beautiful white hair, a vivacious manner, and a brilliant smile. She spoke perfect British-accented English.

"Well, I wasn't going to rent that little penthouse apartment again," Hasan Bey said. "I don't think you'll like it. It's very small, and dusty now. I just use it for storage."

We looked at the apartment. It was indeed tiny, with one minuscule bedroom, a slot of a sitting room, an alcove, a corridor, a closet-like kitchen and a small bathroom; but it had a terrace of decent size, and from the terrace a sweeping view of the Bosphorus. We could see four Ottoman palaces: Topkapı, Dolmabahçe, Çırağan, Beylerbeyi. We took it.

We hired a taxi, a big old 1940s American station wagon with wood trim on the sides, to haul our stuff from Robert College to Ayazpaşa.

"So. Moving to a bigger place?" the driver asked.

"Smaller" I said. "Smaller, but with a panoramic view of the Bosphorus."

"Ah, well then," the driver said, waxing poetic, "then the apartment size doesn't matter. Your *soul* can expand."

But What Good Is It?

We soon fell into a daily routine. I went to the Ottoman archives every day to research my PhD dissertation, which was on the artisans' guilds of İstanbul.

The Ottoman archives are among the world's scholarly treasures boasting sixty million documents, only five million of which have even been catalogued. For a young historian, this is an unbelievably rich treasure. American history is not even four centuries old and all of the important documents have already been studied a thousand times by scholars. There is little opportunity to do new, ground-breaking work with original documents rarely if ever studied before. In the Ottoman archives, studying unseen primary documents is what most people do.

Apparently the Ottomans saved everything, but when the republic was founded and a conscious break was made with the past, Ottoman records were almost forgotten. When the document storerooms in Topkapı Palace were opened after the fall of the empire, it was discovered that the bottom few feet of the document piles had gotten wet and turned to muck. The top documents were salvageable. The bottom few feet were just shoveled out.

The sixty million rescued documents—800 years of bureaucratic records—were taken to the Sublime Porte (*Bab-i Âli*), the former offices of the imperial grand vezirs, and shelved. Scholars from several foreign countries were working in the archives when I got to the Sublime Porte on my first day. I wasn't sure where to start.

"The indexes," one of them said, pointing to some boxes across the room.

I went to the boxes and looked in. There were 12,000 little slips of paper hand-written in Ottoman Turkish. Uh-oh. This was how I was going to spend my youth, deciphering the cryptic handwriting of long-dead government scribes? What on earth was I thinking?

The Turkish archivists in charge were generally quite friendly to us foreign interlopers on their country's history, especially a large, balding man named Turgut Işıksal. One day at lunchtime, Turgut Bey signaled to me to follow him. We went next door to another, smaller archive building. He produced a key, pushed open the door, and led me in. The building held an especially valuable collection of documents. On display in a glass case was a detailed drawing for a Bosphorus bridge that had been planned by Sultan Abdülhamid II late in the 1800s, but never built.

Turgut Bey took me to a locked box of dark wood the size of a large briefcase. It was beautifully made and finished. He turned the key, opened the box, and took out one of several leather-bound books decorated with gilt. From each book dangled a huge wax seal the size of a baseball, attached by ribbons. The seals were stamped with royal arms.

"This is the sultan's copy of the Treaty of Vienna," Turgut Bey said.

I knew that the great international congresses of the world produced final documents recording their important decisions, but it had never occurred to me that these documents would still exist. Of course they would! Here was the very document, recorded in Ottoman Turkish, French, German and English (a separate book for each) that had been signed by the monarchs and prime ministers of the great kingdoms and empires of Europe. As a historian, I was thrilled.

One evening, when I returned from the archives, Jane showed me another old Ottoman document.

"What's this?" she asked. "Can you read it?"

I read what I could. It didn't look particularly important, but I didn't feel that I was a competent judge.

"Where did you get this?" I asked.

"I was just wandering around in some back streets near the Grand Bazaar. I looked through a doorway into a courtyard and saw a man burning a big pile of papers. I went in and took a look. They were all written in Ottoman. I didn't know enough Turkish to ask him about them, but when I picked up a few of them he said I could have them."

The next morning I took the documents to the archives with me and showed them to Turgut Bey.

"Where did your wife get these?" he asked. "Please have her show me!"

We fetched Jane, who showed us the courtyard. There was nothing but a pile of ashes. Turgut Bey talked to a few men there.

"They say that the documents were worthless. How do they know? I don't believe the documents have been properly assessed by an archivist. We may just have lost another part of our history," he said sadly.

It hit me: Turkish janitors have probably burnt more historical documents than early America ever produced.

Texans in a Taxi

We had been in İstanbul for several months. It was time for a vacation, so we took off to Side and collapsed into a room at Ayşe's pension. Ayşe had added two new modern rooms-with-bath to the pension, currently occupied long-term by a Texan family. We chatted with them over tea in the evening and learned their story.

The husband was under contract to an oil prospecting company on the Mediterranean coast. Because the project would take at least six months, his wife and daughter came along. They were not the kind who would normally have chosen to travel outside the USA, but they wanted to be together.

Even though they were based in idyllic Side, the result was not the best. The wife missed her home, its conveniences, and especially her daily dose of TV soap operas. The daughter felt entirely cut off from teenaged American society and consoled herself by creating, in her room late at night after her parents had gone to bed, a soap opera of her own starring herself and a local darkly hand-some Mediterranean romeo good at tiptoeing.

"If you ever get to İstanbul, look us up," I told them.

A few months later our Texan friends from Side came to visit. Having no clue as to how to get from Side to İstanbul, they chose the simple, direct Texan solution: they climbed into a taxi in Side and said "İstanbul." It was a 500-mile fare. The taxi driver immediately fell in love with Texas and its think-big people.

Unfortunately, they had not let us know they were coming. We were on the road ourselves. Disappointed not to find us at home, and without so much as a glance at the Blue Mosque, they climbed back into their taxi and drove back to Side making it a thousand-mile fare, something of a record even for a Texan.

Coffee on Wheels

It was time to check in on Aladdin. I strolled along Çadırcılar Caddesi, and as I neared No 3, I noticed a monstrosity, a five-foot-high copper water pitcher. It was an Ottoman *ibrik*, a ewer of classic design, fancy with spiral indentations swirling around its bulbous shape and a long spout that emerged from the bottom of the vessel and rose to the top in a graceful sinuous curve. It was enormous, and it was standing right in front of Aladdin's shop. I approached it, amazed. What on earth was it, where had it come from, what was it for?

I peered through the door. Aladdin looked up and smiled.

"How do you like it?" he asked.

"It's amazing," I said. "What on earth is it?"

"You see what it is. It's an *ibrik*. I made it."

Okay, I knew that Aladdin, a talented craftsman trained as a coppersmith in his youth, made some strange things. I caught him once making a traditional Turkish coffee pot. It was beautifully, carefully made, but it had wheels on it. Putting wheels on a coffee pot was like putting wheels on a frying pan.

"Why does it have wheels?" I asked Aladdin.

"Why not?"

The best was the time I caught him sitting on his three-legged stool critically inspecting an elaborate *nargile*.

"How do you like it?" he asked as I stepped inside. "It's from the reign of Sultan Ahmet III (1703–1730)."

"Beautiful," I said.

"Thank you," he said. "I finished it yesterday." It certainly looked three centuries old.

The *ibrik*, the ewer, was obviously just decorative. It could barely be picked up by a strong person when empty, let alone full of water.

"What do you plan to do with it? " I asked.

"Sell it, of course. I haven't decided how old it will be yet. From which sultan's reign, I mean."

"But who will buy it? It's so....so *big*!"

"I dunno," he said with a grin. "We'll see."

I was not interested in gigantic *ibriks*, wheeled coffee pots or even in brand-new imperial Ottoman water-pipes. I looked at other things, and found some I liked. I set them before Aladdin, who ignored them.

"I've seen American raincoats," he said. "They look good. Waterproof, too, I'll bet."

I knew a cue when I heard it.

"Would you like me to bring you one?" I asked.

"That would be very kind of you," he answered. I sized him up for it: shorter than I, but heavier. Sort of, well, troll-like.

We completed our bargaining. The prices we ended at were good. Surprisingly low.

I wrote to my mother, the factory-outlet maven, and asked her to look for a raincoat in Aladdin's size.

You Get What You Don't Pay For

My work in the archives was cut out for me, but being in İstanbul was difficult for Jane. She was studying Turkish but languages came hard to her. She had no friends or activities. She was a good sport about it, but it hurt my heart to see how unhappy she was. Her birthday was coming up, and I wanted to get her something especially nice, so I went to the Old Bazaar and Harry's shop.

Harry's real name was Hırant, or Hrand in the more common spelling. He was an İstanbul Armenian of middle age, slender and bespectacled, who spoke fluent English and a half dozen other languages, and enjoyed a brisk trade with the expatriate community of Europeans and Americans. I had visited his shop before. Like most Turkish shopkeepers he remembered every customer he had ever served.

He welcomed me, called out the door to the tea boy, and soon we were chatting over bracing hot sips.

I chose a silver necklace, not ostentatious but finely worked. I asked the price. He tossed it on a jeweler's scale, did a quick calculation, and said "A hundred liras." That seemed too good a price, but one questions only the other sort of price so I said "I'll take it if I can pay you half now and half later."

"No problem. Take as long as you want to pay the rest."

"Can you polish it?"

"I can, but you don't want it polished. The patina is the important thing for a piece like this." I saw that he was right.

By this time we were into our second glass of tea. An old woman appeared at the door holding a small cloth bag. She asked Harry if he was buying old coins. She needed the money. He took a quick look in the bag and said "Auntie, I can't give you very much for them. Go to Ahmet's shop over there. He'll give you more."

"Old coins aren't worth much?" I asked, surprised.

"Some are, some aren't," Harry replied. "I get a dozen people like her every week. Occasionally I find something worthwhile."

Harry launched into a reminiscence:

I was sitting in Nuri's shop chatting one afternoon and an old woman came to the door with coins. She pleaded with Nuri to buy them. Nuri took out a handful of her coins, picked out one particular coin and said "I'll give you a lira for every one of these, but nothing for the others." She wouldn't do it. She wanted to sell them all.

I asked her to tell me what she had been offered for each sort of coin. She gave me the various prices. I told her "I'll pay you that and take all of them."

The old woman was delighted. 'Oh, thank you, sir, thank you, thank you!' she said. We counted through the coins and added it up. It came to 200 liras.

"Nuri!" I said. "Lend me 200 liras. I'll pay you back first thing tomorrow morning."

Nuri handed me the money, and I handed it to the woman. She went away happy.

After she left, Nuri asked me why on earth I had done that. "Those coins are worth shit," he said. "I know it and you know it."

"I wanted to help the old lady," I said. Nuri gave me a "don't take me for an idiot" look.

We closed up shop shortly after. I took the bag of coins, jumped in a taxi, raced down to the ferry docks, got to Kadıköy, jumped in another taxi and raced to my apartment. I sorted through the coins. Most of them were junk, normal stuff, no big deal, but there were five oddball coins in there—like I thought there might be—little old things that didn't look like much. I sat down with my numismatics books and looked them up. It took most of the night, but I found them all. Two of them were not worth much, two were worth at least 50 liras each, and one was worth at least several hundred liras.

The next morning I got to the shop and sure enough, a couple of the guys came around wondering why Harry had bought the old lady's coins. They were thinking, "Harry's not the type to help old ladies out of the goodness of his heart, at least not in the shop." None of us here are. I'm no fool and they know it. They thought I knew something about the coin market that they didn't, such as that it was about to go up.

"What's with the coins?" they asked.

"I think it's a good investment," I said. They looked at one another. "Unfortunately," I went on, "I'm in the middle of a cash crunch, and I can't afford to invest. I need to pay Nuri back this morning."

One of the other shopkeepers offered to buy the coins. "What do you want for them?" he asked.

"Look," I said, "I couldn't really afford to buy them, and you're helping me out by taking them off my hands, so I'll sell them to you at exactly the price I bought them for: 200 liras."

The guy got out his wad but I said, "Just pay it right to Nuri to get me off the hook." He did. I gave him the bag of coins minus the special five. I figure that was okay because that's all the other guys were thinking about, that's all they thought was in there, that's all they were buying.

So now I've got five valuable coins that cost me zilch.

I know some coin collectors. I call them up and easily sell two of the lesser coins, one for 65 liras, the other for 70. Same for the next two. I tell these two buyers that I've got another coin, the real valuable one, and they want to see it. I also know a guy who's a serious, serious collector and this is one of the few coins he's missing from his collection. I make an appointment with each of them to show them the coin, and each appointment is the same: four o'clock on Friday afternoon.

They come to the shop one by one on Friday afternoon. At first they think it's a coincidence, but then they find out they're all interested in buying the same coin. I show it to them and they fight one another to bid on it. The bidding goes on, the time goes by, and soon it's almost 5—closing time. They don't want to come back and start all over on Monday, so the pressure is on.

To make a long story short, the serious collector buys it for 450 liras. I figure I've done him a favor because now his entire collection is worth a lot more.

Harry sits back and smiles.

On her birthday, I gave Jane the necklace. She loved it. "I can't wait to show it to the people at the hospital," she said. We had recently gone to the American Hospital in the Nişantaşı district and asked if they needed the services of a medical technician. The Turkish lab technicians jumped at the chance to tap into the latest American know-how. Jane was hired to teach them.

"This must've been expensive," she said, looking at the necklace. "Can we afford it?"

The Fulbright grant supported us at a below-subsistence level. We were spending our savings to stay in Turkey, at least at the moment. Money was tight.

"I got an incredible price on it," I said, "from Harry."

"Harry? Harry doesn't give bargains," she said.

I told her what I had paid and she agreed that it was a bargain. Had Harry slipped up? *Harry?*

I returned to Harry's shop to pay the other half of the price. He looked up the amount in his book of accounts. He paused for a moment, looked again, then winced perceptibly. He turned to me and smiled.

"I gave you a pretty good price on that necklace, eh?"

I smiled back. "It was a good price," I said. "It's a nice necklace. Jane loves it. I've recommended your shop to several friends."

Harry looked away and was silent for a moment, wistful. He swallowed. He looked back at me and smiled.

"Enjoy," he said.

20

GROWLING DERVISHES

You've probably heard about dervishes, no doubt the whirling ones I saw in Konya, but in fact there are lots of different dervish orders just as there are lots of different orders of monks and nuns. I ran into some dervishes unexpectedly while looking for books in İstanbul.

Whenever I was near the Grand Bazaar or visiting Aladdin I'd stroll through the Sahaflar, the old book bazaar, looking in the shops. I rarely bought anything. I just loved books.

One time I entered the corner shop. It was different. Its shelves were packed with leather-bound volumes, their spines glistening with Arabic letters in gold. I assumed that many were Kur'ans, and others Hadith, the "traditions," or sayings, of the Prophet. Others must have been religious commentaries.

Behind the shop's plain metal desk was a large middle-aged man with graying hair swept back beyond an ample brow and quick, intelligent eyes framed by horn-rimmed glasses. He looked up slowly as I entered, then welcomed me, and asked if there was anything in particular I was looking for. I hemmed and hawed.

"Please have a seat," he said in Turkish. He picked up the telephone and ordered tea, which arrived a few minutes later.

As I sat sipping my tea, a succession of men entered the shop, spoke with the shopkeeper and departed. Some of the talk was of books, but most was of other things. I didn't understand a lot of it because the vocabulary was specialized. It sounded like Ottoman. Something was going on here.

I sat, sipped and watched. The owner expected nothing of me. I was his guest and welcome to stay as long as I wished, as long as I was comfortable. Very Turkish.

I noticed that the people who came into the shop treated him with deference, and he responded with, well, noblesse oblige. A well-dressed young man carrying a briefcase entered the shop, stood in front of the desk, smiled, and addressed the owner formally as Muzaffer Efendi. Because he spoke slowly, as though making a ceremonial pronouncement, I was able to catch some of what he said:

"I bring you the greetings of the Community of the Faithful in Beyoğlu," he said. A succession of antiphonal religious formulas followed, then some business was done. After a formal exchange of well wishes and religious formulas at the end, the young man departed.

Efendi. The term, originally Greek, means "master." It was used in the Ottoman Empire as an honorific for literate men, members of the clergy, princes of the imperial blood, and army officers up to the rank of major. Under the republic, however, it had suffered the usual democratic title debasement, and was now normally used only when addressing men of the lowest social standing: doormen, trash collectors, street sweepers. Every man of any standing at all was now a *bey*, a lord, and anyone with the slightest distinction was a *beyefendi*, a lord-and-master. To a polite taxi driver, his fare was a *beyefendi*. So why was Muzaffer called an Efendi but shown such deference?

As the young man left, a figure filled the doorway, blocking the light and throwing the shop interior into shadow. The figure entered, allowing the light to follow.

It was an old white-haired man with a long white beard. He was wearing a thick light-brown woolen coat and clutching an ancient, battered leather briefcase against his chest with both arms. He greeted Muzaffer Efendi, bowing slowly, very low. Muzaffer Efendi rose from his seat to shake the old man's hand.

I was occupying the only guest chair. I rose to yield it to the old man, but both of them urged me to stay where I was and not to disturb myself. Muzaffer Efendi went to the door, called out an order to a neighboring shopkeeper, and another chair was brought. The old man sat down on it. He nodded to me and greeted me in German.

"This young man speaks Turkish," Muzaffer Efendi said in Turkish.

"Ah, you speak Turkish!" the old man said in Turkish. But are you German? British?"

"American," I said.

"American." The old man said, switching to flawless English. "An American who speaks Turkish. Extraordinary."

"I don't speak it as well as I'd like, and not nearly so well as you speak English," I answered in English.

"The language of Byron and Marlowe," the old man said, "and of course Shakespeare—if there really was a Shakespeare, and if he was Shakespeare and not Lord Dudley...or Marlowe!" he chuckled. The old man's accent was pure

Oxford as was, apparently, his knowledge of English literature. We chatted some more.

"If you're going to be an Ottoman historian, there are several books you should probably read," he said, mentioning their titles. "Muzaffer Efendi won't have them. He has chiefly religious and mystical books. But you should be able to find them elsewhere in the Sahfalar."

"I'll try to remember," I said.

Muzaffer Efendi, who apparently could understand some English though he did not feel confident enough to speak it, handed me a scrap of paper and a pencil.

"There is a saying in Arabic," Muzaffer said, speaking Turkish. "Thinking is hunting. Writing is catching the prey." I jotted down the titles of the books which the old man recommended. They would, indeed, be important to me.

After a few more minutes I paid my respects and left. I never learned who the brilliant old man was. I never saw him again.

Whenever I was in the Sahaflar thereafter, I'd stop in and greet Muzaffer Efendi. I discovered that in certain contexts—Ottoman ones—*Efendi* continued to carry its traditional weight of nobility and authority.

Whenever I greeted him he invited me to sit and have tea. Once when I accepted, he asked, "Would you like to join us early on Friday for our *sema*, our worship service? The Halveti sema. It's the start of Friday to us, Thursday evening to you. Muslim days go from sundown to sundown, you know."

"Yes," I said. Except for the sundown-to-sundown thing, which they had taught us in Peace Corps training, I had no idea what he was talking about.

"Are you married?" he asked. "You can bring your wife. If you're not married you can bring a friend."

"Thank you. Yes, I'm married. I'll bring my wife."

"Meet us in front of the Beyaz Saray in Beyazıt Square at seven o'clock on Thursday evening, Friday to us. We'll have a car and we'll go to the meeting place."

You Gotta Lose It to Gain It

On Thursday Jane and I stood on the crowded sidewalk in front of the Beyaz Saray. I had told her that Muzaffer was some sort of dervish leader, and that we were going to a dervish religious service. A few minutes after seven o'clock a car drew up. The window rolled down and a man asked "Are you waiting for Muzaffer Efendi?"

We got in. Muzaffer was not in the car. The driver made a U-turn and sped westward along the boulevard, then turned off into a warren of narrow, winding residential streets. We drove for perhaps 15 or 20 minutes before coming to a stop in front of the door in a nondescript low building.

We got out of the car. The unmarked door opened and a man ushered us into a fairly large low-ceilinged room painted a restful light green. A small area off to one side was hidden behind latticework. Another small area was separated by a railing, but open to view. On the other side of the room a low *sedir*, or Turkish sofa-bench, ran along the long wall, around the corner and along a shorter wall. The sofa could seat about a dozen people. In the corner, resting on the sofa cushions, was a large white turban. A cast iron post rose off-center to support the ceiling in the odd-shaped room's open space.

A group of perhaps a dozen men, young and old, occupied the open space, standing or sitting and chatting with one another. Other men were arriving in the hall. They were dressed in street clothes of varying sorts. Some looked like shopkeepers, others wore the black suits of bureaucrats, still others the pinstripes of bankers and corporate types.

The man who first greeted us raised his voice and formally introduced us to the group by saying our names. The men smiled, greeted and welcomed us, most in Turkish, some in English, a few in German. A man in a well-tailored suit approached us.

"Welcome! We're glad to have you with us. We're a diverse group," he said. "Many of the shopkeepers in the Sahaflar are members of our order, the *Halveti-i Cerrahi*, but we also have clerks, businessmen, government workers…. Muzaffer Efendi is our sheikh. He'll be here in a few minutes."

Our guide indicated that we should sit behind the railing on the carpeted floor off to the side.

"Would you like a chair?" he asked. We didn't want to disturb them, the floor was fine, but he insisted on bringing a chair for Jane. A few other foreigners were there, a British couple, two Germans, an Australian. Chairs were brought for the women. We men sat on the floor.

The dervishes filled the sofa, sitting relaxed and quiet. Others sat on the floor. All at once everyone rose, so we did too. A door opened to one side and Muzaffer Efendi entered dressed in white loose-fitting garments covered by a flowing cloak. He approached the corner seat on the sofa, lifted the turban, settled it on his head, and sat. Everyone took seats. He looked our way, smiled and nodded in recognition, then raised his eyes heavenward. Led by Muzaffer, all the men held their hands out, palms up, in the Muslim attitude of prayer. Muzaffer began to chant a prayer, a flood of sonorous Ottoman Turkish and Arabic ringing from his throat.

When the prayer was over the men wiped their hands across their faces to receive the blessing. Then they rose and formed a circle. Someone started a tape player and the room filled with lugubrious quarter-tone Ottoman music played by ancient musical instruments accompanying a droning, heavy-voiced choir.

Resting their arms on the shoulders of their neighbors, the men in the circle intoned a prayer in unison. They then began to move sideways, rotating the circle counter-clockwise and chanting "a-HOO a-HOO a-HOO!" which, I later discovered, is one of the names of Allah: "He! (the unnameable)." The men's chanting was breathy and full-lunged, which is why Westerners had nicknamed them the Growling Dervishes.

The circle rotated faster, the men moving vigorously in lockstep around and around. They breathed deeply and chanted with great exhalations. Some of them closed their eyes. Others had their eyes partly closed, as though half asleep or in ecstasy.

Hyperventilation is when the body gets more oxygen than it needs. The mind goes blank—you faint—and the body stops breathing in order to restore the proper balance. When the oxygen dissolved in the blood has been used up and more is needed, you recover consciousness and begin to breathe again.

The dervishes were using music, chant, movement and hyperventilation as means to ecstatic union with the Divine. Every now and then a man would stop chanting, his eyes would roll up, his head loll to one side, and he would appear to lose consciousness. Because his arms were linked with his neighbors', he would not fall. Soon his eyes would open again and he would rejoin the chant.

The only problem was the iron post. In a real dervish hall built for the purpose there would be no obstacles, but dervish orders were banned by law and the dervishes had to meet wherever they could, careful not to draw notice. The government wasn't interested in enforcing the ban vigorously, especially if the dervishes were discreet and stayed out of the public eye, and particularly out of politics. Although this hall served the purpose for the *sema*, it was hardly perfect.

More than one man hit the post as the circle rotated. One old guy kept getting slammed into it on each go-around until his fellow dervishes were afraid he might actually get hurt. They'd work to move the rotating circle away from the post but the old man was in ecstasy, oblivious even to his own safety or pain, and he'd catch the post with a BONG every time he came around. After a particularly loud BONG, which obviously got through his mystic *vurdumduymaz* and threatened to get him into real close and eternal union with the Divine, the men on either side carried him over to the sofa and sat him down to recover.

After ten minutes or so the dervishes stopped, and after a short rest they resumed the chant and dance, rotating and growling to ecstasy. When the fourth rotation ended, the men sat. Three of them went off to a table and sink in a corner, washed and cut up apples, and passed them out to everyone along with cups of water as refreshments. Several of the dervishes approached us foreigners to chat and tell us about their order, the Halveti.

"You know about Sufis, yes? Islamic mystical orders. Sufis seek direct experience of the Divine. 'Halvet' means 'seclusion' or 'loneliness.' We believe that our order is descended from the Prophet Moses, who went into seclusion on Mount Sinai when he wanted to speak with God. Thank you for coming to witness our worship."

Refreshments finished, the dervishes looked to Muzaffer, who raised his hands in supplication and offered a benediction. I caught just enough of the elaborate Ottoman to realize that we foreign non-Muslims were included in his prayers.

Gimme That Fish

My globe-trotting friends Joe and Pam came from Cairo to İstanbul in March on their way back to California. I apologized for inconveniences such as the city's periodic cutoffs of electricity and water.

"Compared to India, Cairo is Paris," they said. "Compared to Cairo, İstanbul is Paris."

My parents arrived in May from Rome, where they had been visiting my brother Steve, who was pursuing a year's additional study there in architecture.

"Here's your friend Aladdin's raincoat," my mother said.

I insisted that we all deliver it to Aladdin together. For this mission I carefully selected a driver from among the noisy pack at the end of Saray Arkası Sokak. His name was Hayri. He was in his late fifties, of medium height, clean-shaven, grey-haired and distinguished-looking. He always wore a tweed jacket, dark brown slacks and a matching sporting cap which perfectly matched his car, an antique Austin. At the wheel, he looked the perfect English gentleman.

As we approached, Hayri got out of the driver's seat, doffed his sporting cap, opened the rear door for my parents and bowed slightly as they climbed in. In one smooth, flowing, graceful motion he closed the door, replaced his cap, glided into the driver's seat, and we were off.

We reached the Bosphorus shore road and Hayri eased into the insane traffic like a matador finessing a huge herd of bulls. Madcap drivers swirled around us, imperiling the Austin's front and rear, threatening its brightly buffed flanks, but Hayri drove on smooth as silk and steady as a rock.

To be imperturbable in the madness of İstanbul traffic is a wonderful thing. I complimented him on his driving.

"Great drivers are born, not made," quoth Hayri.

We drew up in front of Aladdin's. Hayri bowed and handed us out of the Austin, accepted his fare and a considerable tip, and glided back into the traffic maelstrom humming a British ditty.

Aladdin had emerged to see who these important visitors might be who came by taxi. I introduced my parents and we all squeezed into his tiny cluttered shop. The boy magically appeared and was instructed to run and find more stools and to bring tea.

Aladdin unwrapped the parcel I handed him.

"*Ah, güzel, çok güzel!*"(Beautiful, very beautiful!)

I held the raincoat up for him. He put it on and modeled it for us, turning this way and that, looking not into a mirror, for there was none, but into our faces for the reflection of our approval. We beamed and smiled and made low mutterings of praise. He walked outside and looked at his reflection in the dingy glass of the shop window. He beamed with delight and satisfaction.

He came back inside, thanked us again profusely, took off the coat, folded it carefully and set it aside.

Our tea had come. We sorted out the glasses, handed them around, and the conversation paused for an important moment: the commencement of the informal Turkish tea ceremony. Tink tink tink tinka tinka tinklinklinkle, the tiny stainless steel spoons rang against the little tulip-shaped glasses as we stirred in sugar, holding the spoon-end between thumb and index finger, pinkie aloft. Gingerly I held the gold rim of the glass so as not to burn my fingers. Dainty *sotto voce* slurps, mixing cool air with hot tea as it enters the mouth. An audible sigh. Ahhhhh! Good tea.

Our minds had drifted off into the right-brain realm of sensations and dreamy feelings. Aladdin coaxed them back into the left-brain territory of purchase and sale.

"*Tom Bey,*" Aladdin said. "*Rockefeller geldi!*"

"Rockefeller came?" I asked, confused. "Who? What Rockefeller?"

"Rockefeller!" he said and handed me a newspaper clipping. It was a photo of Aladdin in front of his shop next to the huge *ibrik*. On the other side of the *ibrik*, shaking Aladdin's hand, was Nelson Rockefeller. The caption read "Former governor of New York and Vice-President of the USA Nelson Rockefeller visits İstanbul craftsman."

"He bought the *ibrik*," Aladdin said.

He smiled so broadly I was sure his face would crack. Nelson Rockefeller! I would sooner have expected Elvis.

As they sipped their tea, my parents surveyed the shop and picked out a few souvenirs. Aladdin packed up their choices and wouldn't let them pay. We finished our tea, said our goodbyes and left. As we walked away, we looked back to see Aladdin sauntering down Çadırcılar Caddesi on this bright sunny day in his new American raincoat with a rolling walk, chin up, looking to left and right, waiting for the inevitable questions and comments from other shopkeepers on his unusual and newly-acquired sartorial splendor.

Nothing Works Here

My fifteen Fulbright months of reading medieval Turkish legal documents completed, Jane and I returned to Boston early in January 1976. We bought a little house in the working-class suburb of Somerville and settled in just in time. The energy crisis of the mid-1970s hit the world hard, and Turkey particularly hard. I read in *Milliyet* that patients in Çanakkale's hospital wore their overcoats in bed because there was no fuel oil for the central heating system.

By 1977 Turkey was near economic and political collapse. The economy was in dire straits and there was an undeclared civil war raging between radicals and reactionaries. The fighting, which claimed nearly two dozen lives daily, was being fueled by the Soviet government through *agents provocateurs* and arms smuggled in from Bulgaria. It was hardly a great time to travel in Turkey, but the time had come to revise my guidebook for its fourth edition, so I went back. The work was not easy, but living in Turkey was even harder, and far more dangerous. Some of my old friends who loved İstanbul and thought of it as home had left or would soon leave.

The electricity went off several times a day without warning. The telephones rarely worked. Consumer goods, the sorts of things you use every day, were in short supply. There was no coffee. There was no tungsten to make light bulb filaments, and no foreign currency to import tungsten, hence there were no light bulbs. If yours burned out, you lit a candle, sat in the dark, or went to bed.

After racing around Anatolia gathering information I returned to İstanbul. I was staying at the American Research Institute's new quarters in a modern apartment building on a hill in Beşiktaş. It was cheap and friendly, but the mood among the scholars was sombre. Besides the economic difficulties and the danger from terrorists, the government's normal operations had come to a near standstill. Nepotism and political infighting among the ruling coalition parties had produced bureaucratic paralysis. Relatives, friends, party hacks and hangers-on had been appointed to government jobs, and these people knew nothing about administration. It was nearly impossible to get the official permissions necessary to study in the archives, or dig at archeological sites, or even take photographs of historical monuments.

Before leaving İstanbul, I dropped in on my friends Peter and Ella Wallenberg to pay my respects.

"Welcome, welcome, *hoş geldiniz!*" Peter said with a big smile as he opened the door. I noticed a new large outer door of thick steel plate had been installed. "You never know," he said. "Better to be safe."

Their apartment was filled with dinner guests. I tried to beg off but they insisted I stay. The guests included both Turks and foreigners from İstanbul. I was the only out-of-towner. Chatting with one of the Turkish guests, I commented on how the city had changed since I had first arrived in 1967.

"İstanbul used to be the best city in the world," he said. "The most enjoyable place to live. Now it's terrible. *Zevksiz* ("without savor"). What will become of it I don't know."

Peter and Ella's food was delicious, as always, with lots of fish. It brought to mind Peter's story about the gypsy palamut. When I arrived in İstanbul in 1968, fish was "protein for the poor." It was literally free if, as in Peter's story, you happened upon a swarming of the gypsy palamut. If you didn't, you could still buy a nice big palamut in the Balık Pazarı for 10¢. By 1977, a mere ten years later, the new Soviet and Japanese factory ships which literally vacuumed up the sea floor had overfished the ocean to the extent that palamut sold for $2.50 each—twenty-five times more expensive, far too expensive for any but the upper classes.

After dinner I mentioned to Peter that I needed to call and confirm my flight time. He offered to place the call. He lifted the receiver, dialed one digit, then waited, listening intently to the clicks and buzzes in the earpiece. He dialed another digit and listened. He dialed a third, strained to hear, frowned, and hung up.

"Not now. It's not going through. We'll try the call later."

"How do you know it won't go through?" I asked, amazed.

"Experience," he replied. "Some sounds mean there's a chance it'll go through. Other sounds mean it won't."

Later, after several tries we got through, having spent a good half hour at the phone. It was like finally winning on a slot machine.

My flight was to Switzerland. I had written a pocket guidebook to Montréal for Editions Berlitz of Lausanne. They wanted to give me more assignments, and asked if I could come to see them at their offices. It was a sad trip for me because it reminded me of my friend Dux who, though thoroughly cosmopolitan, always thought of himself as Swiss at heart. A year or two ago he had an attack of appendicitis and was rushed to the hospital in his ancestral canton of St Gallen. The doctors first misdiagnosed his condition then botched the appendectomy and he never fully recovered. He died some months afterward.

The day after dinner at the Wallenbergs I got up in the middle of the night and struggled with my luggage down the hill to the main square in Beşiktaş to find a taxi. It was cold, wet, dark, sombre. I was surprised to find myself looking forward to leaving İstanbul.

Clever Gnomes

Arriving in Switzerland from the İstanbul of 1977 was like going from dark into light, from cold to warmth, from a grimace to a smile. The Swissair flight took off and arrived right on time. The airport bus to Lausanne arrived exactly on time at the bus stop where my contact from Berlitz had promised to meet me.

The publisher had reserved a room for me at a lakefront hotel. I checked in and went to my room. After all of the water and heat problems in İstanbul, I wanted a hot bath. I turned the gleaming taps on the gleaming bathtub and gleaming, steaming hot water poured forth in abundance. It was near boiling. I could have made tea with it right from the tap. I undressed and eased into the steaming water.

Ahhhhhhhhhhhhhhhhhhhhhhhhhh!!!!!!!!!!!!!!!!!!!! A dream come true! I lay there in the tub warming up as though I had been chilled on ice for my entire stay in Turkey.

After awhile I felt too hot but I didn't want to cool down the thrilling water, I just wanted to feel some cool air on my face, to blow away some of the suffocating steam. I noticed a curious chain hanging on the tub wall near my head. It was attached to a pulley and a set of louvers. I pulled the chain, the louvers opened, and brisk, chill Swiss air wafted right onto my face. It was unbelievable. The Swiss thought of everything.

After a night of blissful catatonic slumber I awoke and went down to breakfast. I had to be at the Berlitz office at 8 am, so I was in a bit of a hurry. I picked up a coffee cup. It was hot! They had warmed the cups! When I poured the coffee in it would stay hot, not go stone cold because the heavy china cup was cold. Was there nothing these gnomes didn't think of?

From a city that barely worked at all I had flown to a city that worked like a clock, the sort of clock that would not only sing you the hour in the voice of an angel but would caress your thighs, give you an oil change and pick the ticks off your dog at the same time.

What would become of poor old İstanbul?

ॐ

21

LONELY PLANET

We leaned against the heavy marble balustrade by the Baghdad Kiosk in Topkapı Palace, gazing out at the city of the sultans and across the Golden Horn to the Bosphorus beyond. The sultans themselves had relaxed here in the kiosks with their chosen consorts, reclining on the brocade sofas, listening to the women play and sing, watching their mesmerizing dances.

Jane's eyes filled with tears.

"I have something to say."

After a long silence I responded "So do I."

"We're not happy together anymore," she said.

"Yes."

" I think we should separate."

"Yes."

I took her in my arms and we held one another tightly, tightly, for a long time.

"It's such a relief to have said it. I can't imagine it, but I think it's best," I said.

"Yes." She paused. Then, "I still love you."

"I still love *you*," I said. "But you're right. We're not happy. You need something different, maybe somebody different. If you need to leave, I'll let you. We should at least try it."

Each of us felt exultant relief. We had been well and happily married for ten years, but a beast had been gnawing at our hearts for the past two years. Now it was finally acknowledged, and the weight lifted from our shoulders. We knew it would be difficult and painful to live apart after a decade of affection, passion, storm and strife, but we had taken the first step. Having done that, we now had a chance at something better. We had a future again. It might hold pain and suffering or it might hold promise and joy, but the simple prospect of future joy was better than present pain.

"So...what do we do now?" she asked, half-sobbing, half-laughing. "Here we are in İstanbul about to go on a trek through Eastern Turkey, and we've decided to break up. What do we do?"

"We go on our trip. We break up later. When it's convenient."

We both laughed through our tears and held each other tightly again, tightly, holding on for dear life. How could we let go? We laughed and cried, tears of sadness and relief pouring from us both in a cathartic flood.

Tourists eyed us warily—*uh-oh, something going on there!* They slipped past us into the kiosk carefully, willing themselves to vanish.

Nothing was easier than for us to be together—as long as we both saw the possibility of change in the future. The recent past had been a heavy train leading us inevitably toward the crash of heartbreak. Better to jump off, take the bruise of the fall, and find some other track.

But Nobody Goes There

Speaking of tracks, we were in Turkey to follow a long, rough one: a trek through the wild, remote provinces of the east. It was September 1982, and I was writing a new guidebook to Turkey, one that would cover the entire country, not just the most heavily-touristed parts of the more civilized west. I had dropped out of the PhD program at Tufts a year or so before, having looked at the job market in academia and decided there was no point in continuing. When I got my PhD there would be no job available. I was already a successful travel writer, which was more fun that being a professor any day.

My new Turkey guide was for Lonely Planet Publications, a tiny Australian company virtually unknown in the USA. The travel shelves in American bookstores were filled with titles from Frommer's, the best-selling budget series, and Fodor's, the best-selling upscale series. From between the hefty Frommer's and Fodor's tomes, a few slender Lonely Planet titles to exotic destinations peeked out: *Kashmir, Ladakh* and *Zanskar*, for example. Nobody had ever heard of the place, or the author, or the publisher.

I was already the author of Frommer's *Turkey on $10 & $15 a Day*, the best-selling guidebook to Turkey, but so far as I could tell, that book was dead. The civil unrest of the late 1970s had killed Turkish tourism.

On September 12, 1980, the Turkish armed forces carried out another of their gentlemanly coups, which now seemed to be necessary about every ten years. When they finally took over, most Turks asked "what took them so long?" Even so, no one liked the fact that martial law was necessary. It was a defeat for Turkish democracy. The generals were not particularly adept at governing, which meant that people would be just as happy to see them leave as they had been to see them arrive. But the chaos that had gripped Turkish society had been unbearable.

By now everyone knew the script: the army would take over, appoint an interim government to establish a new, workable constitution, hold new elections, cede power back to the civilians, and go back to barracks. Leftists and Rightists would end up in prison, their political parties would be dissolved, and everyone would go back to stopping at red lights and paying their taxes.

To me, this meant that Turkey might just put itself back on the tourist map. I contacted the people at Frommer's and suggested that we bring out a revised fifth edition of the guide.

"Turkey's dead," they said. "No one's going there, and it looks like no one will be going there for the foreseeable future, so we wouldn't sell any books. We can't afford to take the chance."

I was convinced Turkey had potential. By now, I had developed a substantial body of expertise on the destination. I couldn't allow it to lie fallow. I needed to make income from it, so I looked for a different publisher, one willing to take a chance on a new Turkey guide.

On April 1, 1981, I wrote a letter addressed to "Editor-in-chief, Lonely Planet Publications," in Melbourne, Australia:

"I believe that Turkey's return to political, social and economic stability after the bad times of recent years presents an opportunity for increased tourism.... I would love to return to write a Lonely Planet guide."

Two weeks later I received a letter from Tony Wheeler, co-founder of Lonely Planet:

"We probably could be interested in a Turkey guide but our present publishing plans rule it out at the moment due to both time and cash shortages. However, 1982 may be a different story...."

By the end of April, Tony was writing "I must admit I've become a lot more enthusiastic about the idea since I wrote to you....although my knowledge of Turkey and travels in that country have been very minor compared to yours I really do like the place."

By July he agreed that I should return to Turkey as soon as possible in 1981 to do the field research for a brand-new Lonely Planet guide.

Other projects were already on my schedule, however, so my research for *Lonely Planet Turkey* was put off until September of 1982. By then Frommer's, at the urging of the Turkish Ministry of Tourism, had seen the light and contacted me about publishing a revised edition of *Turkey on $10 & $15 a Day*. So now I'd be researching two different guides to Turkey. One, the Frommer's guide, would be mostly for budget-minded Americans, thrifty but not particularly adventurous travelers. The other, the Lonely Planet guide, would be for a worldwide audience of intrepid backpackers.

The difference between the two book contracts was substantial. At Frommer's I was told not to increase the number of maps in the guide "because maps were expensive to produce and print." At Lonely Planet, Tony Wheeler told me, "If you want a hundred maps, we'll include a hundred maps." Lonely Planet also wanted me to shoot photographs. They planned to put eight pages of color photos in the book.

Still, Frommer's, with offices in the Simon & Schuster tower on Manhattan's Avenue of the Americas, was the 900-pound gorilla of travel publishing, and Lonely Planet looked to be little more than a hobby company started in a Melbourne storefront by a bunch of long-haired hippies. I had no idea how this project would work out. I just wanted to get back to writing about Turkey.

Lonely Planet wanted me to cover the entire country, not just the parts accustomed to tourism, which is why I had come to Turkey this time, arriving on August 28, 1982. Jane, always intrepid, wanted to come along, so she flew over after I had finished most of my work in western Turkey. She arrived on September 18th, and we had our little chat in Topkapı overlooking the Golden Horn the next day.

We had been married for ten years. It had not always been easy, but it had always been rewarding. We were very different, one from the other, but we looked upon that as an advantage: we were not similar but complementary, two different halves of a whole. It was certainly that way for years, but at the end of the decade we had ended up with quite different attitudes about important things.

Having decided to break up, we set out together to explore the wild east.

You Live Here Then

We flew to Ankara, rented a cheap, tinny white Renault 12 and drove east to Sungurlu and Boğazkale to see the ancient Hittite capital that Dux and I had explored over a decade before. By nightfall we had reached Amasya, and two days later we were in Trabzon. From Trabzon we explored the ancient, eerie cliffside monastery of Sumela, then headed south, climbing up through the Kaçkar mountains to Artvin, then to Kars, jumping-off place for the medieval Armenian capital of Ani.

Kars gets bad reviews from just about everybody, even the locals. Driving into Kars some years later, I picked up three men in suits who were hitchhiking from the intersection of a village road and the highway. One was a teacher, the other two administrators. All had been born and raised in Kars.

"I like Kars," I said.

"*You like Kars?*" the teacher said with a rueful chuckle. "*Nobody likes Kars. We live here—we were born here!—and even we don't like it.*"

"But it has a special character, partly because it's remote, partly because the Russians held it for awhile and built Russian-style buildings."

"The weather's terrible," the teacher said, "and there's nothing to do."

He was right. The Kars climate is severe. Another time when I arrived it was just after a hailstorm. People were shoveling huge piles of ice out of the streets. This was in August.

Kars's problem, I finally realized, is that it's always been a dead end. The Russian Empire was always trying to grab northeastern Turkey so the Russian border was always closed and heavily defended. The Soviets continued the imperial Russian policies: Stalin tried to grab Kars and Ardahan, and it was only American threats that kept him from doing it.

With the fall of the Soviet Union and the rebirth of the Republic of Armenia, the hostility continued. The border was still closed.

Kars was Turkey's Timbuktu: when you reached it, you could go no further.

Except to Ani, the capital of the medieval kingdom of Armenia, which is most people's ultimate goal when they go to Kars.

The Armenians are an ancient people, perhaps even descended from the ancient Urartians (513–330 BC), who have lived in eastern Anatolia for many centuries. Because they lived on the border between the empires of the west (Roman, Byzantine and Ottoman) and the east (Persian, Arab and Russian), foreign armies have frequently marched through and tromped them. For most of their history they have been ruled by others, but in the 10th century they ruled themselves. King Ashot III (952–977) moved his capital from Kars to Ani, and succeeding kings ruled here until 1045 when the Byzantines took control. So Ani was the independent capital of an independent Armenian kingdom for a mere 84 years, after which it was captured and/or sacked in turn by the Byzantines, Seljuks, Georgians and Kurdish emirs. The arrival of the Mongols in 1239 was Ani's sad closing chapter. In 1319 a severe earthquake reduced it to rubble.

Before the collapse of the Soviet Union, visits to Ani were closely controlled according to a diplomatic protocol signed by the Turkish and Soviet governments. The Sovs elevated paranoia to an art form. Ani, although entirely within Turkish territory, was under Soviet surveillance at all times. Visitors were required by the protocol to obtain written permission from the Turkish regional security officials in Kars, and to have their passports registered prior to arriving at Ani. Visits were only allowed during daylight hours. Visitors must be accompanied by a Turkish soldier at all times while in the ruins, must not take notes or photographs or even point toward the Soviet border, must not picnic or linger in any one spot too long. The reason was that the ruins fell within the one-kilometer-wide no-man's-land which spanned the international frontier.

On the Soviet Armenian side of the frontier, sinister watchtowers looked across the canyon of the Arpaçay creek to the Turkish side.

Even given these strictures, a visit to Ani was spectacular. With our soldier guide in tow, Jane and I penetrated the massive walls at the main gate. Inside was a gently undulating sea of grass on which floated the wrecks of great medieval churches. Birds chirped, a shepherd boy off in the distance shouted at a stray lamb, but otherwise the site was blanketed by a primeval quiet, the non-sound of a city dead for 800 years.

The churches had survived the earthquakes and ravages of the centuries because of their great bulk, but all of the city's other buildings had collapsed and now lay beneath the lush undulating carpet of grass, the undulations being covered piles of rubble which had once been buildings.

We hiked all over the site, which we had completely to ourselves. We knew there were soldiers with high-powered binoculars tracing our movements from the Soviet watchtowers, but it didn't bother us.

We returned to Kars and bought several of the coarse, simple, vigorous local wool carpets: plain, sturdy, honest and forthright, like the town itself, with earthy colors that come right from the undyed wool: sheep colors, the colors of the countryside.

Interesting but Inaccessible

From Kars we headed south for Doğubayazıt on September 27th, early in the morning. It was the first day of Kurban Bayramı, the Sacrifice Holiday.

Local taxi drivers in Kars had recommended that we follow the Erzurum highway southwest to Horasan, then turn southeast and go via Ağrı because the main highway was faster and safer than the secondary roads, although the highway route was longer (310 km). There were alternatives, a secondary road turning southeast at Karakurt, and a rough mountain road through the back country right over the 6630-foot Paslı mountain pass directly to Kağızman. We had got an early start so we decided to chance the mountain pass, hoping that the scenery would make up for the rough road.

You see this coming, don't you? Here I am trusting a map, and not the locals, yet again, as though I were a Frenchman in a frog-like Citroën.

Not long after we left the Kars-Erzurum highway the road deteriorated to unpaved stabilized gravel, then to dirt. It was slow going, and the scenery was bleak: dusty treeless hills with no sign of civilization. Just before the village of Kötek, 10 km northwest of the Karakurt-Ağrı road, a yellow-and-black sign pointed off the road into the hills: *Kaya resimleri,* it read. Rock pictures.

What rock pictures? There was nothing about rock pictures in the guidebooks I had read for comparison. It was my job to find out if these rock pictures were worth seeing. We turned right and followed a rough, badly rutted side road uphill to a small, poor village called Çamuşlu Köyü. We reached the first houses of the village but saw no signs pointing the way to any rock pictures.

We stopped. A man emerged from a house and approached us.

"*Selamün aleykum!*" (Peace be with you), he said. "*Hoş geldiniz, safa geldiniz!*" (Welcome, and well come).

"*Hoş bulduk!*" (We feel welcome) I answered. 'We're looking for the rock pictures."

"Yes, of course, they're up above the village on the cliff. We'll show them to you, but first come have some tea."

The man was Zeynel Demirci, the muhtar. We got out of the car and followed him into his house where his wife and daughters awaited us. He showed us to the seat of honor on the *sedir* in the salon, brought the traditional welcoming cologne, cigarettes and sweets, and asked us about our travels.

"Have you had breakfast yet?" he asked. We had had a snack as we set out from Doğubayazıt, but not a proper breakfast. We were hungry, but we didn't want to inconvenience him or his family, so we said yes, we had had breakfast.

"But are you hungry now?" he insisted. "It's *bayram*, we've prepared the feast, and God has sent you to dine with us. Come, come! Please join us."

Well, actually, we would. It was getting along toward noon, and there wouldn't be any other place along this road to get food.

We gave in. The wife served us roast mutton and freshly-baked village bread. It was delicious.

Word had obviously gone out on the invisible but extraordinarily effective and speedy village word-of-mouth folk telegraph that something was up, and it had to do with oddball beings arriving in a white car with Ankara plates. We knew because with every forkful of mutton a new villager arrived in Zeynel Bey's house to gawk at us. Pretty soon the house was packed, and the porch and the yard out front as well, but everyone was exceedingly polite and courteous. We were a pair of fairly scruffy American gavur vagabonds, probably the first and only non-Muslims, let alone Americans, that anyone in Çamuşlu Köyü had ever seen, and we were being treated like royalty.

Have you ever dined with 100 eyes watching your every move? I mean, you're not being watched by other people at the dinner table. The other people are not eating, they're just watching you, as though you were Madonna having sex, or Brad Pitt doing nothing. Like you're on a stage, at a dinner table, and there's an auditorium full of curious, eager people with laser-like gazes aimed at your fork as you stab a glob of mutton, raise it to face level, part your lips, welcome the glob into your oral cavity, molarize it for a few seconds, then send it south. God forbid you should fight with a piece of gristle, or have a gob of saliva go down your trachea and cause a coughing fit (which was highly likely, as the mutton was delicious, literally mouth-watering). Think what that'd do to your ratings! Lemme tell you, it's not easy to eat like a king. Next time you see a celebrity in the midst of oral gratification, bear this in mind.

We cleaned our plates and were almost surprised, but in fact relieved, when the expected round of applause (hoots, whistles, The Wave) didn't materialize. "*Nefis!*" (Delicious!) I said, which comment was greeted by wide smiles and an appreciative murmur by the throng assembled.

Concerned about the long and perhaps rough road ahead of us, we mentioned the rock pictures again. Zeynel Bey led us outside and back to our car. He, the village teacher and another man of some mysterious significance piled into the narrow, thinly padded back seat of our little car which had been designed only for spindly French endomorphs. The small engine hauled us uphill, wheezing the *Marseillaise*, over the rutted road to a sheer rock cliff.

Carved into the smooth sedimentary rock were pictographs, obviously ancient. In fact, apparently prehistoric.

"Last summer an archeological research team came here from Ankara University" the teacher said. "They made photographs and drawings of the rock pictures, and dug some trenches."

"We did the digging," said Zeynel. "It was pretty interesting, and our men could use the work. Our village isn't rich. We learned something about where we live."

It still amazes me that something as important as prehistoric rock carvings could go unnoticed for centuries, but so it is everywhere. The great Mayan cities of Central America just sat there in the jungle until New York lawyer and amateur archeologist John Lloyd Stephens came along and asked about them. "Oh, sure," the local villagers said, "there're lots of old stone buildings in the jungle. Our ancestors built them. Want us to show you?"

Here in Çamuşlu Köyü, the rock carvings could be more significant than those at Lascaux for all anyone knew, but until the highway department put up the sign, and the team came from the university, and the guidebook author stumbled in by accident, they'd just sit there, unknown to everyone but the villagers. Media coverage is everything, at least if you're an antiquity.

We returned to the village, and the muhtar insisted that we come in for a parting glass of tea. Jane had some free cosmetic samples that she had received in the mail and brought along as travel equipment—things like rouge and eye liner and eye shadow, things you could find easily in New York—or in Ankara, for that matter—but were scarce as moon rocks in Çamuşlu. She gave them to the eldest daughter, a hard-working farm girl with bright eyes and rough hands.

It was the equivalent of the girl giving Jane a tractor coupling.

The girl smiled shyly as Jane gave her the short course in becoming Miss Maybelline. When Çamuşlu Köyü gets its first disco in 2050, she'll be ready, except by then she'll be 83 years old and no amount of makeup will, uh, make up for it.

In Turkey if you give someone a gift, she or he takes it as a challenge and will not rest until she/he has given you something of greater value. The girl's mother loaded us down with the wealth of the village: apples from the village trees, freshly-gathered walnuts, and handmade dried cheese that looked just like rough twine: soak it in water and it plumps up to tasty string cheese. Food for the road. It was just what we needed.

"Please write to us," Zeynel said. He jotted down his name and address on a scrap of paper.

We were about to part. Zeynel had something on his mind. He was too polite—the courtliness of the Turkish villager—to bring it up during our visit, but now the visit was over and we were leaving. It was now or never. He threw politeness to the winds and asked a favor.

"You saw the condition of our village road. It's awful. Sometimes in winter we can't even get up to the village. We complain to the highway department but they don't listen to us. They say they've got more important roads to build. You're a tourism writer, an important man. If you write to us and say it's important to improve our road so that tourists can get to the rock pictures, we can use it as evidence. We may be able to convince them to improve the road. Could you do that?"

I found it hilarious that he thought me important. I warned him not to expect much.

"Oh, they'll listen to you," he said. I didn't have the heart to argue. We said goodbye and drove off.

Some People Never Learn

We soon reached Doğubayazıt, took a room at the brand-new Hotel Ararat, then went out to see the İshak Paşa Sarayı, a striking 17th-century fortress-palace built on a lonely hilltop by the local emir. I took some pictures, one of which ended up as the cover shot for the first edition of my Lonely Planet guide. I wanted to get photos of Mount Ararat as well, but the summit was shrouded in cloud. I asked the reception desk clerk at the hotel if the clouds ever cleared.

"First thing in the morning," he said. "Get up before dawn."

I did, and there it was, the majestic snow-covered summit clear of cloud, in full sunlight. I shot some photos, then watched in amazement as the sun warmed the snow on the summit and the evaporated moisture formed clouds which obscured the mountain, like a woman fresh from the bath covering herself from the prurient gaze of men.

After breakfast we packed the car and asked local taxi drivers about the best way to reach Van.

"Go back to Ağrı, then south via Patnos and Erciş," they said.

"Isn't that the long way around?" I asked. "What about this road along the Iranian border via Çaldıran?" According to the Turkish Highway Department's road map, the Çaldıran road was paved and fairly good, of the same quality as the road via Patnos and Erciş.

"The Çaldıran road's not in good condition. You could get stuck. Besides, it's officially closed after dark because of smugglers. The Jandarma (gendarmes, paramilitary police) are on patrol, and are liable to shoot you because only smugglers are out on that road after dark."

I looked at the map again. The bright red line on the map inspired confidence. Surely the Highway Department in Ankara knows the road better than these local taxi drivers, who probably have no reason to drive that road in any case.

Some people never learn!

We left Doğubayazıt and decided to take the Çaldıran road. We'd just make sure we were off the road by nightfall.

The road was paved and relatively good as far as Ortadirek, but south of there it was unpaved, after which it degenerated to rough, rutted dirt. I began to wonder if we had made the right decision. I could almost hear the hiss of smugglers' bullets in the air.

ಞಞ

22

LOSS AND GAIN

The road got worse and worse. Like the misguided idiots we were, we drove on. Our little Renault was a triumph of wrongheaded French engineering perfectly unsuited to conditions in eastern Turkey—flimsy, low-slung and underpowered, its only virtues being that it was cheap to buy, even cheaper to make, and didn't use much gas—which was no surprise given its dinky engine. The French are great at cross-country bicycling, and this car is why.

In September, dusk comes early in eastern Turkey. By this time it was too late in the day to turn around and return the way we had come. We'd never make it back to the paved road before nightfall. We drove on filled with the mindless confidence of travelers going from bad to worse and depending on blind luck to save their tails.

We got our luck, it was blind, and it was bad. We came over a rise and down a hill, and stopped at the edge of a slough of muddy water. The road ended at the near edge of the slough, and sprang up again from the other shore.

I got out of the car to look at the water. There wasn't enough dry road on either side to get by. I'd have to go through it. Obviously I should avoid the middle, which looked deep. Should I drive along the left edge or the right edge? Which way was shallower? Was the bottom of the slough firm enough to support a car?

The brown mess was opaque. I didn't feel like stripping down and wading into the muck and without doing that there was no way to tell. I chose the left side, put the car in gear and edged forward into the water. The car nosed down into the muck and sank. It stopped. I put the car in reverse and gave it some gas. The wheels wouldn't move. The little engine groaned pitiably, strained toward hernia, did nothing. The front wheels were sucked in worse than someone who had just been sold aluminum siding.

I got out of the dead car and did a quick reality check. We were in a depression in the middle of nowhere only a stone's throw—or a bullet's trajectory—from the Iranian border, with not even a tree, let alone a building or a telephone line, in sight. It was mid-afternoon. The sun was racing toward the horizon like an İstanbul taxi toward a planeload of Japanese tourists.

I'm Sure It's Only a Puppy

Out of the corner of my eye I noticed some movement high above us on the ridge to the west.

A dog?

Another dog appeared beside the first one, then a third. Then a fourth. Tame dogs? Wild dogs? Wolves? Wolves! I couldn't tell.

The situation didn't look good. In fact, it looked bad. Actually, it sucked like a Hoover. I couldn't pick the car up and haul it out of there. Both of us couldn't. We had very little food and water, no bedding, and no weapon. A Swiss Army Knife and a small flashlight constituted our entire tool kit. With these I could perhaps defend us against a determined chicken or a three-legged hamster.

The canines on the ridge above us lifted their butts off the ground and started milling around, always looking at us, as though planning their strategy.

Just then a figure appeared at the top of the rise on the road to the south, in the direction we were going—or, rather, dreamed of going. It was a young man. What the hell? He was dressed in a natty three-piece suit, watch-chain and all. He looked like he was headed for a Harvard Club soirée, except that Harvard was an 8000-mile walk away.

"I must be hallucinating," I thought. The guy approached us.

"Merhaba!" I said.

"Merhaba!" he replied.

"We have a problem," I said, my sense of the obvious hanging out like a beer gut.

He spent a few moments in grave contemplation of the car and the mud pond, now joined at the hip. Raising his eyes to mine, and looking at me with great seriousness, he said "*Evet*" (Yes).

"Would you help us?"

"Evet."

He shucked his jacket, watch chain and vest. We both took off our shoes and socks, rolled up our trouser legs, and waded into the muck. We pushed while Jane put the car in reverse and tried to spin the wheels. We would get covered in mud if the car actually broke free because the spinning tires would churn up a tsunami of muck and send it hurtling our way. But it didn't. Nothing happened except that the engine groaned and cursed in French. We were getting nowhere.

"What are we gonna do?" I wondered out loud.

"Maybe the Jandarmas will help you," he said.

"What Jandarmas?" I asked. "We're in the middle of nowhere."

"There's a Jandarma post over that rise," he said, pointing south. I decided that maybe my sense of the obvious was in fact better than his. Jandarmas were just what we needed. But....

Great, I thought. Is this true or false, good news or bad? Why didn't he mention it before? Now I'm supposed to hike over that rise leaving Jane here with the car, and when I come back the car will be on its way to Tehran in a thousand used-parts boxes and my wife will be on her way to the slave market in Abu Dhabi. Or Jane can come with me and when we come back—which will be in less than an hour because there's not really any Jandarma post on the other side of that rise, just more wolves—the car will be gone along with all our luggage and we'll be standing here in the middle of nowhere with only the clothes on our backs, watching the sun go down and waiting for the wolves to say grace, our only hope being that the air will fill with flying lead from Jandarmas and smugglers soon enough to scare the wolves or at least put us out of our misery. This is great, just great.

I had an idea.

"Tell you what. You go to the Jandarma post and tell them we're here and we need their help," I said.

"They won't believe me," he answered.

"Why not?"

"I'm just a local kid, and a Kurd at that. They'll think it's a joke, or even an ambush. I'm supposed to say 'There's a couple of tourists over that hill stuck in a mudhole and they need your help'? I wouldn't believe it myself."

The thought briefly occurred to me to tell him that it was pretty damned unlikely to be stuck in a mud puddle in a blasted wasteland in extreme eastern Turkey and then have a kid in a three-piece suit saunter over the hill looking like he wanted to sell me hedge funds or asteroid insurance, but this would just be pointing up an absurdity within an absurdity, which seemed a waste of breath at the moment. And after all, the kid had a point. The whole thing was pretty unbelievable.

"Okay," I said, riding a brainwave. "Take this card to them." I got out a business card and wrote on the back in Turkish *Please help us! Our car is stuck. We're nearby.*

The kid nodded, took the card, cleaned himself up as best he could, walked back up the hill and disappeared.

Damn, I thought. That's it. He'll be back in no time with a Kurdish smuggler's posse. About a month from now the Jandarmas, who are probably a hundred miles away, will find only our bleached bones. They'll give us a rough and ready

Muslim funeral then throw our bones into the mud slough to provide traction for any clueless motorists who wander down this road because they don't know how to take good advice from local drivers even when they ask for it. Just what we need. Damn!

We sat in the dirt and contemplated our future. That took about ten seconds because there wasn't a lot to contemplate. Meanwhile, the sun raced toward the horizon.

"I guess we have to at least wait a little while to see if the kid was telling the truth," I said.

"The alternative being…?" Jane asked.

We sat in the dirt and watched the wolves, who seemed possessed of an almost human intelligence. What I mean is that it was easy for us to imagine they could add up the evidence and come to a conclusion:

(a) *two bipeds worth about, oh, 110 pounds of meat on the skinny one, and maybe 180 pounds of meat (well marbled) on the big one;*

(b) *not very lively, so capture is gonna be pretty easy;*

(c) *a little fancy tooth-work to bring 'em down, fairly easy kill;*

(d) *about two hours till nightfall, not enough time for the vultures to see 'em in the daylight, so after they're down they're all ours until tomorrow morning, by which time the vultures are welcome to whatever's left, which should be nothing;*

(e) *Conclusion = fat city! Call the guys! This is gonna be a good one, a hell of a lot better than the last kill, that skinny Iranian smuggler—all bones, no meat—who had a gun and put a bullet in old Roger before we brought him down and chomped him into mincemeat.*

The wolves edged their way over the crest of the ridge and started down the slope, in no hurry, spreading out as they came. Time was on their side.

Suddenly the wolves stopped. They all raised their heads and looked south. So did we.

Over the ridge came a platoon of khaki-clad Turkish Jandarma soldiers led by a sergeant in a creamy white Aegean fisherman's sweater. The sweater was culturally so out of place I would have been no more surprised if he had been dressed in drag and wearing a rubber Ronald Reagan mask. The platoon marched up to us and stopped.

"Merhaba! Thank you for coming. You see our problem," I said.

"No problem," the sergeant answered. He gave an order and led his soldiers into the muck. They lifted up the Renault as though it were a kid's plastic bumper car (which may actually have been the original French design), and hauled it out of the muck.

"Drive around on the other side," he said.

Duh, yeah. Sure it was obvious, but how did he know I wouldn't drive right back into the mud? I had done it once. I had a record.

I drove around the other side, the muddy soldiers watching intently. Safe on the far side of Lake Wolfpack, I stopped. The soldiers, now dripping gobs of mud from the waist down, assembled in ranks. The sergeant came up to the car, his formerly pristine sweater now running with brown goo.

"How can we possibly thank you?" I asked through the open car window.

"Come up to the post for tea," he answered.

"Would you like a ride?"

He looked at himself, covered in mud, chuckled, smiled, and raised his eyebrows in the Turkish gesture for 'no.'

"We'll walk," he said. "See you there."

We Dodge Bullets and Play a Lot of Checkers

We drove up and over the ridge and sure enough there was a tiny cinder block building coated with white stucco, the *Harabe* ("Ruins"—what a name) command post. It didn't look big enough to house a corporation's ethics department let alone a platoon, but that was their post. There was nothing else as far as the eye could see, not a tree, a bush, a wire, not even a piece of junk mail. Nothing. They might as well have been on the moon.

We parked in front of the post and got out. The soldiers quick-marched up a few minutes later. They changed out of their muck-covered uniforms into fresh khaki. The kettle was put on the gas ring. We got out a kilo of shelled hazelnuts we had bought on the Black Sea coast and passed them around.

Turkish soldiers are fed on short rations, the better to accustom them to the privation they may encounter in battle. They are big guys who work hard, so they are usually starved. When we offered them the nuts the sergeant glared at the troops meaningfully. The soldiers took only a few nuts each. They nibbled at each nut, making it last. They took five bites out of a nut which I would have chucked into my mouth whole along with a dozen of its neighbors.

We sipped tea and talked. The sergeant was from Marmaris. Marmaris! A beautiful, balmy Mediterranean town, lush with evergreens and citrus groves.

"Wow," I said. "This must strike you as pretty different." He gave a rueful chuckle. Different wasn't the word for it.

An idea popped into my head.

"How long do you have left to serve here?" I asked. "How many days?"

"One hundred twenty-one," he answered without a second's hesitation. I pointed to the soldiers one by one and each uttered the sacred number that was at the front of his mind at all times. It was like prison inmates counting the days till release, the difference being that even in Turkish prisons the inmates had libraries, and exercise yards, mail call, access to newspapers and medical facilities, and visits from loved ones, and also were unlikely to have their bodies perforated by bullets from Iranian smugglers while they waited out their time.

The soldiers eyed Jane cautiously, unwilling to let their imaginations fly to thoughts of sex because reeling them in when she was gone would be too painful. Nights here were bad enough without introducing dreams of a real live woman—and an attractive one at that—into the equation.

I asked each soldier where he was from, and they were all from the west, or at least no place east of Ankara. This was not surprising. At that time the Turkish army used its power of universal male conscription to educate kids from the relatively rich, developed cities of the west with life in the poor, backward east; and it sent country kids from the east to places like İstanbul and İzmir—and Marmaris— to show them how the other half of Turkey lives. Both sides got quite an education.

I asked if we could take a photo. The sergeant said yes. The soldiers lined up in front of the post, with Jane in the middle.

We had a difficult time leaving. We were the best thing to happen to these guys since their last home-cooked meal. They obviously wanted us to stay longer but were too polite to make a point of it.

I worried out loud that it was getting late, and that we needed to get off the road before night fell.

That did it.

The sergeant said "Yeah, we shoot anybody on the road, because it's only smugglers and they're usually aiming at us."

We thanked them again for saving us, said our goodbyes, and drove on. The road was rough and slow but without any big bad surprises. We reached Çaldıran and the paved highway just as the sun approached the horizon. South of Çaldıran the road was fast. I floored it, the Renault whined like a Frenchman confronted with peanut butter and jelly, and we hurtled toward Van, arriving after dark.

On our way back west we stopped in Sivas, where Dux and I had met the unfriendly desk clerk in the Hotel Köşk years before. After seeing the major sights we wandered off into the back neighborhoods looking for Seljuk *kümbets* (tombs). At one point a crowd of teen-aged boys approached us. A few of them seemed drunk or on their way there, which is a rare occurrence in Turkey as public drunkenness is utterly shameful.

Because foreigners strolling Sivas's back streets are apparently as rare as books by Salman Rushdie in the local library, the boys confronted us as a curiosity. When we came face to face, neither side was sure of the proper protocol. A Sivas Status Battle seemed the best option, at least to the boys. One of them, apparently the alpha—if only by degree of drunkenness—pulled a huge black revolver out of his trouser waistband. He waved it around merrily, but didn't point it at us. Threatening us was not the point, the status battle was. Unless I could produce an even bigger heater—an Uzi or a Kalashnikov would do nicely, and a rocket-propelled grenade launcher would triumph by popular acclaim—he was going to win.

As I had nothing more deadly than a ball point pen in my pocket, I glanced at the revolver and nodded slightly in recognition, thereby acknowledging his alpha-ness to everyone's satisfaction. Rank having been established, he stowed his cannon back in his pants where it no doubt far outranked his other alpha-male equipment in both size and shot.

We wished one another a pleasant day. Jane and I went on looking for Seljuk tombs and he continued his apparently speedy and inexorable progress toward his own.

From Sivas we returned to Ankara, where we got rid of the Renault, hopped on a bus and escaped to Side on the Med coast for four days of rest and relaxation at Ayşe's pension.

Our trip, and our marriage, were over.

Loss and Gain

Jane returned home to Somerville in early October and began to look for a new place to live. I stayed in Turkey another month gathering information for my Lonely Planet guide. As I traveled, I thought about how travel writing was hardly the career for someone who liked being married. My job required me to take long trips—a month, two months, sometimes even three—away from home and spouse. It wasn't always possible for Jane to come with me and besides she had her own professional career. I had no right to demand that she do what my career demanded and come with me on these long trips. But what was the alternative? Being apart so much of the time was not good. We both got lonely, and had grown apart.

I got home on November 5th. A few days later Jane moved out of our mortgaged house and into a rented room. A few months later she found a new condo for sale in Cambridge and we strapped on that mortgage as well.

Considering the wrecked state of my romantic life and the need to write an entire book, it's no surprise that it took until January for me to write the letter to Zeynel Demirci, but when I wrote it I made the petroglyphs of Çamuşlu Köyü sound more important than the Elgin Marbles. I sent off my letter to him and promptly forgot about the whole matter.

Four months later, in April, 1983, much to my surprise, I received a reply:

Dear Writer,

We received your letter of January 4th, which made us very, very happy. What a pity that no writer from a friendly foreign country has ever come as far as our village to have so much as a glass of tea—until you arrived.

Your letter was a godsend to us. We made photocopies of it and sent them to the ministries of villages and cooperatives, the provincial government, the provincial tourism association and the district government.... Thank you so much for including our village in the book you are writing....In the name of the people of Çamuşlu Köyü I send you greetings.

Çamuşlu Köyü Muhtar Zeynel Demirci

PS: The road to the tourist site has been completed.

Wow! Zeynel Bey was right after all: the words of a foreign travel really did have some clout in eastern Turkey.

Back in İstanbul to revise my guide the next time, in 1985, I went to pay my respects to Aladdin. I walked into the shop at Çadırcılar Caddesi No 3, but he wasn't there. Çavuş, now a young man, was sitting on the three-legged stool.

"Merhaba," I said. "Is Aladdin around?"

Çavuş stood and looked at me. He paused for a moment, looked down at the floor, looked back at me, then said quietly "I'm sorry. He passed away."

We stood in silence. "*Başınız sağ olsun,*" I said. It was the traditional Turkish expression of condolence: "May you [at least] be safe."

He opened Aladdin's little money-drawer and took out a newspaper clipping.

"He had incurable cancer," he said, handing me the clipping.

It reported that Alaettin Yanık, an antique dealer with a shop on Çadırcılar Caddesi, having been diagnosed with incurable cancer, had gone to the center of the Bosphorus Bridge, climbed over the guardrail, and jumped to his death.

This was not supposed to happen. My friends in Turkey, indeed Turkey itself, were supposed to stay the same, the way I found them as a callow 21-year-old PCV. Like Ayasofya or the black walls of Diyarbakır, they were supposed to remain constant and unchanging. It was silly to think this way, but I couldn't help it. Besides losing my dear old friends, my mooring-points in the fast-flowing river of life, watching my older friends die off brought me face to face with my own mortality. We all know in our minds that life is not forever, but we don't know it in our hearts until we lose someone we love. Life is short, really short. The longer it goes on, the shorter it looks.

Just Think of the Fights Over Closet Space

I returned home to Somerville. I was now living alone and wondering what to do. My students at İzmir Koleji had taught me the jocular Turkish saying *Bekârlık sultanlıktır,* "Bachelorhood is sultanhood," meaning that a bachelor has his pick of the chicks, but to me this sounded like polygamous fantasizing. The sultan had wives and concubines, and as Turgut Bey, my wise old friend from the

Ottoman archives once said, "Sure, during Ottoman times a man was allowed to have up to four legal wives and as many concubines as he could support, but the catch is that according to Islamic law he had to treat them all equally. He couldn't lavish wealth on one and scrimp on the others."

"You won't want *sultanlık* if you run the numbers," he went on. "Look at the way a pasha lived: each one of his four wives had at least three servants, and the more important servants had servants of their own, and the concubines had servants, and they all had kids. Add it all up and the Big Guy had to write checks to support a hundred people! He had such money problems he couldn't enjoy himself in bed."

Despite the difficulties, I had loved being monogamously married. I had no desire to play the field. But the field was where the women were, so if I wanted to be married again I had better start looking for the essential other half of the equation. I started dating, a strange experience after having been out of the meat market for over a decade.

Middle-aged dating is a lot like leftover pizza. It has none of the freshness of first-time love, the excitement of discovery, the alluring thought that the love of your life might be as close as the next cocktail party or blind date. I met good women with whom I had little in common, which seemed to reinforce the one-and-only theory of romance.

Then came the drunken teenagers, and they saved me.

Know Your Neighbors, but Not This Well

It went like this. Next to our—well, now it was my—little house was a steep wooded hillside, a rarity in Somerville, one of the most densely populated cities in the USA. In Somerville the houses are built so close together that you can hear it when your neighbor flushes the toilet in the middle of the night, even in the winter when you have all your windows closed. When one telephone rings in Somerville it's not uncommon for 45 people in 12 different houses on the same block to pick up the receiver thinking it's for them, and then complain to the phone company about hang-up calls. In Somerville you can come home from work, sniff the odors wafting from the kitchen, say "Mmmmm, pizza!" and get in trouble with your spouse who's actually cooking *Magret de canard au sauce de framboises* because the smell of the pizza really came from the kitchen of the family with seven kids three doors down. Magret de canard is thus not the only dead duck in your house.

So having any open space at all next to your house—let alone a wooded hillside—is a rarity in Somerville.

The trees, several dozen of them, were on the southwest side of my little house. They shaded it from the sun in the summer, which is one of the reasons I had bought the house in the first place. However, the dark shade of the hillside is also a perfect place for teenagers to rendezvous, which usually leads to beer-drinking, loud-music-playing, noise-making, and fleshy genetico-anatomical games of chance. Overcrowded Somerville has precious few places suitable for teenagers to rendezvous, and a superfluity of teenagers wanting to rendezvous in them. The results of any such rendezvous, by the way, not counting STDs and eventual babies, were hours of annoying racket and, the next morning, dozens of empty beer cans, snack wrappers and unrecycled condoms left on the hillside.

Mine was not the only house with the noisy-teenager problem. Several other houses backed onto the hillside, and a few of them were even occupied by people who kept the volume of their TVs low enough that they could hear a 747 passing 20 feet above their house and even, on occasion, the hillside teenagers. For example, the little six-room house at the bottom of the hill, very similar to mine in size and appointments, had been bought by a single professional woman, a Harvard Business School graduate who worked for a fancy management consultancy. Tired of paying rent and tired of waiting for Mr Right to come along and carry her over the threshold, she had bought her own goddamn threshold and strode purposely over it herself.

Unfortunately, shortly after she had bought her little house, it had been burgled, probably by local youths.

Teenagers, while carousing on the hillside, sat directly opposite her kitchen window, the one through which the burglars had breached her domestic sanctuary. She liked the teenagers even less than I did.

Do I sense an ally here?

We met on a Saturday afternoon when the teenagers had arrived and started drinking far too early. I leapt the fence, strode purposefully up to them and told them to clear out. Already drunk, they picked up rocks, pulled their arms back and got ready to pitch them at my head. We stood like that, just outside the professional woman's kitchen window, frozen in a *tableau vivant* of Somerville absurdity, until a police car raced up and squealed to a stop at the bottom of the hillside.

The kids fled. The professional woman came out of her house and looked up at me.

"I called the cops," she said.

She told me about the burglary and how the kids made her jumpy. We both moaned about the noise and the mess. We resolved to form some sort of an anti-noisy-teenager alliance. She was a cute redhead, far more sweet-looking than her hard-bitten HBS shock-troops-of-capitalism training would've suggested.

"By the way, my name's Tom," I said.

"I'm Jane," she answered.

Heh.

I asked her out. We hit it off.

I had a few more dates with other women but all the time a little voice in the back of my mind was whispering to me. You don't hear that little voice unless you are, mentally and spiritually and emotionally speaking, very quiet. At some point in the emotional *sturm und drang* of separation and the heartbreak of divorce there was a lull in my mental turmoil and the little voice came through. By the time I heard it, it was shouting at the top of its tiny lungs.

"What are you doing, fool? You're wasting precious time! She's cute, she's sweet, she's brainy and self-confident. She speaks fluent French and Spanish, she's got red hair and green eyes, loves to travel, has wonderful friends. Her name's even Jane. Duh! Talk about *vurdumduymaz*. Wake up and smell the pheromones!"

We got serious, at least when I wasn't frantically trying to finish my book. My Lonely Planet guide was finally published in July 1985, just as Turkey's 1980s tourism boom was reaching fever pitch. When travelers went to the bookshop to find a Turkish guide, it was just about the only one on the shelf. It flew out of the stores. I made some serious money. I started work on the second edition.

I married Jane, the girl next door, on the autumnal equinox in 1985. Two weeks later we took off for Turkey on our honeymoon. I planned to show her lots of the best parts: İstanbul, Side, Antalya, the Mediterranean and Aegean coasts, Ephesus. Planning comprehensive itineraries was easy. I had done it over and over for my books.

"Wow," she exclaimed. "We can see all that in two weeks?"

"Sure!" I said with a swagger. "I know my way around, babe. Piece of cake. Wedding cake! Heh."

Here, Use My Flashlight

We went first to Side, and Ayşe's pension, where we discovered that tragedy had struck: Hüseyin had been killed in an auto accident.

"*TIR vurdu,*" Ayşe said. Hit by a TIR, an eighteen-wheel *Transport International Routière*, a long-haul cross-border tractor-trailer rig.

Hüseyin had been returning from a business trip to Ankara. The accident killed him and his recent bride—a terrible tragedy, but an increasingly common one in Turkey as development and prosperity filled its highways with more trucks, more cars and more inexperienced drivers. I thought of Professor Abdullah and how the worst thing he had to fear during the "undeveloped" 1960s was an unmarked ditch.

Hüseyin, handsome talented Hüseyin, who "looked just like a German," her favorite son. Ayşe must have been dying inside, but on the outside she accepted the tragedy with equanimity. She was a good Muslim and believed in God's ineffable wisdom.

"I'll build a fountain in his memory," she said, "down by the mosque. That's a proper memorial, don't you think? Let people enjoy a drink of pure cool water as a gift from my son."

Hüseyin's shop accounts were in chaos—they had mostly been in his head, old-fashioned Turkish-style—but Ayşe was committed to straightening it all out and giving him a suitable memorial.

After a night of jet-lag rest in Side we rushed on to Antalya where we raced around the sights. On the evening of the third day Jane said "My head's spinning. Here we are driving out of Antalya at 6 pm. It's dark. Your book says the road along the coast is one of the most scenic in all of Turkey. Why are we driving it in the dark? I can't see a thing."

"I guess I planned a travel writer's trip," I said. "Travel writers have to cover a lot of ground in a short time."

"Darkness," she said. "I really wish I could see the view. Watch out for that cart!"

It was the time of the cotton harvest. The benighted road was filled with wagons piled high with cotton, but lacking any sort of taillights. Instead of a scenic drive I was taking her on the Turkish version of Walt Disney World's Space Mountain.

"On my birthday," she went on—her birthday was coming up in a few days—"we're going to stay in one place. For the whole day. And the place is going to be on the sea so I can swim and sunbathe. And you're going to relax. No taking notes, no grilling people in tourist offices, no researching prices in hotels and restaurants. This is our honeymoon, so on at least one day we're not going to be travel writers. We're going to be honeymooners, or at least act like we are."

We did. We settled in at the Hotel Tusan on the beach north of Kuşadası. Jane swam and sunbathed. I went windsurfing. We took naps and made love and had a romantic candlelit dinner. We were finally on a real honeymoon.

At the end of our trip we returned to İstanbul. We went out to the airport. In those days Pan Am had two daily round-the-world flights. Flight 1 left New York in the evening and went around the world eastbound. Flight 2 left New York each morning and went around the world westbound. It was the airborne equivalent of a Turkish minibus, with its route being the circumference of the earth.

It was Flight 2 that went westbound from İstanbul to New York. We kissed and hugged tightly, then kissed again, and Jane boarded the flight. Pan Am had upgraded us travel-writer newlyweds to first class, so she settled into her first class seat and said yes to a glass of champagne.

During the flight she chatted with the man in the seat next to her. "My husband's still in Turkey finishing up his guidebook," she said. "He'll be home in a few weeks. Yeah, I know it sounds kinda funny, coming home from my honeymoon alone."

"But really, it's okay…I think."

☙❧

23
EPILOGUE

It was okay. We bought a house together, moved in, and a few years later got pregnant. Amniocentesis revealed the baby to be a girl.

"What'll we name her?" Jane asked.

"Well," I said, "as far as I'm concerned there's only one possible name for my daughter."

"No way!" Jane said. "No more Janes! I like my name but it's *mine*, and you've had more than enough Janes already, so the baby will not be named *Jane*." We settled on Lydia, the name of the ancient Aegean kingdom inland from İzmir.

Just Like That İstanbul Taxi Ride

By this time I had acquired something of a reputation as a Turkey expert and was asked to speak at conferences. I spoke at a Turkish-American business meeting in Washington. The hotel was only a short walk from National Airport. I was going to need a one-way plane ticket to get back to Boston the following day, a Sunday, so I walked over to the airport and went to the Eastern Airlines ticket counter.

"I need a ticket to Boston," I said.

The agent rattled on her keyboard, looked at the monitor and said "Two hundred and twenty dollars."

"What?" I shouted. "I don't want to buy the plane, just ride it to Boston. Don't you have a lower fare?" She rattled some more and looked again.

"One hundred fifty-five" she said.

"Look, I've got all day to get there. The flight time isn't important. Put me on any plane you want. You must be able to do better than that on a Sunday."

Rattle rattle. "Ninety-nine dollars," she said.

"That's not bad," I said. "Let me check with some of the other airlines here and I'll get back to you."

"Just a minute," she said, and rattled some more. "Sixty-seven dollars," she said, "and that's absolutely the lowest fare I can give you."

"I'll take it."

In the air flying to Boston it hit me: that experience was precisely the same as haggling for a taxi fare in İstanbul. With this in mind I wrote a book called *How to Beat the High Cost of Travel*, based largely on the realization that just about every pricing mechanism in the travel industry bears a striking resemblance to an İstanbul taxi ride.

Lonely in Side

In 1988 I was back in Turkey to revise my guides yet again. In Side, I went directly to the Hermes Pansiyon as always.

It looked different. Things had been changed, added, subtracted, moved around. I entered, asked for the owner, and was introduced to a woman I had never seen before.

"Is Ayşe Hanım here?" I asked.

"No, no, she sold the pension to us. She's not here any more."

I went to Ayşe's house around the corner. The door was locked, the courtyard—which Ayşe had always kept spotlessly clean—was littered with leaves. The adjoining carpet shop was closed.

I knocked on the door of the house. After a minute a strange woman opened it. I asked.

"She died last year."

Side, now so crowded with pensions, hotels and restaurants and packed with tourists, so friendly and familiar for twenty years, all at once became a lonely place.

A New Kind of Travel Writer

The first edition of my Lonely Planet guide, published in July 1985, was 326 pages long. The second edition (the one with the infamous cover photo of the Harran girls), appeared in January 1988 at 469 pages. The third, in 1990, had 614 pages; the fourth, in 1993, had 748 pages. For the fifth edition, the job had gotten so big that I had to take on Pat Yale, a talented British writer, as my co-author.

"Stop!" said Tony Wheeler, head of Lonely Planet. "We can't afford these huge books. Don't let it get any longer."

But Turkey was growing. The enormous potential I had recognized, however vaguely, in 1967, was being brought to life. Roads, airports and yacht harbors were built, hotels and resorts sprang up by the hundreds, then by the thousands, all over the country. By the 1990s Turkey was one of the top 20 travel destinations in the world, and my Lonely Planet guidebook, the best-seller ever since it appeared, had been translated into French, German, Hebrew, Italian, Polish and Spanish, and Lonely Planet had become the most prominent guidebook publishing company in the world.

My revived Frommer's guide, *Turkey on $25 and $35 a Day*, was republished in 1988 and went through two more editions (1990 and 1992) before it was dropped because of flagging sales, and my Lonely Planet guide took over the market.

Peace Corps Turkey, which started in 1962, was terminated in 1970 when the threats from the leftist radicals were simply too dangerous to ignore. In that eight year period about 1500 American volunteers served in Turkey, and their efforts were not wasted. Peace Corps service was the beginning of a number of significant academic, diplomatic and commercial careers for both American PCVs and their Turkish students. These careers advanced Turkey's development and Turkish-American relations and would not have happened otherwise.

The thousands of dollars lavished on my graduate education through US government programs failed to produce an Ottoman scholar, but considering the acute lack of enthusiasm among the general public for scholarly treatises on matters Ottoman, maybe that's not such a bad thing. I've used my training in other, perhaps more immediately useful ways.

The leading edge of the Baby Boom, and especially the Peace Corps generation of the 1960s, spawned a number of travel writers who took the craft to a new level of sophistication. Traditionally, travel writers had been either upscale casual visitors or scholarly academics. Arthur Frommer broke those molds when he wrote *Europe on $5 a Day*, and the Peace Corps generation of the 1960s went beyond Frommer to produce what might be termed "Third World destination experts." These new travel writers, many of them Americans, lived among the common people in the countries they described, countries well off the beaten track of the European grand tour. They spoke the local language, studied the history, politics and culture, and understood the customs. They didn't start out to be travel writers, but after trying other pursuits (usually academic) they ended up there, using their deep on-the-ground knowledge of a place to enrich the travels of those who followed in their footsteps. They were—and are—truly "the Handsome Americans."

Lonely Planet and Moon Handbooks published guidebooks by a surprising number of these destination experts: Joe Cummings on Thailand, Wayne Bernhardson on Chile and Argentina, Rob Rachowiecki on Peru and Costa Rica, Stan Armington on Nepal, Hugh Finlay on Africa, the intrepid Deanna Swaney on a half dozen countries. The expertise of these writers helped to establish the publishers' fame and associate them with high quality writing and deep local knowledge.

Sadly, the business of guidebook publishing has now made it nearly impossible for a single expert author to earn a living by writing a comprehensive guidebook to a given destination. Most guides are now written by teams of authors, many of whom are professionals but few of whom have any special destination expertise.

My fourteenth Turkey guide was the seventh edition of Lonely Planet's *Turkey* published in March, 2001, weighing in at 720 pages. It was still the best-seller, but the world was changing. At the turn of the millennium the Internet was challenging all other information media, and was obviously the medium of the future for travel writing. After 33 years of writing travel guidebooks for major publishers, I left print behind and moved to the World Wide Web. Drawing on my experience of researching and organizing information for travelers, I began writing pages for TurkeyTravelPlanner.com. By the end of 2004, my 3000-page website was being visited by two million visitors per year, from more than 160 countries, and I had started NewEnglandTravelPlanner.com, StMoritzTravel-Planner.com and several other websites.

The entire world has changed substantially since that champagne-soaked Pan Am 707 filled with eager young PCVs flew eastward from New York to Ankara, but the change in Turkey has been nothing short of astounding. Significantly, in 1990 the entire country waited with bated breath to see if the generals would need to take over again. They didn't. The fact that nothing happened gave a significant psychological boost to Turkish citizens, who saw it as a sign that their democracy had matured.

Despite the ceaseless drama of Turkish politics, some government programs seem to have had an effect after all. Our students at İzmir Koleji actually learned English and moved on to useful careers, some of them becoming quite prominent in the burgeoning tourism industry where knowledge of English is essential. The Ministry of Tourism and Turkish entrepreneurs have made tourism one of Turkey's top revenue-producing industries. Much of Side was preserved from development by the government's plan. The Bosphorus bridge, so hated by the radical students of the 1970s as a symbol of American imperialism, paid for itself in record time, and now no one can imagine the city without it. A second bridge, the Fatih (Conqueror's) Bridge, was built farther up the Bosphorus, and a third bridge is being planned.

The sleepy "underdeveloped" country I landed in has become the economic powerhouse of the eastern Mediterranean and a stronger, more important US ally than ever. Political crises are still common, but political violence is not. University students study hard rather than march in the streets, and they mostly look favorably upon the USA. Although the socialist ideal of common effort for the common good is still respected, capitalism has been eagerly embraced by the very generation which so loudly denounced it a few decades ago. The same thing happened in the USA and in many other countries that lived through the Big Boom summer of 1968.

Resurgent Islam

Among the most surprising changes in Turkey is the resurgence of Islam. It's not surprising that people should turn to religion as a spiritual anchor when radical change sweeps through their society. Consider this: when I first arrived in Turkey it was against the law (though rarely enforced) for a man and woman, even husband and wife, to hold hands in public. Now many Turkish girls wear skimpy bikinis, and there are even topless beaches. Or consider that the residents of Çamuşlu Köyü, out near the Iranian border, had never seen a foreigner, an American, or a non-Muslim before I wandered in, but now they can press a button on a remote control and see the latest American, European and Turkish programs, not to mention "reality TV," which must strike a Turkish villager as outrageously unreal.

In 1995, by a mere 21% of the vote, an Islamist party was elected to lead the country because the centrist political parties, each of which had received about 20% of the vote, were incapable of forming an effective coalition government. Apparently many people voted for the Islamists because they were sick of the traditional parties' corruption and incompetence. It was the Islamists' big chance, but the right wing of the party blew it by saying and doing things guaranteed to upset the military establishment. Accused of unconstitutionally bringing religion into politics, the Islamist party was toppled by the military and an uneasy civilian coalition government was cobbled together.

Despite the noisy Islamist segment on the right end of Turkey's political spectrum—not all that different from the reactionary religious right in America and many other countries—most Turks don't want an Islamist government. They want nothing more of religion than to bring its solace and wisdom into their private lives. The last thing most Turks want is a return to Sharia, Islamic religious law. In fact, a new moderate government "based on the ethics of Islam" came to power in Turkey, and so far has proved to be among the best in recent decades.

I can't help contrasting my first low-key Ramazan in Bornova (1967) with a recent one. I was in İstanbul in December, 2001, near the end of the holy month. Only a few days of fasting remained. I visited the office of my friend Ersan Atsür who runs a travel company called Orion-Tour. About half of his staff—young, well educated, modern and mostly female—were keeping the fast, a far greater percentage than I had observed at İzmir Koleji.

These "modern Muslims" wore standard European office garb, without Islamic head coverings, and worked normally in the office all day. When the customary urge came for a glass of tea or a snack or a cigarette, they thought twice, resisted, and turned their thoughts instead to the deeper meaning of life, to the care of their souls.

"Am I being a good person?" they asked themselves. "Am I helping to fulfill God's plan for humankind? Am I being a good Muslim? Do I care for other people, give alms, deal honestly with everyone?"

One day I arrived at Ersan Bey's office around sundown, the time of *iftar*, the breaking of the fast. If Westerners hear anything about Ramazan it's about the fasting, but that's only half the story and I was about to see the other half. A staffer cleared Ersan Bey's big desk, spread a tablecloth and laid out the simple "break-fast" meal of soup, flat *pide* bread, olives and vegetables. Everyone, whether fasting or not, whether Muslim or not, was invited to share in the celebration. It was a time of warmth, friendship and heartfelt thanks for the goodness of life.

In the evening during Ramazan the İstanbul city government sponsored special concerts, amusements and shows. All the mosques were floodlit and packed with worshippers and sightseers in a holiday mood. The ancient Hippodrome was engulfed in a carnival atmosphere with strings of colored lights and little booths selling snacks, crafts, religious books, trinkets, and souvenirs. There were smiles everywhere.

Imagine a month in which denial of small pleasures during daylight helps you to consider life's big, important questions. It's no wonder Muslims look upon Ramazan as a blessing: it helps them to prioritize, to discover what's important and what isn't, to figure out what we're all doing here—in short, to ponder the meaning of life.

At the end of my stay I went to Atatürk Airport's brand-new world-class international terminal to catch my flight home. Above the passport control booths was a line of big sparkly red letters spelling out WE WISH YOU A MERRY CHRISTMAS AND A HAPPY NEW YEAR in English and also *BAYRAMINIZ KUTLU OLSUN* (Happy Ramazan Holiday). That pretty much says it all.

Last of the Janes

As for me, I'm still happily married to Jane the management consultant, two decades and counting. The Harvard Business School graduate now has her own thriving consulting practice that helps non-profit organizations plan for the future, but her dream-come-true is PieChef.com, her own pie-baking website. So much for the myth that HBS graduates don't know what really matters in life.

Our daughter got her passport when she was a few months old and promptly flew off to France with her mother while I was on yet another guidebook revision trip in Turkey. When she was ten years old we took her to Turkey, which she loved. Now she wants to go back.

Jane, my college girlfriend, found her true love and married him. She and her husband have two talented children and we're still good friends.

Jane, my first wife, had a series of short term relationships. She took off and traveled the world, ever the adventurer, finally ending up in the southwestern USA where she had been born and raised.

Before his death Dux Schneider, ever the mountaineer, realized his dream of exploring the Taurus Mountains of southeastern Turkey on foot and donkey-back. The absorbing, revealing journal of his adventure among the reclusive *Tahtacı* ("Woodcutter") mountain people was published as *Bolkar: Travels with a Donkey in the Taurus Mountains*. It's still in print, with a German edition as well. After Dux's death, Monique and Tamara Schneider moved to England where Monique continued writing fiction as Frances Oliver (*Children of Epiphany*, and her latest: a collection of stories entitled *Dancing on Air*). She's now at work on her memoirs. Unfortunately, Dux's elegantly-written guidebook is long out of print.

As for my twentysomething search for the meaning of life, well—I think I finally found it.

No, I'm not going to tell you what it is. I suspect that what I found is only the meaning of *my* life. It might not even apply to you—although I have a sneaking suspicion that maybe, just maybe, it might.

Here's a hint: Listen to the little voice. Plato was right.

Besides, it's easy enough for you to find it on your own. It's all around you every day. For the more clueless among us, such as Yours Truly, it just takes a lifetime of looking in order to see it.

‌ ‌
‌ **ʂɔ̃**

Turkish Pronunciation Guide

Pronouncing Turkish Words

Turkish is a phonetic language, so every letter is pronounced (with one odd exception).

a   ah, as in art or car

e   eh, as in sell

ı   (undotted 'i') uh, like the 'a' in avert

i   (dotted 'i') ee, like the 'ee' in seek

o   oh, as in for

ö   as German ö (say 'ee' with pursed lips)

u   oo, as in tool

ü   as German ü or French 'eu' as in feu

c   jeh, as English 'j'

ç   cheh, as 'ch' in church

g   geh, as in get

ğ   (soft g) silent; lengthens the previous vowel slightly; ignore it! (Just don't pronounce it)

h   hhh, never silent, always aspirated (pronounced), like 'h' in half or heart

j   zh, as the 'z' in azure

s   sss, always unvoiced as in see; never voiced (zzz) like the 's' in cars

ş   sh, as 'sh' in should

v   a soft sound halfway between 'v' and 'w'

GLOSSARY

acaba…	*Acaba buralarda bir postane var mı?* (AH-jah-bah boo-rah-lahr-dah beer POHSS-tah-neh VAHR muh?) I wonder, is there a post office around here?
Adanalı	(ah-DAH-nah-LUH) "Citizen of Adana," a city at the eastern end of Turkey's Mediterranean coast
agents provocateurs	(French) "agitators," secret agents who instigate violent events
Ağrı	(AII-ruh) Town in eastern Turkey which gets my vote as the most forlorn and godforsaken place in the entire country
Akdeniz	(AHK-deh-neez) "White Sea," the Mediterranean
Akşam	(ahk-SHAHM) "Evening," name of an İstanbul newspaper prominent in the 1960s
alaturka	From Italian *alla turca*, "Turkish-style," in some cases assumed to be inferior to *alafranga* (alla Franca), French- or European-style
Alevi	(ah-leh-VEE) "Alawite," heterodox Muslims whose practices diverge substantially from the main Sunni and Shi'a traditions
Amasya	(ah-MAHSS-yah) provincial capital northeast of Ankara
Amerikan mı?	(ah-meh-ree-KAHN muh) "American?" (Is she/he/it (an) American?)
Anatolia	Asia Minor, the peninsula that forms the larger part of Turkey
ANZAC	Australia-New Zealand Army Corps, troops from those countries under British command in the World War I Gallipoli campaign
ashlar	Huge stone rectangle used to construct monumental buildings, usually without mortar

at arabası	(AHT ah-rah-bah-suh) Horse cart
Atatürk	(AH-tah-tewrk) (Mustafa) Kemal Atatürk (1881-1938), Ottoman army officer who distinguished himself in the Gallipoli campaign of World War I. He went on to organize and lead the Turkish War of Independence, to found the Turkish Republic, and to serve as its first president
ayan	(ah-YAHN) "notables," important people
Ayasofya	(AH-yah-SOHF-yah) Hagia Sophia, [Church of the] Divine Wisdom
ayran	('eye'-RAHN) beaten yogurt churned with spring water and a dash of salt to make a tangy, refreshing beverage especially tasty served chilled on hot days
Ayşe	(AH-yee-sheh) "Aisha," a woman's name; name of Prophet Muhammed's favorite wife
baba	(BAH-bah) "father," "papa," "daddy," often used as an affectionate unofficial title for an older man
Bab-ı Âli	(BAHB-uh ah-LEE) "Sublime Porte," the Ottoman Grand Vezirate (Prime Ministry) in İstanbul, the buildings of which now serve as the Ottoman archives
bak	(BAHK) imperative of bakmak, to look (at)
Balık Pazarı	(bah-LUHK pah-zah-ruh) Fish market, specifically İstanbul's Galatasaray fish market district
barf	(Farsi) "snow"
Başınız sağ olsun	(bah-shuh-nuhz SAAH ohl-soon) "May your head be spared," traditional formula of condolence on the loss of a loved one
bayram	(BAH-yee-rahm) Muslim holiday, especially Kurban Bayramı
bekçi	(BEHK-chee) "watchman," especially a night watchman
Bekârlık sultanlıktır	(beh-kyahr-LUHK sool-tahn-LUHK-tuhr) "Bachelorhood is sultanhood," the idea that bachelors have a wide choice of women available to them while still retaining their freedom
Bereket versin	(beh-reh-KEHT vehr-seen) "May [Allah] give you bounty," said by someone from whom you have just bought something, the implication being that if He does, it will be good for both of you

bêtise	(French) "stupid thing," stupidity
bey	(rhymes with 'grey') "Mr," placed after the given name, as in Süleyman Bey, "Mr Solomon"
Beyaz Saray	(bey-YAHZ sah-rah-yee) "White Palace," a big building in Beyazıt, İstanbul; also the White House in Washington DC
beyefendi	(BEY-eh-FEHN-dee) Ottoman title of high nobility now debased and used commonly, but still signifying greater respect or deference than simple *bey* or the even more greatly debased *efendi*
Beyoğlu	(BEHY-oh-loo) district north of the Golden Horn in İstanbul formerly known as Pera
bimarhane	(bee-MAHR-hah-neh) "insane asylum"
Birinci Kordon	(beer-EEN-jee kohr-DOHN) "First Cordon," the popular name for Atatürk Caddesi, İzmir's waterfront boulevard
Boğazkale	(boh-AHZ-kah-leh) "Castle of the Gorge," name of the village next to the ruins of the Hittite capital of Hattusha
börek	(bew-REHK) stuffed fritters, often of mille-feuille pastry cooked in a variety of ways
Bosphorus	The strait, 20 miles (32 km) long, that divides Europe from Asia at İstanbul
Boş ver!	(BOHSH vehr) "Give empty!" a slang idiom meaning "It doesn't matter!"
Bülbül Dağı	(BEWL-bewl dah-uh) "Nightingale Mountain," the high mountain ridge south of the Ephesus ruins
burma kadayıf	(BOOR-mah kah-dah-yuhf) shredded wheat twisted around a core of pistachio nuts then soaked in honey and syrup
Buyrun(uz)!	(BOOY-roon-nooz) "Help yourself!" or "Be my guest!" also used sometimes in ways similar to the German *bitte*
Buzbağ	(BOOZ-bah) "Ice-vine," a tanniny Tekel red wine made of dark purple Öküzgözü (Ox-eye) grapes
Byzantine	Pertaining to Byzantium, later Constantinople, later İstanbul, or the eastern portion of the Roman Empire governed from that city; the name given to the later Roman Empire in the east (5th to 15th centuries)

cacık	(jah-JUHK) beaten yogurt mixed with grated cucumber and a bit of garlic and salt, served as a hot-weather cold soup
Cadde(si)	(JAHD-deh-(see) "Avenue"
Çadırcılar	(CHAH-duhr-juh-LAHR) "Tent-makers," name of a street adjoining İstanbul's Grand Bazaar
cami(i)	(JAH-mee) "mosque"
Can	(JAHN) "Soul," a feminine or masculine name
Çavuş	(chah-VOOSH) "Sergeant," a masculine name
çay evi	(CHAH-yee eh-vee) "tea house," the social center of every traditional Turkish village or town
Cehennem	(jeh-HEHN-nehm) "Hell"
Celal	(jeh-LAHL) masculine name
Cemil	(jeh-MEEL) masculine name
Cennet	(jeh-NEHT) "Heaven"
Cerberus	In Greek mythology, the three-headed dog that guards the entrance to Hades
chemin de fer	(French) "railway," a card game for gambling, usually with high stakes
çiftçi	(CHEEFT-chee) "farmer"
Çiğli	(CHEE-lee) Name and location (in the 1960s) of a large US Air Force base north of İzmir
Cold Duck	Cheap, sweet sparkling red wine made by the Charmat bulk process
Çorum	(CHOH-room) provincial capital northeast of Ankara, known for its roasted chickpeas
çubuk	(choo-BOUK) "stick," long slender wooden tobacco pipe with a small clay bowl, used in Ottoman times
cumhuriyet	(joom-hoo-ree-YEHT) "republic," name of a prominent Turkish newspaper; Cumhuriyet Meydanı is Republic Square, a plaza in İzmir
Dardanelles	The Hellespont; a strait dividing Thrace from Anatolia, formed by the Gallipoli peninsula and the Anatolian mainland
Darüşşifa	(DAHR-ews-shee-FAH), "Abode of Health," an Ottoman word for health center, hospital

Divriği	(DEEV-ree-yee) town southeast of Sivas known for its Seljuk-era architecture
dolma	(DOHL-mah) "stuffed," vegetable or grapevine leaf filled with rice pilav
efendi	Ottoman title of nobility debased in republican Turkey and usually applied only to workers of the lowest class; title of respect for a Muslim religious leader; originally a Greek term
Efendim	(eh-FEHN-deem) "Sir," "Ms," or "Madam," singular or plural, in Turkish
Eminönü	(eh-MEEN-eu-new) district at the south end of Galata Bridge in İstanbul
epigoni	inferior imitators
eskici	(ESS-kee-jee) "old things person," junkman, buyer and seller of used items, old bottles, etc
Eşrefpaşa	(esh-REHF-pah-shah) a district in İzmir
Etlerimiz buzdolabındadır	(eht-LEH-ree-meez BOOZ-doh-lah-buhn-DAH-duhr) "Our meats are in the refrigerator"
ev pansiyonu	(EHV pahn-see-yoh-noo) "home pension," household renting spare room(s) to travelers
evet	(eh-VEHT) "yes"
falaka	(fah-LAH-kah) painful punishment in Ottoman times in which the soles of the offender's feet were beaten with a flexible stick
Fatimid	Of or pertaining to the descendants of Fatima, daughter of Muhammed, and Ali, second leader of the Muslim commonwealth; usually in reference to the Fatimid dynasty that ruled over North Africa, Egypt and Syria in the 10th and 11th centuries
fayton	(FAH-yee-tohn) "phaeton," four-wheeled carriage with a convertible top drawn by two horses, popular for short leisure rides within the city
Frenk	(FRENK) Ottoman term for a "Frank," a European
Fruko	(FROO-koh) orange soda made in Turkey under license from the Coca-Cola Company
Galatasaray	(gah-LAH-tah-sah-rah-yee) "Galata Palace," a district in European İstanbul centered on the historic 19th-century Galatasaray Lycée, the first European-style

	institution of higher learning funded by the Ottoman government
gastarbeiter	(German) "guest worker," a foreign worker (including many Turks) in Germany during the 1960s and '70s when the German economy created more jobs than it could fill with local workers
gavur	(gah-VOOR) "giaour," infidel, non-Muslim, a light-duty or jocular insult in Turkish
gazöz, gazoz	(gah-ZEWZ, gah-ZOHZ) from French *(eau) gazeuse*, carbonated (water) which, with a bit of syrup added, becomes a soft drink
Geçmis olsun!	(getch-MEESH ohl-soon) "May it be in your past," a formulaic phrase said to someone who has had a bad experience, finished a trip, etc
gider	(gee-DEHR) "to go"
göbektaşı	(gew-BEHK-tah-shuh) raised platform in the hottest room of a Turkish bath on which bathers lie to rest or to receive a massage
gravitas	(Latin) gravity, seriousness
Güzel Marmara	(gew-ZEHL MAHR-mah-rah) "Beautiful Marmara," a Tekel white wine made from grapes grown near the Sea of Marmara
Hacı Salih	(hah-JUH sah-LEEHH) famous old İstanbul restaurant
hafız	(hah-FUHZ) person who has memorized the entire Kur'an, often asked to chant passages at religious occasions
Halveti	(HAHL-veh-TEE) short for Halveti-i Cerrahi, a sub-order of the "Growling Dervishes"
hamal	(hah-MAHL) porter willing to carry anything and often able to carry huge heavy loads
han	(HAHN) "caravanserai," caravan way-station, either in a town or out in the countryside on a major trade route
Hanım	(HAH-nuhm) "Ms," placed after the given name, as in Ayşe Hanım, "Ms Aisha"
Hatay	(HAH-tah-yee) Turkish province, formerly the Sanjak of Alexandretta, centered on the city of İskenderun
Hatice	(HAH-tee-jeh) feminine name
Haydar	('HIGH'-dahr) masculine name

Hayri	('HIGH'-ree) masculine name
Hay hay!	('HIGH'-'high') "Certainly! Right away!"
hazırlık	(HAH-zuhr-luhk) preparation, preparatory
heurige	(HOI-rig-eh; German) wineshop in a Vienna Woods village
Hijri	(HEEJ-ree) "(Year) of the Hegira" (Muhammed's 'flight' from Mecca to Medina): date in the Muslim lunar calendar, calculated starting in 622 AD
hocam	(HOH-jahm) "my teacher," an honorific title applied to any teacher or former teacher by Turks of all ages, whether they had ever been the teacher's students or not
Hoş geldiniz!	(HOHSH gehl-dee-neez) "Welcome!"
Hoş bulduk!	(HOHSH bool-dook) "We are welcomed!" Formulaic response to the welcome greeting Hoş geldiniz!
ibrik	(ee-BREEK) ewer, Ottoman-style water pitcher; in Ottoman households a servant poured water from the ewer over the hands of dinner guests to cleanse them before and after eating
iftar	(EEF-tahr) breaking of the daily Ramazan fast by eating a light supper, traditionally including pide
Işık	(uh-SHUHK) "light," also a feminine name
işkembe(ci)	(eesh-KEHM-beh(-jee)) "tripe soup (maker/shop)"
Istakoz	(uhss-tah-KOHZ) "lobster"
Jandarma	(zhan-DAHR-mah) Turkish gendarme(s), the national force of paramilitary police; Jandarmas are usually the sole police service in the remote countryside
jeu d'esprit	(French) joke, witticism
Kabataş	(KAH-bah-tahsh) a Bosphorus shore district of European İstanbul just south of Dolmabahçe, known for its ferry docks
kaffee mit schlag	(German) Viennese coffee (topped with whipped cream)
kale	(KAH-leh) "fortress," castle, citadel
kapıcı	(KAH-puh-juh) "doorman," factotum
Karaköy	(KAH-rah-kewy) formerly Galata, the district at the northern end of İstanbul's Galata Bridge

Karşıyaka	(kahr-shuh-YAH-kah), "Opposite Shore," a suburb north of İzmir across the bay
Karum-Kanesh	site of an ancient trading center near modern-day Kayseri
kaya resimleri	(KAH-yah reh-seem-leh-ree) "rock pictures," petroglyphs
kayık	(kah-YUHK) traditional wooden coastal freighter, originally driven by sail but lately by diesel engine
kebab, kebap	(keh-BAHP) roasted food: meat, fish, chicken, chestnuts; anything roasted
kebapçı	(keh-BAHP-chuh) person who makes kebap, or restaurant where kebap is prepared and served
keyf	(KEH-yeef) pleasure, delight, joy; tipsy, slight intoxication
kiralık daire	(KEE-rah-luhk dah-yee-REH) "apartment for rent"
Kızılay	(KUH-zuh-lah-yee) "Red Crescent (Society)," Muslim equivalent of the Red Cross; also a main square in Ankara where the Kızılay headquarters was located in the 1960s
Kızıldereliler	(KUH-zuhl-deh-reh-lee-LEHR) "Redskins," aboriginal inhabitants of North America
kleine braune	(German) "little brown (one)," strong, aromatic medium-roast express coffee served in Austria
kola	(KOH-lah) "cola," Coca-Cola or one of its local imitations
kolej(i)	(koh-LEZH(-ee)) school of lycée/high school level teaching foreign languages
konak	(KOH-nahk) mansion, sometimes short for Hükümet Konağı, "Government House;" name of İzmir's main square, location of the city's historic Government House
köfte	(KURF-teh) meatballs of ground mutton, usually grilled
Köprülü	(KEW-prew-lew) distinguished Ottoman noble family that provided numerous generals, grand vezirs and other high government officers
kümbet	(kewm-BEHT) vaulted or domed tomb, especially those constructed by the Seljuk Turks
Kur'an	(koor-AHN) short for Kur'an-i Kerim, the Holy Koran

Kurban Bayramı	(koor-BAHN bah-yee-rah-muh) "Sacrifice Holiday," the Muslim festival known as 'Eid el-Adha or 'Eid el-Kebir in many countries, commemorating Abraham's near-sacrifice of his son Isaac with the ritual slaughter and cooking of a sheep
lâle	(lyah-LEH) tulip; official name of İstanbul's "Pudding Shop," renowned during the 1960s hippy era—and still going strong!
leblebi	(LEHB-leh-BEE) roasted chick peas eaten as a snack
Levantine	"Of the Levant" (the eastern end of the Mediterranean), descendant of European traders living in Turkey
lokanta	(loh-KAHN-tah) "restaurant" (from Italian locanda)
Maşallah!	(MAH-shahl-lah) "Gift of God!" an exclamation of joy and blessing at seeing something beautiful or pleasing
maden sodası	(mah-DEHN soh-dah-suh) "mineral soda," fizzy mineral water
meclis	(mej-LEESS) "assembly," legislative council
medrese	(MEH-dreh-seh) "madrassah," Muslim theological seminary
Merhaba!	(MEHR-hah-bah) "Hello!" all-purpose greeting
meşrutiyet	(mehsh-roo-tee-YEHT) "constitution;" name of a street in Beyoğlu, İstanbul
meydan	(meh-yee-DAHN) "plaza," public square
meze(ler)	(MEH-zeh(-LEHR)) Turkish hors d'oeuvres, salads and purées
mihrab	(MEEHH-rahb) prayer niche in a mosque, indicating the direction of Mecca
Milâdi	(MEE-lah-DEE) the Gregorian (Christian) calendar now commonly in use throughout the world; Common Era calendar
mufti	müftü in Turkish: mosque official/prayer-leader (not a "priest" as there is no priesthood in Islam)
muhtar	(muh-TAHR) village headman, "mayor"
Muzaffer	(moo-zah-FEHR) "Victorious" (Arabic); masculine name
Nacide	(NAH-jee-deh) feminine name

nargile	(NAHR-gee-leh) Turkish water-pipe, hookah, hubble-bubble
Necdet	(nedj-DET) "Bold," a masculine name
nefis	(neh-FEESS) "excellent" (often said of a sensual pleasure, particularly fine dining)
neşe	(NEH-sheh) "joy," merriment; also a masculine name
oruç	(oh-ROOCH) "fasting," not eating
Osmanlıca	(ohss-MAHN-luh-jah) Ottoman Turkish, written in the Arabic script
palamut	(PAH-lah-moot) "bonito" (*sarda sarda*), a small tuna fish
palatschinken	German version of *crêpes-suzettes* (thin pancakes filled with jam)
paşa	(PAH-shah) "pasha," Ottoman military general or high government official
pastane(si)	(pahss-TAH-ne(-see)) "pastry shop"
patron	(pah-TROHN) "owner" (of a business, and often its manager)
pavyon	(PAHV-yohn) from the French *pavillon*, a semi-legitimate nightclub with singers, comedians, belly-dancers, and usually prostitutes
PCV	Peace Corps Volunteer
petit four	(French) small rich sweet cake or biscuit with icing
pide	(PEE-deh) flat bread (pita), traditionally an essential ingredient of *iftar*
pilav	(pee-LAHV) rice cooked in broth, often with spices or other ingredients
PKK	Kurdistan Peoples' Party, a terrorist organization which carried out attacks on military and civilian targets within Turkey during the 1980s and 1990s, until its leader, Abdullah Öcalan, was captured by Turkish commandos
post hoc...	*Post hoc ergo propter hoc* (Latin) "After this, therefore because of this," the logical fallacy that because something happens after something else it was necessarily caused by the first event
rahle	(RAHH-leh) book stand made of two wooden rectangles, usually used to hold Kur'ans,

rakı	(rah-KUH) grape brandy flavored with anise (like arrack, ouzo and pastis), Turkey's "national (alcoholic) drink," usually cut with water, which clouds it milky-white, earning it the nickname *aslan sütü*, "lion's milk"
Ramazan	(RAH-mah-zahn) Ramadan, ninth month of the Muslim lunar Hijri calendar, during which observant Muslims fast from sunrise to sundown, and feast during hours of darkness
rédacteur des bêtises	(French) "Stupidities Editor"
Sachertorte	(ZAH-kehr tohr-teh, German) "Sacher cake," a rich chocolate confection invented at Vienna's Hotel Sacher
şadırvan	(SHAH-duhr-vahn) fountain near a mosque for performing ritual ablutions before prayers
Safa geldiniz!	(sah-FAH gehl-dee-neez) An extension to the traditional formulaic greeting *Hoş geldiniz!*
Sağ ol!	(SAAH ohl) "Thank you!" (literally "May you be well and strong!" the Turkish equivalent of "Yes, sir!" or "Very good, sir!"
Sahaflar	(sah-hahf-LAHR) İstanbul's old book bazaar
sahlep	(sahh-LEHP) hot drink of milk thickened with, and flavored by, orchid-root powder, served in winter
şalvar	(SHAHL-vahr) baggy Turkish cotton trousers ("bloomers"), usually of small floral prints, worn by peasant girls and women
Şam fıstığı	(SHAHM fuhss-tuh-uh) "Damascus peanuts," pistachio nuts
Saray Muhallebicisi	(sah-RAH-yee moo-HAH-leh-beh-jee-see) "Palace Rosewater Pudding Maker," a pastry shop on İstanbul's İstiklal Caddesi near Taksim Square
saz	(SAHZ) "musical instrument," specifically, the traditional long-necked, oval-bodied Turkish stringed instrument
scaena	(Latin) the wall-like structure behind the stage in a classical theater
Second Empire	(suh-GOND ohm-PEER), style of French architecture and decoration prevailing during the reign of Napoleon III (1852-1870)

sedir	(seh-DEER) low bench seat along a wall, topped by cushions covered in embroidered cloth or Turkish carpets
şeftali	(shef-tah-LEE) "peach"
Şehir Kulübü	(sheh-HEER koo-lew-bew) "City Club," a common name for the bar-restaurant-nightclub patronized by the leading (male) citizens of a provincial town
Selamün aleykum	(she-LAHM-ewn ah-LEY-koom, Arabic) "Peace be unto you," a traditional Muslim greeting
Selçuk	(SEHL-chook) "Seljuk," pertaining to the Seljuk Turks who invaded Anatolia in the 11ᵗʰ century; name of the town nearest Ephesus, which marks the farthest westward advance of Seljuk rule
sema	(SEH-mah) dervish (Muslim mystic) worship service which in many orders involves physical activity, such as dance
sheikh	(*şeyh* in Turkish) leader of a religious group such as a dervish order, usually elevated to the leadership because he is worthy of respect
Şifaiye	(shee-FAH-yeh, Ottoman) "health center"
sigara böreği	(see-GAH-rah bew-reh-yee) "cigarette fritters," tube-shaped rolls of pastry dough stuffed with white cheese and parsley and deep-fried
Sirkeci	(SEER-keh-jee) district between Eminönü and Seraglio Point in İstanbul; Sirkeci Garı, İstanbul's European railway terminus
Sıtkı	(suht-KUH) masculine name
sokak	(soh-KAHK) "street"
STDs	sexually-transmitted diseases
sturm und drang	(SHTOORM oont DRAHNG, German) "storm and strife"
Sufi	(SOO-fee) Muslim mystic, someone who seeks direct communion with the Divine through special rites or actions
sünnet	(sur-NEHT) "ritual circumcision," customarily performed on Muslim boys approaching puberty
sütlaç	(SEWT-lahtch) rice pudding made with milk

Tahtakale	(TAHH-tah-kah-leh) market district near Eminönü, İstanbul
taramasalata	(TAH-rah-mah-sah-lah-tah) red caviar spread
Tekel	(teh-KEHL) Turkish State Monopolies, which once made most of the country's matches, tobacco products and alcoholic beverages, and still manufactures important quantities of some of these
Tekel Birası	(teh-KEHL bee-rah-suh) beer made by Tekel
Tepebaşı	(TEH-peh-bah-shuh) "at the hilltop," name of a district in Beyoğlu, İstanbul
Thrace	geographic region which includes the European portion of Turkey and parts of eastern Bulgaria and northern Greece
Toz olur!	(TOHZ oh-loor) literally "Become dust!" slang: Run away! Disappear!
troglodyte	cave-dweller
tumulus	low mound resulting from centuries of human community habitation, usually prehistoric; excavated by archeologists
Turgut	(toor-GOOT) masculine name
Ulu Cami	(oo-LOO jah-mee) "Great Mosque"
Üsküdar	(EW-skew-dahr) Scutari, an Asian district of İstanbul
vindaloo	extremely spicy-hot Indian curry
vurdumduymaz	(voor-doom dooy-MAHZ) "I hit him, he didn't feel it," insensitive, a blockhead
weltschmerz(lich)	(German) "world-weari(ness)"
Wienerschnitzel	(German) "Vienna cutlet," breaded veal cutlet Austrian-style
yakamoz	(YAH-kah-MOHZ) sea-water phosphorescence generated by plankton
yalı	(yah-LUH) Ottoman-era İstanbul seaside villa, usually on the Bosphorus, typically of wood frame construction
Yassou!	(YAH-soo, Greek) "Hello!"
Yazılıkaya	(YAH-zuh-LUH-kah-yah) "Inscribed rock," a sacred Hittite site near Boğazkale (Hattusha)
Yener	(yeh-NEHR) "Victorious;" "edible" (literally "it is eaten")

Yeşil Cami

(yeh-SHEEL jah-mee) "Green Mosque," an early Ottoman mosque in Bursa

Yeşilırmak

yeh-SHEEL-uhr-mahk) "Green River," a major river northeast of Ankara, flowing through Amasya

yoğurtçu

(yoh-OORT-choo) "yogurt-maker" or -seller

zevksiz

(zehvk-SEEZ) "without savor" or taste, unpleasant

Zincirkıran

(zeen-JEER-kuh-rahn) "Chain-breaker," one of the many fantasy names which probably originated in the name reform of 1935, when the government required all Turks to adopt surnames

züppe

(zewp-PEH) "presumptuous," stuck-up, snooty

About the Author

Tom Brosnahan, a veteran guidebook author, photographer and consultant on travel information, has written over 40 guidebooks for Berlitz, Frommer's and Lonely Planet covering Belize, Canada, Egypt, England, France, Guatemala, Israel, Mexico, New England, Tunisia and Turkey, with over four million copies in print worldwide in more than 10 languages.

His company, Travel Info Exchange, Inc, develops travel and other websites, including TurkeyTravelPlanner.com, NewEnglandTravelPlanner.com, StMoritzTravelPlanner.com, WritersWebsitePlanner.com, PieChef.com and InfoExchange.com.

He has been a Contributing Editor to Arthur Frommer's *Budget Travel*, and has had many articles and photographs published in leading periodicals including *Travel & Leisure, The New York Times, The Daily Telegraph* (London), *Chicago Tribune, New York Daily News, BBC World, Journeys, Odyssey* and *Travel Life*.

He is a member of the American Society of Journalists and Authors, the Authors Guild, and the Society of American Travel Writers, of which he has been a Director. He is a co-founder and faculty member of the SATW Institute for Travel Writing and Photography.

He is married to Jane A Fisher, co-owner of Cambridge-Concord Associates, a management consultancy (CambridgeConcord.com). They have one daughter, and live in Concord, Massachusetts.

Acknowledgements

Thanks to many friends for taking the time to read and make valuable comments on the manuscript of this book, including Linda Allen and Peter Hiscocks for their enthusiastic support; Elizabeth Caney for her usual deep Taurean insights; Jamie Dunford-Wood of TravelIntelligence.net, who knows good travel writing; Barbara Fisher, expert in both art and literature; Judy Foreman for the priceless insights of a veteran newspaper reporter; Carol Harper, whose wisdom and experience in communicating with an audience are infallible; Joe and Pamela Helms, ever deeply insightful about the meaning of life; Alice Kaufman, Elaine Kuttner and Peter Kuttner, who judged it through the lens of summer reading; Betsy Peterson, Jonathan Rubin and Sheri Scully, who gave the book-group report. Your generous help went beyond the bounds of friendship, and I thank you deeply.

Special thanks to Pamela Talbot for both commenting in detail on the manuscript and for coming up with such a brilliant title. Pamela, you do have a talent for titles! Finally, and extra specially, thanks to Jane Fisher, my wife, for being my first and best reader, editor and impartial critic (Ow!), my inspiration, and the treasure at the end of my quest.

—*Tom Brosnahan*

Where This Book Was Written

Home, Concord, Massachusetts
Concord Free Public Library, Concord, Massachusetts
Thankful Stow Road, Guilford, Connecticut
The Bryn Mere, Annisquam, Massachusetts
Room 315, Hotel Balıkçılar, Konya, Turkey
Room 305, The Grand Summit Hotel, Sunday River, Bethel, Maine
KLM Flight 1610, İstanbul-Amsterdam
Northwest Flight 37, Amsterdam-Boston
Ketchum Run Lodge, Forksville, Pennsylvania
Room 41, Hotel Empress Zoe, Sultanahmet, İstanbul
Room 615, Hotel Eresin Crown, Sultanahmet, İstanbul
Fairmont Hamilton Princess Hotel, Hamilton, Bermuda
Chelsea Arts Club, Chelsea, London
Room 3293, Williamsburg Inn, Colonial Williamsburg, Virginia
Business Class, Acela Regional train 94 (Newport News to Manhattan)
Grand atrium lobby of Wilderness Lodge, Walt Disney World, Orlando,
    Florida